Enterprise Applications
Administration

Enterprise Applications Administration

The Definitive Guide to Implementation and Operations

Jeremy Faircloth

AMSTERDAM • BOSTON • HEIDELBERG • LONDON
NEW YORK • OXFORD • PARIS • SAN DIEGO
SAN FRANCISCO • SINGAPORE • SYDNEY • TOKYO
Morgan Kaufmann is an imprint of Elsevier

Acquiring Editor: Steve Elliot
Editorial Project Manager: Kaitlin Herbert
Project Manager: Punithavathy Govindaradjane
Designer: Russell Purdy

Morgan Kaufmann is an imprint of Elsevier
225 Wyman Street, Waltham, MA 02451, USA
The Boulevard, Langford Lane, Kidlington, Oxford, OX5 1 GB, UK

Library of Congress Cataloging-in-Publication Data
Faircloth, Jeremy.
Enterprise applications administration:the definitive guide to implementation and operations/Jeremy Faircloth.
pages cm
Includes bibliographical references and index.
ISBN 978-0-12-407773-7 (pbk.)
1. Application software--Management. 2. Computer systems--Management. 3. Business enterprises--Data processing. I. Title.
QA76.76.A65F35 2013
005.3068′8--dc23
                                    2013039245

British Library Cataloguing-in-Publication Data
A catalogue record for this book is available from the British Library.

Dedication

To My Wife, Christina Faircloth

I don't think you expected this when you said "for better or for worse," but you've stuck with me through all of it anyway. Thank you, Chris, for supporting me, loving me, and putting up with the life of an "IT Widow."

Contents

Acknowledgments

A full year went into this book and I still feel that I could have spent another year working on it to make it right. Three laptops met their doom, multiple mice met walls in frustration, and there is now a permanent dent in both my desk and my forehead. Through all of that, there are many people who still decided it was worth sticking through this with me and supporting this effort along the way.

My family, as always, are my greatest fans, best supporters, and the people that suffer the most when I'm running behind schedule. I'd like to thank my wife Christina and my son Austin for all of their support year after year as I continue to try to get the words out of my head and onto paper. Thank you both so much for everything that you do to support me and keep this dream of mine alive.

I'd also like to thank all of my other family members who helped and supported me with this in some way or another: Jeff Landreth (I can never call you Scott), Joann Faircloth, John and Mary Faircloth, Barbara Landreth, and all the rest of you good folks. I'd list you all, but I only have so much space and there are **so many** of you that I appreciate! Thank you all so much!

A big thank you also to Steve Elliot and Kaitlin Herbert, my editor and project manager with Elsevier. You really helped keep me on track and keep this moving even when the going got rough. Your support through this project is very much appreciated and none of us authors could be successful without a great team like you guys.

Finally, I want to thank all of the individuals that have worked with me in supporting enterprise applications through the years. There have been great times, huge challenges, and many surprises that have affected all of us. Through it all, we have all learned a lot and I appreciate all of the things that each one of you has taught me through the years. Chuck Chilton, Mark Seely, Scott Bilyeu, Travis Perry, Mike Mashburn, Mike Angeloff, Christina Angeloff, Albert Zhu, and so many more of you all taught me many things about working with systems, working with applications, and most of all, working with people. Thank you all so much for everything that you let me learn from you.

Inevitably, I end up missing someone when writing any acknowledgments, so if you have been with me on this journey and I haven't mentioned you here, please forgive me. Your help has surely been appreciated and I thank you. I'll probably owe you a beer for my oversight!

Preface

BOOK OVERVIEW AND KEY LEARNING POINTS

This book addresses a need within the information technology field to bring back a level of generalization needed to support today's enterprise applications. Over the years, there has been a trend toward technology specialization to such a high degree that many information technology professionals no longer have the breadth of skills necessary to support multiple technology disciplines with the same level of expertise. This trend is acceptable when dealing with silos of technology but begins to be an issue when working with large, complex enterprise applications.

Enterprise applications administration is the skill and art of working in a cross-discipline role with a holistic view of the enterprise application and all of its component technologies in mind. This book is intended to provide a knowledge base to the reader that covers the primary technologies that enterprise applications administrators work with on a daily basis. In addition, some of the softer skills needed within this role are covered so that there are no gaps in the basic knowledge necessary to become or lead enterprise applications administrators.

BOOK AUDIENCE

The intended audience for this book is any technical professional who has an interest in working with enterprise applications, any instructor who is teaching the skills needed to become an enterprise applications administrator, and any manager who needs to manage high-performing enterprise applications administration teams. In addition, technical experts specialized in any technical area will find value here by learning the basics of other disciplines and better understanding the entire ecosystem utilized by enterprise applications. Database administrators can learn about server hardware and operating systems. Security professionals can learn about networks and applications. Developers can learn about databases and architecture. All technical specialties associated with enterprise applications are discussed and present learning opportunities to any technical professional.

HOW THIS BOOK IS ORGANIZED

This book begins by focusing on defining enterprise applications administration and how this job role differs from any other technical role. We then move into technical training on each of the core technologies used within enterprise applications administration: Networks, Servers, Databases, Information Security, and Architecture. Each of these technologies has their own dedicated chapter where we go into a medium level of detail on the technology itself as well as its relation to enterprise applications. We then begin to move into softer skills and discuss Enterprise Applications Administration Teams. This is followed by a look at the full enterprise applications ecosystem and how Automation and Monitoring fit into the administration role. Finally, we discuss that most dreaded of topics by focusing on Documentation for the final chapter.

The organization of this book is intended to take you through the journey of enterprise applications administration. This journey starts by ensuring that you understand what enterprise applications administration really is and why it requires such a breadth of knowledge across so many technical areas. The journey continues as you learn each of those technical disciplines, expand your knowledge in areas that you're already familiar with, and standardize on terms in areas where you already specialize. With that knowledge in mind, you can then better understand how the team approach works with enterprise applications administration and how crucial the appropriate management of these teams can be. The final two chapters focus on concepts that fall across all technical disciplines as well as the management of teams as we look at how to automate processes, monitor applications, and document all of the critical information associated with this work.

CONCLUSION

After many years of working with enterprise applications, there is a clear need for more education on this topic. It is my hope that this book can serve as the start of that education and help provide some guidance as to what is needed to become a truly great enterprise applications administrator. There are always changes to technologies, changes to applications, and changes within corporate environments. With a firm foundation of knowledge, skills, and experience, you can weather these changes and be successful. The success of enterprise applications administrators is truly the path to success for the organizations that hire them and know how to properly use their skills.

CHAPTER 1

Introduction to Enterprise Applications Administration

PURPOSE OF THIS BOOK

As the information technology (IT) field has grown over the past few decades, there has been a shift in the mind-set of those who work in this field. Early on, any IT professional had to have a solid understanding of electrical engineering, programming, networking, data storage, and all other aspects of the field. This later changed into a trend of specialization where IT professionals learned to be very deep in their knowledge of certain aspects of technology. This gave rise to titles such as "Network Administrator," "Database Administrator," "Developer," and the like. This change toward specialization is identical to what has happened in other fields such as medicine where doctors can specialize in a specific type of medicine rather than be a general practitioner.

This shift toward specialization has its benefits as IT professionals are able to focus on a single aspect of the field, such as relational databases, and become true experts in that technology. However, that level of expertise comes with a cost. As your focus becomes more and more defined on a specific technology, your knowledge of other technical areas naturally tends to reduce over time. Eventually, you can become so specialized that you can no longer work in or understand other areas of IT.

This has become a big problem in the industry today, as there tends to be too few generalists who understand multiple technical areas and an overabundance of specialists who only understand one. At the point that you start to deal with applications across a corporate enterprise, the problem of specialization quickly becomes apparent. It is very common to run into situations where 10 specialists are all working on the same problem, but are unable to communicate amongst each other to actually solve the problem because none of them can speak the technical language of the others.

The growing trend to solve this is the evolution of "enterprise applications administrators" who have a breadth of knowledge across many technical areas and depth of knowledge in one or more. These administrators help to bridge the gap between various technical specialists and provide the knowledge and expertise necessary to facilitate solutions for applications across corporate enterprises. This "new breed" of technical professional brings the older concepts of generalization in the IT field into the present and effectively provides the glue to bond all of the other aspects of IT together.

To Teach

This book focuses on teaching IT professionals the breadth of knowledge and skills that are necessary in order to become an enterprise applications administrator. This involves all of the core technology areas of:

- Networking
- Servers
- Operating Systems
- Relational Database Management Systems
- Security
- Architecture
- Process Automation
- Monitoring

as well as the softer skills in the areas of:

- People and Team Management
- Documentation

As we look at each of these areas, we will discuss each at a medium level of technical knowledge. Again, the goal is not to be an expert in all of these areas but knowledgeable in all of them. Should you choose to gain more knowledge in one or more technical areas, that is excellent and will only serve to increase your skills. However, it is important to remember to maintain your knowledge across all of these areas in order to continue to be able to be a competent enterprise applications administrator.

Many longer-term certification programs such as Microsoft's Microsoft Certified Solutions Expert (MCSE) program or Cisco's Cisco Certified Internetwork

Expert (CCIE) program require a breadth of knowledge in a number of areas similar to what we will be discussing. These certification programs can absolutely help you in validating your IT knowledge across several areas; however, there are still limitations in their validation due to their vendor-specific focus. For example, you won't run across many questions related to Linux systems on the Microsoft MCSE exam. It is certainly recommended that as you progress through your enterprise applications administration studies that you take the appropriate certification exams to demonstrate your knowledge, but it's important to again recognize that breadth of knowledge is critical.

Therefore, one of the primary purposes of this book is to teach you not only the basic knowledge for each of the subject areas mentioned above but also to expand on each so that you can develop a better understanding of the technology and how each area relates to each other. The level of knowledge that we discuss may not be sufficient to pass a vendor-specific certification exam, but it should help you on your way to becoming a good enterprise applications administrator.

To Refine

It is expected that many of you reading this already specialize in at least one IT knowledge area and are looking to expand on what you already know. With that in mind, this book is organized into sections based on each technology area. Where it makes sense, you may find it valuable to skim the areas where you're already an expert and focus more heavily on those areas that are new to you. However, it is recommended that you do at least skim the areas where you already feel comfortable, as we will be discussing how each technical area interacts with the others.

Through better understanding how each technical area interacts with others, you will be able to refine the skills that you already have and learn how to use them in new ways. In many instances, you can take your technical expertise in one area and apply the same troubleshooting or analysis skills into another. This cross-functional use of technical knowledge is one of the things that make enterprise applications administrators a highly sought-after technical resource.

If you already have a strong knowledge across all of the technical areas that are discussed in this book, you will probably still find value in our discussions on the softer skills required to perform enterprise applications administration. Whether it's working with people, building a team, or putting together good documentation, these soft skills are absolutely necessary in the enterprise applications administrator role. Most technical books do provide a great deal of focus on the technical area that they're addressing, but few show how that technical area bleeds into other parts of the role.

Understanding those additional skill areas will help you to further refine what you already know and put it into practice in new ways.

To Standardize

We will also put focus into standardization throughout this book. This affects multiple areas of knowledge and is critical to becoming an enterprise applications administrator. In most cases, it is desirable that actions taken be consistent, repeatable, and reliable. For this to happen, all activities must be standardized as much as possible and precedent set to rely on those standards so that the process can be repeated. However, there are other standards that must be in place in order for standardized processes to even be possible. These include standardization of both terminology and documentation.

Terminology

As we look at standardization, we will focus on the three areas of terminology, documentation, and processes. Each chapter will not only include a deep dive into its topic area but also call out specific standardized terminology that will be used throughout the book. Part of the goal of an enterprise applications administrator is to be able to successfully communicate across other specialized teams. In order to do this, the same language must be used. Therefore, it is critical that as much attention is paid to the terminology used in a technology as is paid to the technology itself.

Just as in the medical or legal fields, IT has its own language, and many "dictionaries" exist which attempt to document this language. They are mostly successful as many terms do work across all areas in IT; however, what is often not noticed is that each specialty area in IT has its own distinct dialect of language as well. For example, "locking" to a database administrator would indicate that a record is blocked from access whereas to a system administrator, it would indicate a system hang.

As we discuss each topic throughout this book, specific terminology that relates to that topic will be used so that you can gain a general understanding of the terminology within that context. Where there is potential terminology confusion, this will be called out so that you can be aware of the term and its different meanings.

In addition to technology-specific terminology, there is also a need to standardize on general IT terminology. Many frameworks such as the Information Technology Infrastructure Library (ITIL) exist primarily to help IT professionals align on a standardized way of communicating and referring to various functions and events. For example, the ITIL framework goes to great lengths to define the differences between an "incident" and a "problem." While this may seem excessive, it's actually quite necessary to have standardized terminology explicitly defined in this manner so that we can be 100% certain that we're referring to the same concepts when having IT discussions.

This also aids us in being able to assign objective measurements to IT functions. For example, if you are attempting to justify the cost of additional headcount for an IT area, it can be incredibly helpful to be able to measure the value of filling that role. However, that measurement must be as objective as possible so that the need can be justified to groups outside of the one requesting the headcount. Being able to express that by filling a specific role, incident response time will decrease by 30% while being able to increase volume by another 20% can be more effective than simply stating that the team "can respond faster and handle more work."

Processes

As previously mentioned, being able to repeat a set of actions consistently and achieve the same results is a key part of enterprise applications administration. In order to successfully achieve this, the actions must become part of a standardized process. When the actions are performed in the same way every time, the expectation can be set that there is less likelihood of an error occurring in the execution of this process. This leads to higher reliability whenever any process is used.

There are typically a number of different ways of accomplishing the same tasks in IT. For example, changing file permissions on a Linux system requires use of the chmod command along with specific parameters. These parameters can vary depending on what it is that you're attempting to accomplish. When it is necessary to change these file permissions on a regular basis, it may make sense to put these actions into a standardized process. The process could include:

1. Log into the system
2. Change to the appropriate directory
3. Confirm that the file exists
4. Verify current file permissions
5. Change file permissions with the following command:
   ```
   chmod 755 [filename.ext]
   ```
6. Verify new file permissions
7. Log off

With this process, you'll notice that there are some steps in here that might not be performed in a normal "quick" permissions change such as the file existence validation and the verification of current permissions. These extra steps put a little more rigor into the actions being taken and help reduce the possibility that something is missed or performed incorrectly. When a standardized process is defined, this level of attention to detail can be taken into account and included in the process. Then, of course, the process must be documented so that all enterprise applications administrators on the team can follow it in a consistent manner.

Documentation

The last area of standardization that we'll be covering is documentation. There is a huge amount of documentation that is typically generated in association with any enterprise application implementation, but much of it is not helpful to enterprise applications administrators and much of the documentation that they really need doesn't exist. Therefore, it is typically up to the enterprise applications administrator to create or augment documentation to suit their needs. With this in mind, we'll go over documentation in depth and discuss some of the most critical documents that you'll be working with.

Documentation is probably one of the least-loved aspects of doing enterprise applications administration. Most administrators hate doing documentation, see it as a tedious chore, and question the value. However, the instant that they run into a situation where they know that they've already solved a problem in the past, can't remember how, but are able to find the fix procedure in a document, they begin to see how important documentation is. Additionally, there are the benefits of being able to rapidly train new administrators, pass on repetitive tasks to less-skilled team members, and quickly reference critical data about the application in question.

After being exposed to the process of good documentation and having the opportunity to see its value, most administrators become evangelical of this documentation philosophy and take it with them for the rest of their career. They typically find that the long-term value of well-documented information is worth the tedious effort that goes into producing it and, while it may never become less of a chore, at least they know that the chore is worth doing.

TIPS & TRICKS

Documentation: A Love/Hate Relationship

Most technical experts hate writing documentation. Working with technology is fun and exciting while writing out documentation is boring and monotonous. However, it's a necessary evil and one that every administrator learns to appreciate, if not enjoy. Enterprise applications administrators tend to love the results of good documentation but hate the process of creating it.

When it's time to do documentation, it helps to isolate yourself from other distractions (including access to your favorite social media or news sites), focus on the documentation that you need to complete, and set a strict amount of time that you're going to dedicate to the task. It may also help to set goals as you go along such as completing a certain number of pages or getting some number of sections of the document completed. This work has to be done, so focus on making sure you have the tools and attitude necessary to complete the task instead of focusing on how painful it may be. Then reward yourself by playing with something fun!

DEFINING ENTERPRISE APPLICATIONS ADMINISTRATION

Enterprise applications administration is a fairly vague term and many definitions have been created associated with this capability in the past. Here, we will attempt to put a strong definition behind what enterprise applications administration is, and almost more importantly, what it isn't. First and foremost however, let's consider what an enterprise application is and move forward from there.

An enterprise application is an application built and developed for supporting the business needs of large enterprises. These can run the gamut of purposes ranging from web content management systems to customer relationship management systems to supply chain management systems. Regardless of the business need that the application is supporting, the application design will typically reflect certain principles that are unique to large-scale enterprise systems. For example, enterprise applications typically support varying levels of high availability, have many simultaneous users, and are broken up into a variety of modules.

As a contrasting example, a small-office application may:

- Be locally hosted on a single workstation or server
- Provide minimal multiuser support
- Contain all functionality of the application within a single executable

Many examples of enterprise applications exist. A few of the more common examples typically seen within major corporations are:

- JD Edwards
- PeopleSoft
- Siebel
- SAP
- Hyperion
- Oracle ERP
- SalesLogix
- Oracle BI
- Microsoft Dynamics

Many of these applications provide solutions to multiple business needs, but in all cases they are complex, multitier enterprise applications that require a different set of skills to support as compared to their lower-complexity small-office counterparts.

What Is Enterprise Applications Administration?

Now that we have a solid definition for what an enterprise application is, we can move on to defining the concept of enterprise applications administration. Enterprise applications administration is, at its most basic, the planning (architecting and requirements gathering), implementation, training, support, and ongoing maintenance and upgrades associated with enterprise applications. This comprises a number of specific services and tasks associated with various phases of the enterprise application lifecycle. As we look at enterprise applications administration as a whole, we'll spend a little time focusing on each of these.

Implementation

When an enterprise application is first being introduced into the corporate enterprise, there is typically a fairly large implementation project that is begun to support the build-out and integration of the enterprise application. This project will often include project managers, architects, subject-matter experts for different areas within the technology stack, developers, testers, trainers, and a legion of other people that help ensure the successful rollout of the enterprise application. The most successful projects also include enterprise applications administrators who play a critical role in the long-term success of the implementation.

During the implementation phase, enterprise applications administrators tend to provide a variety of services that help move the project forward. A sample of these include:

- Assisting in defining nonfunctional application requirements
- Aligning application architecture/design with infrastructure architecture/design
- Determining hardware/software configuration necessary to meet defined service-level agreements
- Determining application technology stack layers
- Identifying and resolving dependency software requirements
- Identifying infrastructure requirements and defining infrastructure build order
- Determining nonproduction and production environment layout
- Installing and configuring dependency software and the enterprise application
- Supporting the software development life cycle through life cycle management, code/configuration migration, and other tasks
- Documenting standard operating procedures, application runbooks, and work instructions
- Implementing and administering user access controls
- Determining run schedules for batch-based integration jobs

Please note that this list is not intended to be a comprehensive list of all tasks that an enterprise applications administrator does during the application implementation. This is just a sample and all of these may or may not apply on any given implementation project. However, these are all tasks that an enterprise applications administrator should be prepared to perform.

Support

When working with enterprise applications, there is a lot of ambiguity around the term "support." In some cases, "support" refers to helping provide for developers' needs so that they have all of the tools and systems at their disposal for creating and modifying application code. In other cases, "support" refers to incident and problem management and thereby supporting the end users of the application. And in other instances it means doing all of the tasks necessary to keep the enterprise application up and running.

In this book, we will try and relieve some of that ambiguity by defining a set of tasks and work associated with each type of support, but be aware that many companies are not nearly as clear in their definition. One of the more important tasks for any enterprise applications administrator is to try to clearly understand what the company's expectations are from a support standpoint and ensure that those expectations are met.

Ongoing Development

After an enterprise application has gone through its initial implementation, there tends to be an ongoing cycle of development intended to continue to refine and improve the application. This development can be done using a variety of methodologies including Waterfall, Agile, and Extreme Programming, but in the end it boils down to creating new code and configurations that need to be put into place in the production enterprise application environment. This is another area where enterprise applications administrators play a crucial role.

As the development process takes place, there are a few critical needs that the developers have in order to get the work done. These include ensuring that development and testing environments are available, configured correctly, and able to accept code and configurations as needed during the development lifecycle. It is frequently the responsibility of the enterprise applications administrator to take on these tasks and ensure that everything works smoothly for the developers. The enterprise applications administrator will normally be the primary point of contact for developers to get environment support and may also be the party responsible for the code deployment itself.

CORPORATE MEMO...

Segregation of Duties

In many corporate environments, there are specific rules in place associated with segregation of duties. One of these is usually a rule stating that the developer of code cannot be the person who migrates the code into test or production environments. To fill this requirement, enterprise applications administrators are usually best positioned to perform the code deployments. Segregation of duties is also a way to ensure the integrity and security of systems and to protect from fraud and error. In addition to segregation of duties, many companies also have policies for job rotation and mandatory vacation.

When doing development for an enterprise application, it's common to have a software configuration management (SCM) system in place, which handles code versioning, checkouts of code for work, approvals, etc. It is frequently the responsibility of the enterprise applications administrator to help ensure that the SCM processes and technology work correctly with the enterprise application. They may also play a role in the software development lifecycle itself by being responsible for deploying newly developed code into nonproduction and production environments.

Aside from providing support to the developers from an environment perspective, enterprise applications administrators frequently act in a consulting role and help provide advice on how the developers should implement specific functionality into the application. In many cases, when a new application module is being implemented, the developers will request assistance from the enterprise applications administrator to better understand how that specific module of the application works and how it could best be implemented based on the specific architecture being used for the application instance. In this consulting role, the enterprise applications administrator is able to use their knowledge and experience to help ensure that new functionality is implemented in the best way possible.

Incident and Problem Management

The concepts for incident and problem management have been around for a very long time, but they're formalized within the ITIL framework. In essence, these revolve around fixing issues that occur within the enterprise application. In many cases, there is a corporate helpdesk which can assist with many issues that end users face including password resets, questions about basic functionality, etc. They may even be able to help with some application-related errors and function as "frontline" support to help quickly resolve end-user issues.

Enterprise applications administrators typically step in as a level 2 or level 3 support expert when it comes to providing end-user support. In this role, the enterprise applications administrator resolves more difficult problems within the application, troubleshoots issues to determine their root cause from a systems perspective, and coordinates with developers or other technical teams to resolve underlying code or infrastructure issues. Using their knowledge of both the application and the infrastructure that it runs on, the enterprise applications administrator can provide a much deeper level of expert assistance when it comes to resolving these more difficult problems.

Monitoring

Another role that falls under the "support" umbrella is keeping the enterprise application running. This includes maintenance activities (which we'll cover next), but also all of the tasks necessary to ensure that the system has the highest level of availability possible. A key component of this is monitoring the enterprise application to ensure that everything is working as expected. The key idea here is for the enterprise applications administrator to be aware of issues before the application fails or end users report an issue.

Monitoring falls into several areas including monitoring the utilization of hardware, operating systems, network utilization, database performance, and application performance. In most cases, there are three levels of monitoring that are performed. The first is simple availability monitoring, that is, making sure that each component of the enterprise application is "up." The second is functionality monitoring, which involves making sure that not only is the application available, but that it's working the way that it's supposed to. And the last is performance monitoring, which is watching to be sure that the application is performing at the speed that it's supposed to.

There are a number of tools available for performing this monitoring, but in the end, it's typically the responsibility of the enterprise applications administrator to make sure that some form of monitoring is in place and that there are processes in place to react to any issues discovered by the monitoring. It doesn't help much from an availability perspective when an automated monitoring system determines that there's a problem if no one is notified or paying attention to the monitoring system.

Maintenance

After an enterprise application has been implemented, there is a need for ongoing maintenance to occur to support the application. This maintenance may include patching the application, patching dependency applications, deploying new code or features, cleaning up log data, re-indexing databases, and coordinating patching or maintenance of core application infrastructure. Each of these is a task that doesn't really fall under typical job roles for developers, systems administrators, or other IT roles due to the specific yet broad set of skills that are necessary to perform the tasks. They do, however, fit well with the skills of an enterprise applications administrator.

Patching is an important aspect of maintaining any system and should be considered a key maintenance item for the enterprise applications administrator. Patching is the installation of new executable code or libraries to fix bugs or add new features to the application. These patches may be applied to the core enterprise application itself, other applications that are considered dependencies, operating systems, or even the firmware for various hardware devices. In some cases such as with the application patches, it may be the enterprise applications administrator who coordinates and installs the patch. In other cases, another team may do the installation but the enterprise applications administrator assists in impact analysis, coordination, and testing.

Many enterprise applications have a number of different logging options and these options may exist at all layers of the application. This can lead to the generation of a large amount of log data that can eventually fill up system drives or impact performance if not carefully maintained. While it's important to keep some level of log data for problem analysis, auditing, and other purposes, it's equally important to clean up the logs that are no longer necessary. This is a task that is also well suited for the skillset of an enterprise applications administrator.

Other maintenance tasks such as re-indexing databases or renewing web site X.509 certificates may or may not fall to the enterprise applications administrator depending on the organizational structure of the corporation. There are frequently dedicated teams that perform activities such as these, but the enterprise applications administrator may be responsible for requesting that the work be done or coordinating it across the appropriate teams. In cases where there is no dedicated team for these functions or the specific tasks fall outside of the team's role, it will typically be the enterprise applications administrator performing the tasks.

What Isn't Enterprise Applications Administration?

We've gone through a lot of explanation of what enterprise applications administration is, but it's also important to know what it isn't. Enterprise applications administrators obviously have many roles and duties as we've already discussed in this chapter. There are some general guidelines that we can use to specify what typically falls outside of the role of an enterprise applications administrator and into other roles within the IT organization.

Typically speaking, an enterprise applications administrator is not an expert in all areas of IT and infrastructure. This may vary based on the administrator's personal experience, but it should not be an expectation. Rather, the expectation is that an enterprise applications administrator should be a generalist with a mid-level knowledge of all IT systems areas and expert-level knowledge in one or two. This gives the administrator the breadth of knowledge necessary to understand and properly communicate with experts in various areas while also maintaining expertise in a chosen core area of knowledge.

In most cases, an enterprise applications administrator is not a developer. They may be able to write some code, do some level of development, or work through the application development lifecycle, but in most cases they are not developers. This is one of the most frequent mistakes that the author has experienced in working with a variety of organizations. The assumption that development skills directly translate to enterprise applications administration skills is incorrect and can lead to mistakes made due to skill gaps. That is not to say that developers cannot become enterprise applications administrators, but the skills necessary to perform enterprise applications administration must first be developed.

Enterprise applications administrators are not project managers. Many tasks within enterprise applications administration do require managing "microprojects" and enterprise applications administrators do frequently contribute to projects, but project management, as a role, typically does not fall under the enterprise applications administration umbrella. Improving project management skills can certainly aid an enterprise applications administrator in their work, but it should not be expected that this administrator could easily fit into a true project manager role.

Enterprise applications administration is not frontline support or a helpdesk function. Typically, individuals with a lower level of experience and knowledge than enterprise applications administrators can perform helpdesk-level support. By properly managing resources and ensuring that the right skill level is associated with each job function, the overall enterprise IT operations function can be made more efficient and cost-effective. By utilizing less-skilled resources for frontline support, enterprise applications administrators used for higher-level support can apply more focus to difficult problems without being distracted by any number of minor, easily resolved issues.

And lastly, enterprise applications administration is not a replacement for vendor support or maintenance agreements. While enterprise applications administrators can do a great deal to maintain and fix enterprise applications, there are limitations on what can be done without vendor support. Please note, of course, that this applies primarily to commercial off-the-shelf

(COTS) software and not open-source software or software developed in-house. For COTS software, there are usually limitations on how deep the customer can get into the application to fix various problems. Usually, the source code for the core application itself is not available to the customer and therefore the vendor must be engaged to develop a software patch to fix certain bugs or provide enhancements.

ENTERPRISE APPLICATIONS ADMINISTRATORS

So far we've discussed the concept of enterprise applications administration and how it fits into the overall IT organization in general. Now we'll focus more on the administrators themselves, their role, and their job definition. Enterprise applications administrators, by necessity, must have a very broad understanding of most areas within IT. Gaining this knowledge is neither easy nor quick and often requires many years of experience. With that in mind, what differentiates enterprise applications administrators from other professionals in the IT field? Where is the line drawn between a server administrator and an enterprise applications administrator?

The true differentiators are experience and breadth of knowledge. Since enterprise applications administration requires knowledge from such a large number of IT functional areas, IT professionals in any of these areas can, in turn, become enterprise applications administrators. The key requirement to do so is to widen their knowledge base to encompass other IT disciplines and gain experience in those additional areas. This can be done through training and reading books focused on each area or through books, such as this one, that cover multiple disciplines. In addition, changing positions to other functional areas in IT in order to gain work experience in these areas can be an option.

For example, a Windows server administrator is well positioned to become an enterprise applications administrator in that they already have a core knowledge of at least one operating system as well as some hardware and networking knowledge due to the necessity of ensuring that the operating system interacts correctly with the hardware that it's installed on and the network that it's connected to. In order to make the transition to enterprise applications administration, this server administrator would need to gain knowledge and experience in the areas of database administration, IT security, architecture, and, of course, the enterprise applications in question. They may also need to increase the depth of their knowledge of networking technology, but with their background, they're already well on their way to becoming an enterprise applications administrator.

Experience is generally harder and more time consuming to obtain than knowledge. While books such as this one strive to teach as much as possible about a topic, there truly is no replacement for actual experience acting in roles associated with the knowledge that you've gained. While you may have excellent theoretical knowledge that has been derived from practical knowledge that others have gained, performing the work yourself to gain that practical knowledge will provide you with the experience necessary to do the job right.

Anyone who has worked in IT will tell you that things simply never work the way they're supposed to. From undocumented, required steps to bugs to odd idiosyncrasies, IT is a field where even the simplest task can become a nightmare. Problem solving is a critical component of performing well in any IT role and it's even more critical for enterprise applications administrators. The benefit of this is that real-world experience with a specific technology will help you to learn more about it *because* of the additional work that has to be done to get the technology to work correctly. This is the experience that is necessary to perform well in the enterprise applications administration role.

Job Role

Knowing the role of an enterprise applications administrator is critical to filling the role with the right people or becoming a good enterprise applications administrator yourself. We've already discussed some of the key services that an enterprise applications administrator offers and the tasks that they perform. Now we'll drill into those a little more deeply and discuss how the enterprise applications administrator provides these services.

Project Implementation

In most projects involving the implementation or modification of an enterprise application, enterprise applications administrators are a critical resource. These individuals are responsible for ensuring that the application is able to do what is necessary to fulfill the project needs based on a technical point of view. As mentioned earlier in this chapter, this involves a number of specific, highly technical tasks that enterprise applications administrators are uniquely positioned to perform. These tasks take place at various times throughout the project lifecycle and will typically involve actions that are required to happen for the project to progress.

There are a number of different project methodologies that are used across organizations or even within the same organization. For the purposes of this book, a generic project methodology will be used that is comprised of the following phases:

- Scoping
- Design

- Development
- Testing
- Delivery

In this methodology, the scoping phase is when requirements are gathered and initial project architectural decisions are made. Design is the phase where high-level and detailed designs are developed and some proof-of-concept development may be done. Development is the core work of the project where new code is developed or new configurations are made. In the testing phase, all of the code will be functionally tested as well as regression tested if a current system is being modified. Finally, the delivery phase is when the code and configurations are locked down and deployed into the production environment.

It's important to note that the enterprise applications administrator is a critical resource associated with every phase of the project lifecycle. The tasks listed previously in this chapter are integral components to ensuring that any implementation or modification project is executed correctly. Throughout this book, we'll discuss project-related aspects of an enterprise applications administrator's work as they fit in with the various topic areas.

Ongoing Development

Whether it's part of a large implementation project or a small modification project, the role of an enterprise applications administrator is necessary for any ongoing development associated with an enterprise application. This role serves to support the developers in their work as well as ensuring the integrity of the SCM process. Some of the tasks associated with ongoing development naturally overlap with those associated with implementation projects, but there are a few differences that should be noted.

When supporting ongoing development, a critical need is to have a stable, reliable set of environments that support development, testing, and staging. It is often the responsibility of the enterprise applications administrator to ensure that these environments exist, that they are maintained and up-to-date, and that they are available for use by authorized developers. This may include ensuring that environment configuration is replicated across multiple environments, software patch levels are identical across multiple environments, environments are available and accessible, and the environments are ready to accept code or configurations as needed to support development efforts.

Outside of environment support, the enterprise applications administrator may play a role in the SCM lifecycle itself. In many cases, code deployment requires a number of steps that require a high level of access to the enterprise application or the infrastructure that it runs on. This level of access is typically not granted to developers across all environments, therefore a surrogate must be used for deploying the necessary changes. Depending on the policies of the company, the access restrictions may only apply to production environments, all environments in the enterprise, or just a subset. Whatever the case may be, the enterprise applications administrator can act in a role that provides support to the developers while maintaining the integrity of the corporate systems.

The last, and arguably most important, role of the enterprise applications administrator in ongoing development is their knowledge as a subject-matter expert of the enterprise application and the infrastructure that it utilizes. In the development process, questions arise as to the best manner to implement new or changed functionality. In some cases, this is a simple development decision, but in others, more expertise may be necessary. For example, a standard developer decision related to how to update images for a web-based application might be to simply place the images in a specific directory on the server hosting the application. However, the enterprise applications administrator may instead recommend implementing a shared cache or use of a distributed file system for hosting the image if the application hosting is spread across a large number of servers or across a wide geographical area.

Another example of applying the expertise of an enterprise applications administrator in this consulting role could be the choice of specific libraries for use in the development process. There are incompatibilities that the enterprise applications administrator may be aware of that the developer may not know about that would restrict the use of a specific library. Again, the knowledge of the enterprise applications administrator is crucial in ensuring that this incompatibility is discovered as soon as possible to prevent development time and money being spent using a technology which could not be used within the production environment.

CORPORATE MEMO...

Always ask Your Admin

An example of the enterprise applications administrator providing value in a consulting role from the author's own experience lies within the area of software compatibility. In one particular instance, a developer had made a decision to use a specific code library to simplify the development effort associated with adding new functionality to an enterprise application. This code library worked fine on the developer's Windows workstation when the developer tested it, but the developer requested a review to ensure that use of the library would be acceptable. Upon further research, the author discovered that the library worked well in Windows, but a specific function necessary for the development project was isolated to only the Windows platform and did not exist within the UNIX version of the library. In this case, the enterprise application's production environment used UNIX and therefore the library was not compatible with the production technology stack. If the enterprise applications administrator had not been consulted, it's possible that development would have continued using the library and rework would have to be done later to correct for the incompatibility.

Support

Another key role of the enterprise applications administrator is "support". As previously mentioned, the definition of what support means varies widely between companies and even within the same company. It is outside the scope of this book to try and outline all the different definitions of support, but there are some common themes in this area that any enterprise applications administrator should understand.

We've already discussed some of the common areas associated with support including supporting developers in the ongoing development process, performing monitoring, and performing maintenance of the enterprise application and its dependencies. These support tasks are very common and frequently fall to the enterprise applications administrator to perform as part of their job role. The technical details associated with monitoring will be covered in Chapter 8, and maintenance will be discussed as we go through each technology area in the remaining chapters in this book.

Our focus now, therefore, will shift to the concepts of incident and problem management and how the enterprise applications administrator fits into these efforts. Depending on the organization, incident and problem management may be referred to under different names such as "trouble tickets," "help desk tickets," "problem reports," and so on. The terminology used in this book is from the ITIL framework in an effort to use the most common standardized terminology to refer to what is essentially the same work. In the end, these terms refer to fixing things that are not working as expected in the enterprise application.

In most cases, there is a helpdesk or other Level 1 support personnel that acts as a buffer between the end users of the application and the enterprise applications administrator. This supporting role is intended to speed up the resolution of common problems, provide a more highly available resource to respond to end-user needs, and reduce the overall workload for the enterprise applications administrator. In most organizations, the Level 1 support will build a knowledge base (KB) or frequently asked questions (FAQ) document or web site to provide a means for users to "help themselves" instead of waiting for the helpdesk to respond. In addition, the support organization may have their own KB built using experience gained in their supporting role. In cases where the Level 1 support role does not exist, the enterprise applications administrator may be overloaded with the work necessary to perform basic support tasks and be unavailable for more complex support tasks or other tasks associated with their job role. Therefore, it is critical that the Level 1 support role exist in order to provide the best customer experience for the enterprise application end users as well as distribute support workload in a manner that best utilizes the skill level of the personnel involved.

When a support issue arises that needs a higher level of expertise than what the Level 1 support personnel can provide, the issue is typically escalated to Level 2 support personnel or directly to an enterprise applications administrator depending on the organizational structure of the company. If a Level 2 support layer is in place, the personnel associated with this role will typically have a higher level of access within the enterprise application and will be trained to handle more complex support tasks. Level 2 support may also involve personnel from other groups outside of the enterprise application support structure such as an independent security administration team, desktop support team, or even support teams for certain infrastructure components. Again, the goal here is to provide a higher level of support while maintaining a fairly rapid response to the end-user needs and freeing up higher-level resources to work on more complex tasks.

Level 3 support is typically provided by the enterprise applications administrator and is usually the highest level of support for the enterprise application outside of the vendor or development group. When an incident or problem reaches this level, it's implied that none of the other support levels have the knowledge or system access necessary to resolve the issue. The enterprise applications administrator is then responsible for analyzing the issue, determining the cause, identifying a solution, and implementing that solution. In some cases, this may require involving the enterprise application software vendor or developer, working with various infrastructure groups to fix an enterprise application dependency, or implementing a change into the enterprise application that requires a high level of access and knowledge.

The skills associated with being an enterprise applications administrator are very visible in this type of support role. In order to analyze the problem, the enterprise applications administrator may have to use their knowledge of the enterprise application, all of its software components, infrastructure that it utilizes, and their experience in troubleshooting other complex issues. In many cases, it is in this role that many companies are able to justify the high cost of training or hiring experienced enterprise applications administrators as they are able to more quickly work through and resolve issues that would baffle administrators that focus solely on a particular technology stack.

An example of this would be a problem where an end user reports that the enterprise application is locking up when they perform a particular function. The enterprise applications administrator would work with the end user to understand exactly what steps they are going through that causes the behavior to manifest and attempt to replicate the behavior. Through the analysis, the enterprise applications administrator may find that the behavior only occurs for this specific user and no others. Based on their experience, that may imply that the differentiator may be the setup of the user account.

After building a duplicate account, the enterprise applications administrator may be able to replicate the locking behavior and, by using extensive logging, determine that the "locking" is actually the application waiting on a response from the database to a query that uses details associated with the user's account information. In coordination with a database administrator, the enterprise applications administrator might discover that this particular query is doing a join incorrectly due to a specific attribute on the user account and is taking 3–4 hours to execute against the database. This could, in turn, lead to a timeout within the enterprise application. The enterprise applications administrator would then work with a development team to put better logic behind the query being used and support the software development lifecycle to get the fix moved into the production environment.

All of these tasks require a very high level of knowledge of the enterprise application itself as well as the infrastructure and database being used by the application. A database administrator may be able to identify the long-running query, but wouldn't be able to find the cause. An enterprise application security administrator may see the attribute on the end-user account, but not know that it has any effect on application performance. And a server administrator may be able to increase logging to provide visibility to the query being run, but not be aware of what they should be looking for. It is the coordination of the various teams associated with supporting the enterprise application and the ability to troubleshoot highly complex issues such as this that truly show the value of enterprise applications administrators and their role in supporting the enterprise application.

Production Acceptance and Production Control

The most important role of an enterprise applications administrator is that of a gatekeeper for the production application environment. If appropriate segregation of duties rules have been implemented within the corporate environment, it is the job of the enterprise applications administrator to be the final word on whether or not changes are moving into the production environment and how those changes are moved. Enterprise systems that lack this level of control and rigor set themselves up for failure by ignoring the added value of protecting the production enterprise application environment.

This is not to say that other roles within the change management process such as change approvers or change control boards should be replaced by enterprise applications administrators; far from it! These change management roles and processes ensure that the appropriate rigor around changes to the enterprise application have been followed throughout the change lifecycle. Rather, the enterprise applications administrator is able to apply their skills and knowledge in a role that gives them both the accountability and the authority to ensure that the production enterprise application environment is kept stable while still supporting the natural need to make changes to the environment.

This breaks down into two key areas: production acceptance and production control. Production acceptance is the methodology used to ensure the consistent and successful implementation of change into a production environment. In order to accomplish this, the enterprise applications administrator should perform a thorough analysis of what is changing, how it is being changed, and what the impact of the change is throughout the entire collection of hardware, software, people, and processes that comprise the enterprise application. After this analysis, the enterprise applications administrator should ensure that any gaps that could cause issues in any of these areas are resolved and that the change conforms to all appropriate requirements necessary to ensure a successful implementation. This covers the accountability aspect of the role that was mentioned previously.

The authority portion of the role is filled through the concept of production control. If a change is being requested that will cause a substantial negative impact to the production enterprise application environment, the enterprise applications administrator responsible for the environment should have the authority necessary to prevent the change from being made until the appropriate issues are addressed. This is akin to a gatekeeper who ensures that only those who are authorized may pass the gates into a protected environment.

Many organizations initially resist the concept of production control as it has historically been associated with the closed world of mainframe IT departments where all changes moved slowly and required a huge amount of rigor and process to make even minor changes. However, IT has evolved to become more nimble and with that the concept of production control has morphed into more of an "enabler" than a "resistor." The goal of production control is not to stop or slow down change but to ensure that the change is safe and will not cause more harm than good. As an organization sees the positive impact of this role, they tend to recognize the value and eventually support the role wholeheartedly as a very positive contributor to the change process.

KEY CONCEPTS

Production Acceptance and Production Control

Two very important concepts associated with well-run enterprise applications administration departments are those of production acceptance and production control. We discuss these at a high level in this chapter, but it's important that you spend some time familiarizing yourself with the technologies associated with enterprise applications administration and how these two concepts fit into each other. Throughout this book as we discuss each technology or soft skill, ask yourself how that technology or skill plays a part into the analysis associated with production acceptance and the authority associated with production control. Each technology and skill has a direct relationship to these concepts and you should strive to understand that relationship.

Key Technical Knowledge and Skills

We've discussed the key knowledge areas and skills that an enterprise applications administrator should have at a high level. Let's now take a more detailed look at each area so that it's clear as to what the essential knowledge and skills are for each individual technology. As we discuss each of these, you'll see the common theme that an enterprise applications administrator should have a mid-level knowledge of the technology and matching skills. Again, the goal of an enterprise applications administrator is not to be an expert in all technologies, but to be at the level of competence necessary to successfully fulfill their role within the enterprise.

Networking

Networking involves all of the hardware, cabling, firmware, software, logical topology, and other components necessary to ensure that the enterprise application systems are able to communicate end-to-end. It has been said that the most secure systems are not connected to any others, and while this is true, that concept simply cannot apply in the world of enterprise applications where connectivity is crucial. Ensuring that each system or device is able to successfully connect to all of the other appropriate components of the enterprise applications is a critical part of enterprise applications administration.

In most organizations, there is a separate operations team that is responsible for ensuring the availability of the corporate network. This team may run a Network Operations Center (NOC) or utilize some other method of ensuring rapid response to network issues. They are usually responsible for the administration of most network devices with the possible exception of security-related devices such as firewalls or intrusion detection systems. Services provided by teams like this typically involve support and operations of the corporate network, consulting on projects to ensure appropriate use of network technology or infrastructure, and performing monitoring and testing of network changes.

The enterprise applications administrator needs to have a solid understanding of networking technologies as well as very specific details of the network being used by the enterprise applications that they are responsible for in order to be able to successfully work with the corporate network team. As with most other technical teams, it is the role of the enterprise applications administrator to facilitate conversations that bridge the gap between core technology knowledge and enterprise application knowledge. To successfully do so, the enterprise applications administrator must be able to speak both languages as mentioned previously in this chapter.

The role of the enterprise applications administrator as a technical liaison with the corporate network team comes into play during project implementation, production acceptance, and support tasks. During the project implementation, the enterprise applications administrator is typically responsible for ensuring that the network team is aware of what the project is doing, what their needs are, and what the impact might be to the enterprise network. They play a similar role in the production acceptance process by fully understanding the changes being made and their effect on the corporate network. They can then work with the corporate network team to ensure that the network supports what the enterprise application needs as well as ensure that the enterprise application will not have a negative impact on the corporate network.

Finally, the enterprise applications administrator will need to have a clear understanding of networking technology in order to properly apply their troubleshooting skills to determine the cause of network-related issues or eliminate the network from the potential cause list. While it may be the corporate network team that is responsible for identifying the root technical cause of network-related issues, it is the enterprise applications administrator who can help identify that the issue is actually network related and help guide the corporate network team as to where in the network the problem may exist. This greatly reduces the amount of effort that the corporate network team must put into troubleshooting and speeds up the resolution of issues caused by network problems tremendously.

Operating Systems

Enterprise applications are, in the end, pieces of software and every piece of software runs within some form of an operating system. Knowing the technical details of the operating system being used by each software component of the enterprise application is critical to serving in the role of an enterprise applications administrator. Every operating system has its own nuances related to how the enterprise application interfaces with the hardware that the operating system resides on. Each operating system also has its own logic and rules that dictate how the various core functions provided by the operating system work. For example, displaying a line of text in the Windows operating system is distinctly different from displaying a line of text in the AIX operating system.

Again, the enterprise applications administrator does not have to have expert-level knowledge of the operating systems they're working with in order to be successful. They may never have to perform highly complex tasks like creating mount points to external network devices and associating the mount points with appropriate directory structures within the file system. But, they should understand concepts like this so that they can identify failures, understand the impact of those failures on the enterprise application, and facilitate finding the cause of the failure. Acting in the role of liaison with other corporate support teams that may be responsible for operating system maintenance, the enterprise applications administrator must be able to understand the technology and communicate appropriately with the technology experts.

In many cases, it will be the enterprise applications administrator who is responsible for installing and maintaining the enterprise application components upon the various servers used by the enterprise application. When that is the case, the enterprise applications administrator must know how to work within the operating system and have the appropriate skills necessary to perform installations, file manipulation, permission changes, and various other required tasks. The execution of each of these tasks varies widely between each operating system and the enterprise applications administrator must be able to perform them on whichever platforms are required by the enterprise application.

Database Administration

Most enterprise applications use some form of database back-end to store the data needed by the enterprise application. In addition, there are typically databases associated with other external applications that are accessed by the enterprise application either directly or via interfaces to those other applications. Lastly, there are frequently databases that link to the enterprise application database, which are intended specifically for reporting purposes. We'll get into all of these scenarios as we go on to discuss database design in Chapter 4 and integrations in Chapter 6.

Regardless of the location or purpose for each database, an enterprise applications administrator must understand what databases are for, how they work, and how to use them correctly in order to be successful. This involves all aspects of database technology from usage, to indexing, to high-availability architectures. It also includes understanding how to properly request data from a database and, almost more importantly, how *not* to request data in order to prevent overloading database resources.

The mid-level knowledge and skills that an enterprise applications administrator has in this area will again facilitate conversations with technology experts. Database administration is one of the more complex technology areas to specialize in due to the huge amount of knowledge that is necessary to be able to properly troubleshoot, tune, and operate large or complex databases. Many people are able to spend an entire career specializing in database technologies and retire without mastering all areas of the technology. With this in mind, it is certainly not an expectation that the enterprise applications administrator is an expert at database technologies, but they should understand enough of the topic in order to be able to intelligently converse with the experts in the field and perform an appropriate level of troubleshooting and analysis.

Information Security

Throughout all technology areas, there is a common thread that should tie them all together. That is the concept of information security. Information security is a critical component of every technology associated with enterprise applications including every layer of the application stack, every component of the infrastructure, every piece of code associated with the application, and every phase of the implementation or change process. With enterprise applications, information security is even more critical than ever and needs the constant diligence of the enterprise applications administrator in order to be effective.

Information security involves the confidentiality, integrity, and availability of the enterprise application. This is known as the "CIA triad" in security terminology. We'll go over each aspect of this in detail in Chapter 5, but as with the other technical areas, the expectation is that the enterprise applications administrator has a medium level of knowledge and skill in this area. In many cases, even more knowledge related to information security may be necessary depending on the type of enterprise application that is being supported, the type of data that it has or uses, and the way that the application is accessed. All of these factors change the information security footprint associated with the enterprise application and can change the approach to security within and around the application.

Architecture

Lastly, at least as it relates to technical skills, the enterprise applications administrator should have a solid understanding of enterprise architecture and technical architecture. This topic includes the logical connections between multiple enterprise applications, data sources, and systems from the perspective of enterprise architecture. From a technical architecture perspective, it involves the connections (physical or logical) between various hardware and systems associated with the enterprise applications.

Architecture itself is a very broad topic, but having a good understanding of all of the other technical areas that we've discussed will help a great deal in understanding how architecture works. After you have a firm understanding of each technical area, the concepts of enterprise and technical architecture help define how to tie it all together. This is the process of ensuring that technologies are implemented in the right way to support the goals of the company while understanding the constraints of the technologies in use.

In many organizations, there are various levels of architecture support and governance. These may include application architects, software architects, solution architects, technical architects, enterprise architects, service architects, and so on. The list goes on and on as there is potentially an architect associated with every aspect of every technology. Obviously, no one person could be an architect responsible for all of these areas simultaneously, but it is the role of an enterprise applications administrator to understand the key elements of architecture associated with all of these as well as be able to either support or fill each role as needed. As with any of the other technical areas that we've discussed, the enterprise applications administrator doesn't have to be an expert architect, but they should understand architecture concepts well and be able to perform at a medium level of proficiency in that role.

SUMMARY

This chapter really serves as a crash course into what an enterprise application is and what enterprise applications administrators are and do. We started by going over the purpose of this book and what the author's intent is in writing it. Hopefully, this aligns with your goals in reading it. We discussed the primary goals of the book being to teach, refine, and standardize with the standardization focusing on terminology, processes, and documentation used by enterprise applications administrators.

In order to clearly understand the concepts that we'll be discussing throughout the book, it's important to have a clear understanding of exactly what an enterprise application is. We defined this and went into some detail on enterprise applications, their role within corporations, and some examples of common enterprise applications. We also discussed what an enterprise application is *not* which is a critical part of clearly defining any subject.

Moving on past the enterprise application itself, we discussed the role of enterprise applications administrators and what that term means. As we examined the concept of what an enterprise applications administrator does, we were able to clearly define some of the job roles associated with enterprise applications administrators. Part of this includes specific services provided by the enterprise applications administrator and specific tasks that they are expected to perform.

Lastly, we briefly touched on the various technical areas that enterprise applications administrators are expected to comprehend. Each of these technical areas should be studied, practiced, and understood by the enterprise applications administrator and we'll be covering each in detail throughout this book. Additionally, there are softer skills that an enterprise applications administrator should have and we'll discuss those as well in later chapters.

CHAPTER 2

Networks

INFORMATION IN THIS CHAPTER

- Network Fundamentals
- Network Troubleshooting

NETWORK FUNDAMENTALS

The first technical area that we're going to discuss is that of networking and its relationship to enterprise applications. As mentioned in Chapter 1, a system connected to no others is considered the most secure, but this concept could never apply in the world of enterprise applications. Therefore, it is important to understand the technologies used to network various components of the enterprise application together and how those technologies work.

We will start with a discussion of network fundamentals. This will cover networking concepts, the most common protocols that you'll be working with, and the logical and physical aspects of networking. The term "physical" in this case includes networking hardware, cabling, and even wireless communications. The hardware that we'll discuss goes across the board from network interface cards (NICs) all the way to firewall devices. If you already have an understanding of these areas, then this will be more of a review than anything new. However, it is important to set an initial baseline of knowledge across all of these technical areas so that all enterprise applications administrators share the same core knowledge.

Networking Concepts

When you consider the basic concept of networking, a network is really just a connection between multiple systems and devices that allows communication between them. This connection can be made via a variety of methods including copper wiring, optical fiber cable, or even radio signals (wireless). When working with enterprise applications, the complexity of a network grows tremendously, but you should always remember that at its core, it is simply communication between multiple systems and devices. Sometimes this simplification will help focus your troubleshooting as it's very easy to become distracted by the sheer complexity of networking technologies and forget what it is that you're really trying to accomplish.

With that basic concept in mind, there are a few different types of networks that you need to be aware of. We'll only discuss two of them here, as the third, metropolitan area network or MAN is not as commonly used as it once was. The first is a local area network or LAN. A LAN is a network that is isolated within a single building, floor, or limited area. It allows for communication between devices close by and no others. The second major network type is a wide area network or WAN. A WAN covers a much larger area and can cross a city, state, country, or even work across the world. The most common design is to have a LAN in place to handle local communication and then connect that LAN to a WAN in order to facilitate communication with nonlocal systems. A perfect example of this is as simple as the LAN in your home connecting to a WAN in order to gain access to the Internet.

In the world of enterprise applications, you'll typically deal with the structure of LANs connecting to WANs in order to provide global connectivity. Depending on the application design and needs, an enterprise application may be limited to only communicate within the boundaries of the LAN. However, with the global footprint of most large enterprises, it is much more common for the enterprise application to be available in multiple locations by routing its traffic over WANs to those locations. This communication may also be further limited to allow the enterprise application to be available across all of the company's locations, but not be externally accessible to the Internet at large. We'll talk about how this works as we discuss network designs as well as security.

Topologies

There are multiple network topologies that exist and are used under various circumstances. Depending on the network design, one or more of these topologies may exist in any given enterprise network. Each topology has its own benefits and detriments, therefore, it is pretty common for multiple topologies to be implemented in order to work around each other's limitations. Network topologies can be categorized as being either physical or logical. In addition, a network's physical topology may or may not match the network's logical topology.

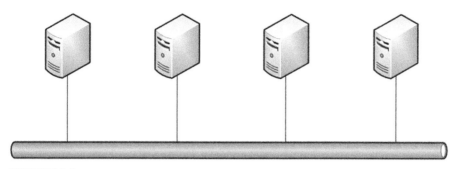

FIGURE 2.1
Bus topology.

Bus Topology

The earliest network topology (outside of just connecting two systems together with wires) was the bus topology. In this topology, the network was effectively a single physical line with a bunch of systems tapping into it. All systems could "hear" all communications that were sent along the line. To connect to the network, it was as simple as adding a "vampire tap" which would penetrate the cable shielding and attach metal prongs to the copper wires in the cable or adding a break to the cable and doing a similar connection with metal adapters. A diagram of this network topology is shown in Figure 2.1.

This topology allowed communication between all of the systems connected to it, but it had a couple very limiting factors. First, any break in the cable would disrupt communications network wide. Even if the break was intentional, such as modifying the cable to add a new system or removing a system from the network, the entire network would go down until the cable break was rectified. The network failure was due to two factors. First, obviously the systems on either side of the cable break would be unable to communicate. However, due to the very strict electrical tolerances required for the network to operate, even communications between multiple systems on the same side of the break would fail.

A second limitation to this topology is the number of systems that can communicate on any given network bus. All network communication using copper cabling is based on electrical signals generated by the systems on the network. If too many systems are communicating using the same cable, the messages can conflict with each other and cause the receiving system to never get the message that was sent to it. Due to the way that networking software is designed (we'll discuss protocols and software later), the sending system could, in some cases, identify that the message wasn't received due to the lack of an acknowledgment and resend the message. This would cause even

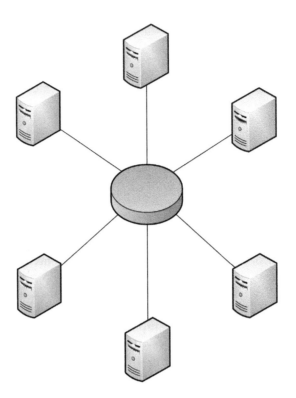

FIGURE 2.2
Ring topology.

more network traffic and make the problem even worse. Eventually, communications on the network would slow down to a crawl or fail entirely. Even with those limitations, the bus topology is still in use today due to its speed and usefulness under specific circumstances.

A logical bus topology means that when a system sends a message it will be received by all other devices on the network. Using the design shown in Figure 2.1, you will achieve a logical bus topology with the example of the use of a single cable. You can also get the same logical bus topology by using a physical star topology, as shown in Figure 2.3, with the central core being a device such as a network hub or repeater.

Ring Topology
Ring topologies are similar to a bus topology with the ends connected together so that it forms a ring. You can see an illustration of this in Figure 2.2. Ring topologies are not as common as they used to be, but they can still be found in some enterprise networks that have legacy systems in place. This means that some enterprise applications still have ring topologies

as part of their overall network structure. In a ring topology, any given communication is passed around the ring from system to system until a system determines that the communication was intended for it and "pulls" the communication out of the ring.

The ring topology worked well and eliminated a lot of issues around conflicting messages due to the way that the networking software utilized the topology. However, there were still some limitations to the topology that caused it to be less effective as the network grew. Since ring topologies are dependent on each system helping to pass messages along, problems with any system on the network could cause all communications on the network to fail. These system problems could be due to an actual failure or a simple misconfiguration. Since all of the systems have to communicate in exactly the same way and at the same speed in a ring topology, setting up the network configuration of a single system incorrectly can cause it to be unable to perform its duty in facilitating network communication. To help create a more fault-tolerant ring topology, companies can explore the option of using a dual-ring topology, eliminating the risk of a break in the ring.

TIPS & TRICKS

Token Ring Topology

If you encounter an enterprise application that is using a token ring network design, understand that this is referring to the logical ring topology and not necessarily the physical topology. The physical topology of a token ring network could be a physical ring topology or it could be a physical star topology.

Star Topology

A star topology is a network that is designed to look very similar to a star with a central core and many systems connected directly to that core. The systems in a star topology do not connect to each other, but instead pass messages to the central core that, in turn, passes the message to either all other systems or the specific destination system depending on the network design. This topology works well for many smaller networks and works around many of the detriments associated with bus or ring topologies. You can see the general design of this topology in Figure 2.3.

A star topology does have its own limitations but there are effective ways of working around them. In reality, you can only connect so many systems to the same star network before you begin to run into physical limitations, such as cable length or the number of ports available on the hardware used for the network. The star topology handles this by being easily extended into multiple stars with a central core in the middle. This design can be seen in

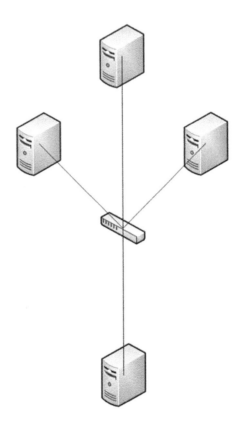

FIGURE 2.3
Star topology.

Figure 2.4, where there are multiple distinct star networks connected into a central core. In networking terminology, this core could be considered the *backbone* of the overall network. Messages intended for each system are transferred from the initiating system, to its star, into the core and then back out to the appropriate star and destination system.

Mesh Topology

The last topology that we'll discuss is the mesh topology. This topology is intended to allow a very high level of redundancy by connecting each system within the network to every other system on the network. Obviously, as more systems are added to the network, the number of connections between them grows tremendously. This can be seen in Figure 2.5, where there are a number of systems on the network with connections between all of them. This means that it is incredibly difficult to scale a network using a mesh topology.

So why would a mesh topology ever be in use if it is so complex and difficult to manage? The high level of redundancy in this topology makes it very

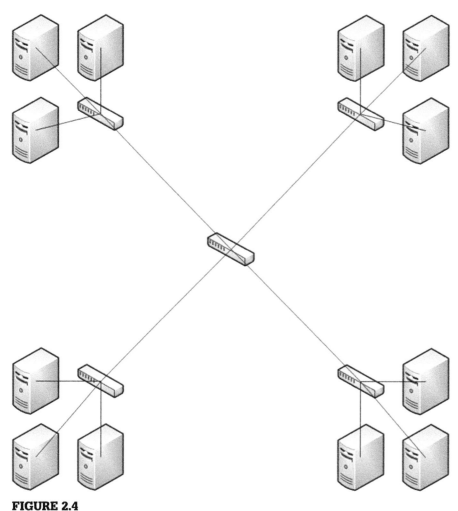

FIGURE 2.4
Star topology with backbone.

appealing for networks that absolutely must remain available at all times. Any single system or cable failure within a mesh topology cannot, by design, cause the network to fail, as there is always an alternative path that can be used for moving communications through the network. When working with WANs that require extensive redundancy or very small LANs with incredibly high availability requirements, a mesh topology could be a good fit. An illustration of how a mesh topology could be set up in one of these situations is shown in Figure 2.6. Companies can use a partially connected mesh topology, creating redundancy and fault tolerance where it is needed and nowhere else.

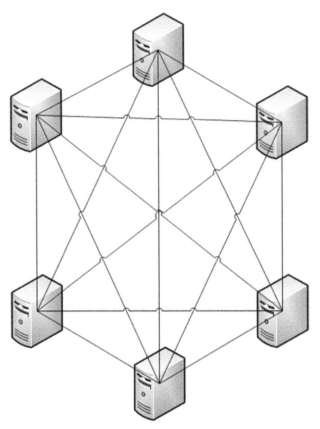

FIGURE 2.5
Fully connected mesh topology.

Protocols

When working with any network, it's important that the communication on the network follows a specific sequence of steps and very prescriptive rules. For example, you wouldn't want a system to send a communication that acknowledges the receipt of a message prior to it receiving the message. The set of rules that are followed for network communications is known as a protocol. Protocols work at various layers within the network, so let's first take a look at what layers we're dealing with.

OSI Model

In order to ensure that hardware and software created by multiple manufactures can communicate with each other effectively, a number of standards have been created. One of the standards most commonly referred to when discussing network concepts is the OSI model or Open Systems Interconnections

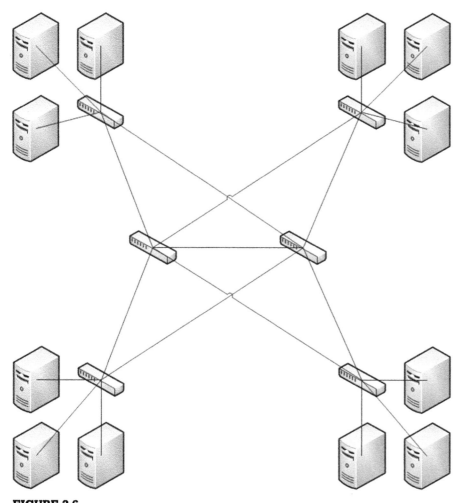

FIGURE 2.6
Star topology with mesh backbone.

Reference Model. This standard describes a seven-layer approach to network communications that breaks apart the communication process into layers associated with the type of communication being performed. The OSI model is intended as a reference framework and while it is leveraged in developing protocols, there are no protocols that use the OSI model exactly as it is defined. However, understanding the OSI model can really help in understanding the concepts behind all protocols that exist today.

The OSI model is comprised of seven layers. These are:

1. Physical
2. Data Link

3. Network
4. Transport
5. Session
6. Presentation
7. Application

Each layer deals with a specific type and method of communication. By definition, each layer is intended to communicate only with the layers above and below it. For example, the Transport layer should be able to communicate with the Network and Session layers. We'll now take a brief look at each layer and what it is intended to do.

Physical The physical layer deals with standardizing the physical connections between network devices. This includes cables, connectors, the electrical signals that go across the cables, and the NICs used by systems to connect to the physical network. This layer is intended to very explicitly define everything from the voltages used in the electrical signal to the sizes associated with various connectors and everything in between. Some other examples of definitions at this layer include the twist rate of wires within a cable, the length of various types of cables, and the topologies that can be used (such as those we discussed previously).

Data Link The Data Link layer, also known as Layer 2, starts moving towards more logical concepts versus the physical layer below it. These concepts include identifying individual systems on a network based on some form of addressing scheme, definitions of how packets of data should be formed for network communications, and how the integrity of the communication should be maintained through error correction routines. The Data Link layer has two sublayers, logical link control (LLC) and media access control (MAC).

Media Access Control The MAC sublayer is the interface between the Physical layer and the LLC sublayer. At this sublayer, every device is assigned an address. In today's common use, this is a MAC address. On any given network, each device must have a unique MAC address that can be factory set when the device is manufactured or set manually.

Logical Link Control The LLC is the Data Link layer closest to the Network layer. The LLC header will contain the protocol stack of the packet.

For example, if you are on a TCP/IP (Transmission Control Protocol/Internet Protocol) network and request access to a resource, the LLC sublayer will identify that the Network layer protocol being used is IP.

Network The Network layer, also known as Layer 3, abstracts itself even further from physical concepts and deals with routing traffic between systems at a logical level. While every device on a network has a MAC address that defines the physical address of the device, it also has some form of logical address, such as an IPv4 or IPv6 address, that provides a higher level logical address. The definitions associated with the Network layer help standardize how these addresses work, how communication is routed between devices at a logical level, and how communication is routed between multiple logical networks. The advantage of having a logical addressing scheme at the Network layer is that devices can communicate via the Network layer protocols regardless of whether or not they're using different Data Link layer protocols.

Any given network device must be able to translate between its Data Link layer address and its Network layer address. In addition, network devices that route communications between devices on the network must understand this translation in many cases to ensure that a communication intended for a specific Network layer address is sent to the correct Data Link layer device. Standards are defined which designate how this translation is performed depending on the protocol in use.

Transport The Transport layer starts to get into what is called the "upper layers" or "host layers" of the OSI model. This layer defines protocols that help even further ensure the integrity of network communications. At this layer, definitions are created that provide even more granular error correction for any messages that are sent between two devices on the network. In some cases, this involves taking large messages that are sent from the Session layer and splitting them up into more digestible chunks that increase the likelihood of the message getting to its destination successfully. Obviously, the larger a message is, the higher the probability that some small part of the message could get mangled causing the entire message to be unreadable. Protocols at the Transport layer help in preventing this. The Transport layer also handles creating the logical "end-to-end connection" between devices and adding the appropriate messages to maintain that active connection. We'll discuss this in a little more detail when we get into specific protocols and the difference between connection-based and connectionless protocols.

Session While a logical connection is maintained at the Transport layer, a specific session is maintained at the Session layer. This may seem confusing, but there are specific rules that differentiate a connection from a session.

A session is based on maintaining a two-way conversation between two devices based on simplex (only one device can "talk"), half duplex (both devices can "talk" but only one at a time), and full duplex (both devices "talk" at the same time). If you contrast this against a Transport layer protocol, the Transport doesn't care who "talks" when; it just cares about making sure that the "words" are able to get to each system correctly.

Presentation The Presentation layer starts getting closer to things that humans can actually understand. Instead of electrical impulses (physical) or binary code (data link), the Presentation layer deals with standards that define actual characters and how data gets presented to devices. This layer also has definitions associated with compressing characters to require less data to represent them so that they take less time to transmit or receive on the network. Along with compression, there are also encryption standards that function at this layer. We'll discuss encryption in a little more detail in Chapter 5 when we discuss the topic of security.

Application Finally, we make it to the top of the OSI model, which is the Application layer. This is the layer that defines how software interacts with the network. While we typically think of "application" in the context of software such as enterprise applications, the OSI model intends for the definition of "application" to really be that interface between the software and the functionality that the network can provide. Obviously, technology has changed a great deal over the years and our terminology has changed with it so it's important to be aware of how the term "application" applies in the OSI model concepts versus our concepts of information technology today. Protocols at the Application layer in the OSI model include examples such as File Transfer Protocol (FTP), Domain Name System (DNS), Simple Mail Transfer Protocol (SMTP), and other similar standards that you may have heard of before.

TCP/IP Model

TCP/IP is probably the most commonly used set of protocols in the world today. It is not a single protocol, but rather a combination of a few different protocols. In fact, "TCP/IP" in this context refers to a model that carries various names, such as the "internet protocol suite," "DoD model," "Arpanet reference model," and "Internet model," but is commonly referred to by the two most important protocols within the suite/model, TCP and IP. For ease of use, we'll refer to this model as the TCP/IP model within this book since this is the most common nomenclature today.

The TCP/IP model is comprised of a number of layers that loosely match up with various layers within the OSI model. Depending on who is defining the model and what text it is in, the number of layers and their alignment with

Table 2.1 OSI and TCP/IP Models with Example Protocols

OSI Model Layer	TCP/IP Model Layer	Protocol Examples
Application		DHCP, DNS, FTP, HTTP, IRC, LDAP, RPC, SSH, TLS/SSL, SMTP
Presentation	Application	
Session		
Transport	Transport	TCP, UDP, SCTP
Network	Internet	IPv4, IPv6, ICMP, IPsec
Data Link	Link	ARP, RARP, L2TP, DSL, PPP
Physical		

the OSI model differs. These layers all have functions similar to the OSI layer definitions and have distinct protocols associated with the layers. Table 2.1 shows the various layers of the OSI model, the TCP/IP model layers that match them (based on the "Internet model" defined in RFC 1122), and then some of the protocols that exist within each of these layers. This list is by no means exhaustive, but it should give you a general idea of how the model translates into its various protocols.

As you can see in Table 2.1, the TCP/IP model doesn't really have alignment with the Physical layer of the OSI model, but all other layers are represented. This has been debated in the past and some texts document an additional layer for the TCP/IP model that aligns with the Physical layer of the OSI model. Since the TCP/IP model does not have any specific protocols or standards that define physical requirements, it is the opinion of the author that the intent of the TCP/IP model is to be abstracted from any physical requirements and provide definition for various functionality regardless of the medium used.

Link Layer The Link layer within the TCP/IP model includes protocols, such as ARP (Address Resolution Protocol), RARP (Reverse ARP), DSL (Digital Subscriber Line), Ethernet, L2TP (Layer 2 Tunneling Protocol), PPP (Point to Point Protocol), NTP (Network Time Protocol), and others. The intent of protocols in this layer is to provide for network communication within a LAN exclusively. Each of these protocols is able to provide for that functionality or support it in a variety of ways. For example, L2TP allows for creation of a virtual private network (VPN), which basically extends a local network so that the system connecting to the network appears local to any other system on that network. The DSL protocol performs a similar function but includes definition of the use of telephone lines to create the "local" network.

The last protocol that we'll talk about in this layer is ARP. This protocol is very commonly used and performs (obviously) address resolution between the Internet layer of the TCP/IP model and the Link layer. This is most commonly used to translate IP addresses into MAC addresses allowing for the layering approach between physical and logical addressing as defined in the OSI model. It is important to note that since this protocol resides in the Link layer of the TCP/IP model, it is not routed and is therefore only used for address translation within the local network.

ARP plays a large role in enterprise applications as it performs a critical address translation role necessary for most enterprise applications to function and can sometimes be a source of problems. We'll discuss this further in Network Troubleshooting section as well as in Chapter 5 when we talk about security.

Internet Layer Within the TCP/IP model, the Internet layer is where the "IP" part of the model lives. This layer also includes other protocols, such as Internet Control Message Protocol (ICMP), Internet Group Management Protocol (IGMP), and IPsec. In the context of the TCP/IP model, the term "Internet" does not refer to the large network comprised of millions of systems which evolved from the original ARPANET, but rather the concept of internetworking or allowing multiple smaller networks to communicate with each other. It is in this layer that definitions exist that allow for addressing, routing, and some level of error detection for communications intended to cross local network boundaries.

Internet Protocol IP is a protocol within the Internet layer of the TCP/IP model or the Network layer of the OSI model, which defines addressing and how individual messages are routed to their intended destination. IP addresses in IPv4 (the prevailing numbering system) follow a format of xxx.xxx.xxx.xxx, where each decimal value (0−255) translates into 8 binary bits called an octet. For example, 10.5.0.1 translates into 00001010.00000101.00000000.00000001. You'll typically deal with IP addresses in the decimal format, but knowing the binary translation becomes important when dealing with subnetting which we'll discuss in a little bit.

One important thing to note about IP addresses is that every machine on a TCP/IP network will have one or more IP addresses assigned to it. Unlike MAC addresses where only one address can be associated with a device, multiple IP addresses, through their nature of being a logical address versus a physical address, can be assigned to a single device. This leverages the capabilities provided by the ARP protocol in the Link layer to perform the address translation appropriately.

IPv6 is a newer addresses scheme and was created to address the shortage of IP addresses under the IPv4 scheme. IPv6 uses a 128-bit address as compared to IPv4 32-bit addressing scheme. This change increases the number of available addresses tremendously (from 2^{32} to 2^{128}) and changes quite a few things about how IP works. Due to these changes, IPv4 and IPv6 are not interoperable which has slowed the transition between the two versions of the protocol. Most enterprise applications as of the time of this writing work on networks that are still using the IPv4 protocol so most of our focus will be on how IPv4 works rather than IPv6.

Subnetting Subnetting is a way of breaking up TCP/IP networks into smaller segments that are easier to manage, isolate traffic like broadcasts, and make system identification a little easier. This is done by applying a subnet mask to identify how much of a network address space is available for a specific subnet. This gets back into the binary conversion mentioned previously.

Any given IP address is split into a network value and a host value. The network value determines which network the address belongs to and the host value identifies a specific host within that network. A series of "classes" define generic network/host value combinations. The most common classes are A, B, and C. These break down as follows with X identifying the network and Y identifying available host values:

- Class A—XXX.YYY.YYY.YYY
- Class B—XXX.XXX.YYY.YYY
- Class C—XXX.XXX.XXX.YYY

As you can see by this, a Class A address space can (theoretically) have only 256 networks, but can host 16,777,216 hosts per network. A Class C on the other hand can have (again in theory) 16,777,216 networks but only 256 hosts each. There are some numbers that are reserved and others that cannot be used within each address space, so the full number of networks and hosts are not really available in practice.

Each class is associated with a subnet mask. These are as follows:

- Class A—255.0.0.0 or /8
- Class B—255.255.0.0 or /16
- Class C—255.255.255.0 or /24

These subnet masks are values that are used to define how the network/host split works for the IP address. This is done by performing a logical AND operation between the subnet mask and the IP address in binary. Typically you won't have to deal with much of this math when performing enterprise applications administration, but it's important to understand what you're working with.

The way this works is that you take an IP address such as 10.5.0.1 and first convert it to binary:

```
00001010.00000101.00000000.00000001
```

Then you take the defined network subnet mask. In this case, let's say we're using 255.255.255.0 or Classless Inter-Domain Routing (CIDR) 24. Convert that to binary as well:

```
11111111.11111111.11111111.00000000
```

CIDR notation is determined by counting the 1s within the subnet mask. As you can see in the string above, there are 24 1s. Once the subnet mask is converted, you know that every binary value within an IP address that matches a 1 in the subnet mask is part of the network address. Any binary value within an IP address that matches a 0 in the subnet mask is part of the host address. In this example, that means any value in the last octet is a host.

There is a mathematical method that can be used to determine the "network address" specifically. You basically do a logical AND operation. That means that if both values are 1, the result is a 1. If both values are 0, the result is a 0. And if the values differ (1 and 0), the result is a 0. So, for our example, we get the following:

```
00001010.00000101.00000000.00000001
11111111.11111111.11111111.00000000
00001010.00000101.00000000.00000000
```

Translating this back into decimal gives us 10.5.0.0, which means that the network address in this example is 10.5.0. This would be written as 10.5.0.0124.

Transport Layer The Transport layer of the TCP/IP model is intended to define how messages are communicated between an application on one system and a matching application on another system. Again, keep in mind that the layering approach of both the OSI and TCP/IP models intends for messages to flow between each layer in sequence with each providing its additive functionality within the communication process. In the case of the Transport layer of the TCP/IP model, there are two primary protocols that provide for connectivity, error detection and correction, flow control, and multiplexing. These are the TCP and the User Datagram Protocols (UDP).

Transmission Control Protocol/User Datagram Protocol TCP and UDP differ tremendously, but the one area where they are similar is their concept of multiplexing. Multiplexing is the concept of having multiple connection endpoints on a single system. Just as a system with one MAC address can have multiple IP addresses, a single IP address can have multiple ports. A port is a reference to a specific endpoint on the system and the multiplexing associated with handling messages with different port definitions is part of the functionality of both the TCP and UDP protocols. Within these two protocols, a port is a value from 0 to 65,535 that identifies a specific channel to use when communicating to a system. TCP and UDP ports are separate and communicate in different ways, so you can have the same port number assigned for both TCP and UDP with no conflict. However, you cannot have two applications listen on the same protocol and port.

There are quite a few ports that are considered "well known" because they're assigned to specific Application layer protocols to use. Depending on the application, these may be TCP ports, UDP ports, or both. Some examples are listed below:

- 20—FTP—Data
- 21—FTP—Control
- 22—Secure Shell (SSH)
- 23—Telnet
- 25—SMTP
- 53—DNS
- 69—Trivial File Transfer Protocol (TFTP)
- 80/443—Hypertext Transfer Protocol/HTTP Secure (HTTP/HTTPS)
- 110—POP3
- 115—Simple File Transfer Protocol (SFTP)
- 161—Simple Network Management Protocol (SNMP)
- 389—Lightweight Directory Access Protocol (LDAP)

Typically ports below 1024 are considered reserved for "core" protocols and sometimes require extended permissions on an operating system to use them.

TCP is a connection-based protocol and provides for a high level of reliability. Every TCP connection involves a "three-way handshake" to set up the connection prior to communicating any application data across the communications channel. Because of its connection-based operation, TCP provides a confirmation to acknowledge every message that it receives. This allows the sending application to rely on TCP to ensure that the destination application receives each message or to let the application know if there is a communications problem of some type. Applications using the TCP protocol tend to be those which require reliability and a high confidence level that each message sent is received at its destination.

UDP on the other hand is a connectionless protocol that requires no handshake and functions on a "fire and forget" model where each message is sent and hopefully received by its recipient. The UDP protocol does not provide any confirmations that a message has been received and is therefore only used in cases where it's considered okay for a message or two to be lost. Because of the lack of back and forth communication required to handle confirmations, UDP is able to function at a higher rate of speed and works very well for applications that need to operate very quickly, such as DNS,

SNMP, and Dynamic Host Configuration Protocol (DHCP). In addition, many audio or video streaming services use the UDP protocol for communications.

Application Layer All of the protocols that fall within the TCP/IP model layers that we have discussed so far exist to support the protocols in the Application layer of the model. It is these protocols that provide the base functionality that we have grown to rely on in the world of enterprise applications today. While many enterprise applications have their own internal protocols, port assignments, and communications requirements, they all rely on the same concepts used by the core protocols that exist within this layer. In addition, while protocols in the TCP/IP model Application layer may not precisely match the functionality of enterprise applications, they can frequently mimic the functionality to such a degree that troubleshooting can be done at a more granular level than within the enterprise application itself. We'll discuss this more in Network troubleshooting section.

Ethernet

With the concepts of the OSI and TCP/IP models in mind, let discuss a few of the protocols commonly used and how they align with it. First on the list is Ethernet. Ethernet is one of the most common protocols used today for communications between systems and operates at the first two levels of the OSI model (physical and data link). Ethernet has a variety of speeds available (10 megabits per second (Mbps), 100 Mbps, 1000 Mbps (also called Gigabit), and 10 GbE) and can use many different types of cable. These combinations of cable and speed all fall under various permutations of Ethernet, such as 100BaseTX (100 Mbps using Category 5 cabling) or 1000BaseLX (1000 Mbps using optical fiber cabling), but they're all technically still Ethernet and follow specific standards for the two OSI model layers that they operate at.

As you'll recall, the Physical layer of the OSI model deals with the connectors, cabling, and other physical requirements. The Data Link layer deals with addressing and message integrity. In the Ethernet protocol, the Physical layer is handled with the specification of cable requirements, connectors, etc. The Data Link layer is actually broken up into two more granular layers called the MAC layer and the LLC layer. The MAC layer handles addressing, collision detection, and collision correction while the LLC handles error control and multiplexing. In some modern network environments, the LLC sublayer is no longer responsible for error correction and this work has moved up to the Transport Layer. Multiplexing in this context is the ability to combine multiple messages into a single transmission and then break them apart when they're received.

TIPS & TRICKS

Acronym Reuse

If you've had any experience in information technology at all, you're sure to have noticed that there are a lot of acronyms used in this industry. Entire dictionaries exist to help define the most commonly used acronyms. The biggest problem with acronyms, however, is that there are only so many combinations of letters that can be used. Consequently, many acronyms have different meanings depending on their context or usage. It's even more challenging when identical acronyms are used within the same context. This is the case for the acronym "MAC." When referring to the sublayer of the OSI model, MAC means "media access control." However, the hardware that implements the MAC such as an NIC is also a "MAC" itself. In this case, "MAC" means "medium access controller." So you have a NIC which is a MAC assigned a MAC. Perhaps IT really means "Insane Terminology"?

Application Layer Protocols

As we've gone through the various layers of the TCP/IP and OSI models, we've touched on a number of the protocols that reside in the Application layer already. The list showing protocol ports in the Transport Layer section is a good example of many Application layer protocols. Each of these leverages the functionality of the Transport layer protocols of TCP and UDP to perform its communications and provides a variety of functions. Since most enterprise applications do require a few of these protocols, let's go through some of the most frequently used protocols and discuss how they apply to enterprise applications administration.

Dynamic Host Configuration Protocol DHCP is used for automatically configuring devices that join a TCP/IP-based network. This configuration can include elements such as an IP address, subnet mask, DNS server addresses, a default gateway address, and other configuration information. A server set up to use DHCP and host the configuration information in a local data store provides this configuration information. DHCP uses UDP port 67 on the server side and UDP port 68 on the client side. DHCP also has two versions: DHCPv4 and DHCPv6 to support IPv4 and IPv6, respectively. These two versions, much like the two versions of IP, are very different and are therefore considered separate protocols and use separate ports. DHCPv6 uses UDP port 546 on the client side and UDP 547 on the server side.

The process for obtaining DHCP configuration information is pretty simple: Discover, Offer, Request, and Acknowledge (DORA). The DHCP client broadcasts a message called a DHCP discover message. The server will reply with a DHCP offer message that includes an offered IP address, subnet mask, and some other data. If the client agrees to accept the address, it will respond with a DHCP request message to let the server know that it will be using the offered address. Finally, the server responds with a DHCP acknowledge message that includes the time that the address lease is valid as well as any other information requested by the client.

There are two additional message types used with DHCP. The first is a DHCP information request which is sent by the DHCP client. This is effectively a request for additional configuration information that may not have been included in the initial DHCP offer message. There is also a DHCP release message that can be used by the client. This isn't required as the DHCP lease will expire at its configured expiry time, but it can be used optionally prior to requesting a new address or new lease of the same address if there is a need.

Most enterprise applications are configured to use static IP addresses for the servers that host the application, but it is also possible for those servers to use a dynamic address with a DHCP reservation. A DHCP reservation will offer the same IP address lease to a system by using the NIC's MAC address to identify it. Client systems, on the other hand, are usually configured to use DHCP without address reservations except under special circumstances. There are some potential issues that can arise with DHCP configuration that can cause the enterprise application to be unavailable or act oddly for the client system. We'll discuss this further in the Network Troubleshooting section.

Domain Name System DNS is a protocol that is designed to perform name to IP address resolution services. DNS provides multiple types of records for a domain name. The main types of records are:

- Address Record (A or AAAA)—Domain name to IPv4 or IPv6
- Name Server Record (NS)—Where to find an Authorative name server for a particular domain
- Mail Exchanger Record (MX)—Tells the name of the e-mail servers for a domain
- Pointer Record (PTR)—Opposite of A record; IP address to domain name lookup
- Canonical Name Record (CNAME)—Name alias record

At its core, DNS takes a domain name such as WWW.FAIRCLOTHSEC.COM and translates that into its actual IP address so that IP-based systems can communicate. This name-based system is used both internally within corporate enterprises as well as worldwide on all Internet-based systems. The configuration and use of DNS is very complex and we won't be going into much depth on the topic here, but we will be covering some of the basics.

The DNS protocol is based on a hierarchical structure. There are top level domains (TLDs), such as COM, ORG, and NET. These TLDs serve as the root-naming source for all Internet-based systems. Below that are some example subdomains, such as FAIRCLOTHSEC and SYNGRESS. When separating the subdomain from the TLD, a period is used so this is written as

FAIRCLOTHSEC.COM and SYNGRESS.COM, respectively. Finally, as we continue to move down the hierarchy, we get to individual hostnames, such as WWW (World Wide Web) and FTP. When writing these, we continue to move from right to left and separate with periods so we have WWW. FAIRCLOTHSEC.COM and FTP.SYNGRESS.COM.

All of the storage of this naming data are based on a hierarchy of name servers using the DNS protocol. Any given domain must have at least one server that is set as the authoritative server for the domain. There are also name servers that are defined for the TLDs that are called root name servers. These name servers are technically responsible for handling the initial DNS request for resolving any name associated with the TLD that they are responsible for. In reality, this information is cached in many, many name servers and those caches are usually called instead of communicating with the root name servers directly.

When a name needs to be resolved, a request is made to the root name server (or an appropriate cache) to find out which name server is the authoritative server for the next subdomain in the domain name being searched for. This authoritative server is then called to determine the authoritative server for the next subdomain until finally the authoritative name server for the specific host is called and an IP address for the host is returned. In practice, there is a lot of caching performed in this process so the authoritative servers are not called directly in all cases. To speed the process of name resolution and reduce server load, caches are typically used for most resolution requests. These caches will hold a copy of the appropriate DNS data for a specific duration called a "time-to-live" for the data.

File Transfer Protocol The next protocol that we'll talk about is FTP. FTP is a protocol designed specifically to transfer (surprise!) files between two hosts. FTP is not as commonly used as it once was as many file transfers are now being done using HTTP or other protocols. However, when a large file needs to be transferred and security isn't a big concern, FTP is the protocol of choice. If a secure transfer is needed, FTP can be used with Transport Layer Security (TLS)/SSL (discussed later in this chapter) for encryption and the combination is referred to as FTPS. Combining FTP with SSH can also be used to provide a layer of security with this combination being referred to as SFTP. To add to our acronym list, SFTP can also stand for Secure File Transfer Protocol.

The FTP protocol works in two modes: active and passive. They follow this sequence of events:

Active mode

1. The FTP client initializes a control connection from a random port higher than 1024 to the server's port 21.

2. The FTP client sends a PORT command instructing the server to connect to a port on the client 1 higher than the client's control port. This is the client's data port.
3. The server sends data to the client from server port 20 to the client's data port.

Passive mode

1. The FTP client initializes a random port higher than 1024 as the control port and initializes the port 1 higher than the control port as the data port.
2. The FTP client sends a PASV command instructing the server to open a random data port.
3. The server sends a PORT command notifying the client of the data port number that was just initialized.
4. The FTP client then sends data from the data port it initialized to the data port the server instructed it to use.

Hypertext Transfer Protocol HTTP is arguably the most common Application layer protocol in use today. This is the protocol used for most nonsecure WWW communication. HTTP functions in a standard request—response mode where the HTTP client makes a request to the HTTP server, which in turn processes the request and responds. HTTP relies on uniform resource identifiers (URIs), typically in the form of uniform resource locators (URLs), in order to identify the requested file to request.

TIPS AND TRICKS

URIs? URLs? URNs?

There is a lot of confusion between uniform resource identifiers (URIs), uniform resource locators (URLs), and uniform resource names (URNs). In many cases, you'll hear the first two used almost interchangeably while never hearing the third. The truth is, they're all related. A URI can be a URL, a URN, or both. The concept behind a URI is to identify a resource in some manner. How this is done varies on whether a URN or a URL is used.

A URN refers to a resource by name and is used for identifying books by ISBN, magazines by ISSN, and movies by ISAN. When any of these resources are assigned a number or "name" within their respective URN namespace, they can in the future be located by requesting the resource by that name. URNs use the syntax of urn: <namespace identifier>:<namespace string>. For example, urn:isbn:1597496278 would refer to another book by this author.

A URL refers to a resource by its location. This is typically a web location that is using a designated protocol to transfer a specific resource. The format for a URL differs and follows the syntax of scheme://domain:port/path. Scheme can refer to a protocol, such as HTTP or FTP, or it can refer to some other application or function. For example, http://www.syngress.com is a valid URL as are http://www.mkp.com:80/ or about:blank. Depending on the software used, each of these may perform different functions, but all are URLs.

HTTP has a number of different methods that can be used as part of the request–reply framework. Some of these are:

- CONNECT—Switches the current connection to a TCP/IP tunnel
- DELETE—Deletes a specified resource as defined by the URI
- GET—Requests a specified resource as defined by the URI
- HEAD—Requests just the headers of a specific resource as defined by the URI
- OPTIONS—Requests information on what HTTP methods the server supports
- PATCH—Requests that specific modifications be made to a specified resource as defined by the URI
- POST—Requests that the data included in the request be passed to the specific resource as defined by the URI
- PUT—Requests that the data included in the request be stored as the resource defined by the URI
- TRACE—Requests that the server respond with a message that duplicates what it received in the request

Not all servers support all of these methods and some are explicitly turned off for security purposes. In addition, as the HTTP protocol evolves over time, more and more methods are added as options in the protocol definition. The bare minimum methods necessary to support HTTP are GET and HEAD. Anything else is useful, but not required.

Lightweight Directory Access Protocol LDAP is used for directory services. These directory services can be any type of data stored in a hierarchical manner and are frequently used for storing corporate identity information or server configuration information. Active Directory, for example, is Microsoft's implementation of a directory service used for a number of different purposes, but is accessible via LDAP.

LDAP works in a request–response model similar to HTTP, but does have a couple of unique differences. First, with LDAP, multiple requests can be sent to the LDAP server without waiting for a response from the last request. With this in mind, the replies may come back out of order. The design of LDAP is built to handle this method of communication and reorders the incoming data if necessary.

Also similar to HTTP, LDAP supports a number of different methods, which are considered "operations" in LDAP terminology. These operations include:

- Add—Insert new entry into the directory
- Bind—Authenticate and establish a compatible LDAP version for communication

- Compare—Check to see if a specific attribute exists for a directory entry
- Delete—Delete a directory entry
- Modify—Modify the data associated with a directory entry
- Search—Search for directory contents and retrieve those contents
- Unbind—Close the connection

All entries in an LDAP compatible directory service have a specific hierarchy that is used to store and present the data that they contain. This hierarchy is based on each entry having a unique distinguished name (DN) and one or more attributes. Each attribute can have one or more values associated with the attribute. The DN is where the hierarchy of the directory entry is stored and is comprised of both the relative distinguished name (RDN) and the DNs of the parent objects in the hierarchy. For example, in the DN `dn: cn:fairclothj,dc=fairclothsec,dc=com`, the full string is the DN while the substring "`cn:fairclothj`" is the RDN. The DNs of the parent objects are "`dc = fairclothsec`" and "`dc = com`." CN is the acronym for Common Name and DC is the acronym for Domain Component.

Each DN can have multiple attributes as mentioned above. These could look similar to the following:

```
dn: cn=perryjct,dc=fairclothsec,dc=com
cn: perryjct
givenName: John
middleName: Clarence
middleName: Travis
surName: Perry
telephoneNumber: +1 800 555 1212
telephoneNumber: +1 800 555 1213
mail:perryjct@fairclothsec.com
objectClass: person
```

As you can see in this example, the individual specified has a number of attributes including givenName, surname, mail, etc. There are also attributes that have multiple values, such as middleName and telephoneNumber. In this example you'll also notice that the CN is included in both the DN as well as specified as a distinct attribute. This is because the DN is not technically an attribute and can, in theory, change if the directory entry is moved to a different relative path. In order to maintain a consistent CN, this value is stored as an attribute.

Simple Mail Transfer Protocol SMTP is designed for sending email. This may seem like a pretty obvious protocol that doesn't warrant much discussion, but with email being considered a critical communications channel, it's important to understand how SMTP works so that you know how to troubleshoot and fix it. SMTP is comprised of a mail submission agent (MSA), a mail user agent (MUA), a mail retrieval agent (MRA), a mail exchanger (MX), a mail delivery agent (MDA), and potentially multiple servers in between known as mail transfer agents (MTAs). As you can see, the transfer of email is complex from the start just due to the number of servers and agents involved in the process.

The process flow for sending an email goes as follows:

1. The MUA (client) sends the properly formatted email to the MSA or directly to an MTA
2. The MSA sends the mail to its MTA
3. Additional MTAs may be routed through until the email is on a "boundary MTA"
4. The boundary MTA performs a query using DNS to identify the MX for the domain the email is intended for
5. The MTA connects to the MX and transfers the email
6. The MX transfers the email to the MDA
7. At this point, the mail is transferred to the appropriate internal mail server and stored until the MUA or MRA connects to it and retrieves the message on behalf of the user (usually using the POP or IMAP Protocols)

The actual sequence of commands to construct and send a message using the SMTP protocol is actually a little easier than following the email delivery path. It consists of a "HELO" message to open the communications channel followed by the commands "MAIL," "RCPT," and "DATA" each with the appropriate data to form the email header and message. Finally, the connection is terminated using the "QUIT" command. When we get to the Network Troubleshooting section, we'll go over how to manually construct an SMTP message to check email functionality.

Simple Network Management Protocol The next protocol on our list is SNMP. This protocol is primarily intended for managing network devices including switches, routers, and even servers. For this to happen the device being managed must have an SNMP agent installed and there must be another system with an SNMP client. This can be as simple as an administrator's computer with a basic client or as complex as a server with a full Network Management System (NMS) software suite. The client can then connect to the agent to read and write data or the agent can connect to the NMS to push out management data.

The SNMP model supports both reading and writing of configuration and management information depending on the configuration of the agent and the device. When in read-only mode, the agent can be queried in order to gather information from the device or the agent can be configured to push its information to the NMS. When configured for read/write mode, the agent can not only provide information but also accept new configuration data on behalf of the device allowing it to be remotely configured.

The definition for SNMP includes details on how the protocol should work, a basic schema that should be used for the data, as well as some basic data objects. However, it does not define which variables any given device should have or which ones should be available via the agent. Due to this, SNMP is incredibly extensible and can work for both older devices as well as new devices which may have additional variables that need to be defined. With that in mind, the client does need to understand the variables available from the agent in order to properly query it or accept pushed data. This is accomplished through the use of a management information base (MIB). The MIB is basically a file that shows all of the variables that are available through the agent presented in a hierarchical manner.

In order to use SNMP to manage a device, you will need a client that supports the SNMP protocol, the MIB for the agent that you are going to connect to, the address for the device where the agent is set up, and a community string. This community string is used to determine whether or not the client is authorized to read or write data from or to the agent. In early versions of SNMP, there was no authentication and all of this was passed in cleartext which led to a number of vulnerabilities. Later versions improved on this by adding authentication and encryption to the protocol. After importing the MIB into the client and adding the appropriate configuration information necessary to connect to the agent, you should be able to successfully connect to the agent and retrieve data. You'll most frequently use this as an enterprise applications administrator when trying to gather information from remote devices.

KEY CONCEPTS

Application Layer Protocols

Each Application layer protocol can be used by enterprise applications to provide for specific services. For example, the enterprise application may use SMTP to send emails to customers or TLS to create a secure communications channel between various application components. Understanding how each of these protocols work can help you to better understand the enterprise application and how it performs various tasks.

Secure Shell SSH is designed to be an encrypted communications channel between two systems for the purpose of either allowing remote control of a system or encrypting other traffic being transferred between the two. The primary focus of SSH is around security and ensuring that the communications between these two systems are encrypted. It uses a client—server model wherein the system making the remote connection is the client and the system receiving the connection is the server. SSH is most commonly used for securely connecting to a "shell" or terminal on a remote UNIX-based system replacing Telnet and other unsecure connection methods. However, SSH can also be used for creating a secure tunnel that can be used by other protocols that cannot create a secure connection by themselves.

SSH does support standard username/password authentication, but its primary design is around the use of keys using public-key cryptography. We'll talk more about public-key cryptography in Chapter 5 when we discuss security, but for now, be aware that public-key cryptography is based on the existence of a public key and a private key. The public key can be shared, but the private key is only intended for use by the person who generated the keypair. In the case of SSH, a public key can be added to the authorized key list for the server. When this is done, the owner of the keypair can then use their private key as part of the connection routine from their SSH client and the SSH server will authorize them to connect.

Telnet Telnet is a basic protocol that allows for a terminal connection to a remote machine. It functions similar to SSH in that it is a client/server based application, but does not offer any of the security mechanisms available with SSH. In fact, data transferred using the Telnet protocol is completely unencrypted including any passwords sent across the communications channel. Therefore, it is very rarely used for actual terminal sessions when a more secure protocol, such as SSH, is available. However, a Telnet client is one of the most useful tools available for any enterprise applications administrator.

Telnet is a very simple protocol, which means that the client implementing the Telnet protocol is pretty simple as well. In the case of Telnet clients, this works out very well because the client can be used for purposes other than creating a connection to a remote Telnet server. Basically, a Telnet client makes a socket connection to a defined port on a remote host. After this connection is established, it passes any data sent from the client to the server and vice versa. Due to this, you can use a Telnet client to connect to a system using the SMTP protocol on the appropriate port and manually send mail commands. You can also connect to a system serving as an HTTP server on the appropriate port and send or receive data using HTTP. This makes Telnet clients very useful as a troubleshooting tool even if they shouldn't be used for remote terminal sessions due to the security risks.

Transport Layer Security The last protocol that we'll discuss is TLS. TLS is the replacement for SSL and is a protocol that allows for the creation of a secure communications channel using encryption. TLS does this using a few different methods including performing key exchanges using public-key (asymmetric) cryptography, shared-key (symmetric) encryption for confidentiality, and hashing to ensure integrity. This combination of security techniques allows for TLS to ensure a secure communications channel between two systems and is used with HTTP to create the HTTPS protocol as well as with other protocols.

The establishment of a TLS session happens relatively quickly making it transparent for the most part, but it's actually a pretty complex process. When dealing with enterprise applications, you'll frequently need to work with and understand how TLS works and how these communication sessions are established. This is critical for understanding security issues such as man-in-the-middle attacks (discussed in Chapter 5) and how TLS connections can be terminated at a proxy or load balancer to allow for external security and internal transparency.

The session starts with the client requesting a secure connection with the server. This request includes some important data, such as version numbers, encryption settings, and any other information necessary for the server to be able to respond back to the client correctly. The server then responds with much of the same data regarding its own configuration as well as its certificate. If the client's initial request specified that a two-way secure connection should be created (authentication of both the client and the server versus just authentication of the server), the server will also include a request for the client's certificate in its response. The client then authenticates that the server's certificate is valid and that the server represented by the certificate is indeed the one that the client is communicating with. Next, the client creates a key to use as a premaster secret key (used for symmetric-key cryptography) and encrypts it using the public key that is included in the server's certificate. If two-way encryption is being used, the client also includes its own certificate in the response.

When the server receives the response, it authenticates the client if two-way encryption is being used in a manner similar to how the client authenticated the server previously. The server then uses its private key to decrypt the premaster secret key that the client generated. The server then uses an algorithm to generate a master secret key using the premaster secret key. The client uses the same algorithm so that in the end they both have a copy of the master secret key. Both the client and the server then take this master secret key and generate session keys. It is these symmetric session keys that are then used to encrypt every message transferred during the secure session between the client and the server. Finally, the client sends a message to the server indicating that all future messages will be encrypted using the session key followed by a message encrypted with the session key indicating that the client is done with its part of setting up the connection. The server responds with a similar message to let it know that all future responses will be encrypted using the session key, again, followed by an encrypted message using the session key that indicates that the server-side setup of the secure channel is complete. The secure connection is then available for all future messages as each are in turn encrypted with the session key and decrypted when they arrive on the opposing system.

This complex sequence of events is required in order to set up a secure channel using the TLS protocol. Once established, this channel can then be used by other Application layer protocols to securely transfer data. We've already touched on its use with HTTP, but TLS is also used to provide secure channels for FTP, Network News Transfer Protocol (NNTP), and SNMP among others. The use of TLS overcomes any encryption deficiencies inherent with the definition of these other protocols and allows for a standardized method of creating secure communications channels within the TCP/IP model.

Networking Hardware and Cabling

Now that we've discussed the logical part of networking and the key concepts associated with this technology, it's time to move to the physical aspects. When working with networks, physically you're primarily dealing with hardware network devices and the cabling which connects them. Again, this book is not intended to give you the expertise to immediately jump in and become a network administrator, but you should gain enough knowledge to be able to successfully communicate with experts in the field and understand the basic concepts behind networking technology.

Network Hardware

The first aspect of physical networking that we'll be discussing is the hardware. Network devices tend to be dedicated pieces of hardware that serve one or more networking functions. In large enterprise networks, you will typically find that devices are more dedicated to a single function and that there are many devices that do the same thing. For example, in a small office network, you could have a single device that performs switching, routing, firewall, and VPN functionality. At home you may have a single device that performs switching, routing, firewall, and wireless access point functions. When dealing with large enterprise networks, you'll typically find that a dedicated device provides each of these functions and there may be dozens of the same device on the premises.

With that in mind, we're going to go over some of the most common devices found in enterprise networks and discuss what functions they serve and how they work. Again, in smaller networks you may find that these functions are combined in multifunction devices, but you need to understand the functions individually in order to fully relate the device to what it does in the enterprise environment.

Network Interface Card

An NIC is the core piece of hardware used for networking connectivity. While traditionally associated with PCs, laptops, and servers, NICs can exist in almost any networked device including printers, telephones, and scanners. In some networking hardware, such as switches used for network storage arrays, there are replaceable modules that allow for the use of different connection types. These modules are technically NICs as well.

As we discussed previously in this chapter, every NIC has a MAC address in the Ethernet or Token Ring topologies. This unique hardware address defines how the NIC is identified to ensure that the data gets to the correct system. The MAC address can usually be modified when needed, but all NICs will have a preassigned MAC address associated with the NIC. Depending on the way that configuration management is handled in the enterprise, these MAC addresses may be set following a specific standard, recorded for inventory purposes, or potentially used to determine whether or not a specific system should be allowed on the network. This security function is most typically associated with wireless networks where MAC address filtering is a standard configuration option.

Switch

A switch is a core networking component used in all present-day networks. Switches work at OSI Layers 2 and 3 and basically route communications between network devices. When a switch operates in both OSI Layers 2 and 3 (which is the most common currently), it is considered a multilayer switch. Basic switches are OSI Layer 2 devices and are becoming less common due to the decreasing prices of technology necessary to add the OSI Layer 3 functionality.

The reason that switches are considered OSI Layer 2 and 3 devices rather than Layer 1 devices is that they do more than simply pass all data along to every physical port of the switch. Instead, they actually inspect the packet to determine the MAC address of the destination system and, if that system is connected to a port on the switch, it sends the traffic to that port exclusively. No devices on any of the other switch ports see the message as it is passed along. The switch does this by keeping a table that lists the MAC address of each device associated with each of its ports. By looking up the MAC address in this table, the switch is able to determine the correct destination port for the communication.

Multilayer switches that support OSI Layer 3 add some functionality to the standard switch. Instead of relying exclusively on the MAC address, they can further dissect the packet being transferred to determine the OSI Layer 3 address (such as an IP address) that the message is intended for. By being able to understand OSI Layer 3 addressing, the switch is able to perform some functions similar to a router and route messages based on this address. This also gives the switch the ability to send multicast messages to only the appropriate ports rather than broadcasting these messages to every port on the switch.

One additional function that most enterprise-quality switches have is the ability to perform port mirroring. Port mirroring takes all of the data going to and from a port on the switch and duplicates it in a read-only mode on another port. This allows for monitoring of the traffic for analysis or trouble-shooting which is known as "sniffing" the traffic. When administering enterprise applications, you'll find that there are many instances where you'll need to examine the traffic going between different systems that are part of the enterprise application stack. Examining this traffic can help find routing issues, problems with malformed packets, and other issues that can effect the operation of the enterprise application.

Router

A router is a device intended to route communications based on their OSI Layer 3 addressing. As we discussed in the section on IP addressing, an address at this layer is comprised of both a network and a host address. The router uses the network address to determine which network it should route the message to and then sends the message on its way. Routers can also apply some intelligence to their routing and, based on information available to the router, move communications to faster or less congested networks as needed as long as there are multiple paths between the router and the destination network.

Another function that is available with most enterprise-quality routers is quality of service (QoS) routing. This feature is also available within some switches. Based on specific rules that are configured in the router, the router will apply priority to the processing of specific types of traffic. For example, some home routers are adding functionality which allow for the application of QoS rules to streaming media to ensure that communications for video and audio streams get priority. Enterprise networks may apply QoS rules to ensure that voice over IP (VOIP) communications take priority over other traffic. When a router uses QoS, it takes a look at all of the messages that it has been sent to process, moves the messages into a specific order based on the QoS rules, and then processes them in priority order. If another message comes in that has a higher priority, it will be moved to the front of the line.

Load Balancer

A load balancer is a device or service that is intended to route traffic to specific systems or networks based on a variety of algorithms. There are a few different types of load balancing, so let's first discuss the load balancing concept and then move to the hardware that supports it. Many enterprise applications implement load balancing at multiple layers, including the web, application, and database layers, depending on the complexity or size of the application. At any given layer, load balancing distributes the load across two or more systems in order to reduce load on a single system and, in most cases, provide redundant paths in the event of a system failure on one or more of the load-balanced nodes. Figure 2.7 shows one way that load balancing can be implemented in an enterprise application.

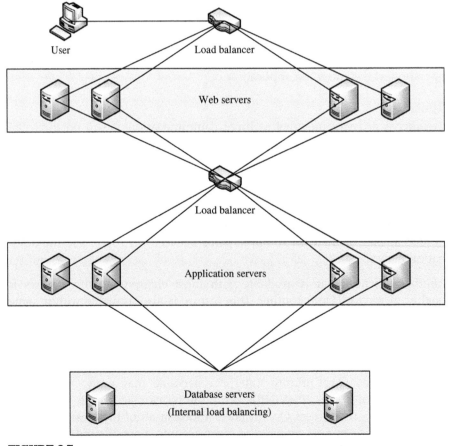

FIGURE 2.7
Enterprise application load balancing example.

The load balancing can be accomplished through a basic round-robin algorithm or something as complex as an algorithm which bases routing decisions on actual system utilization statistics or other factors. If round-robin load balancing is used, the load balancer will simply route each incoming connection or message to the next system in its ordered list. For example, if round-robin load balancing was in use in the enterprise application architecture shown in Figure 2.7, the first connection would go to webserver 1, the second to webserver 2, and so on.

A more complex algorithm could use either internal or external data to make routing decisions. If the load balancing is using internal data, it might be able to determine the number of active connections that it has routing through it to each system at any given time and route new connections to the system with the lowest connection count. Another option would be to determine the type of message coming in based on protocol, URI, or other details and route to a chosen subset of systems based on this more extensive message analysis.

External data includes information sent back to the load balancer from the systems that it is routing traffic to. This data can be system metrics, such as processor, memory, input/output (I/O), and other critical operational data, that can help the load balancer to determine which system would be the best destination for incoming messages. The load balancer can use complex algorithms to compute the least utilized system based on this data and route the message accordingly.

The hardware associated with load balancing can be either a dedicated device or the same hardware used for other functions. For example, DNS can be used for a simple method of round-robin load balancing therefore the DNS servers could be considered load balancers in this situation; however, DNS records are cached so this load balancing scenario will only be valid for initial requests. In addition, there are software-based load balancing utilities that can run on the same system as certain application components and provide a level of intersystem message routing accomplishing the load balancing function. If a dedicated device is used, it is essentially an OSI Layer 3 device that performs a level of packet inspection and routing. This routing can be done at the port level similar to a switch or at the network level similar to a router. In most cases, the device functions more like a router and therefore must be configured as the default route for the systems that it is load balancing.

Load balancers can also provide a level of redundancy as previously mentioned. At the system level, load balancers can check to ensure that the destination system is up and available before routing messages to it. This check can be as simple as an ICMP ping request to ensure that the system is up or as complex as an HTTP request of a specific page with an associated content check to ensure that the service required is available. If the system is not available or not functioning normally, the load balancer can remove the destination system from the pool of available systems and send an alert to let an administrator know that there is a problem.

Another layer of redundancy can be implemented with load balancers by adding multiple network cards to the destination systems and connecting each network card to a different load balancer. With this configuration, if the load balancer itself fails, there is an alternate path for the traffic to get to the destination systems. This is a common practice in highly available environments.

Firewall

A firewall is the most common device used to protect an internal network from outside intruders. When properly configured, a firewall blocks access to an internal network from the outside (ingress filtering) and blocks users of the internal network from accessing potentially dangerous external networks or ports (egress filtering).

There are three primary firewall technologies to be aware of as an enterprise applications administrator:

- Packet filtering
- Application layer gateways
- Stateful inspection

A packet filtering firewall works at the network layer of the OSI model and is designed to operate rapidly by either allowing or denying packets. An application layer gateway operates at the application layer of the OSI model, analyzing each packet and verifying that it contains the correct type of data for the specific application it is attempting to communicate with. A stateful inspection firewall checks each packet to verify that it is an expected response to a current communications session. This type of firewall operates at the network layer, but is aware of the transport, session, presentation, and application layers and derives its state table based on these layers of the OSI model. Another term for this type of firewall is a "deep packet inspection" firewall indicating its use of all layers within the packet including examination of the data itself.

To better understand the function of these different types of firewalls, we must first understand what exactly the firewall is doing. The highest level of security requires that firewalls be able to access, analyze, and utilize communication information, communication-derived state, application-derived state, and be able to perform information manipulation. Each of these terms is defined below:

- Communication information—Information from all layers in the packet
- Communication-derived state—The state as derived from previous communications
- Application-derived state—That state as derived from applications
- Information manipulation—The ability to perform logical or arithmetic functions on data in any part of the packet

Different firewall technologies support these requirements in different ways. Again, keep in mind that some circumstances may not require all of these, but only a subset. In that case, the administrator will frequently go with a firewall technology that fits the situation rather than one that is simply the newest technology.

Firewall Rules The defined instructions that are used by the firewall to determine what to do with specific traffic are called firewall rules. These rules in a basic firewall (packet filtering) identify the packet source IP and port, destination IP and port, and the definition of what to do with the traffic. Should it be allowed to pass? Denied? Or, if using a firewall as part of the intrusion detection system, should an alert be sent indicating that there is a potential intrusion?

Rules for application layer gateways or stateful inspection are more complex and add more criteria that can be used for identifying the type of traffic or what its intent is. For example, rules can be put in place to capture attempts at directory traversal (strings like "../../../../" in the URL) and drop those packets so that they never even make it to the web server.

Firmware
Firmware is not a network hardware device *per se*, but is a component of all network devices. Every network device has its own software and configuration that is used to control how the device functions. This software and configuration is typically stored on one or more chips on the hardware rather than a hard drive or other storage device, as you would see with a server. The software and configuration information stored on this chip is considered the device's firmware. In some cases, a distinction is made between the software and the configuration where the software is considered the firmware and the configuration is considered separate from the firmware itself.

As an enterprise applications administrator, you may or may not be responsible for performing firmware updates on network devices, but you do need to be aware of firmware and what it does to ensure that the enterprise application works correctly. Just like any software product, firmware is subject to defects and enhancements between different versions. Some enterprise application components may require that the firmware of specific pieces of hardware be at or above a certain revision level due to known issues in earlier firmware versions. Being aware of these requirements and ensuring that compatibility with various firmware revisions is maintained is very important.

In addition, you can see different behaviors in different versions of a device's firmware. Because of this, if multiple identical devices exist within the enterprise application architecture but the devices have different firmware revisions, you could see intermittent errors depending on which device is in use at any given time. From a change management perspective, it is best to ensure that all identical devices that comprise an enterprise application also have identical firmware versions.

Network Cabling

Network cabling has changed a lot over the years and has gone through many stages of development. Early on, coaxial cable was one of the most common cable types used in networks, but that has changed. In the present day, the most common cable type for general use is copper-based shielded twisted pair (STP) and unshielded twisted pair (UTP). When dealing with very high-speed networks, long-distance networks, or in situations where electromagnetic interference (EMI) is a concern, optical fiber cables are frequently used.

For the purposes of enterprise applications administration, we will not be going into the details of network cabling that a true network administrator needs to know such as maximum cable length, appropriate twist rates for various wire pairs, or other highly technical information. Instead, like with all of our other technical topics, we will be touching on the basics of each of these cabling types and how they apply to enterprise applications administration. If, in your specific environment, you need more detailed explanations on when to use different cable types and the properties of those cables, by all means, continue to enhance your education on the topic. The goal for this book is to provide the basic information that all enterprise applications administrators must have in order to be effective in their role.

Twisted Pair Cables

STP and UTP cabling are very similar and are both based on a number of insulated copper wires that are twisted in pairs and encased together within an outer sheath as a bundle. The difference between the two is the existence of an additional layer of wrapped metal that acts as an electromagnetic shield. This shield can be applied to individual pairs of wires or the bundle as a whole and is intended to reduce the effects of EMI.

STP and UTP are the most commonly used cable types within most corporate networks with UTP being the more popular of the two. This is due to the additional cost associated with STP. However, in some larger enterprises, the cost of STP cable is outweighed by the advantages provided by the EMI resistance. If a very high level of EMI is identified as a cause for network-related issues, a move to STP may make financial sense. This all depends on the environment, the equipment in use, and the issue tolerance of the organization in question.

STP and UTP are defined by a number of standards known as categories. This is abbreviated as "Cat" and will commonly be seen with a number representing the category definition such as Cat5. Each category of STP and UTP cable has a number of defined attributes including the number of wire pairs, the twist rate for each wire pair, and even the insulation color for each wire. We won't be going into each of those attributes in this book, but will touch on some of the most common categories and what they're used for. Table 2.2 includes a list of common STP and UTP categories.

Table 2.2 STP and UTP Cable Categories

Category	Usage
Cat3	Analog telephone cable
Cat5	100BASE-TX and 1000BASE-T Ethernet
Cat5e	100BASE-TX and 1000BASE-T Ethernet (higher testing requirements than Cat5)
Cat6	10GBASE-T Ethernet
Cat6e	10GBASE-T Ethernet (slightly modified standard)

In most cases, any higher rated category can be used for the purposes of the categories beneath it. For example, Cat5 or Cat6 cables could be used for analog telephone communications. However, Cat3 cable could not be used for 10GBASE-T Ethernet due to its limited bandwidth and other considerations.

Optical Fiber Cables

Optical fiber cables use the concept of light conduction rather than electrical conduction. From a physical perspective, instead of a series of 1's and 0's going across a cable being defined by varying electrical signals, the data is instead defined by light being transmitted in optical waves. This makes for much faster communication, more available bandwidth in any given cable, and protection from issues such as EMI or snooping of electromagnetic signals. Optical fiber cable is also more expensive than STP and UTP and devices that support optical fiber tend to have a higher cost as well.

Optical fiber cable uses strands of either glass or plastic that act as conductors for light. On either end of the cable is an optical transceiver that is capable of sending and receiving optical signals. The network data is converted from electrical signals into optical signals by the sending transceiver and transmitted to the receiving transceiver where the optical signals are then converted back into electrical signals for use by the receiving device. This process occurs very quickly and is used for the fastest networks in use today.

Within most enterprise networks, you'll often find optical fiber cables used for connections where high speed, high bandwidth, or long distance is a requirement. For example, many network storage devices use optical fiber for their interconnections between other storage devices or even the servers connected to them. Some corporate datacenters are starting to move towards using optical fiber connections for anything in the datacenter and using STP/UTP cabling only for connections going to user workstations outside of the datacenter. In addition, many WANs rely on optical fiber for part or all of the network.

NETWORK TROUBLESHOOTING

Troubleshooting networking connectivity is a critical skill for enterprise applications administrators. Many of the issues that occur with enterprise applications can be traced back to issues with connectivity; however, it is important to recognize that generally these connectivity issues are not due to problems with the network itself. In most cases, a misconfiguration, an error with a destination service, or some other related issue is the underlying cause of the connectivity issue. This is a very important distinction as it is incredibly common for newer enterprise applications administrators without a strong understanding of network troubleshooting to simply blame the "network" during the initial steps of troubleshooting rather than working to determine the true root cause of the issue.

In this section, we will be covering some basic troubleshooting techniques that can be used at the various layers of the TCP/IP model as well as with various network hardware devices. The focus on the TCP/IP model at this point is due to the high prevalence of TCP/IP as the communications protocol of choice for the majority of enterprise applications. We will also discuss some of the more critical services associated with enterprise applications and how to troubleshoot issues that may occur with those services.

When troubleshooting network issues, the most common process is to start at the Application layer and work your way backwards from there. We will be covering the flow of troubleshooting in the order of Physical layer to Application layer since that is the order in which we discussed networking concepts in general. When performing actual troubleshooting, start at the Application layer and go through each layer until you get back to the Physical layer, although starting with a quick ping may prove to be helpful. The probability of issues being present in higher layer technologies is much higher than the probability of issues existing at the lowest layer.

Physical

From the physical perspective, there are two main areas where an enterprise applications administrator may find a need for troubleshooting. These are the network cabling and the NICs themselves. While it frequently isn't the enterprise applications administrator who does this level of troubleshooting, it is important to be aware of what sort of errors can occur at this layer in order to better communicate with the network administrators who would perform the actual testing.

Cabling

When it comes to network cabling, the main issues that you can run into are breaks in the wires within the cables, problems with EMI, and problems with cable connectors. An issue in any of these areas can lead to intermittent or complete communications failure. You'll typically see symptoms such as connections to machines being up for a short amount of time and then dropping, connectivity lights being lit but no ability to see the network from the device, and a high number of communication errors with the device.

The troubleshooting of these issues involves a few basic steps. First, a cable test can be performed to see if there is an issue with the cable itself. This will necessitate taking any device connected to the cable offline, so if it is an intermittent error, this troubleshooting step will take the device offline entirely. If the cable test passes, the next step is to try replacing the physical connectors on the cable. This may be more complex than it is worth in some environments, so some administrators will skip directly to the next step, which is replacing the cable entirely. If all of these steps are done, the cable and/or connector can typically be ruled out as the source of the problem.

Network Interface Cards

The other potential problem area within the Physical layer is the NIC for the devices in question. Problems with the NIC can either be physical such as a bent pin or malfunctioning card, or it could be a configuration issue that causes the card to work incorrectly. These configuration issues are most commonly speed or duplex settings mismatching between the NIC and the switch or customized parameters that don't work effectively on the network that the NIC is attached to.

When troubleshooting issues with NICs, the first step is to ensure that any link lights or other functional indicators show that the device is active. From the operating system perspective, the device should be able to identify the NIC and recognize that it is functioning. Changing the NIC to its default configuration, replacing the NIC driver with the latest version, and ensuring that the NIC firmware is at the latest version are all good troubleshooting steps as well. If all of this is done and there are still issues, there are some manufacturer-specific testing utilities that can be used to test the network card to ensure that it is functioning normally. The final step is, as with any physical device, to try replacing the NIC with a new one and see if the issue is resolved by the hardware replacement.

Link Layer

At the Link layer, there is limited troubleshooting that an enterprise applications administrator can do. Any issues around a high number of Ethernet collisions, for example, would require a higher level of expertise than the normal expectation for this role as well as very powerful analysis tools. However, one area that an enterprise applications administrator may be able to analyze revolves around the Link layer address resolution using ARP.

Address Resolution Protocol

As previously mentioned, ARP is used to translate between Internet layer addresses (IP addresses) and Link layer addresses (MAC addresses). In some cases, something can go wrong with this address resolution and translation causing a variety of connectivity issues such as the inability to reach a specific host. Knowing how ARP works is the first step to understanding how this can happen; but, just as important, is being able to positively identify an ARP issue to ensure that it isn't something else causing the problem.

Most network devices that use ARP maintain an ARP table that caches the translation between MAC address and IP address. In some cases, this table can contain incorrect data either through configuration errors such as adding a system to the network with a duplicate IP address or through malicious intent such as an ARP poisoning/spoofing attack. When this happens, the system with the incorrect ARP table will attempt to send messages to the wrong MAC address. A sample ARP table is shown in Figure 2.8.

```
? (10.211.55.3) at 0:1c:42:fb:31:e0 on vnic0 ifscope [ethernet]
? (192.168.1.169) at 0:1e:58:b4:8c:be on en0 ifscope [ethernet]
? (192.168.1.200) at 0:16:b6:ce:64:6c on en0 ifscope [ethernet]
? (192.168.1.222) at 0:90:a9:b3:93:d1 on en0 ifscope [ethernet]
```

FIGURE 2.8

Sample ARP table.

If it appears that a system should be up and available on the network, but no traffic can reach the device, it is possible that there is an ARP problem. The easiest way to confirm this is to run the arp–a command on a Windows or Unix-based system that is trying to communicate with the destination system. If the MAC address in the ARP table matches that set on the destination device, then it is unlikely that there is an ARP problem. If the address does not match, you can try clearing the ARP cache and try again. If that is not effective, you will need to determine where the erroneous ARP data is coming from and correct it at the source.

Internet Layer

The Internet layer is where IP lives within the TCP/IP model and is also the location of a very useful troubleshooting protocol called ICMP. At this layer, the most common issues are around addressing for both network and host addresses. Incorrect configurations, such as duplicate IP addresses, incorrect subnet masks, or incorrect default gateway addresses are very common and can cause many issues. The best troubleshooting technique for working with the Internet layer is to confirm with absolute certainty that the IP configuration is correct, confirm it again, and then have a second person confirm it just in case you missed an error the first two times.

ICMP

The most common tool associated with ICMP is called ping. ping utilizes ICMP packets to verify that a given destination network device is reachable from the source device. It does this by sending a message from the source to the destination using the ICMP protocol that includes specific flags to designate the type of ICMP message being sent. If the destination device responds, then it is considered available and the ping utility will typically show how long it took for the destination device to respond and other useful information. A simple example of how this is used is shown in Figure 2.9.

```
                              $ ping -c5 192.168.1.200
PING 192.168.1.200 (192.168.1.200): 56 data bytes
64 bytes from 192.168.1.200: icmp_seq=0 ttl=64 time=7.453 ms
64 bytes from 192.168.1.200: icmp_seq=1 ttl=64 time=5.813 ms
64 bytes from 192.168.1.200: icmp_seq=2 ttl=64 time=3.629 ms
64 bytes from 192.168.1.200: icmp_seq=3 ttl=64 time=7.766 ms
64 bytes from 192.168.1.200: icmp_seq=4 ttl=64 time=4.527 ms

--- 192.168.1.200 ping statistics ---
5 packets transmitted, 5 packets received, 0.0% packet loss
round-trip min/avg/max/stddev = 3.629/5.838/7.766/1.608 ms
```

FIGURE 2.9
Sample ping test.

ping is often used when troubleshooting to confirm connectivity to the destination device at the Internet layer, however, there are some valid cases where a ping test will fail but connectivity between the devices is still functional. Based on the original Request for Comments (RFC) that defined ICMP, it was intended that ICMP support be required on all network devices and that the device should respond to all ICMP requests. Due to security concerns however, ICMP is frequently disabled or blocked which prevents ping from being used to check for connectivity to a network device. If ICMP is enabled and nothing is blocking the transmission of ICMP packets, the test should be successful.

Traceroute

Another useful tool for checking connectivity is traceroute. This tool is included by default with most operating systems although it may be called a couple of different names. For example, in Unix-based operating systems, the tool or command is called traceroute. Microsoft Windows offers the same capability under the name tracert. Both tools work in a similar manner although the specific command syntax varies.

traceroute effectively determines the path that traffic takes to get from the source system to a destination system and identifies all devices in that path. Network devices, such as routers and load balancers, can typically be seen in traceroute results. Firewalls may be able to be seen although this isn't guaranteed. Network devices, such as bridges and repeaters, cannot be seen in traceroute results since they operate at a lower level of the TCP/IP model than IP. A sample traceroute can be seen in Figure 2.10.

As you can see in Figure 2.10, there are quite a few network devices between the source system and the destination. Each of these has been identified by name as well as IP, but the display of this data is a configurable option. In addition, the response time for each device along the path is recorded. This can be helpful in determining where a slowdown in communications is occurring.

Transport Layer

Moving up in the TCP/IP model, we next come to the Transport layer. Troubleshooting at this layer primarily involves working with TCP and UDP connections and determining the causes for communications failures using these protocols. If address resolution is working correctly then your next area to look at is the ability to communicate with specific TCP and UDP ports directly. This communication can be tested using simple tools, such as a telnet client or netcat. Telnet works great for testing TCP communications and netcat is able to test both TCP and UDP connections.

```
███████████████████████$ traceroute www.fairclothsec.com
traceroute to fairclothsec.com (74.124.211.102), 64 hops max, 52 byte packets
 1  192.168.1.200 (192.168.1.200)  11.462 ms  20.446 ms  31.242 ms
 2  ████████(█████████)  37.324 ms  29.183 ms  35.787 ms
 3  ████████ (███████)  30.053 ms  39.179 ms  28.584 ms
 4  ███████.martin.mn.minn.comcast.net (████████████)  31.981 ms  36.903 ms  2
3.243 ms
 5  ███████████.martin.mn.minn.comcast.net (███████████)  16.593 ms  36.380 ms
47.187 ms
 6  ██████████.roseville.mn.minn.comcast.net (████████████)  34.881 ms  26.70
3 ms  40.111 ms
 7  pos-0-13-0-0-cr01.350ecermak.il.ibone.comcast.net (68.86.94.73)  53.271 ms  59
.968 ms  30.312 ms
 8  he-1-12-0-0-cr01.denver.co.ibone.comcast.net (68.86.85.250)  59.943 ms  64.850
ms  79.380 ms
 9  he-0-3-0-0-cr01.denverqwest.co.ibone.comcast.net (68.86.89.34)  71.063 ms  60.
576 ms  81.780 ms
10  he-4-15-0-0-cr01.sanjose.ca.ibone.comcast.net (68.86.89.137)  82.992 ms  104.8
38 ms  88.913 ms
11  pos-2-13-0-0-cr01.losangeles.ca.ibone.comcast.net (68.86.86.206)  80.769 ms  8
2.075 ms  120.997 ms
12  pos-0-5-0-0-pe01.600wseventh.ca.ibone.comcast.net (68.86.88.194)  86.880 ms  8
6.902 ms  111.653 ms
13  173.167.57.138 (173.167.57.138)  98.290 ms  93.580 ms  90.110 ms
14  ae0-110g.cr1.lax1.us.nlayer.net (69.31.127.141)  105.528 ms
    ae0-110g.cr1.lax1.us.nlayer.net (69.31.127.137)  113.491 ms
    ae0-110g.cr1.lax1.us.nlayer.net (69.31.127.141)  96.601 ms
15  ae1-50g.ar1.lax2.us.nlayer.net (69.31.127.130)  88.079 ms  99.047 ms  101.887
ms
16  as17139.xe-5-0-5.ar1.lax2.us.nlayer.net (69.31.127.58)  96.646 ms  82.330 ms
95.886 ms
17  po10-dc1-core-1.corporatecolo.com (74.124.220.129)  96.117 ms  109.259 ms  117
.652 ms
18  tge4-1-dc1-core-1.corporatecolo.com (66.117.1.86)  89.664 ms  83.564 ms  80.60
7 ms
19  biz130.inmotionhosting.com (74.124.211.102)  99.676 ms  85.270 ms  97.059 ms
```

FIGURE 2.10
Sample traceroute results.

Telnet

Telnet is a client application intended for use with the telnet protocol and is included by default with most operating systems. Some additional work may be needed to install it with later Microsoft Windows desktop operating systems and some bare-bones Linux distributions may require the installation of a telnet client package. If you are working on a Windows desktop system and cannot find the telnet client, you can generally add it by going into "Turn Windows features on or off" in the Windows control panel and selecting the telnet client. On Windows servers, it's in the Features Summary section of Server Manager.

While the telnet client is intended to work with the telnet protocol, it actually comes in very useful for testing general TCP connectivity. This is really because of the simplicity of the telnet protocol itself. Telnet basically requires establishing a TCP connection to a port and then sends and receives ASCII characters to and from the destination system through that connection. Since

```
                               $ telnet www.fairclothsec.com 80
Trying 74.124.211.102...
Connected to fairclothsec.com.
Escape character is '^]'.
```

FIGURE 2.11
Sample telnet client TCP connectivity test.

there is nothing exceptionally complex about this type of connection, a telnet client can be used for testing any protocol that requires the same sequence of events. We'll discuss testing specific Application level protocols later in this chapter, but for now, we'll focus on the TCP connection itself.

When testing TCP, the most basic test is to simply see if you can establish a connection to the remote TCP port. This can be tested by using telnet with the following syntax: `telnet <host> <port>`. The telnet client will attempt to connect to the remote system on the specified port. If this is successful, you'll see the message shown in Figure 2.11. If it is unsuccessful, you'll see a message indicating that the connection request has been rejected or timed out. Either of these latter responses can indicate that the remote machine is not listening on that port or that the communication has been blocked. The best next step is to check the destination system and ensure that the port you're expecting actually has a service listening on that port. If so, the communication may be blocked by a firewall or another network device.

Application Layer

Performing troubleshooting at the Application layer means testing the underlying Application layer protocols as directly as possible. Most enterprise applications use these protocols natively or in conjunction with functions within their host operating systems, however, they may not provide a high amount of visibility into how they're using the protocols. By knowing how to test the protocols manually, we can work to eliminate the protocol and remote service from the list of potential root causes for any given issue.

Dynamic Host Configuration Protocol

As mentioned previously in this chapter, DHCP is a protocol used for performing dynamic IP addressing for DHCP clients. This addressing includes not only configuring an IP address, subnet mask, and default gateway but also other configuration items, such as DNS servers and WINS servers. In most enterprise applications environments, the servers hosting the enterprise applications are set to use static IP addresses versus relying on DHCP. However, there are environments where DHCP is relied on for providing even server addressing via DHCP reservations so any enterprise applications administrator should know the basics behind DHCP troubleshooting.

Most issues encountered with DHCP typically involve being unable to obtain a leased IP address, receiving an incorrect IP address, or receiving incorrect DHCP configuration information. If the DHCP client is unable to lease an IP address, the first step in troubleshooting is to ensure that the DHCP client system can communicate with the DHCP server. This test can be performed by using `ping` as previously demonstrated in this section. If the DHCP server responds to the ping request then you should try a few DHCP client-side actions to eliminate the client from the equation.

DHCP clients typically have a few commands that can be used to force them to try to get a new address. Depending on the operating system that you're using, the syntax for these commands and the executable name for the DHCP client itself may vary. Ensure that you use the correct tool for the operating system that you're working with and then use the appropriate command to "release" the leased IP address. After the current address is released, use the correct syntax associated with the "renew" function of the DHCP client. After a release/renew operation, the DHCP client should have new configuration information available.

If the IP address is still not correct, the DHCP server may have a configuration problem. Most DHCP servers allow for addresses to be configured in such a way that they will always be issued to a specific MAC address when the DHCP client requests an address. Sometimes this configuration is erroneously removed or corrupted causing incorrect addresses to be issued. In addition, all of the optional DHCP configuration items like DNS server addresses are configured within the DHCP server. If this configuration has errors, it can cause all DHCP clients to receive incorrect configuration information as well.

Domain Name System

DNS is used for name resolution and when it fails, it can appear that all connectivity isn't working. However, there are a few simple tests you can run to determine whether DNS is the problem or if it's something else. Remember that the primary purpose of DNS is to resolve host and domain names into IP addresses. Therefore, the most basic test for DNS failures is to determine if there is a difference between contacting a host directly by IP versus resolving the name into an IP and then contacting the host. So start your troubleshooting by trying to ping or connect to the destination system by IP address. If this is successful, you can then test basic name resolution by using the hostname with `ping` to see if DNS resolution works.

If DNS resolution fails, then there are a few things to look at to find out why. The most common causes are generally due to configuration errors. An incorrect DNS server may have been set up either manually or by using DHCP so always check your DNS server address configuration to ensure that it is correct. If local names are resolving (i.e., names within your domain) but remote names are not, then there may be a problem with communicating with an external DNS server or an issue with your DNS forwarder. The DNS forwarder is what handles finding a DNS server to resolve your requested host and domain if your local DNS server does not have the appropriate information.

Another avenue for testing DNS is to use the `nslookup` tool. This tool is available for most operating systems and allows you to test resolution using the DNS protocol. Within `nslookup`, you can view your default DNS server, set an alternative DNS server, and attempt various DNS lookups including querying for specific types of records, such as MX or PTR. Performing this type of test can help you to isolate where the failure is occurring. By trying alternate DNS servers, you can identify whether it's actually your local DNS server that is having a problem or some larger network issue such as DNS traffic being blocked by a firewall.

One additional thing to keep in mind with DNS is that most operating systems have a distinct order of operations when it comes to performing name resolution. They will normally check their local cache first, a `.hosts` file if it exists, then a primary DNS server, and finally a secondary DNS server. With this order of operations, if there is a problem with the local cache or `.hosts` file, resolution for some hosts may fail even though the DNS server is fine. Some malware actually modifies the `.hosts` file or corrupts the operating system to force DNS names to resolve to incorrect servers in order to create revenue through forcing advertising views. Always be sure to check for issues locally as well to confirm that there are no problems with the source system's configuration.

Hypertext Transfer Protocol

HTTP is the protocol most frequently used for viewing web pages, but it is also used to accomplish file transfers, perform web service communications, and accomplish other tasks where the protocol seems well suited due to its flexibility. It uses TCP and, for web servers, is typically found on TCP port 80. It can, however, be used on any TCP port depending on the needs of the system.

Troubleshooting HTTP is done in a manner very similar to checking any given TCP port. Using a tool such as a telnet client, a TCP connection is established to the remote system on the appropriate port as a starting point in testing the HTTP functionality. After this connection is established, a series of manual commands can be entered which cause the remote system to provide very specific data in return. A basic set of testing commands is:

```
HEAD/HTTP/1.1
Host:www.domain.com
```

```
█████████████████████$ telnet www.fairclothsec.com 80
Trying 74.124.211.102...
Connected to fairclothsec.com.
Escape character is '^]'.
HEAD / HTTP/1.1
Host: www.fairclothsec.com

HTTP/1.1 200 OK
Date: Sun, 03 Mar 2013 03:01:50 GMT
Server: Apache
Set-Cookie: lang=english; expires=Mon, 03-Mar-2014 03:01:50 GMT
Content-Type: text/html; charset=utf-8

Connection closed by foreign host.
```

FIGURE 2.12
Sample manual HTTP test.

Keep in mind that after entering the "Host" command, you must press enter twice. If you are able to successfully connect to the remote port and run these commands, there is a high likelihood that the HTTP server itself is functioning correctly. You should see a return dataset similar to that shown in Figure 2.12, which shows a HTTP code of 200 (success). This particular test just gets the file header of the default file. If you want to retrieve a specific file header, replace the "/" in the command between "HEAD" and "HTTP" with the correct path and filename. In addition, if you'd like to retrieve the entire file instead of just the header, you can replace "HEAD" with "GET".

Simple Mail Transfer Protocol

Many enterprise applications use SMTP for sending various emails from the application. In some cases the enterprise application will have a remote SMTP server set up and in others it will rely on a local SMTP server to accept the message and relay it to the next SMTP server in line. Regardless of the SMTP server location, it is important to be able to verify that these services are working and are accepting messages.

Testing SMTP can be done in a manner similar to that used for testing HTTP above. A TCP connection using a telnet client will enable you to connect to the SMTP server on the appropriate port and send specific commands that simulate what a SMTP client would send to create and send an email. To perform this test, use a telnet client to connect to port 25 (assuming that the default port is used) of the SMTP server in question. After establishing the connection, send the following commands:

```
HELO mail.fairclothsec.com
MAIL FROM:backdoor@fairclothsec.com
RCPT TO:letmein@fake-inc.com
```

```
DATA
Subject: Backdoor

.

QUIT
```

Please note that similar to the HTTP test, an extra "enter" is required after the final "." in the SMTP test message. If everything is working correctly, you'll receive a response similar to that shown in Figure 2.13. Keep in mind that the syntax for SMTP may vary slightly depending on the server type and version. For example, "HELO" on some systems is "EHLO" on others if Extended SMTP (ESMTP) is supported. ESMTP supports authentication, the use of TLS, and other features in addition to the core SMTP command set.

In addition to differences in command syntax, different servers respond in different ways to each command. In the example shown in Figure 2.13, you see that the server returned a message of "250 OK" when sent the "MAIL FROM" command. Other servers may respond with a more descriptive message such as "250 2.1.0 Sender OK". Regardless of the messaging, the response code of "250" should be consistent.

```
                              $ telnet localhost 25
Trying ::1...
telnet: connect to address ::1: Connection refused
Trying 127.0.0.1...
Connected to localhost.
Escape character is '^]'.
220 GenericMail 1.01.01.0
HELO mail.fairclothsec.com
250 OK
MAIL FROM: test@fairclothsec.com
250 OK
RCPT TO: test@fairclothsec.com
250 OK
DATA
354 Start mail input; end with <CLRF>.<CLRF>
Subject: Test Message

.

250 OK
QUIT
221 Closing connection
Connection closed by foreign host.
```

FIGURE 2.13
Sample SMTP manual test.

When manually testing SMTP, there are a few different tests that you may want to run to help diagnose where a particular problem lies. First, send a message from a local (within the same server) user to another local server user. This will tell you whether or not the local SMTP server is at least handling basic message transfers correctly. The next test is to send a message from a local (within the same domain) user to another user within the domain. This test allows you to pinpoint whether or not the problem is a domain-specific issue. And finally, test sending a message from a local user to a user in a different domain. A failure in this test indicates that there is a problem routing mail externally.

Transport Layer Security

The last Application layer protocol that we'll discuss troubleshooting is TLS. As we've already discussed, TLS is used to add a layer of encryption to a number of other Application layer protocols and requires that a secure communications channel be able to be established. Due to the complex nature of public-key encryption, it is sometimes difficult to establish this secure connection and some troubleshooting may be necessary to help identify where in the connection process the problem lies.

CORPORATE MEMO...

Internal Certificates

Many corporations opt to set up their own Certificate Authority (CA) and use internally signed certificates when securing internal communications. This has a very high value to the company as they don't have to pay a third-party CA for every certificate issued, however, it can cause some issues when establishing secure connections if everything isn't configured correctly. When using an internally signed certificate, you must ensure that any device communicating with the certificate holder trusts the internal CA. Also, watch the validity dates on certificates, as some systems require that every certificate have a valid expiry date and it's possible to internally sign certificates with no expiration or an expiration date far in the future. Being aware of these potential issues can help you to ensure that the use of internally signed certificates works correctly within your organization.

We've already discussed how TLS works and how a working communications session is established. To troubleshoot this process, you need to gain access to the TLS layer directly rather than relying on any other Application layer protocol routing through it. One of the best methods for doing this is to use the OpenSSL tool to create a TLS session without involving the other Application layer protocols. OpenSSL is an open-source tool that is frequently utilized by applications to provide encryption services on their behalf. While some enterprise applications build in their own TLS services, others rely on external providers like OpenSSL.

```
██████████████$ openssl s_client -connect www.google.com:443
CONNECTED(00000003)
depth=1 /C=US/O=Google Inc/CN=Google Internet Authority
verify error:num=20:unable to get local issuer certificate
verify return:0
---
Certificate chain
 0 s:/C=US/ST=California/L=Mountain View/O=Google Inc/CN=www.google.com
   i:/C=US/O=Google Inc/CN=Google Internet Authority
 1 s:/C=US/O=Google Inc/CN=Google Internet Authority
   i:/C=US/O=Equifax/OU=Equifax Secure Certificate Authority
---
Server certificate
-----BEGIN CERTIFICATE-----
MIIDgDCCAumgAwIBAgIKFIUNngAAAAB9QDANBgkqhkiG9w0BAQUFADBGMQswCQYD
VQQGEwJVUzETMBEGA1UEChMKR29vZ2xlIEluYzEiMCAGA1UEAxMZR29vZ2xlIElu
dGVybmV0IEF1dGhvcml0eTAeFw0xMzAyMjAxMzM0NTZaFw0xMzA2MDcxOTQzMjda
MGgxCzAJBgNVBAYTAlVTMRMwEQYDVQQIEwpDYWxpZm9ybmlhMRYwFAYDVQQHEw1N
b3VudGFpbiBWaWV3MRMwEQYDVQQKEwpHb29nbGUgSW5jMRcwFQYDVQQDEw53d3cu
Z29vZ2xlLmNvbTCBnzANBgkqhkiG9w0BAQEFAAOBjQAwgYkCgYEA4PUVszIbQhPw
k6LYSXpFVyIEmngQ19O5kna+f8dSr6COmuZQ3EtK9wr4Py8GmSrw3jVC/7zY/JO5
kgHSmDYIl+zTsLn5kBCfCbTUOJCMz+PaMpvkZ6A4FFieBtGQA9IYK5/MnL5AFZt3
WG2px4hEQQj8kfulQaCD3RdRCAF10FsCAwEAAaOCAVEwggFNMB0GA1UdJQQWMBQG
CCsGAQUFBwMBBggrBgEFBQcDAjAdBgNVHQ4EFgQUCBmaAp7Irw9cgY4BT7/mv/E3
LmEwHwYDVR0jBBgwFoAUv8Aw6/VDET5nup6R+/xq2uNrEiQwWwYDVR0fBFQwUjBQ
oE6gTIZKaHR0cDovL3d3dy5nc3RhdGljLmNvbS9Hb29nbGVJbnRlcm5ldEF1dGhv
cml0eS9Hb29nbGVJbnRlcm5ldEF1dGhvcml0eS5jcmwwZgYIKwYBBQUHAQEEWjBY
MFYGCCsGAQUFBzAChkpodHRwOi8vd3d3LmdzdGF0aWMuY29tL0dvb2dsZUludGVy
bmV0QXV0aG9yaXR5L0dvb2dsZUludGVybmV0QXV0aG9yaXR5LmNydDAMBgNVHRMB
Af8EAjAAMBkGA1UdEQQSMBCCDnd3dy5nb29nbGUuY29tMA0GCSqGSIb3DQEBBQUA
A4GBAJvolyDMFonlbMzlMEnldcFmTRrCdoLl38pA2gASQL5FY4CwMIzdw8odva9y
PPNiL7Gwdl2U/XdxeWPjc/7x19gyfZavVng4KGGXfqKZaxw7scFqSu0p//l4Emr6
Q0eccUWKGlcizUsWFdLVzLnhT4ZvFLTbLjlOHNKduxezw4mI
-----END CERTIFICATE-----
subject=/C=US/ST=California/L=Mountain View/O=Google Inc/CN=www.google.com
issuer=/C=US/O=Google Inc/CN=Google Internet Authority
---
No client certificate CA names sent
---
SSL handshake has read 1752 bytes and written 316 bytes
---
New, TLSv1/SSLv3, Cipher is RC4-SHA
Server public key is 1024 bit
Secure Renegotiation IS supported
Compression: NONE
Expansion: NONE
SSL-Session:
    Protocol  : TLSv1
    Cipher    : RC4-SHA
    Session-ID: 2B59D3F1F3FDC438E0E0302CDBB999CEBA78E549C4938E64FFFAA059A74597FA
    Session-ID-ctx:
    Master-Key: BB2223131190411AE07832F43437CAF9EAC09C5298ADBDC508698E4A20238259DD2E86F0294F71B80FEFDDF6C607013E
    Key-Arg   : None
    Start Time: 1362334443
    Timeout   : 300 (sec)
    Verify return code: 0 (ok)
---
```

FIGURE 2.14

Establishing an OpenSSL secure connection.

To create a basic one-way TLS connection to a remote web server, you can use the following command with OpenSSL: `openssl s_client -connect www.google.com:443`. The results of this are shown in Figure 2.14. When this is run, OpenSSL will create a secure connection to TCP port 443 on the server `www.google.com`. You will then be left with an open channel where you can run other tests such as the manual HTTP test demonstrated previously.

You may notice in Figure 2.14 that there is a verification error early in the establishment of the secure communications channel. The text associated with this error is "verify error:num = 20:unable to get local issuer certificate." This error means that we didn't specify a particular list of CAs for OpenSSL to trust. You can use the OpenSSL command "`-CApath`" to specify the path to a location for CA certificates that you wish for OpenSSL to trust.

```
Certificate:
    Data:
        Version: 3 (0x2)
        Serial Number:
            14:85:0d:9e:00:00:00:00:7d:40
        Signature Algorithm: sha1WithRSAEncryption
        Issuer: C=US, O=Google Inc, CN=Google Internet Authority
        Validity
            Not Before: Feb 20 13:34:56 2013 GMT
            Not After : Jun  7 19:43:27 2013 GMT
        Subject: C=US, ST=California, L=Mountain View, O=Google Inc, CN=www.google.com
        Subject Public Key Info:
            Public Key Algorithm: rsaEncryption
            RSA Public Key: (1024 bit)
                Modulus (1024 bit):
                    00:e0:f5:15:b3:32:1b:42:13:f0:93:a2:d8:49:7a:
                    45:57:22:04:9a:78:10:d7:d3:92:92:76:be:7f:c7:
                    52:af:a0:8e:9a:e6:50:dc:4b:4a:f7:0a:f8:3f:2f:
                    06:99:2a:f0:de:35:42:ff:bc:d8:fc:93:b9:92:01:
                    d2:98:36:08:97:ec:d3:b0:b9:f9:90:10:9f:09:b4:
                    d4:38:90:8c:cf:e3:da:32:9b:e4:67:a0:38:14:58:
                    9e:06:d1:90:03:d2:18:2b:9f:cc:9c:be:40:15:9b:
                    77:58:6d:a9:c7:88:44:41:08:fc:91:fb:a5:41:a0:
                    83:dd:17:51:08:01:75:d0:5b
                Exponent: 65537 (0x10001)
        X509v3 extensions:
            X509v3 Extended Key Usage:
                TLS Web Server Authentication, TLS Web Client Authentication
            X509v3 Subject Key Identifier:
                08:19:9A:02:9E:C8:AF:0F:5C:81:8E:01:4F:BF:E6:BF:F1:37:2E:61
            X509v3 Authority Key Identifier:
                keyid:BF:C0:30:EB:F5:43:11:3E:67:BA:9E:91:FB:FC:6A:DA:E3:6B:12:24

            X509v3 CRL Distribution Points:
                URI:http://www.gstatic.com/GoogleInternetAuthority/GoogleInternetAuthority.crl

            Authority Information Access:
                CA Issuers - URI:http://www.gstatic.com/GoogleInternetAuthority/GoogleInternetAuthority.crt

            X509v3 Basic Constraints: critical
                CA:FALSE
            X509v3 Subject Alternative Name:
                DNS:www.google.com
    Signature Algorithm: sha1WithRSAEncryption
        9b:e8:97:20:cc:16:89:e5:6c:cc:e5:30:49:e5:75:c1:66:4d:
        1a:c2:76:82:e5:df:ca:40:da:00:12:40:be:45:63:80:b0:30:
        8c:dd:c3:ca:1d:bd:af:72:3c:f3:62:2f:b1:b0:76:5d:94:fd:
        77:71:79:63:e3:73:fe:f1:d7:d8:32:7d:96:af:56:78:38:28:
        61:97:7e:a2:99:6b:1c:3b:b1:c1:6a:4a:ed:29:ff:f9:78:12:
        6a:fa:43:47:9c:71:45:8a:1a:57:22:cd:4b:16:15:d2:d5:cc:
        b9:e1:4f:86:6f:14:b4:db:2e:39:4e:1c:d2:9d:bb:17:b3:c3:
        89:88
```

FIGURE 2.15

Decoded x509 certificate details.

Another useful trick with OpenSSL is to have it display the validity dates and other information associated with the server-side certificate. This is actually included in the response we received in Figure 2.14, but we can't read it because it's in the encoded certificate. We can use the following command to force OpenSSL to route any incoming data including the certificate through its x509 certificate translator: openssl s_client -connect www.google.com:443 | openssl x509 -text. Figure 2.15 shows the resulting certificate information displayed after using this altered command.

If you need to test two-way TLS communications, you can use the "-cert" option to specify a local client X.509 certificate. Keep in mind, however, that this will only be used if the server is set to use client certificates for client authentication. In addition, if you'd like to see all of the TLS connection

```
███████████████████$ openssl s_client -state -nbio -connect www.google.com:443 | grep
"^SSL"
SSL_connect:before/connect initialization
SSL_connect:SSLv2/v3 write client hello A
SSL_connect:error in SSLv2/v3 read server hello A
SSL_connect:SSLv3 read server hello A
SSL_connect:error in SSLv3 read server certificate A
SSL_connect:error in SSLv3 read server certificate A
depth=1 /C=US/O=Google Inc/CN=Google Internet Authority
verify error:num=20:unable to get local issuer certificate
verify return:0
SSL_connect:SSLv3 read server certificate A
SSL_connect:SSLv3 read server done A
SSL_connect:SSLv3 write client key exchange A
SSL_connect:SSLv3 write change cipher spec A
SSL_connect:SSLv3 write finished A
SSL_connect:SSLv3 flush data
SSL_connect:error in SSLv3 read finished A
SSL_connect:SSLv3 read finished A
SSL handshake has read 1752 bytes and written 316 bytes
SSL-Session:
```

FIGURE 2.16

TLS connection summary.

process in a nice summarized format, you can use the following command: `openssl s_client -state -nbio -connect www.google.com:443 | grep "^SSL"`. This should give you the summary shown in Figure 2.16.

In most cases, issues with TLS can be found using OpenSSL to troubleshoot a direct connection to the remote system. A very common problem with TLS is invalid certificates caused by the certificate being expired, issued by an untrusted CA, or a mismatch between the server configuration used to present the certificate versus that used to generate it. Another very common issue has to do with the certificate chain. Each host certificate tends to be signed by an intermediate server that, in turn, has its own certificate signed by either a primary CA or another intermediate server. If the client does not trust each intermediate server in this chain, then validation of the certificate path will fail. This generally means that you have to have a copy of each intermediate server's certificate in your trusted certificate store.

Additional Tools

There are countless other tools that are available for troubleshooting. Two other tools that will prove to be useful to an enterprise applications administrator are `netstat` and `nmap`. `netstat` is a tool that can be found on most systems and is used to identify any incoming or outgoing network connections, the protocol, and the state of the connection. A tool that compliments `netstat` nicely, but may need to be downloaded, is `nmap`. `nmap` will aid in identifying which ports are open on a remote machine. `nmap` is capable of much more than this, but for basic troubleshooting, using `nmap` in this capacity gets the job done.

SUMMARY

This chapter has been a deluge of information around networking concepts and how to troubleshoot various aspects of networks. Obviously, networking is a very specialized field and it takes a great deal of effort to become an expert in this technical area. However, any enterprise applications administrator should have a good understanding of these basic networking concepts and understand how each part of the network performs its role in the communications critical to a functioning enterprise application.

As we discussed general networking concepts, we talked about various topologies and how each type fits into the corporate enterprise. This discussion transitioned into protocols and a couple of different models which are commonly used as reference points when working with networking technologies: the OSI and TCP/IP models. We went into depth on each model and discussed the various layers associated with the model as well as examples of the protocols used at each layer.

From concepts, we moved forward into the physical realm of hardware and cabling. We discussed many of the common network devices that are used to create the network infrastructure used by our enterprise applications. We also talked about common types of cables and how they are used to create the connections between these network devices. Without this combination of networking hardware and cabling, we would not have the critical infrastructure necessary for any enterprise application to be functional.

Finally, we talked about troubleshooting at various levels of the OSI and TCP/IP models. Every layer has its own protocols and troubleshooting techniques. By being proficient in these testing processes, we can leverage our knowledge of networking technology to help troubleshoot where communications issues are occurring within an enterprise application. Part of this troubleshooting includes manually simulating the same protocol usage that the enterprise application may perform natively using a variety of tools. These simulations can help further isolate issues and point us in the right direction to find the root cause.

Since networks are so incredibly critical to the operation of any enterprise application, it is important that we, as enterprise applications administrators, know a sufficient amount about networking technologies. While we may not be responsible for maintaining the network or even working with any of the network devices directly in our role as an enterprise applications administrator, it is very important to be able to properly communicate with those who do. Being able to speak the right language to the right people can facilitate rapid issue resolution and help to ensure that the correct troubleshooting is being done.

Servers

HARDWARE

When working with enterprise applications, the core services provided by the application are typically run on a variety of servers. These servers are specialized pieces of hardware that provide a higher level of capacity, availability, and reliability than workstation-class machines. In most cases, an enterprise application will have anywhere from one to hundreds of servers as part of the application infrastructure.

Most large companies have teams dedicated to running the company's server infrastructure. These teams may further specialize into people responsible for hardware, others for architecture, and still others for operating system installation and maintenance. There may even be teams that further specialize between installation, ongoing maintenance, and security management for the server infrastructure. Depending on the organization, the enterprise applications administrator may have very little or a great deal of access to and responsibility for the server infrastructure.

With this in mind, however, all enterprise applications administrators should have a basic knowledge of server hardware and software so that they understand the interaction between the enterprise application and the server infrastructure that hosts it. In order to properly troubleshoot and support enterprise applications, the enterprise applications administrator needs to have a firm grasp of the concepts associated with various server hardware components and the core operating systems typically used with server-class machines.

In this chapter, we will be discussing some of the core hardware components that all enterprise applications administrators should know about. Again, the level of detail provided for each of these components and for server infrastructure in general is not intended to give you expert-level knowledge. The intent, rather, is for you to have a general understanding of core hardware components and how they can affect the operation of the enterprise applications that you are responsible for.

Later in the chapter, we'll also be talking about the operating systems used by these servers. We'll discuss both Windows and *NIX-based operating systems and go into a little bit of detail around how they're architected and how they work. Understanding the basics of the operating system upon which your enterprise application resides is critical to being able to effectively administer the application.

Processor

For any computer, the processor is often referred to as the "brain." This is the piece of hardware responsible for executing instructions and coordinating all tasks that various pieces of hardware will perform. In many cases, server-class machines will have multiple processors in order to increase efficiency and capacity. Each processor is then able to perform some level of parallel functionality in conjunction with the other processors in the server.

There are a few different processor architectures that exist, each with their nuances. Many of the differences between them affect how memory and cache are used, how tasks are split between processors, and how the processor performs its functions. As an enterprise applications administrator, this information may be helpful, but it isn't necessarily critical as all processors tend to function in a pretty similar manner from the perspective of performing operations. However, if you are responsible for helping to drive choices between different server options, be aware that different processor architectures do perform different types of tasks better than others. For example, some processors can perform high I/O tasks such as database operations very quickly while others may be better at handling a high number of simultaneous users. Make sure that you pay close attention to this aspect of your server options before making a processor recommendation.

Processor Architecture

There are two primary processor architectures used in today's environments: 32-bit (x86) and 64-bit (x86-64, IA64, and AMD64). These architectures differ in the datapath width, integer size, and memory address width that the processor is able to work with. A 64-bit processor can support processing of larger "chunks" of data and address more memory than its 32-bit counterparts. Although most new hardware comes with 64-bit hardware, it is important to know what the underlying processor architecture of existing hardware is for compatibility purposes.

In order to support a 64-bit architecture, operating systems and their applications must be rewritten to work differently if they were originally designed to function with a 32-bit processor architecture. In some cases, operating systems written or rewritten to support 64-bit processor architectures will offer a "compatibility mode" feature that emulates a 32-bit processor for applications that have not yet been rewritten. With that in mind, many 32-bit applications can successfully run on 64-bit processors. The opposite is not true, that is, 64-bit applications cannot run on a 32-bit processor. For example, if an enterprise application required a Microsoft Exchange 2013 mail server to operate, that mail server could not use a 32-bit processor since it would not be compatible with the software design.

Cores

Many present-day servers not only have the ability to run multiple processors but also the ability to support processors that have multiple "cores." These multicore processors are designed to provide parallel processing within a single processor by adding one or more processor cores. These processor cores may share some level of on-chip cache as well as have their own independent caches in order to both facilitate information sharing and provide for fast operation.

In many cases, the additional cores in the processor are identical and allow for execution of multiple copies of the same types of operations in the same way, just faster. In other cases, processor technology is evolving to support multiple types of cores within a single processor with each core being specialized to a specific type of function. For example, a quad-core processor could have two cores that work best in performing normal computing operations while the other two cores are designed to provide a performance boost when performing math-intensive operations such as cryptography. The processor can then allocate the appropriate tasks to the correct cores providing an even greater performance boost.

Depending on the operating system, each core can appear to be a separate processor and can show independent statistics. For example, you can see the number of transactions occurring in each processor core as if it were its own processor. This can aid in understanding the capabilities of a system but can mask the actual processor architecture to a degree since it may be more difficult to identify whether you're looking at cores or processors.

The architecture of multicore versus multiprocessor is pretty important when looking at how a system is designed. Since multicore processors frequently share a cache as well as a bus connection, these single points can limit how much processing the multicore processor can perform. With enough cores, you can eventually get to the point that the processor is able to process data faster than the data can get to it. In the case of multiple processors, each processor is more independent than the cores within it as it relates to the bus and other hardware around it. This independence can be limited, however, based on the motherboard design and how the processor connects to memory and other I/O functions in the system.

There are some advantages and disadvantages in both designs. Most server-class systems actually use a combination of architectures by providing multiple multicore processors within a single system. This arrangement tends to allow the advantages associated with each architecture to be used and minimizes the disadvantages as much as possible.

Processes

Any executable can spawn multiple processes in order to improve efficiency. While this is not technically a hardware topic, it is important for enterprise applications administrators to understand processes and threads along with how to utilize processor resources. Between processes and threads, applications can utilize multiple processors and multiple cores in the most effective ways possible so that they can get the greatest benefits from this hardware.

Processes, from an operating system perspective, are independent instances of a given executable that has its own memory space and processor time slices allocated to it. Because of this, processes function very independently and can be spread across multiple processors in order to allow for simultaneous operation. However, independent processes cannot access each other's memory space, and therefore, each must maintain its own variables and other data. This can be worked around by using Inter-Process Communication (IPC), but there are still efficiency losses using this method. An executable with multiple processes does make good use of multiprocessor system architectures and can speed up overall system operations.

Threads

Threads are an even more granular method of breaking out individual tasks within an executable or process. A process can have multiple threads with each thread operating simultaneously on multiprocessor and multicore systems. The advantage with threading is that the memory space across the threads is shared and, therefore, there is no IPC necessary for the threads to share variables and other data. All threads can simply pull the data from the same memory space.

Each core is able to execute a single thread at a time, but there are technologies, such as multitasking, where the operating system switches between running threads so that they appear to be executing simultaneously. In addition, there is hyper-threading available in some processor designs, which allows for simultaneous execution of two threads by duplicating some, but not all, of a processor's functional components. This creates the concept of an additional "logical processor" that can handle an additional thread of work if the operating system supports this technology.

Most enterprise applications use a combination of processes and threads in their construction in order to create the most efficient application possible. This architecture works in conjunction with multitasking capabilities provided by the operating system to add further performance gains. Figure 3.1 shows a breakdown of processes and threads within a multiprocessor, multi-core system architecture.

As you can see in Figure 3.1, each processor has one or more processes and each process has one or more threads. In this figure, both processes 1 and 2 can run simultaneously. Process 3 can run simultaneously with processes 1 and 2 *only if* it multitasks at the thread level. At the thread level, threads 1–4

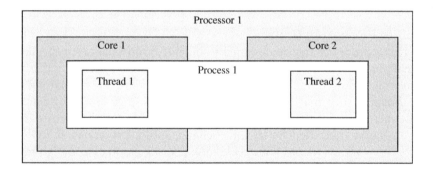

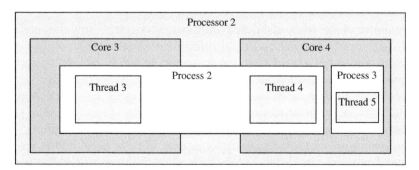

FIGURE 3.1
Processors, cores, processes, and threads.

can run simultaneously, but thread 5 from process 3 must time share with thread 4 from process 2. Due to this, core 4 will end up with a higher utilization than the other three cores since it is handling work for two threads instead of just one. In the real world, most cores are time sharing between many processes and threads, but this illustration serves as an example of how processors, cores, processes, and threads all work together. When the enterprise application starts performing a number of simultaneous tasks, it could split them up in this method in order to gain the fastest possible execution of any given set of work.

Nontraditional Processors

In most cases, when someone refers to a "processor," they're referring to the primary system processor or "central processing unit" using the terminology from decades past. However, there is a growing trend within information technology to use nontraditional processors to perform certain tasks. This can help to offset the load for specialized work off of the primary processor and onto other processors within the system. The two most common nontraditional processors are graphics processing units (GPUs) and cryptographic cards.

Graphics Processing Units

A GPU is a processor that is designed to quickly build images for display for external devices. This is the processor on any given system's video card whether that card is integrated with the motherboard or standalone. The GPU design is such that it can very quickly process large blocks of data in a parallel manner with the intent that this processing be used to create image data. As gamers required better and better graphics processing in order to handle the work associated with generating realistic graphics at a high rate of speed, GPUs evolved to become even more efficient at this task and have been improved to function incredibly fast.

The majority of the work associated with image processing involves performing a high number of mathematical operations to generate shading details, polygons, and other graphics-related concepts. As GPUs evolved to perform these tasks with such efficiency, it was realized that GPUs could also be used for performing other math-intensive functions or other tasks that required large sets of data to be processed simultaneously. This led to the use of GPUs for performing tasks such as generating hashes for Bitcoin "mining" and building rainbow tables for password cracking. Both of these efforts are very math and processor intensive and, by offloading the work to GPUs, the tasks can be executed more quickly due to the design of the processors as well as the number of video cards that can be added to a system.

Cryptographic Cards

Cryptographic cards are another type of nontraditional processor that are built for rapidly performing cryptographic functions. Similar to GPUs, cryptographic cards perform math-based tasks incredibly quickly and therefore provide a performance boost over traditional system processors when executing this type of work. In addition, cryptographic cards can improve overall system performance by allowing the primary processor to handle normal operations while shifting all cryptographic work to the cryptographic card. These cards are primarily used in web servers and other systems where a large amount of encrypted traffic needs to be generated.

Memory

Memory is a critical part of any server infrastructure and tends to be one of the primary areas to look at when dealing with system utilization or capacity planning. The system memory is a temporary storage location where the system stores parts of running applications, variables, and other data. This temporary storage location is wiped upon system restart and is constantly read from and written to while the system is in operation.

Memory from the enterprise application perspective is comprised of two basic types: hardware (physical) and virtual (page file or swap file). Hardware-based memory refers to the physical memory chips installed in a server that allow for very rapid read/write operations when storing temporary data. Virtual memory is a concept of disk-based memory that acts as if it were hardware-based and presents itself as an extension of the server's hardware-based memory. Another definition of virtual memory pertains to memory that is allocated to a virtual machine within a virtualized hardware environment. We'll discuss this type of memory in Chapter 6 when we discuss architecture.

Hardware-Based Memory

Hardware-based memory, as has already been mentioned, refers to the actual physical memory chips installed in a server. This type of memory comes in many different types and varies depending on the desired memory size, bus speed, hardware architecture, and other factors. In most cases, the purchase and installation of memory is not done by the enterprise applications administrator, but should you find yourself in that situation, rely heavily on the hardware vendor's specifications to ensure that the correct memory is used. The use of incompatible memory can cause a number of system problems and potentially void your warranty or service contract.

The most important aspect of memory from the enterprise applications administration perspective is generally that of sizing. Enterprise applications require a very large amount of memory to run, and there are typically tuning options within the application's configuration that allow the administrator to make the most efficient use of memory resources possible. This may be in the form of providing minimum and maximum amounts of memory to use per process or even determining the maximum number of threads that can be started within a particular memory space. Knowing the amount of memory that the system has and how the specific application that you're dealing with utilizes memory is critical to ensuring system availability.

In some cases, the enterprise application vendor may not provide good information on how the application uses memory or the information that they do provide may be of questionable quality. When this is the case, the enterprise applications administrator can rely on performing load tests to determine the true memory utilization patterns of the enterprise application.

A load test can be performed in a number of ways depending on the purpose of the test. The two most common load tests are (i) to ensure that a system can handle a predetermined number of simultaneous users, system calls, or transactions and (ii) to determine how many simultaneous users, system calls, or transactions a system can handle before failing. In both cases, various performance aspects of the system will need to be monitored and recorded for analysis. One of these is the memory utilization of the system.

When performing a load test, watching the memory utilization can tell you several important things. Before the application is started, the initial memory utilization value tells you the memory use of the system "at rest." After the application is started, but before the test is begun, the memory utilization tells you what the application uses upon initialization. A typical load test will ramp up users at a predetermined rate. As the number of users increases, the memory utilization will typically increase in parallel; however, there may be an initial jump in memory utilization as the application moves from an initialized state to an active state. The amount of this jump as the first few users hit the system can typically be recorded as the application activation overhead. When the load test has added all of the users that it's going to add, you can get the memory utilization at that time and record it as the active application value. Finally, after the load test is concluded and all user sessions have been closed, record the memory utilization value again as the ramped down value.

Using this method, you should end up with the following numbers:

- At rest value
- Application initialization value
- Application activation value
- Active application value
- Ramped down value

These values can give you a really good idea of what the application's memory utilization profile looks like. By subtracting the application initialization value from the active application value, you can determine the user utilization value. Dividing this by the number of users in the load test gives you an estimated amount of memory used per user. Using this number, you can estimate the amount of memory that a system will need in order to support 100, 1,000, or 10,000 users. This may also determine the number of users that can be on a single server before it exhausts its resources.

The ramped down value gives you an idea of what the memory utilization should look like when the activity on the server is low. If memory utilization drops down to this figure during a peak time of the day, it may be an indicator that there is something wrong in the application. We'll talk about that more in Chapter 8 when we discuss monitoring. Under normal conditions, the memory utilization of your application when operating in the production environment should always be somewhere between the application activation value and the active application value. This range can be considered your memory utilization baseline for the application.

Virtual Memory

Virtual memory is a function provided by many operating systems where the operating system creates a virtual memory space that applications can access as if it were a single piece of contiguous memory. This virtual memory space can be a combination of actual physical memory as well as disk-based resources in concert. Most operating systems have a method to configure their virtual memory and, in this context, they're typically referring to the amount of disk space to allocate for virtual memory use.

Disk-based virtual memory tends to be slower than true hardware-based memory, but that's acceptable under many circumstances. If the majority of an application needs to be stored in memory but isn't used frequently, this portion could be moved to virtual memory leaving the faster hardware-based resources available to data which needs to be read from or written to often. With the increased utilization of solid-state drives (SSDs), virtual memory is getting faster if the disk-based virtual memory is on a drive of this type. It still doesn't match the speed of hardware-based memory, but it is much faster than traditional disk-based resources that utilize magnetic platters instead of flash memory.

I/O

I/O is the term used to refer to a server's input and output. This is effectively the data coming in and out of various components in the system including disk reads/writes and network communication. Under certain circumstances, the system may be powerful enough from a processor and memory perspective to work well, but constrained when trying to move data around. For an enterprise applications administrator, this concept is pretty important and can drive decisions around system configurations as well as provide insight into potential performance problems.

Disk

An important element of I/O is the storage of data. When discussing virtual memory, we briefly touched on the fact that hard disks perform slower than memory. This performance difference manifests due to the design of hard disks as well as how they function. From a terminology perspective, most organizations refer to this type of storage simply as "disk."

The intent behind disk-based storage is to handle long-term storage of data for much longer than could be maintained in memory. In addition, disk-based storage is intended to retain data even if the device loses power, which is contrary to the function of memory-based storage. With this in mind, we will discuss disk-based storage based on the two primary types that relate to enterprise applications: local and remote.

Local Disk

Local disk is essentially hard drives that are installed within the server itself. These hard drives can come in a number of configurations along with varied specifications in operating parameters such as speed and size. Most server-class systems accept the use of multiple drives and many include hardware that allows those drives to support the concept of "redundant array of inexpensive disks" (RAID). We'll talk about RAID in Chapter 6 when we go over redundant architecture.

Depending on the server's configuration, it may support as few as two and as many as several dozen hard drives. For example, many blade-based servers will only support two local disks and rely on remote storage, also discussed later in this section, for any additional needs. These local drives are attached to I/O controllers that are specific to the type of drive interface such as Serial AT Attachment (SATA) or Serial Attached SCSI (SAS). These controllers are, in turn, connected to the system bus so that all other devices within the server can communicate with the controller. By sending the appropriate commands and/or data to the controller, the drive can be written to or read from.

From the performance perspective, the areas to look at for local disk start with the drives themselves. At a drive level, the following statistics all play a part in determining the performance of the drive:

- Cache size
- Revolutions per minute (RPM)
- Data transfer rate (TR)
- Seek time

There are other values that help determine the appropriate fit for your enterprise including power consumption, failure rate, and others, but for the purposes of this book we're focusing on I/O performance and its impact on enterprise applications.

There are many benchmarks that can be used for gauging the overall performance of a hard drive based on all of these values, but it helps to have a quick way to compare similar drives in order to get a good idea of how they rate against each other. Taking the caching out of the equation since cache is pretty straight forward, that is, more + faster = better, we'll focus on the other data elements of RPM, TR, and seek time.

The RPM of a drive directly translates into its latency. Latency is how long the system spends waiting on the drive to spin the platter around to where it needs to be in order to read the required data. The speed that the drive spins then has an automatic relationship to this latency. Some common values are given in Table 3.1. To derive these values, there is a fairly simple formula to determine latency from RPM:

$$\frac{1000}{X/60}/2$$

In this equation, X is the RPM for the drive in question. We first determine the revolutions in a second by dividing the RPM by 60. We divide 1000 by the result to get the number of milliseconds. This result is divided by 2 which represents the time to move the disk a half turn, the average distance that the disk would need to travel to get the appropriate data underneath the read head.

The seek time is the amount of time it takes the drive to move to the right part of the disk to read the data. This value is impacted by a number of more granular factors such as the read head motor speed, the speed of the processing components within the drive, and the even drive vibration. Most hard disks manufacturers will publish this value along with the other statistics that they provide in their drive information.

The last value we'll discuss is the transfer rate. This is dependent on the drive interface and defines how fast it can transfer out the data that is being read.

Table 3.1 Hard Disk RPM and Latency Correlation

Revolutions per Minute (RPM)	Latency
15,000	2.0 ms
10,000	3.0 ms
7200	4.17 ms
5400	5.56 ms

Manufacturers will often publish two values associated with the transfer rate. The first is the theoretical transfer rate for the drive, which is a metric in part based on the interface being used and the second is a sustained data rate based on the drive itself. In reality, it doesn't matter which value between these you use to compare two drives as long as you use the same value for each. For example, don't compare theoretical transfer rate for one drive against the sustained transfer rate for the other as the theoretical rate will always be much, much faster.

TIPS & TRICKS

Measuring Performance

If you actually purchase drives and run performance tests against them, you'll have a very solid way to compare the performance of each. But how do you use the performance figures that we've talked about to get a solid understanding of drive performance without actually purchasing the drives? I use a fairly simple formula to give me a pretty good idea of which is the faster drive when comparing a few from different vendors that are similar. This does not take into account caching, special features, operating temperature, vibration prevention, or other important drive characteristics into account. Only pure performance based on latency, seek time, and transfer rate are considered.

$$\frac{2 \log X}{\sqrt{(Y + Z)}}$$

In this equation:

- X = transfer rate
- Y = seek time
- Z = latency

Table 3.2 gives some sample drive data and the resulting performance values. Based on these results, we can see that drive 2 should, in theory, be the fastest based on the data that we have available to compare since it has the highest overall performance value. However, even with a lower transfer rate, drive 3 should perform faster than drive 1 due to the reduced seek time.

Note that by no means is this intended to be an all-encompassing formula to cover all potential variations or changes in technology over time. It's simply a quick and easy way to determine the relative performance of hard disks when compared.

Table 3.2 Hard Disk Performance Analysis

Drive Name	Transfer Rate (X)	Seek Time (Y)	Latency (Z)	Performance Value
Drive 1	6000	16.96	4.17	1.824
Drive 2	6000	8.5	4.17	2.122
Drive 3	3000	8.5	4.17	1.953

In general, most enterprise applications rely heavily on disk performance and perform a very large number of read/write operations in certain parts of the application. Other parts of the application may rely primarily on data stored in memory. The application as a whole, however, may be entirely reliant on the speed of the network connecting the various application components. For example, the database tier of an enterprise application will cache as much as possible but will still utilize a high number of disk accesses, so it's critical to ensure that this system has high performance storage. The web server, on the other hand, may be able to cache all static content and rely on dynamic content to be provided via network transfer. This makes disk performance less of a critical factor at this application tier.

Remote Disk

Many enterprise applications rely on remote disk for their servers. This comes in the form of Network Attached Storage (NAS) or Storage Area Networks (SANs) for the purposes of this discussion. The concept of cloud-based storage will be discussed in Chapter 6. These two forms of remote storage both provide the ability to use disk resources from an external device to augment the local disk capabilities of a given server. This can provide gains in administrative efficiency and allow you to use storage that exceeds the capacity of the server itself. However, by using remote storage, there is typically a change to the I/O performance of the system, as remote storage may not have the same access speed as local storage. This, naturally, depends on the configuration and hardware used for the remote storage.

NAS is the simpler and cheaper of the two remote storage options that we're discussing. With NAS, an administrator adds a NAS device to the network and configures the appropriate file shares and permissions on the device and its drive partitions. The servers are then configured to communicate with the remote storage device through either private or shared directory locations on the device. The NAS can be backed up independently from the servers and can also provide replication or other capabilities.

A SAN is a large step up from NAS and is much more complex and powerful. SAN systems involve arrays of drives that are configured to provide very high levels of availability, capacity, and speed. SAN is made visible to remote servers through more complex configuration than a drive share, typically through the configuration of special software or hardware devices such as a SAN card. This makes the SAN allocated to the server appear to the operating system as if it were a local drive and the operating system, in turn, can format it with its own file system and store files using the same mechanisms as it would for local disk; however, some NAS manufacturers are beginning to offer the ability for their customers to connect in this same means with iSCSI connections. NAS devices tend to be slower than storing files on local disk, but advancements in technology such as 10GbE and adding the iSCSI standard are making NAS units a faster solution.

The degree of performance degradation depends on several factors including the type of network used, the file system of the NAS, and the performance of the NAS device itself. SAN tends to be much faster than NAS as a rule due to the design and configuration of the SAN. In addition, many SAN devices provide the consumer the ability to choose the storage network that best fits their environment. Furthermore, some SANs are now using SAS Expanders creating yet another way to increase SAN performance.

The best practice for ensuring high-performing enterprise applications is to perform appropriate performance tests for each part of the system as a whole, which includes the I/O transactions associated with disk resources. Using the same techniques that we discussed for processor and memory performance analysis, you should be able to determine a performance baseline for disk resources and understand how those resources affect the holistic performance of the enterprise application.

Network

Network I/O is another critical component of server performance. We've already discussed general network concepts and networking hardware in the last chapter. From a server performance perspective, it is the use of this network and its capacity that should be our focus.

Any time that a server communicates to the network, it consumes I/O resources on the system bus, the network card, and the network itself. If taking a theoretical approach, you would consider just the network speed such as 100Mb, 1000Mb, etc. as your baseline and the number of transactions that the server performs per second as your utilization factor. This would give you a theoretical network I/O utilization of the server.

However, reality isn't quite that simple. Other factors come into play that could limit the overall network I/O such as:

- High number of erroneous packets causing retries
- Other hardware components taking up too much I/O bandwidth on the system bus
- High processor or disk utilization reducing the speed at which data can be fed to the network for transmission
- Unexpected additional network I/O on the system due to backups being scheduled to occur over the network during high system utilization
- High overall network utilization due to other systems consuming network resources

Based on this, it's always important to look at network I/O on the server in question and also the utilization of the network at a whole. There is some tuning that can be done at the network level to improve efficiency, but only if a problem is identified. By performing an analysis of network I/O and using other I/O factors to correlate true system utilization, you can isolate the cause of performance issues and ensure that the correct technology area is further analyzed.

Multihoming

Multihoming is a method used to increase the number of network connections that a system has. In some contexts, a multihomed machine refers to a system that has multiple IP addresses from different networks assigned in case there is a routing problem for one of the networks. Multihoming in the I/O context means having multiple network cards installed in the server in order to increase the network bandwidth available.

This can be done via two techniques. The first, and least common, is to logically tie the cards together via software so that it appears to be a single interface. This allows the system to use both cards simultaneously to increase the total bandwidth for the server. This is rarely done due to the complexity of setting it up and issues with routing that can reduce the reliability of the network connection.

The second is to route specific traffic over one network card while other traffic is routed over another. For example, one card may be dedicated to traffic to external backup devices, network-based storage, or monitoring systems while the other card is dedicated to end-user and general system transactions. This design allows for a split in the I/O utilization within the system and in essence isolates specific network traffic. Systems that are set up in this way are able to better tune their network I/O utilization and improve overall performance for the enterprise application that they're hosting.

WINDOWS

Microsoft Windows is one of the most popular server operating systems in use for corporate enterprises today. This operating system has gone through many revisions over the years starting with Windows NT Server and moving through various versions up to the most recent as of the time of this writing, Windows Server 2012. Each version has an increasing number of new features as well as removal of lesser-used functions. As the operating system has evolved, it has become more powerful, easier to use, and more stable as an enterprise-quality network operating system.

Basic Concepts

Windows Server is comprised of a number of features that are critical for enterprise applications administrators to understand. These basic concepts include some important differences between Windows versions, the architecture of the operating system, how it handles the logical concepts of a network, its file system, various aspects of file system management, and troubleshooting. Each of these concepts will be examined as they relate to newer versions of the operating system. Older versions may have similar concepts, but implement them in different ways.

Versions

As previously mentioned, Microsoft's first "real" network operating system geared for enterprise use was Windows NT. Windows NT 4 was the most popular version of this series and included some very powerful features such as the Windows Explorer, taskbar, and Start menu. Windows NT 3.1 was the first Microsoft operating system to support 32-bit architecture in comparison to the 16-bit architecture used previously.

Windows NT also introduced NTFS (New Technology File System) as a powerful file system architecture. This file system included many additional features that did not exist in the FAT (File Allocation Table) file system previously used by Microsoft products. Lastly, Microsoft introduced its first move toward domain-based system and user management. This involved the concept of each system and user making use of the Windows NT server being part of the same "domain" and centralizing access control and permissions based on this membership.

Windows 2000 Server was the next major release after Windows NT Server and involved many upgrades and new features. While Windows NT is becoming almost nonexistent in many corporate environments (it's 20 years old as of the time of this writing), Windows 2000 Server systems can still be found in many enterprises. This operating system version introduced the concept of Microsoft's Active Directory as a major enhancement of the domain concept. We'll be discussing Active Directory in more detail later in this section.

Windows 2000 Server also improved the server's fault tolerance through better use of RAID, Distributed File System (DFS) services, and logical server redundancy for domain controllers. Server security was enhanced improving the protocol used for authentication as well as the model for applying permissions both to network services as well as individual workstations. Security was a major concern for Windows 2000 Server, however, requiring very frequent updates to patch security vulnerabilities. Windows 2000 Server also provided a new version of NTFS that further enhanced its capabilities including support for Encrypting File System (EFS).

Windows Server 2003 was an upgrade to Windows 2000 Server, but wasn't as much of a jump in functionality as compared to the transition between Windows NT and Windows 2000 Server. Windows Server 2003 included some new features and enhancements including support for the Microsoft .NET Framework, enhanced clustering capabilities, improved Active Directory functionality, local firewall functionality, other security enhancements, and a vastly improved version of Internet Information Server (IIS). Windows Server 2003 also included the ability to use "shadow files" in order to allow real-time backup of files that are presently in use by the system.

Windows Server 2008 was the next major network operating system release from Microsoft. This version was based on the same operating system code-base as Windows Vista and included some improved core features because of this. This included rewritten networking components such as the support of IPv6. From the security perspective, Address Space Layout Randomization (ASLR) was implemented which makes some vulnerability exploits more difficult to write, the internal firewall was improved, and security in Active Directory was further improved.

Windows Server 2008 also improved its hardware management through the use of Dynamic Hardware Partitioning (DHP). This allows the operating system to address processors and memory individually and reallocate these hardware resources in real time. The benefit of this is the ability to maintain the server's availability while replacing processor and memory components, which was previously not possible from the operating system perspective.

Microsoft also changed its approach toward Active Directory, splitting its functionality up into a variety of components. These are Active Directory Certificate Services (ADCS), Active Directory Domain Services (ADDS), Active Directory Federation Services (ADFS), Active Directory Lightweight Directory Services (AD LDS), Active Directory Metadata Services (ADMS), and Active Directory Rights Management Services (AD RMS).

As of this writing, the most current version of Microsoft's Server line is Windows Server 2012. This version includes enhanced DNS and DHCP functionality, additional enhancements to Active Directory, and a new file system called Resilient File System (ReFS). This new file system changes the way that data is stored and indexed in order to increase the amount of storage supported by the operating system to a yottabyte (10^{24} bytes) and improves resilience. It doesn't support all of the same features as NTFS, however, including quotas, streams, file level encryption, and extended attributes. Also, the server will not boot from a partition formatted with ReFS, so this file system cannot be used for the root server file system. Windows Server 2012 also includes improved Hyper-V virtualization support, which was originally introduced with Windows Server 2008.

Yotta-what?

The Resilient File System that we discussed supports a yottabyte of storage. But what is a yottabyte? The following chart should help translate what this really means:

$$Kilobyte = 10^3$$
$$Megabyte = 10^6$$
$$Gigabyte = 10^9$$
$$Terabyte = 10^{12}$$
$$Petabyte = 10^{15}$$
$$Exabyte = 10^{18}$$
$$Zettabyte = 10^{21}$$
$$Yottabyte = 10^{24}$$

So, a yottabyte is 1,000,000,000,000,000,000,000,000 bytes or one quadrillion gigabytes. That would probably successfully hold your digital movie collection.

Operating System Architecture

Windows has a complex architecture that is used to provide a high level of security and functionality. This architecture is based on the concept of a "kernel" which embodies all of the low level functions of the operating system with layers of abstraction both outside the kernel as well as within the kernel itself. The kernel concept itself is based on a ring security model where various layers of the operating system reside in different security "rings." This ring model, illustrated in Figure 3.2, defines the boundaries between various layers of both hardware and software protection.

As you can see in Figure 3.2, the innermost layer of the rings is Ring -1. This is a relatively new concept in the ring security model and is made available in a couple of different processor architectures specifically to allow for virtualization. We'll discuss the virtualization concept further in Chapter 6 when we go into details on architecture. For now, understand that the Ring -1 functions exist in order to allow virtualized hosts to perform Ring 0 functions independently without affecting other virtualized hosts.

Ring 0 is the layer where the operating system kernel resides and provides direct access to processor and memory functions. Anything run within this ring is considered running in "kernel mode." Ring 3, the outermost ring, is where user applications reside and this is referred to as "user mode." In order for any user mode applications to work with the system hardware, it must request an operation from the operating system running in kernel mode.

There are various interfaces between the user applications in Ring 3 and the operating system in Ring 0. In Windows architecture, there is a layer that resides primarily in kernel mode, but also partially in user mode called the

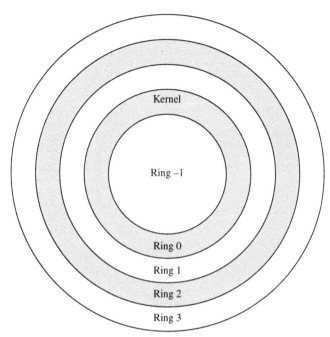

FIGURE 3.2
Ring security model.

Windows "executive." The Windows executive serves as a layer of protection for the kernel and provides functions that allow user mode applications to access kernel mode operations. In this context, the Windows executive serves as an interface between user applications and the kernel.

Within the user mode of Windows, there are a variety of components that operate in this layer and provide various types of functionality. These are broken up into the following component types:

- System processes
- Environment subsystems
- User applications
- Service processes

These are illustrated in Figure 3.3. As you can see, each component type has a number of components, some of which are shown in Figure 3.3. For example, "service host" and "print spooler" are both examples of service processes. User applications can call some of these components to perform specific operations and others run independently with no user application interaction. Again, each of these components runs within user mode and therefore does not have direct access to the system hardware.

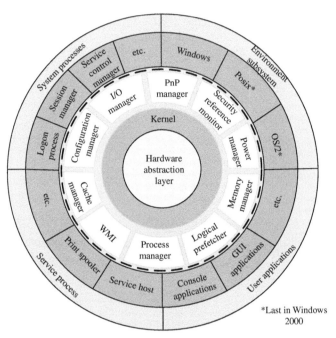

FIGURE 3.3
Windows architecture.

The Windows executive contains another set of components that can be called by user mode components or applications. These components in the Windows executive serve as an interface with the operating system kernel. The Windows executive is considered as a kernel mode layer; however, it does span across both kernel mode and user mode to some degree. Figure 3.3 illustrates the components of the Windows executive within the dashed line separating the user mode layer from the kernel mode layer. These change somewhat between various Windows versions, but the concept of the Windows executive as an interface between user mode components and kernel mode operations is consistent across all versions.

When user mode components or applications call the Windows executive, they use various application programming interfaces (APIs), dynamic-link libraries (DLLs), and other access methods. Each call is then routed through the Windows executive to the appropriate kernel mode function as needed. Within the Windows kernel, code exists which orchestrate calls to internal kernel functions as well as system hardware. This is split between kernel functions and a hardware abstraction layer (HAL) that allows the kernel functions to be identical across multiple hardware platforms.

The Windows HAL serves as an interface between kernel functions and the physical hardware itself. This abstraction layer is what allows Windows functions to operate the same regardless of which motherboard, processor, or memory types are installed in the system. The kernel function calls the HAL that, in turn, translates the call into the appropriate format for the hardware installed in the system. The HAL then communicates with the hardware and passes any responses back to the kernel function that called it. There are some exceptions to this process, such as calls to graphics drivers that bypass the HAL and call the hardware directly.

The core architecture of Windows is very complex and takes up several volumes to explain in detail. For the purposes of enterprise applications administration, you should understand the core concepts of kernel mode, user mode, and the components that run within each including the Windows executive. You should also have an understanding of the layered security approach that Windows uses and how this aligns with the ring security model. The components within each layer of Windows provide critical functions that all Windows-based enterprise applications use, and it's very important to have a solid understanding of how this architecture works.

Active Directory

Active Directory is Microsoft's implementation of a directory service and, as mentioned earlier in this chapter, is included in Windows 2000 Server and beyond. This directory service is similar in many ways to other LDAP-based directory services and stores objects in a hierarchical manner as described in Chapter 2 in the section on LDAP. In fact, Microsoft Active Directory supports multiple versions of LDAP and also implements technologies such as Kerberos and DNS as part of its suite of functions.

In Active Directory, objects exist for all resources and "security principals." Objects that fall under the latter definition include computers, users, and services, whereas resources are objects such as printers, file shares, and other shared network devices. Each active directory object can have multiple attributes as specified by the LDAP protocol and exists in a defined hierarchy.

Within Active Directory, the hierarchy starts at the top with a concept called "forests" that contain one or more "domain trees" that, in turn, contain one or more "domains." This goes back to the Windows NT concept of a domain structure where every computer and user is part of the same domain. Within each domain, there exists one or more "organizational units" (OUs), although these are merely logical groupings and not actual containers themselves. Therefore, any object that is assigned to an organizational unit falls directly under the domain in the hierarchy. Figure 3.4 shows the Windows

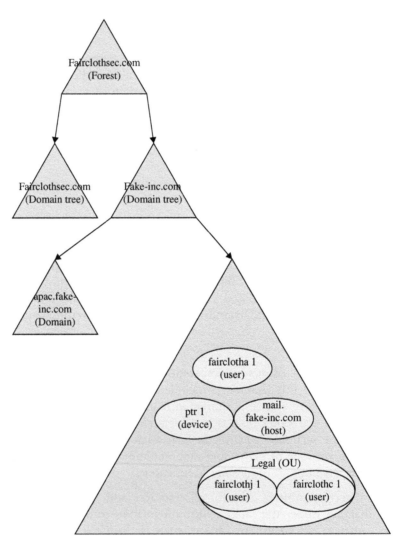

FIGURE 3.4
Active directory hierarchy.

Active Directory hierarchy and illustrates some of the logical grouping that can be done with Active Directory.

In addition to logical grouping, Active Directory supports grouping from the physical aspect as well. This type of grouping relies on objects called "sites" and is used to segment locations based on subnet. From an Active Directory perspective, the site object is very important as it drives behaviors around replication of the Active Directory information along with other functions.

Active Directory supports enterprise applications in a few different ways. For example, some enterprise applications rely on Active Directory to authenticate users as well as provide authorization details for the user. In some cases, the attributes for the user object in Active Directory may contain various pieces of data that tell the enterprise application what level of application access the user is authorized to have. This may also be based on the OUs that the user is a member of. In some cases, enterprise applications can build an in-application organizational hierarchy based on data made available from Active Directory.

From the other perspective, in order to establish trust relationships between the various servers that comprise the enterprise application, the servers all need to have appropriate objects within Active Directory. These trust relationships allow the servers to communicate securely and function properly as the hosts for the enterprise application. Another great feature in Active Directory pertaining to trusts is the ability to create external trusts and realm trusts. These trusts are key when establishing business-to-business processes, accessing hosted environments outside your forest, or even creating trusts amongst non-Windows systems that support Kerberos v5. The enterprise application itself may also operate under named service accounts that reside in Active Directory with appropriate permissions and policies assigned.

Group Policy One of the Windows features frequently used is its application of group policies. Group policies are Windows settings that are applied to Windows systems upon startup or login and control many aspects of the user experience within the operating system. Group policies can be applied either through local group policies stored on the Windows system itself or through domain group policies made available in Active Directory. The domain group policy will always win if there is ever a conflict between local and domain group policy. Most corporate environments that implement group policies and have an Active Directory infrastructure choose to implement these policies through Active Directory.

Group policies are split into functions based on whether they are intended to affect the computer's core functionality or the user's experience. This means that many system-related settings can be controlled through group policies including networking, file system usage, and security. While it typically isn't the enterprise applications administrator who is setting up group policies, it is important to understand what they are and the effect they can have on both the operating system and the application users.

Group policies do provide a convenient method of administering large numbers of Windows servers and workstations and can provide huge benefits to large enterprises. Many basic configuration tasks can be automated and made consistent across many systems with very little effort, which reduces administrative workload and decreases troubleshooting time for Windows system administrators.

From an enterprise applications perspective, group policies can have an effect on the configuration of the servers hosting the application, the workstations being used to access it, and the users of the application. If you, in the course of working with an enterprise application, need a setting added, changed, or removed to or from all servers/workstations/users, you might consider the use of group policies. While it is not within the scope of this book to walk through how to perform group policy modifications, keep this technology in mind as a potential option for helping you in your administration work.

Registry

Windows relies on the Windows registry as the primary configuration store for most system settings. The registry is comprised of several files that contain both system-specific and user-specific settings. The registry is arranged in a hierarchical format and is split into five trees (also called hives). These trees are:

1. Hkey_Classes_Root
2. Hkey_Local_Machine
3. Hkey_Users
4. Hkey_Current_User
5. Hkey_Current_Config (Only in some versions)

CORPORATE MEMO...

Hives?

In most of the Corporate Memo sidebars, you will find various tips on how the text relates to real-world corporate environments. In this case, this is more of a tip of what not to do in a corporate environment.

When Windows was being developed, one of the developers shared with his fellow Microsoft employees that he really, really, really hated bees. Therefore, another developer who wrote a lot of the code for the Windows registry did his best to implement as many bee-related references as possible. Thus, registry trees are "hives" and the registry entries are in "cells."

The real tip is to be careful what you share with your fellow employees! You never know where that information may crop up!

The Windows registry is technically stored as a database in binary format, which leads to faster load speeds and data queries. In addition, the registry supports permission-based editing, which is effectively the application of an access control list (ACL) on the registry itself. Modifications to the registry can be done via the Registry Editor, command-line tools, or through applications using the registry. The Windows Registry Editor also supports imports and exports as well as direct editing of the registry through the use of .REG files.

Many enterprise applications store their configuration information in the Windows registry, in local .XML files, or internal application-specific configuration stores. In the case where this information is stored in the registry, the enterprise applications administrator will need to understand in which hive the configuration is stored, what the various configuration options control and how to navigate to and change these settings. It is also important to understand how individual user accounts use the registry settings especially in a Terminal Services or Citrix environments. When configuring user-specific application settings saved in the Windows Registry, a Terminal Services environment could require logon and logoff scripts that import and export the registry settings.

File System

Windows supports a number of file systems including two Windows-specific file systems: NTFS and ReFS (in Windows Server 2012 and later). These file systems are improvements over the FAT file system previously used by MS-DOS. With the use of improved file systems, Windows increases its abilities to manage data at the file level and apply file system-specific functions.

NTFS is a file system that uses a database called a master file table (MFT) to store information about every file and directory stored in the file system. This replaces the file allocation table used by the FAT file system. NTFS does perform a little slower than FAT, but provides recoverability options and extended features such as compression, encryption, long file names, and the ability to apply permissions that makes the speed reduction worthwhile.

TIPS & TRICKS

Encryption and Compression

NTFS supports both encryption and compression capabilities. The encryption function encrypts all or part of the files on the disk in order to apply additional security. Compression allows you to shrink the amount of space that the files take up on the disk and therefore store more data. However, it's important to note that these two functions absolutely do not work together. You cannot apply both NTFS-based encryption and NTFS-based compression to the same files.

ReFS is a new file system introduced with Windows Server 2012. For the most part, ReFS and NTFS are fairly similar, but there are some important differences that you need to be aware of. ReFS does not support the following NTFS functions:

- Ability to boot from a ReFS partition
- Compression
- Disk quotas
- Encryption
- Extended attributes
- Hard links
- Object identifiers
- Removable media
- Short file names
- Streams

ReFS supports very large file systems, scales very well, and supports Microsoft's new Storage Spaces concept (a storage virtualization system). In addition, it supports some new mechanisms to help prevent file system corruption such as automatic detection of errors in file metadata and autocorrection using redundant copies. This level of error detection and correction can also be applied to the files themselves as well as the metadata making ReFS a file system that supports very large file systems with a high level of integrity.

Permissions A critical feature of NTFS and ReFS is their ability to support file-based permissions. This is done through the application of ACLs and allows you to restrict access to individual files or directories to specific security principles as well as control what operations they can perform with the files. These permissions are applied at the file system level and therefore control access to the files beyond what can be done with a network share pointed at the file system location. The combination of the share permissions and the file system permissions creates the effective permissions for any security principle accessing the files.

Every file or directory in NTFS and ReFS has an assigned owner. This may or may not be the person who created the file, but is always the person who is assigned as having the most control over the file. The file owner can assign ownership of the file to someone else, change file permissions, or do anything they'd like with the file. The permissions assigned by the file owner modify the ACL associated with the file and provides the mechanism to set the access rights at a very granular level.

Within the ACL, various permissions can be set for any security principle to allow or deny specific operations. These include:

- Full control
- Modify

- Read and execute
- List folder contents
- Read
- Write
- Special permissions

These vary a little bit depending on whether you are working with a file or a directory. The "special permissions" operation allows even more granular control over what the security principle can do with the file or directory. These additional permissions include items such as reading/writing attributes, changing permissions, and traversing a folder (without the ability to read its contents).

From an enterprise applications perspective, it's very important to understand file permissions as they can have a tremendous impact on the application and its ability to function correctly. If, for example, the user account that the enterprise application runs under doesn't have access to critical files, the application may fail to run correctly or may generate errors. This is also critical as you cross system boundaries and read/write to files on remote systems. The user context within which the application runs will either need access to these remote resources or be able to authenticate as a user who does have the appropriate level of access.

Troubleshooting Tools

Troubleshooting Windows is a very complex topic and can span dozens of books this size. The intent here is to cover some of the basic troubleshooting necessary from an enterprise applications administration perspective and some of the tools that you may find useful when working with enterprise applications running on Windows systems. We will discuss troubleshooting as it relates to some of the key areas associated with Windows architecture covered previously in this chapter.

GUI Tools

With Windows systems, there are a number of tools included that can help you in troubleshooting any issues that you run into. This section focuses only on those tools included with the operating system and does not cover the many excellent third-party tools that are available. All of the tools in this section have a graphical user interface (GUI) and are generally available in most Windows versions.

Task Manager

Task Manager is one of the most frequently used tools in Windows. The quick way to access it is to right-click on the Taskbar and click the Task

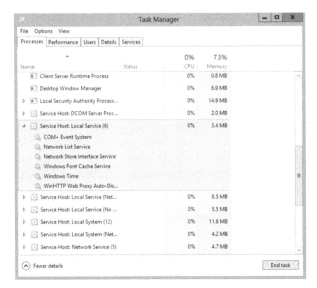

FIGURE 3.5
Windows Server 2012 Task Manager.

Manager option or press Ctrl-Shift-Esc. The example screenshot in Figure 3.5 shows the Task Manager from Windows Server 2012 with the "More Details" selection expanded. From here, we can see running applications, background services, and other processes running on the system as well as the memory and CPU resources that each process is consuming. By expanding the process similar to the "Local Service" process shown in the example, you can see any subprocesses or services associated with the parent process.

By changing to the various tabs within the Task Manager, we can perform additional functions. The Performance tab shows the current utilization of CPU, memory, and network resources and allows you to view other important system information. The Users tab lists the users currently on the system, the applications that they have running, and the system resources that each user is utilizing. Moving to the Details tab gives you more insight into the processes currently running on the system and provides a number of actions that you can perform with those processes including killing them, changing their priority, opening the directory that they're running from, and other useful functions. Finally, the Services tab shows you processes that are running as services on the system and allows you to start or stop them.

Resource Monitor

The Windows Resource Monitor is available in Windows to provide you even more extensive details on resource utilization on the system. It's available

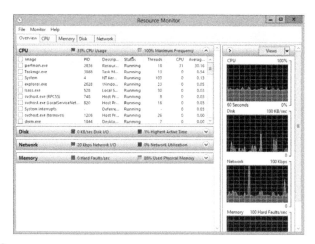

FIGURE 3.6
Windows Server 2012 Resource Monitor.

through Start- > All Programs- > Accessories- > System Tools- > Resource Monitor in some versions of Windows, in the Tools menu of Server Manager in others, through clicking on the Resource Monitor link on the Performance tab in Task Manager, or Start- > Run- > "resmon". The Windows Server 2012 version is shown in Figure 3.6.

While Task Manager can show you some resource utilization information, the data available in Resource Monitor is much more extensive and granular. Through the various tabs, you can view general statistics or detailed CPU, memory, disk, and network data.

Performance Monitor
Just as Resource Monitor provides more extensive resource data than Task Manager, Performance Monitor provides more extensive performance data than either of the tools that we've discussed so far. Performance Monitor, which can be accessed by going to Start- > Run- > "perfmon", is designed to allow a Windows administrator to collect very detailed performance data associated with the system hardware or operating system. This includes many performance counters that aren't available to Resource Manager such as kernel statistics, .NET Common Language Runtime (CLR) data, and other important data elements. For example, in Figure 3.7, we're adding a counter associated with pagefile usage to the current session.

Performance Monitor also allows you to define and save collections of various counters that you use for specific purposes. For example, if there is a particular set of data that you like to look at every time to analyze the system's overall capacity as a database server, you can define that data collector set

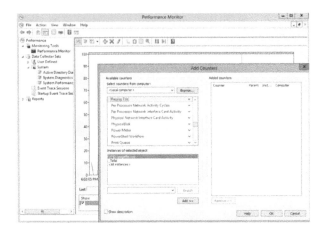

FIGURE 3.7
Windows Server 2012 Performance Monitor.

once and then just use the saved set in the future. The results of a scan for these data sets can be saved as Performance Monitor reports and reviewed in an easy to use report format.

Performance Monitor also allows you to save the results of monitoring sessions for later review, viewing on a different system than the one being monitored, or importing into other tools. This allows you to gain more use from the collected data and compare results between multiple sessions or multiple systems easily. There are a number of other features available through Performance Monitor, but this should get you started on the areas that are important from an enterprise applications administration point of view.

Registry Editor
As we discussed previously in this chapter, the Windows registry is a critical storage location for system and application configuration and settings. To edit the registry, we can use a tool called the Registry Editor. Registry Editor can be executed quickly by just running the regedit executable file. This works across all Windows versions and should bring up the Registry Editor as shown in Figure 3.8.

We are not going to cover any details on settings that you can change with the Windows Registry Editor here. As with most powerful administrative tools, mistakes made in Registry Editor can leave a system unbootable or in a highly unstable condition. The default recommendation is that you should not use Registry Editor unless you have a firm understanding of what you're doing with it and are willing to risk damaging the operating system if you make a mistake.

FIGURE 3.8
Windows Server 2012 Registry Editor.

From the enterprise applications administrator perspective, the Registry Editor should generally be considered a read-only research tool and should not be used for making changes without discussion with a qualified Windows administrator. That said, Registry Editor could be great for finding hidden settings that can potentially be modifying the behavior of your enterprise application. For example, if the enterprise application that you're working with is supposed to use Microsoft Word templates for generating correspondence but for some reason is failing because it's trying to open Notepad instead, it could be because of a file extension association mistake. This can be found through Windows Explorer, but you can also see the problem using the Registry Editor as shown in Figure 3.9.

FIGURE 3.9
Erroneous file association viewed in Registry Editor.

Group Policy Editor

The Group Policy Editor is used (obviously) to edit group policies associated with a domain, site, or other object. However, for an enterprise applications administrator, it's not necessarily the editing capabilities that we need, but rather, the viewing capabilities. Group Policy Editor can show you what the effective policy is for any given object and help you understand if there are any restrictions in place that could be causing problems for your enterprise application or its users.

The Group Policy Editor can be executed from the Server Manager tools in Windows Server 2012 and is also available in earlier Windows versions. Again, for this example, we're using Windows Server 2012. Figure 3.10 shows Group Policy Editor running with the default domain policy for a specific domain displayed. Within the Settings tab, we can view any settings that are in place per this policy. In this example, there is a security policy restricting a specific path. This could potentially cause issues if access to this path is required for the user that the enterprise application runs under and it doesn't have sufficient privileges.

Command-Line Tools

Many of the tools that you will need to use are command-line tools, so you will need to get familiar with the Windows command line. You can access this by running `cmd` or by executing the Command Prompt application within the Windows Accessories application folder.

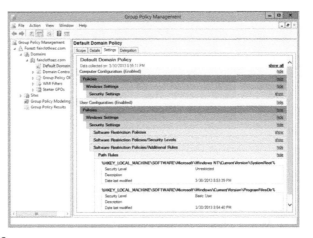

FIGURE 3.10
Windows Server 2012 Group Policy Editor.

Network

There are a number of tools within Windows that can help you in diagnosing network-related issues on your server. A few of these are listed below:

- `ipconfig`—Shows network configuration information
- `ping`—Sends ICMP packets to a specified host or IP address
- `tracert`—Performs a traceroute to a specific host or IP address
- `pathping`—Combines both ping and tracert
- `netstat`—Shows all network ports in use on the system
- `route`—Used to view, add, delete, or modify routes in the system routing table
- `nslookup`—Used to troubleshoot and verify DNS configuration
- `telnet`—Used for testing TCP connectivity

We discussed many of these in Chapter 2 when we went over network configuration and troubleshooting. From a Windows server, you should be able to execute these commands and interpret the results. Let's walk through some of the tools as examples so that you can see what the results could look like in your own testing scenarios. We'll start with viewing the basic system network configuration information. Figure 3.11 shows the results of running `ipconfig` within the Windows Azure cloud platform on a Windows Server 2012 system.

Within the `ipconfig` information shown in Figure 3.11, you can see the enabled network adapters, IP addresses, and other network configuration information for the system. More extensive information can be seen by using the `/all` switch as shown in Figure 3.12.

Now that we have an understanding of the network configuration of the system, we can perform some testing using the `ping` and `tracert` commands. Figure 3.13 shows the results of running a `ping` test against an unknown host, a host that is listed in DNS but not responding, and a host that is responding.

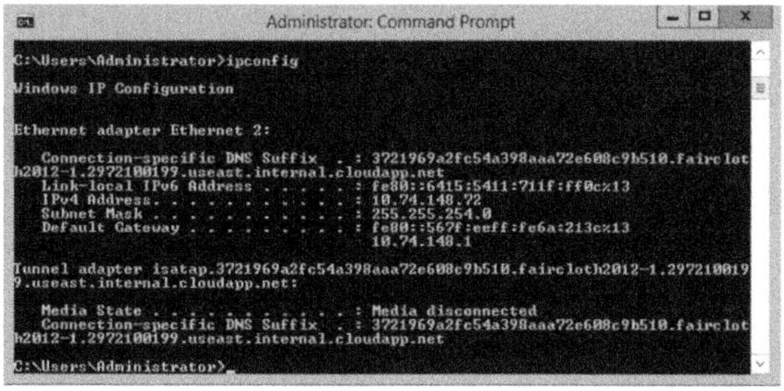

FIGURE 3.11

`ipconfig` command results.

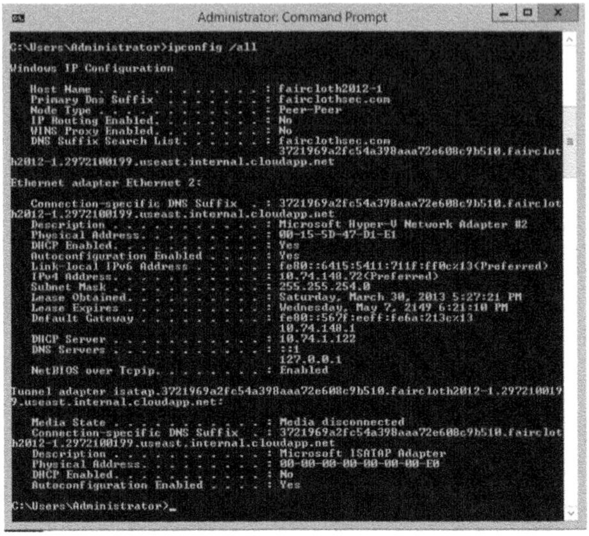

FIGURE 3.12
`ipconfig/all` command results.

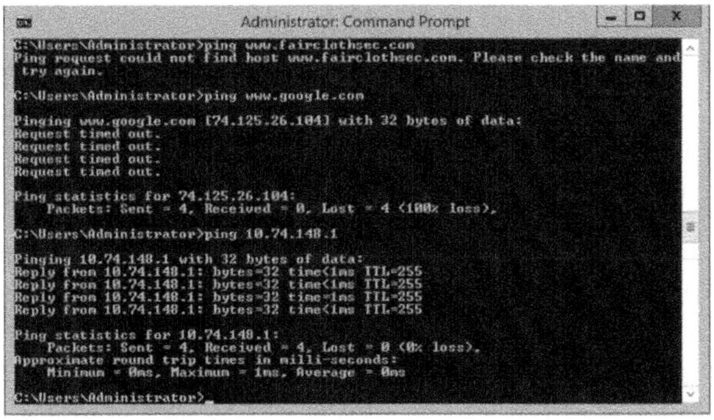

FIGURE 3.13
`ping` command results.

Running the `tracert` command is just as simple, but provides a great deal of additional information related to the route your traffic is taking to get to a specific host. Figure 3.14 shows a successful execution of the `tracert` command. As you can see from the results, there are a number of routers in place between the system running the test and the destination host. Each of these hops adds a little bit of latency to the request which cumulatively results in the amount of time it takes to send or receive any packet to or from the destination host.

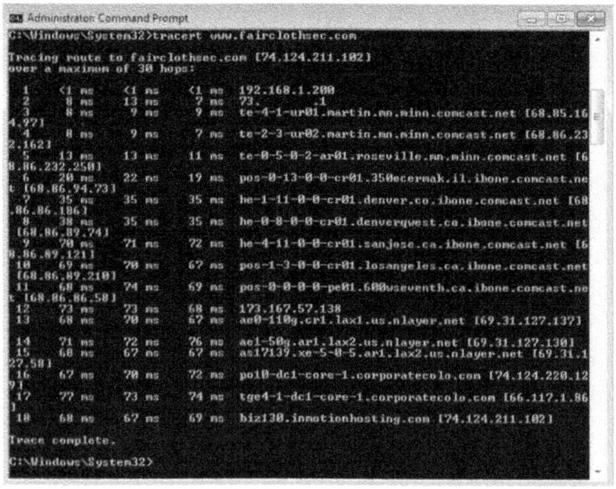

FIGURE 3.14
tracert command results.

Finally, let's take a look at netstat. This tool is used for displaying local port utilization on a Windows system. There are a wide variety of options available when running this tool to fine-tune the results that are presented. However, just running the command by itself can provide a wealth of data about connections that are in use on the system. Figure 3.15 shows the results of a basic netstat command execution.

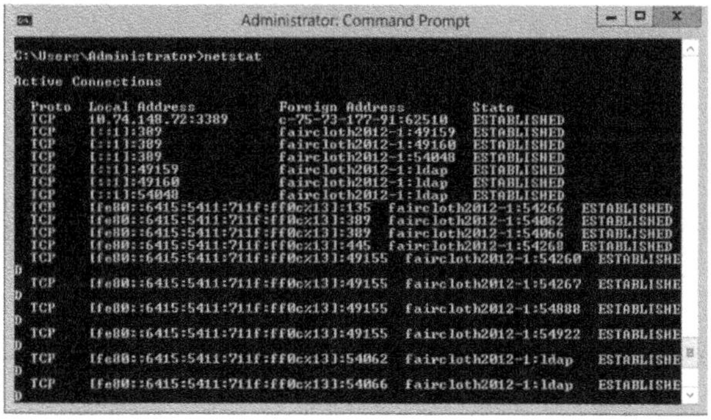

FIGURE 3.15
netstat command results.

As you can see from the example in Figure 3.15, netstat shows us the protocol in use, the local address and port where the connection is established, the remote host and port, and the state of the connection. By using other parameters (shown by running netstat -h) you can view other details such as listening ports, the executable which is utilizing the port, and a huge amount of other useful data.

File System

Working with the Windows file system presents its own challenges. With the support of encryption, compression, and permissions comes the added complexity of each of those features. From a tools perspective, there are a number of built-in tools that help manage and troubleshoot file system-related issues. In this section, we will not be covering basic file system navigation, but rather some of the more advanced tools that will aid you in diagnosing enterprise application issues associated with the Windows file system.

For the first tool, we're going to be looking at a utility that can help with remote file system connections as well as many other Windows networking related functions such as accounts, group assignments, and others. However, since this is a section devoted to file system tools, we'll just look at that aspect of the utility and leave the other functions as an exploration exercise for you. This tool is the net utility included with Windows. By running the command net use, we can see all network drive connections on the local machine. In addition, by running the net share command, we can see shares that are present on the local server. An example is shown in Figure 3.16.

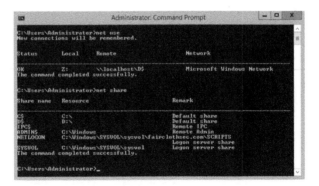

FIGURE 3.16
net use and net share command results.

Another very useful tool is icacls or, in previous Windows versions, cacls. This tool allows you to view and manipulate file and directory permissions on Windows servers. By running the command with no parameters, an extensive list of available commands is shown. If you specify a file or folder following the icacls command, the permissions on that object are displayed. A couple of examples are shown in Figure 3.17.

FIGURE 3.17
icacls command results.

Other Tools

There are a few other tools that require mention when it comes to working with Windows servers. The first is the powershell tool. A full explanation of how to use this incredibly powerful utility is beyond the scope of this book, but you need to be aware of the Windows PowerShell and what it does. PowerShell can be executed simply by running powershell from the command line by itself or by adding a number of command-line parameters. This tool is effectively a powerful scripting language that allows you to leverage various Windows internal components to provide more flexibility and capabilities than basic scripting languages.

Another useful toolset for Active Directory environments are the Directory Service Tools or DS tools. These tools include:

- dsadd—Adds objects to Active Directory
- dsquery—Searches objects in Active Directory
- dsget—Displays properties from objects in Active Directory
- dsmod—Modifies objects in Active Directory
- dsmove—Moves or renames objects in Active Directory
- dsrm—Removes objects from Active Directory

For example, the dsquery tool allows you to perform various queries against the Active Directory or use its sibling tools to make modifications to the directory. Running the command dsquery with no parameters will display the help file for the utility and describe how to use it for various tasks. For example, if you'd like to see the users and computers available in the directory, you can run dsquery user and dsquery computer. This is shown in Figure 3.18. In addition to simple searches with dsquery, you can pipe the results to other DS tools. For example, if you wanted to find the phone numbers of all users in a specific OU you could simply type:

```
dsquery user "ou=accounting,ou=departments,dc=fake-inc,dc=com"
-name * -limit 0 | dsget user -samid -tel
```

FIGURE 3.18

dsquery command results.

This has been just a small sampling of the hundreds of tools available to help you in working within the Windows environment. Many of these can help in troubleshooting issues associated with enterprise applications that you are responsible for administering. By following good troubleshooting principles and using the right tools, you can quickly diagnose a number of different problems that can occur in these critical enterprise applications.

*NIX

UNIX has a long and convoluted history in the information technology world. From its initial creation in 1969 until today, the concepts behind UNIX have morphed into dozens of distinct operating systems. In present day, these are considered *NIX operating systems, UNIX-like operating systems, or "traditional" UNIX operating systems. The Open Group currently owns the UNIX trademark and certifies some operating systems to wear that official UNIX badge of honor.

KEY CONCEPTS

Why *NIX?

There has been a great deal of debate over the years on what to call UNIX-like operating systems. The original name for UNIX was written as "Unix," but quickly morphed into UNIX in a number of official publications and conference presentations. The actual trademark for UNIX is "UNIX" and is owned by The Open Group after changing hands several times. UNIX systems based on some of the original UNIX code, compliant with certain standards, and with a paid certification fee can license the UNIX trademark (and pay ongoing royalties to the trademark holder).

But what should we call all of the operating systems that look and act similar to UNIX without actually *being* UNIX? Some call them UNIX-like as has been done in this text. Others use an asterisk or question mark as a wild card and refer to them as *NIX or ?NIX. Still others just call them UNIX informally and don't think anything of it. In this text, we'll be using *NIX and UNIX-like interchangeably.

As UNIX has morphed over time, it has either had some of its source code rolled into new operating systems or new operating systems have very closely emulated core UNIX functionality. For example, BSD is actually derived from UNIX source code; however, Linux is simply developed to function in the same way as UNIX and does not actually use any UNIX source code elements. Some of the more common UNIX-like operating systems are BSD and its children FreeBSD and OpenBSD, AIX, HP/UX, Solaris and later OpenSolaris, Mac OS X, Minix, and Linux.

We won't be going over the history of UNIX-like operating systems in this section, but rather will be discussing the core concepts of UNIX, its architecture, some nuances of the variants and distributions of UNIX, and some basic UNIX troubleshooting tools.

Basic Concepts

UNIX-like operating systems all use some of the same basic core concepts. These are typically implemented in different ways thus justifying the variant, but the principles are very similar. For example, all UNIX-like operating systems are designed to be multitasking, support multiple users, and use file system structures to represent system devices.

As we look through the concepts behind UNIX-like operating systems, you'll see a lot of similarities with things we've already discussed in the Windows section of this chapter. That's because a lot of these UNIX concepts were used in the development of Windows even though it isn't really considered a UNIX-like operating system. As with many things, good ideas tend to stick around and many of the core decisions made when developing UNIX stand the test of time and still make sense for operating system design today.

Operating System Architecture

To start with the similarities, refer back to Figure 3.2 showing the ring security model. This model found its roots in UNIX and is still used today. UNIX-like operating systems use the same concept of a kernel being separate and protected from anything outside of the kernel. In UNIX-like operating systems, these two distinct areas are called kernel space and user space. The concept is that core operating system code is in the kernel running in kernel space while everything else runs in user space.

All UNIX-like operating systems include the kernel, but they also tend to include a lot of other components as part of their distribution. These include some form of a compiler or development environment, a lot of libraries that contain reusable functions, various tools and utilities, and a lot of documentation for all of the preceding components. In the UNIX-like variants that are considered "open," the source code for these components are included as well.

Figure 3.19 shows an illustration of the UNIX-like system architecture. There is a core kernel that handles interaction with hardware devices but does not have the same form of HAL as Windows systems. Between the kernel and core operating system capabilities lies a layer of protection similar to the Windows Executive layer. In UNIX-like systems, this is called the system call interface (SCI). The way this is implemented differs a great deal from Windows architecture, but performs similar functions.

Outside of the SCI is a layer of functions that provide for all of the calls used by various applications in the UNIX world. These functions include all aspects of foreground and background functionality, command shells, communications (drivers and protocols), etc. It is through these types of functions that each UNIX application retains its portability across different UNIX-like platforms with minimal changes.

File Systems

There are a few different file systems associated with UNIX-like systems. Many UNIX-like systems can now use file systems associated with other operating systems such as FAT and NTFS as well as their own native file systems. Some examples of these native file systems are UNIX File System (UFS), Linux Third Extended File System (ext3), Enhanced Journaled File System

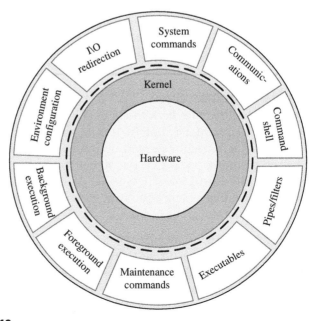

FIGURE 3.19
UNIX-like operating system architecture.

(JFS), IBM General Parallel File System (GPFS), and Hierarchical File System Plus (HFS+). There are others, but these are currently the most common.

Each of these has its own set of features and implements its file storage and metadata management in slightly different ways. From the enterprise applications administrator perspective, you need to understand the variety of file systems that exist for UNIX-like system as well as which file systems are recommended for the various tiers of your enterprise application. For example, some databases perform really well on GPFS if they're running on an AIX system, but may not perform as well if UFS is used. This is where performance testing really comes into play even at the file level to ensure that you are maximizing application performance in the I/O arena.

Directory Structure

UNIX-like systems tend to share a common directory structure that helps in the transition between different operating systems. This is based off of a base root directory referred to simply as "/". Underneath this root in a hierarchy are a series of common subdirectories which each holds a certain type of files. Underneath those, of course, are a myriad of additional subdirectories. This is how that structure looks like in most UNIX-like systems:

- /—Root directory
  - bin—Critical binary files
  - dev—Hardware devices
  - etc—Configuration files and some applications
  - lib—Library files
  - opt—Some applications
  - public—Public shared files
  - root—Home directory for "root" user
  - sbin—System binary files
  - tmp—Temporary files
  - user or home—User home directories
    - fairclothj—Each named user has their own home directory
    - fairclothk—Each named user has their own home directory
    - fairclothm—Each named user has their own home directory
    - faircloths—Each named user has their own home directory
  - usr—Some applications
  - var—Variable files that change frequently

These directories change a little bit depending on which UNIX-like system is being used, but are generally pretty consistent. In many cases, you will find application configuration files in "/etc" or "/opt". Log files can often be found in "/var" or "/var/log" as well as in application directories. When working with hardware devices, you'll typically find the references to those devices in "/dev". Lastly, the home directory for any given user is generally where user-specific settings are stored as well as any personal-use binaries.

Permissions

UNIX-like operating systems provide very granular control of file and directory access through the use of permissions. This is very similar to how Windows works with ACLs, but predates the Windows implementation. With UNIX file systems, it is important to understand the concepts of owners, groups, and "everyone else." We'll talk through these concepts and go through how UNIX permissions work in this section.

First, let's talk about file and directory ownership. A specific user owns every file or directory in a UNIX file system. This user may be an actual user account, the root account, or some other service account associated with an application on the system. Typically, the creator of a file is defined as its owner by default. Each file or directory can also have a group associated with it. When this is the case, any member of that group has the same file permissions as any other group member for the associated file (with exception of the file owner). Finally, there is the "everyone else" or "other" category. This is a catchall for any other user of the UNIX system.

Each of these three security principals (owner, group, other) can have specific permissions applied to each file or directory. These permissions are read, write, and execute. The permissions are chained together in order based on the security principal. This looks similar to the following:

```
(own|grp|oth)
(rwx|rwx|rwx)
```

So, for example, if the file had the following permissions assigned:

- Owner: Read, Write, Execute
- Group: Read, Execute
- Other: Execute

The permissions string would be `rwxr-x--x` for this file. An example of this can be seen when viewing a directory listing of files as shown in Figure 3.20.

FIGURE 3.20
UNIX-like operating system file permissions example.

In addition to the "rwx" nomenclature for file permissions, UNIX-like systems support numeric permissions assignment. This is based on a binary representation of the permissions wherein each assigned permission is represented by a binary 1. For example, permissions of "r-x" would be numerically represented as "101" which when converted from binary to decimal would simply be 5. Table 3.3 shows each possible permission, its binary representation, and its decimal representation.

Variants and Distributions

There are a number of UNIX-like operating systems that you may encounter as an enterprise applications administrator. Some of the more common in corporate environments are AIX, HP/UX, Solaris, and Linux. Each of these is available in a number of different versions and Linux is available in a huge number of distributions as well. A "distribution" is a modified version of the Linux operating system that includes the Linux kernel and any number of modified libraries or applications.

A deep analysis into the differences between each of these UNIX-like operating systems or Linux distributions is beyond the scope of this book; however, as an enterprise applications administrator, you need to be aware of them as well as the fact that there are differences. Each variant or distribution may implement certain core pieces of functionality in very different ways so that the commands that you use in one UNIX-like operating system may not transfer to another. The core concepts do remain the same however, thus the "UNIX-like" designation for the operating system. This means you can apply conceptual knowledge about UNIX that we've discussed in this section across all UNIX-like operating systems.

Table 3.3 UNIX File Permissions

Permission	Binary	Decimal
r--	100	4
rw-	110	6
r-x	101	5
rwx	111	7
-w-	010	2
-wx	011	3
--x	001	1
---	000	0

X Window System

Many people consider UNIX-like systems to be solidly in the realm of command-line only capability and don't think of it as a graphical environment. However, UNIX-like systems typically support the X Window System, which provides a very full-featured graphical environment for users of the system both locally and remote. The X Window System was introduced in 1984 and is now included in almost every UNIX-like operating system variant and Linux distribution.

The X Window System uses a client–server architecture where the host system runs the client service and the server is executed either on the same system or on a remote system. This may seem a little counterintuitive at first, but it is based on the general architectural design of the X Window System. On the user's system, all keyboard, mouse, and graphical I/O is routed through the X server, which then passes this data to and from the X client running on the remote (or local) UNIX-like system. In this design, the X client actually does a connection back to the X server on the user's computer rather than the traditional client–server architecture, which is reversed. This windowing system allows for a flexible GUI that can be used regardless of how you are accessing the UNIX-like system.

Troubleshooting Tools

Just as with Windows systems, there are a number of tools within UNIX-like operating systems that can aid you in troubleshooting enterprise applications. While there are some GUI tools available, for the purposes of this book we're going to focus on command-line-based tools since they are more common across all UNIX-like operating systems and generally easier to access.

Performance

There are a number of tools available in UNIX-like systems that allow you to monitor and understand the performance of the system. As with Windows tools, these tools focus on things like processes running on the system, memory utilization, I/O statistics, and others. Depending on the UNIX-like operating system or Linux distribution that you're using, some or all of the tools that we'll discuss may be available. If they are not available for your specific operating system, there is a high likelihood that a similar tool is available.

First, let's take a look at the processes running on the system itself. A common tool for this is ps. ps lists the running processes on the system, their process IDs, and other useful information. As with any UNIX tool, a number of command-line parameters are available for ps that modifies the information that it shows and its output. In addition, you can pass the output from ps to other tools such as grep to search for a specific process. An example would be the use of the following syntax to show all running processes with "entapp" in the name: ps –ef | grep entapp.

If you're interested in the processes that are consuming the most resources on the UNIX-like system, another useful command is top. top shows the top resource consumers on the system and displays a number of pieces of information about each of those top processes including their memory utilization, CPU utilization, time running, the user that ran them, and others. top is a little different from most of the other tools that we'll discuss because it runs in an interactive mode. Rather than simply display the appropriate data and quit, top keeps running and constantly updates the display with the latest information about the top processes. A number of commands are available while top is running that allow you to change the display or the information being provided. A similar tool that also shows system utilization is vmstat.

iostat is a tool that shows the performance of various I/O components on the UNIX-like system. This includes disks used by the system and displays data about the disk transactions per second, blocks read or written, and the speed of those reads and writes. iostat is useful for troubleshooting disk performance issues and viewing the ongoing operational statistics of the system's I/O functions.

Network

Many of the network troubleshooting tools that we've discussed for Windows also apply to UNIX-like operating systems. While some of the command syntax may change, the basic tools for ping and netstat are practically identical. However, there are a couple of naming differences for other tools to be aware of. For example, whereas in Windows you would use ipconfig to view network adapter configuration information, UNIX-like operating systems use ifconfig (or iwconfig for wireless) for the same purpose. Also, instead of the shortened form of tracert used for Windows, you would use the full command of traceroute under UNIX.

File System Working with a UNIX-like operating system's file system can be a little challenging if you are unfamiliar with the appropriate tools. Keep in mind that with UNIX remote file shares and even devices show up as part of the local file system. In order to work with these, you need to be able to understand how to view the file system in the appropriate ways. UNIX does provide a few tools that can help.

First is the df tool. This utility is used to show all mounted file systems, where that file system is mounted within the local file structure, and even the disk utilization of the file system. It's executed from the command line of course and shows an output similar to that generated by the first command run in Figure 3.21.

As you can see in Figure 3.21, there are a couple of other commands that have been run on this system aside from df. The second command in this sequence is the du -hs /root command. du is a utility that shows disk utilization. The two command-line parameters included with this (-hs) change the output to human readable format and summarize the result. Thus, we end up with a simple response of 3.8G instead of a full directory listing that includes the number of bytes that each file is consuming. By adding a specific directory, in this case /root, we further focus the tool to only provide information about a single directory and its contents.

The last command shown in Figure 3.21 is the mount command. This command is used to show all devices currently mounted and where in the file structure any given mounted device can be found. In this example, we have a mount for device /dev/sda1 mounted as our root (/) directory. There is also some extended information about each mount available in this command output.

Other Tools

Another useful tool for troubleshooting in UNIX-like operating systems is the which command. This tool will identify where in the path any given executable is. This does assume that the executable exists somewhere in the system path as shown with the echo $PATH command. For an example, look at Figure 3.22 where the result of running which to search for a common utility is shown.

```
root@bt:~# df
Filesystem      1K-blocks      Used Available Use% Mounted on
/dev/sda1       25014616  16869436   6891036  71% /
none              504704       236    504468   1% /dev
none              512740         0    512740   0% /dev/shm
none              512740       176    512564   1% /var/run
none              512740         0    512740   0% /var/lock
none              512740         0    512740   0% /lib/init/rw
root@bt:~# du -hs /root
3.8G    /root
root@bt:~# mount
/dev/sda1 on / type ext4 (rw,errors=remount-ro)
proc on /proc type proc (rw,noexec,nosuid,nodev)
none on /sys type sysfs (rw,noexec,nosuid,nodev)
none on /sys/fs/fuse/connections type fusectl (rw)
none on /sys/kernel/debug type debugfs (rw)
none on /sys/kernel/security type securityfs (rw)
none on /dev type devtmpfs (rw,mode=0755)
none on /dev/pts type devpts (rw,noexec,nosuid,gid=5,mode=0620)
none on /dev/shm type tmpfs (rw,nosuid,nodev)
none on /var/run type tmpfs (rw,nosuid,mode=0755)
none on /var/lock type tmpfs (rw,noexec,nosuid,nodev)
none on /lib/init/rw type tmpfs (rw,nosuid,mode=0755)
root@bt:~#
```

FIGURE 3.21
UNIX file system command results.

FIGURE 3.22

which command results.

FIGURE 3.23

umask command results.

The last tool that we're going to talk about is the umask command. This command isn't usually used for troubleshooting per se, but understanding what umask is may help in resolving some default permissions-based issues. Previously in this chapter, we discussed UNIX file permissions. As you'll recall, every file and directory in a UFS has permissions associated to it for the owner, group, and everyone else. Changing the owner is done with the chown command and changing the permissions is done with the chmod command, but how does the system know what to do with a brand new file when it is created on the system? UNIX-like operating systems use the umask value to determine the default permissions for any new file created under a user account.

Running umask alone will tell you what the current umask value is. In the example shown in Figure 3.23, our umask value is 0022. We'll discuss the math behind how this works in a moment, but for now, just trust that this will result in default file permissions of 644 or rw-r--r-- per the translation table given in Table 3.3. This too can be seen in Figure 3.23 with the new file that we've created using the touch command.

So how is the umask value calculated? Start with the value 666 and simply subtract the decimal value of what you want the default permissions to be. For example, if we want to automatically apply permissions rwxrwxrwx instead of the current default, we'd subtract 666 from 666 leaving us with 000. You would then set the umask value by running the command umask 000. This probably isn't a good idea as any newly created file would be open for anyone to read or write. You can also view the umask value in rwx format by running umask -S.

Another great set of tools to use in *nix is the tail or head command coupled with the grep command. tail will allow you to see the last X lines of text in a file and `head` will allow you to see the first X lines of text in a file. In addition, these tools can use the `-f` option to force the commands to keep the selected file open. The `grep` command comes into play while using tail or head to automatically look for a specific piece of text. For example, if trying to look at traffic from a single client to a web server, use the `tail -f` command with `grep`: `tail -f /var/log/httpd/access_log | grep "192.168.1.100"`.

TIPS & TRICKS

My File Doesn't Execute...

In many UNIX-like operating systems, newly created files do not get created with execute permissions. Even if the `umask` value is set to apply the "x" permission, the operating system may prevent this from working. You'll have to set the execute permission manually using `chmod`.

SUMMARY

This chapter has been an introduction to server technologies and their relation to enterprise applications administration. We began by going over the hardware concepts associated with server technologies. This included not only a description of various components such as processors, memory, and disk, but also how the performance of those components can affect the operations of an enterprise application. We talked a little bit about the concepts of cores, processes, and threads as well as how all of these relate to the multitasking capability of enterprise applications.

Moving on to operating systems, we started with one of the more commonly used enterprise application host operating systems, Microsoft Windows. The various versions of Windows as well as some of the nuances associated with those versions were discussed with a focus on capabilities used by enterprise applications. This led to an overview of Windows architecture including the core concepts of the HAL, kernel, Windows Executive, and all of the Windows components that leverage that core. Some tools that can be used to troubleshoot Windows was our final discussion about the world of Windows and its place in enterprise applications administration.

Next up was the UNIX world and the complexities associated with various UNIX-like variants and Linux distributions. With the wide variety of UNIX-like operating systems available, we weren't able to go into a great deal of depth for each one, but we did cover core foundational architecture that is shared across most, if not all, UNIX-like operating system. Again, this included a kernel and the system capabilities that use it. As with Windows, we also talked about useful tools for troubleshooting UNIX-like operating systems.

In general, this chapter should give you a good general overview of servers and their role in enterprise applications administration. Again, our goal is not to cover server technologies or operating systems at a depth sufficient to give you expert-level knowledge. Rather, you should leave this chapter with a solid foundation on this topic that will allow you to communicate appropriately with systems administrators for both hardware and operating systems as well as support the mid-level knowledge needed to support enterprise applications.

Databases

BASIC CONCEPTS

In almost every enterprise application, there is a database on the back end to store the application data. This database may be hosted by any of a wide variety of database management systems (DBMSs). Some of the more common DBMS hosts are Oracle Database, MS SQL Server, IBM DB/2, MySQL, and others. In this chapter, we'll look at some concepts that are common across all of these without getting into too much detail on the nuances that differentiate each DBMS from the others.

Being able to successfully work with these databases is critical for any enterprise applications administrator as it is typically the best way to get right to the source of truth for any data-related issue and bypass much of the enterprise application logic. In addition, the performance of the database makes a tremendous impact on the performance of the application, so knowing how the database for the application works can help its administrator in ensuring that the application performs well.

Terminology

When working with databases from the perspective of an enterprise applications administrator, the first thing to understand is the terminology associated with databases. Many of these terms may seem basic, but it's important to ensure that the appropriate terminology is consistently used. This goes back to one of the core responsibilities of an enterprise applications administrator to speak the language of each respective technology area to facilitate communications with experts in those areas.

We've already discussed the first term, DBMS. In some cases, depending on the system in use, the term relational database management system (RDBMS) may be used as well. This refers to the software products, such as those listed above, which provide database services. This is very different than the database itself! In many cases, the term "database" is incorrectly used to refer to the DBMS. It's important to delineate between these two topics to ensure that you're referring to the correct object. The context may make that clear, but it never hurts to be precise.

The database itself is an object hosted by the DBMS. This object will have its own configuration, settings, design, storage, access control, logging mechanism, and other details associated with it. A DBMS can host a single database or multiple databases depending on how it is configured. This can allow for better utilization of hardware resources whether it's making use of free system resources by adding more databases to a single system or ensuring high performance for a single database by providing dedicated hardware.

Within the database is an internal definition of the structure and design of the database itself. This is known as the database schema. The database schema describes in explicit detail all of the objects within the database and how they are configured. Please note that this does not include the data hosted within this structure, just the structure itself. When working with databases, you can take the schema from one database, apply it to a new database, and you'll have an exact replica of the structure from the original source. However, it will be completely blank and contain no data.

The structure that is included with the schema starts with a concept called tables. A single database can have many tables and each can have its own distinct design and definition. That design is based on the columns, sometimes referred to as fields, that each table holds. Every column will have a particular type of data that it can accept which is referred to as the datatype. The datatype determines the type of data (string, date–time, number, blob, etc.) that is allowed to be stored in any given column. In addition, columns can have a defined width, which indicates the largest piece of data that can be stored in that column. For example, a table could have five columns with the first defined as a number with a width of 100 characters and the rest defined as strings with 255 characters. The table structure shown in Table 4.1 shows what some sample data in this table could look like.

Table 4.1 Sample Database Table				
ID	**Title**	**FirstName**	**MiddleName**	**LastName**
123	Dr.	Steve	Tiberius	Rosoff

Finally, we come to the data itself. Each entry in a database table is known as a row, a record, or a tuple depending on whom you're talking to. Most relational DBMSs use row for their official terminology while other database structures may lean toward the term tuple. There are some slight differences here in that a row, by the strictest definition, stores its data in a specific order (as defined by the table's column structure) whereas a tuple is a data set where the order can change and each piece of data returned is usually comprised of a key-value pair. The use of tuples using this definition is becoming popular with the move toward "NoSQL" databases for handling very large unstructured data sets but you may still hear rows referred to as tuples. Either way, it's still a set of data.

SQL

Okay, now that we have our Database 101 class glossary out of the way, let's move on to Structured Query Language (SQL) so that we can actually work with some of this data. Each DBMS implements its use of SQL a little differently so syntax that works perfectly in one DBMS may fail in another. Therefore, you'll need to make sure to set up your SQL requests to match the requirements of the DBMS that you're working with. We will not be covering those DBMS-specific syntax changes in this book, as it is more granular than our intended scope.

When you consider SQL, think of it as a language that is used to ask questions. By asking a question in just the right way, the DBMS will respond with an answer. In theory, if you asked the question correctly, the response will include all of the data that you need to serve the purpose that prompted you to ask the question in the first place. For example, if you have a database that stores customer information for all of the customers that your company works with, you could form an SQL query (a question) that asks for the entire list of customers. You could further refine that query to define exactly what you want to know about the customers, how you want the response sorted, and all sorts of other useful operations.

Requesting Data

Let's start by showing an example database. The database shown in Figure 4.1 is intended to represent a basic customer database. We'll talk

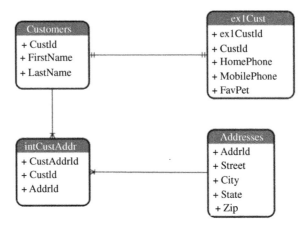

FIGURE 4.1
Example customer database.

about some of the design elements that are used in this example structure later in the chapter, but for now just consider this an example data source for building out our requests.

As you can see in the example shown in Figure 4.1, this is an incredibly simple database with only four tables. Many enterprise applications have hundreds or thousands of tables handling many data elements, but this example is intended to demonstrate basic use of SQL, so we'll keep the complexity down a little.

The database shown in Figure 4.1 has a table called Customers that contains columns for a record identifier (CustId), and the customer's first and last names. There can be many cases where a customer has the same first and last names, so the record identifier keeps them separated or *distinct*. Otherwise, when you go to use this data, you wouldn't be able to positively tie the customer name with any information stored in other tables.

The ex1Cust table serves as an extension table for the customer table. In this particular database design, there's really no reason that the additional columns stores in the extension table couldn't be part of the core Customers table, but it's important to understand the relationship between extension tables and core tables from a query perspective. We'll discuss extension tables more when we talk about database design, but for now understand that with a true extension table, there is a one-to-one tie between records in the core table and records in the extension table. That means that for every record in the core table called Customers, there will be one and only one matching record in the ex1Cust table.

To handle address information, this database has a table called Addresses. This table holds very basic address information, and based on its limited design, cannot handle data such as a second address line, non-US addresses, etc. Again, this design is simply for demonstration purposes and would not be something that should exist in a practical database design.

Any given customer could have multiple addresses and any address could have multiple customers at the same location. This is common in the business world where a single business location houses multiple independent businesses. So to handle this, we consider the tie between customers and addresses a many-to-many relationship. To link those together, an intersection or junction table called intCustAddr has been created.

SELECT

With this basic table structure in place within our example database, we can start looking at how to request data from the database. This is done through the use of the SELECT SQL statement. SELECT requires two things when you use it to ask a question of the database; what you want to know and where that information is. The "what" value should be the column or columns that you're interested in. The "where" value should be the tables where those columns reside. So, for example, if we simply wanted a list of all customer last names, we'd use the statement:

```
SELECT LastName FROM Customers;
```

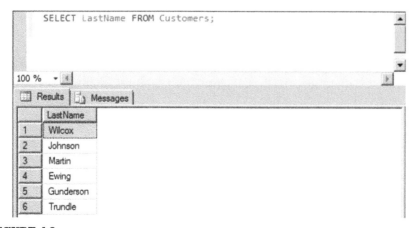

FIGURE 4.2
SELECT query for LastName.

This results in a list of customer last names as shown in Figure 4.2. This list can contain duplicates, doesn't appear to be in any specific order, and only includes the customer's last name. Based on the SQL statement that we used, this is exactly what we asked for. That's part of the joy of working with computers; they are always quite literal.

ORDER BY

So now that we have a basic SELECT query, let's modify it a little bit to do some sorting. For example, if we wanted to sort that data alphabetically using the last name, we could use the query:

```
SELECT LastName FROM Customers ORDER BY LastName;
```

This would give us the result shown in Table 4.2.

Table 4.2 Ordered LastName Query
LastName
Ewing
Gunderson
Johnson
Martin
Trundle
Wilcox

We can also reverse the order by using the command:

```
SELECT LastName FROM Customers ORDER BY LastName DESC;
```

Now, let's say that we want more data. For example, if we want to add the customer's first name to our request, we could use the command:

```
SELECT FirstName, LastName FROM Customers ORDER BY LastName;
```

Running this query gives us the data from both columns as shown in Table 4.3.

Table 4.3 Query Result with Multiple Columns	
FirstName	**LastName**
Tracy	Ewing
Lief	Gunderson
Amanda	Johnson
George	Martin
Bobby	Trundle
Jason	Wilcox

Wildcards

In addition to specifying the fields that we're looking for, we can also use a wildcard to query for all fields in the table. By using the command:

```
SELECT * FROM Customers;
```

the DBMS will return all columns and all rows from this table. This can be seen in the output displayed in Table 4.4.

Table 4.4 Wildcard Table Query

CustId	FirstName	LastName
4	Tracy	Ewing
5	Lief	Gunderson
2	Amanda	Johnson
3	George	Martin
6	Bobby	Trundle
1	Jason	Wilcox

Let's get back to that concept of a duplicate name that we mentioned earlier. If we were to add a new row to this table for a customer with the name "Lief Gunderson," we would end up with two customers sharing the same name. If we perform a query specifying just the LastName field, we would be unable to tell which customer is which. By adding the CustId field either explicitly or implicitly by using a wildcard, we can now identify that customer using their ID in addition to their name.

DISTINCT

What if all we wanted was a list of names regardless of how many customers we have with the same name? There is an SQL query parameter called DISTINCT that can be used to only show rows that have unique values in the requested fields. So, if we used the following query, we'd only receive unique first name and last name combinations:

```
SELECT DISTINCT FirstName, LastName FROM Customers ORDER BY LastName;
```

As you can see from our growing query string, SQL query can become very long and unwieldy. To prevent this, most DBMSs ignore any whitespace within a query. So the following query is identical to the previous one but is easier to read. Using this formatting style makes your queries easier to quickly read and interpret.

```
SELECT FirstName, LastName
FROM Customers
ORDER BY LastName;
```

WHERE

So far our focus has been around returning all rows from specific columns in a table, but now it's time to start reducing that returned data a little bit. Obviously, in an enterprise application, any given table can have millions of rows and no one could parse through that much data manually. This is where SQL gives us the ability to search for specific things using the WHERE clause. WHERE allows you to define certain criteria for your query that limit the results that are returned. For example, if we wanted only the customer record with a CustId of 3, we could use the query:

```
SELECT *
FROM Customers
WHERE CustID = 3;
```

This would provide the result shown in Table 4.5.

Table 4.5 Query by CustId

CustId	FirstName	LastName
3	George	Martin

Since we're querying for a number, we perform this query without using quotes around the value that we're searching for. If we were searching for text, singles quotes would be required. Some DBMSs will also accept double quotes, but the SQL standard specifies the use of single quotes so this works universally.

When performing a search, there are a number of operators that can be used. In our example, we used the = operator to search for records matching an exact value. Other operators can search based on numeric functions (greater than, less than, etc.) or text patterns. There is also an operator available which allows you to specify multiple values that the resulting row can contain. These operators are shown in Table 4.6.

The mathematical operators are self-explanatory, but let's go over the last three operators shown in Table 4.6 in a little more detail. The BETWEEN operator is used to specify a range of values. So, if we wanted to query for all rows with a CustId value between 2 and 5, we could use the query:

```
SELECT *
FROM Customers
WHERE CustId BETWEEN 2 AND 5;
```

Table 4.6 Basic SQL WHERE Operators

Operator	Function
=	Equal
< > or ! =	Not equal
<	Less than
>	Greater than
< =	Less than or equal
> =	Greater than or equal
BETWEEN	Within a given range
IN	Within a given set of values
LIKE	Matching a specific pattern

Table 4.7 Query Using BETWEEN Operator

CustId	FirstName	LastName
2	Amanda	Johnson
3	George	Martin
4	Tracy	Ewing
5	Lief	Gunderson

This query returns the rows shown in Table 4.7.

The IN operator allows us to specify explicit values that we want to match in the given column. For example, if we wanted to use IN rather than BETWEEN to return the same results in Table 4.7, we could use the following query:

```
SELECT *
FROM Customers
WHERE CustId IN (2,3,4,5);
```

Keep in mind that these operators, though they may appear numeric in nature, also work with text. The same results could also be returned with the following query:

```
SELECT *
FROM Customers
WHERE LastName IN ('Johnson', 'Martin', 'Ewing', 'Gunderson');
```

Finally, let's take a look at the LIKE operator. This operator is used with wild-cards in order to perform rudimentary pattern matching within SQL queries.

The wildcard used is % and this can exist anywhere in the query string. So if we wanted to query for all rows where the last name starts with a 'T', we could use the following query:

```
SELECT *
FROM Customers
WHERE LastName LIKE 'T%';
```

You can also use multiple wildcards within a query. As an example, we can query for all customers that have the string 'un' in their last name using the following syntax:

```
SELECT *
FROM Customers
WHERE LastName LIKE '%un%';
```

This query returns the results shown in Table 4.8.

Table 4.8 Query Using LIKE Operator

CustId	FirstName	LastName
5	Lief	Gunderson
6	Bobby	Trundle
7	Lief	Gunderson

With all of these operators, we can filter down our results substantially, but there are cases where the filtering needs to be a little more complex. For example, we may need to return results based on data in multiple columns, negative operators, or missing data. SQL provides the ability to modify operators in the WHERE clause to support these additional needs.

Using the AND modifier allows you to specify multiple data matching operations to further refine a query. For example, if we wanted to search for all rows that contain 'un' in the last name field as well as a first name of 'Bobby', we could use the following query:

```
SELECT *
FROM Customers
WHERE LastName LIKE '%un%' AND FirstName = 'Bobby';
```

This query returns a single result for Bobby Trundle. You can also use an operator modifier called NOT to reverse any given operator's function. For example, performing the operation NOT LIKE would provide results that *don't* match the given query string. If we wanted to perform a query for customers that have a last name containing 'un' but specifically exclude customers with a first name containing 'ob', we could use the following query:

```
SELECT *
FROM Customers
WHERE LastName LIKE '%un%' AND FirstName NOT LIKE '%ob%';
```

Another useful operator modifier is NULL. This, like the other modifiers, does not work alone but is used with the IS operator. If you wanted to run a query returning all of the customers with no first name, you could use this example:

```
SELECT *
FROM Customers
WHERE FirstName IS NULL;
```

In our sample data set, this returns no results because all of the customers have a first name. However, the NOT modifier works with this as well. So you could perform a query like the following one to return all of the rows where a customer *does* have a first name:

```
SELECT *
FROM Customers
WHERE FirstName IS NOT NULL;
```

Joins

All of our queries so far have focused on a single table within our database; however, the power of a relational database is in its relationships. There are a number of additional tables in our database schema that contain additional useful customer information. In order to use these other tables in relation to our primary Customers table, we need to join them together.

Joins are an integral part of performing queries and can get quite complex. For the purposes of this book, we'll discuss basic joins, how they work, and how you can use them to leverage the relationships between tables. A join effectively creates a link between multiple tables and presents the resulting data in a format of your choosing. This join can be formed in a couple of different ways and the type of join can be either implicitly or explicitly defined.

Let's start with some simple examples. In our database, we have a Customers table as well as a table called ex1Cust. We can easily display the data from both tables as they are related based on the CustId field. To do this, we create a join based on this field being equal in both tables. An example query using this type of join is:

```
SELECT *
FROM Customers, ex1Cust
WHERE Customers.CustId = ex1Cust.CustId;
```

This example joins the two tables together based on the matching field that we defined. In this case, the results shown in Table 4.9 show all of the data from both tables where the customer ID matches. One difference between these and preceding queries is the definition of a second table in the FROM clause. You'll also notice that in the WHERE clause, we've specified each field with the [table].[column] nomenclature. This is part of the SQL language definition and provides a mechanism to explicitly identify a column within a given table even if the same column name exists in multiple joined tables.

The type of join done here is referred to as an inner join. This is a join where you are linking values that are equal between the specified tables. In this case, we're implicitly defining that join as an inner join based on the specification of values in the WHERE clause. You can also explicitly define the join, which requires different syntax. To explicitly define this join, you could use the following query:

```
SELECT *
FROM Customers INNER JOIN ex1Cust
ON Customers.CustId = ex1Cust.CustId;
```

Running this query will return the exact same results as shown in Table 4.9. Either syntax is technically correct and in this particular case is just a matter of style. In other cases, the construction of queries in slightly different manners can result in the same returned data set but have very different performance profiles thus returning the results at different speeds and potentially consuming hardware resources differently. This is sometimes referred to as query tuning; one of the services typically performed by very experienced database administrators when complex queries are involved.

Now let's look at a more complex operation involving even more tables. Per our database design, we also have an Addresses table that has a many-to-many relationship with our Customers table. Let's say that we need to know the address for every customer. We can't do a join in the manner shown in

Table 4.9 Example Implicit Inner Join

CustId	FirstName	LastName	ex1CustId	CustId	HomePhone	MobilePhone	FavPet
1	Jason	Wilcox	1	1	742-186-3294	648-279-1955	Snarf
2	Amanda	Johnson	2	2	999-592-2013	170-564-7285	Texas
3	George	Martin	3	3	369-721-4622	984-127-6632	Tinker
4	Tracy	Ewing	4	4	473-652-3524	523-748-5291	
5	Lief	Gunderson	5	5	380-142-8820	489-338-6719	Biscuit
6	Bobby	Trundle	6	6	271-434-8789	218-519-0042	Lily
7	Lief	Gunderson	7	7	765-432-1212	119-352-1123	Gizzy

the last example because the address table doesn't have a CustId value, which is appropriate considering its relationship type. So instead, we leverage the intersection table. A sample query for this would be:

```
SELECT A.FirstName, A.LastName, C.Street, C.City, C.State, C.Zip
FROM Customers A, intCustAddr B, Addresses C
WHERE A.custId = B.custId AND B.AddrId = C.AddrId;
```

This query has a few differences from our prior examples. First, of course, is the specification of the intersection table intCustAddr. This leads to the two inner joins specified through the use of the WHERE clause. However, you'll also notice that we're not using the full [table].[column] nomenclature for specifying the fields. Instead, we're defining an alias for each table in the FROM statement and then utilizing those aliases throughout the query. The results of this query are shown in Table 4.10.

An outer join is another join type that we can use when querying for data. This type of join relies on using data where no relationship exists. Let's go back to our address example. Did you notice that in the results shown in Table 4.10, only one instance of Lief Gunderson exists? In our other example queries, there were two customers that shared that name. In this case, the customer is missing from this result set because we performed an inner join, which excludes rows where there isn't a match.

To summarize the different join types, we can use the following definitions:

- JOIN (INNER JOIN)—Returns rows where there is a match in each table
- LEFT JOIN—Returns rows from "Left" table regardless of whether or not there is data in the right table
- RIGHT JOIN—Returns rows from "Right" table, regardless of whether or not there is data in the left table
- FULL JOIN—Return rows from all tables. Not supported in all DBMS
- UNION JOIN—Two (or more) SELECT statements in one output. Number of columns must be the same

Table 4.10 Example Query using an Intersection Table

FirstName	LastName	Street	City	State	Zip
Jason	Wilcox	1212 Main St.	Elizabeth	CO	12345
Amanda	Johnson	2121 1st St.	Clinton	NC	54321
George	Martin	2121 1st St.	Clinton	NC	54321
Tracy	Ewing	5432 1st St.	Minnehaha	MN	44444
Lief	Gunderson	6336 Purgatory Rd.	Eden Prairie	MN	55347
Bobby	Trundle	1010 Binary Ln.	Hardin	TX	80808

KEY CONCEPTS

Query Performance

How a query is constructed can have a huge impact on how the query performs. The query used to generate the results shown in Table 4.10 used inner joins to perform define the relationship between three tables and display the appropriate data. A list of only customers who have addresses in the Addresses table could also be generated using the following query:

```
SELECT A.FirstName, A.LastName
FROM Customers A
WHERE A.CustId IN
(SELECT B.CustId
FROM intCustAddr B
WHERE B.AddrId IN
(SELECT C.AddrId
FROM Addresses C));
```

Aside from being more difficult to read, this query will also perform slower since most DBMSs process joins faster than nested SELECT statements.

Different DBMSs have distinct ways that they operate and they perform queries in slightly different ways. Aside from differences in syntax, queries may have to be constructed a little differently when switching between DBMSs in order to ensure that they perform correctly. This is, again, a task for experienced database administrators.

You can perform an outer join in order to show data where relationships don't exist. This is useful when trying to identify customers that (for example) haven't ever filed a service request assuming that customer information and service request information is stored in two (or more) tables. The following example shows an outer join associated with our example address query:

```
SELECT A.FirstName, A.LastName, C.Street, C.City, C.State, C.Zip
FROM Customers A
LEFT OUTER JOIN intCustAddr B ON A.CustId = B.CustId
LEFT OUTER JOIN Addresses C ON B.AddrId = C.AddrId;
```

Performing the query in this manner allows us to see the full data set regardless of whether or not a customer has an address in the address table. You can see the results of this query in Table 4.11.

There are a few other ways of querying data such as UNION queries that are a little more advanced. The SELECT statements, operators, and operator modifiers that we've discussed should cover most basic scenarios and help you in formulating the queries that you need as an enterprise applications administrator. Based on this discussion, you should now be able to perform basic queries that span multiple tables and relationship types, filter the

Table 4.11 Example Outer Join

FirstName	LastName	Street	City	State	Zip
Jason	Wilcox	1212 Main St.	Elizabeth	CO	12345
Amanda	Johnson	2121 1st St.	Clinton	NC	54321
George	Martin	2121 1st St.	Clinton	NC	54321
Tracy	Ewing	5432 1st St.	Minnehaha	MN	44444
Lief	Gunderson	6336 Purgatory Rd.	Eden Prairie	MN	55347
Bobby	Trundle	1010 Binary Ln.	Hardin	TX	80808
Lief	Gunderson	NULL	NULL	NULL	NULL

returned data based on the criteria that you specify, and then change the order of the results to fit your needs.

Adding, Modifying, and Deleting Data

Now that you have an understanding of how to request data from a database, let's spend some time talking about how to change that data. In many cases, you'll need to add, modify, or delete data within a database. These data changes have their own SQL commands and syntax that we'll discuss in this section.

INSERT INTO

We'll start off with adding new data. The concept of adding data is based on inserting new records or rows into a table. This insertion is done via SQL statement using the INSERT INTO statement. The syntax for performing a basic data addition is:

```
INSERT INTO Customers
VALUES (8,'Leroy','Jenkins');
```

This statement will add a new row into our Customers table with a CustId of 8, FirstName of 'Leroy', and LastName of 'Jenkins'. As you can see in this example, the table name is included in the INSERT INTO statement and the VALUES statement is used to define what needs to be inserted. A value should exist for each column when using this particular syntax. If the value is intended to be null, just put in a comma to close out that value. For example, a row with just a CustId and LastName value would use (8,,'Jenkins').

Another method of inserting a row using INSERT INTO is to explicitly define the appropriate column names. Using another example, we could insert a row with just CustId and FirstName values by using the following syntax:

```
INSERT INTO Customers (CustId,FirstName)
VALUES (9,'Scot');
```

Modifying data in a table follows a similar method but requires a little more diligence to ensure that the correct record is modified. This is one of the reasons that it's always wise to have a unique identifier for every record such as our CustId value. We'll talk about that a little more in the section on design, but for now, go with the guidance that it's critical to be able to positively identify the record that you're looking for to ensure that you do not modify the wrong data.

UPDATE

Modifications are done using the UPDATE statement in SQL. The syntax for an update is:

```
UPDATE Customers
SET FirstName = 'Scott', LastName = 'Bilyeu'
WHERE CustId = 9;
```

When this is executed, the DBMS should report back the number of rows modified. This should be equal to the number of rows returned when a SELECT statement is run using the same table(s) and WHERE clause. In this case, our update modified one row.

TIPS & TRICKS

WHERE Clauses for Record Modification

The criticality of getting the WHERE clause correct for record updates or deletions cannot be stressed enough. If, for example, the WHERE clause is forgotten in an SQL UPDATE statement, the DBMS will probably not report an error. It will simply do what you requested and *update every row in the table with the new values!* This can cause a huge amount of damage to any database.

When working with enterprise applications, it should be a very rare occurrence to have to manually make data changes in the database. In most cases, the enterprise application should be left to its own devices to update data, as it will typically incorporate business logic, enforce relationships, and provide other constraints to the data update. In the event that you do have to perform a manual update, the best practice is to follow these steps:

1. Perform a SELECT query using the same table(s) and WHERE clause as you plan to use for the update or deletion.
2. Note down the number of rows returned.
3. Back up the results of the SELECT query.
4. Perform the update.
5. Ensure that the number of rows updated matches the number recorded in step 2.
6. Perform a SELECT query using the appropriate WHERE clause to show the updated data.

DELETE

Finally, there's the DELETE statement used for removing data from a database. This uses syntax similar to the UPDATE statement in that you specify the appropriate table and WHERE clause. Just as with UPDATE statements, the correct specification of the WHERE clause is absolutely critical! If this is missed, the entire contents of the table are removed. If the WHERE clause is incorrect, it can lead to the removal of critical data. Always be very careful when modifying data in any database. The syntax for a DELETE statement is:

```
DELETE FROM Customers
WHERE CustId = 8;
```

TIPS & TRICKS

Table Truncation

When deleting all rows from a table, it often makes sense to perform a TRUNCATE rather than a DELETE operation. When you perform a DELETE, depending on the DBMS, all of the rows are potentially copied to a "rollback" or backup location so that they can be restored if you change your mind before committing your deletion to the database. In addition, any operations in the database that are set to occur when data is deleted are triggered to run. These two steps can cause deletions to take additional time.

If you're absolutely sure that you want to erase all of the data in a table and you have no need for any triggered functions to run, a truncate will operate much faster. It does not perform the data backup and is therefore irreversible. It also doesn't trigger operations that watch for deletions. This causes truncates to run quite fast.

One additional benefit is that truncates reset the "high water mark" for the table. When a table has all of its data deleted, it can still consume the same amount of space within the database. This is because the DBMS tracks the usage of a table and does not free up space consumed by the table when deletions are performed under the assumption that the table may need that space again in the future. Truncating a table removes this high water mark value and allows those resources to be released.

Modifying Database Schemas

All of the SQL that we've discussed so far has related to the viewing and modification of data within a database. SQL also supports the creation, modification, and deletion of database objects as well through the same language structure. In this section, we'll be focusing on how to use SQL for performing these operations on database schemas. As with any other SQL commands, these may vary in syntax and style across different DBMSs. Always consider the documentation of the specific DBMS that you're working with the definitive source of how to construct SQL queries for that DBMS.

Let's start by discussing creation and modification of tables within a database. We will not cover creation and modification of actual databases in this book, as there are many very technical details that must be configured by a database administrator when it comes to database creation. Things such as automated backup schedules, database file storage locations, and database-specific configuration options are typically best left to the experts on the DBMS in use and the environment where it's being used.

CREATE TABLE

Creation of new tables is done using a CREATE TABLE SQL statement. Additional parameters are included with this that define the name of the table, the columns to create, what type of data will be stored in those columns, default values, any conditions or rules around the use of the table, and other configuration elements based on the DBMS in use. For example, the following statement creates a table called ServiceRequests:

```
CREATE TABLE ServiceRequests
(
SrId char(50) NOT NULL PRIMARY KEY,
CustId char(50) NOT NULL,
SrTitle char(50) NOT NULL,
SrDesc char(255)
);
```

As you can see in this example, we have created a column for a service request ID number, a column to relate this to a customer ID, and two columns to store service request-specific information. Running this query will result in the creation of the table within the database.

ALTER

After a table has been created, you may need to modify the table. These modifications can include adding new columns, removing columns, changing datatypes, and many other table-level configuration changes. In SQL, using the ALTER statement performs these changes. ALTER statements are used in combination with modifiers such as ADD or DROP to control what change is made. Again, different DBMSs implement the ALTER statement in different ways and some greatly restrict what changes can be made to existing tables.

For the table that we just created, let's assume that we need to add another column called SrCode to hold a coding value associated with different types of service requests. To do this, we could run the following ALTER statement:

```
ALTER TABLE ServiceRequests
ADD SrCode CHAR(50) NOT NULL DEFAULT '101';
```

This SQL statement would add the new column, define its datatype and length, and add in a default value. The default value will be used whenever a new row is created unless the default is overridden with an actual value. This feature is useful when there is a need to predefault values such as auto-generating row IDs, populating the current timestamp, or performing other similar tasks.

In some cases, you may need to change the datatype, default value, or other configuration of a column within a table. For these types of changes, you can use the ALTER COLUMN modifier within an ALTER TABLE statement. For example, let's increase the length of the data in the SrTitle column. To do this, use the following statement:

```
MS SQL:
ALTER TABLE ServiceRequests
ALTER COLUMN SrTitle CHAR(100) NOT NULL;

Oracle/MySQL:
ALTER TABLE ServiceRequests
MODIFY SrTitle CHAR(100) NOT NULL;
```

Keep in mind that some DBMSs do restrict the modification of datatypes or lengths after a table has been created. Others may allow changes as long as the table or the columns do not have any data. In many cases, changing a datatype can be a major change to the database and require exporting the data, deleting the table, adding the table back with the modified schema, and finally reimporting the data. This is why it's critical that the up-front database design be as future-proof as possible.

Another table-level modification is the removal of a column. This operation is performed in a similar manner and uses the DROP modifier with the ALTER TABLE statement. To remove the SrCode column, we could use this syntax:

```
ALTER TABLE ServiceRequests
DROP COLUMN SrCode;
```

When this statement is run, the SrCode column will be removed. Keep in mind again that some DBMSs will put constraints on this operation depending on several factors including whether or not there is data in the column. Also, this type of change is irreversible. There is no "undo" command after this change has been committed to the database so be certain that you really intend to remove the column in question.

In addition to removing columns, you can also remove entire tables from a database schema. Table removal is done using a similar DROP statement. In this case, it takes the form of:

```
DROP TABLE ServiceRequests;
```

This is a very simple way to remove a table and cause permanent damage to any database, so be very careful when running commands like this. A typo can cause such extensive damage that you may need to restore the database from a backup.

TRUNCATE

If you don't want to actually remove a table but instead wish to remove just the data that exists in the table, there's an easy way to perform that operation as well. This is done using the TRUNCATE statement. TRUNCATE removes data but leaves the actual database schema alone. While you could perform this activity by simply using a DELETE statement, most DBMSs that support using TRUNCATE perform the operation slightly differently and may free up more disk space when a TRUNCATE is performed versus a DELETE. Again, this differs under each DBMS. A sample TRUNCATE statement would be:

```
TRUNCATE TABLE ServiceRequests;
```

This particular statement would remove all data from the ServiceRequests table while leaving the table structure intact. In some cases, a truncate would be performed to handle the data deletion as part of the overall "export, delete, modify schema, and import" sequence of operations mentioned previously.

NoSQL

There is a lot of buzz going on at the time of this writing on the concept of "NoSQL." NoSQL is the generic term being used to refer to just about any database that does not work in the typical relational manner that we've described so far in this chapter. Relational databases use table structures, relationships between tables, datatypes, data lengths, and other design elements to create a relationship between all of the data elements within the database. NoSQL databases go in another direction and intentionally remove the reliance on typical data relationships and store information in "collections" instead of tables. There are four main categories when talking about NoSQL: Key value stores, Tabular, Document stores, and Graph.

The type of data stored in NoSQL databases varies widely but include key-value pairs, blobs of data, and other nonrelational data formats. There are a number of DBMSs which call themselves "NoSQL Databases" and each one varies in function even more widely than the relational DBMSs that we've already discussed. The concept of NoSQL is still evolving at a very rapid pace and is highly expected to morph dramatically over the next few years.

Some of the key differentiators between NoSQL DBMSs and relational DBMSs are the interfaces, the architecture, and the features of the DBMS. In many NoSQL DBMSs, application programming interfaces (APIs) are used instead of traditional SQL-compatible clients. Contrary to the name, there are cases where NoSQL DBMSs actually use SQL-like statements in their queries through these alternative interfaces. From an architecture perspective, most NoSQL DBMSs have the ability to run in a distributed fashion as a core part of its system design. This creates the ability for NoSQL databases to be very highly scalable and an excellent fit for cases where very large amounts of data are being managed or very high performance is required. Lastly, the features of NoSQL DBMSs differ, primarily based on the differences in interface methods and architecture. For example, data integrity features may not be on par with traditional relational DBMSs due to the distributed architecture supported with NoSQL DBMSs.

NoSQL is starting to become more common in large enterprises and may be a core component of enterprise applications going forward. With their support for very large data stores and high performance, NoSQL DBMSs can be a fit for large web-based architectures where performance and scalability are critical. While most current enterprise applications are generally based on relational databases, this may change in the future as NoSQL DBMSs evolve and find their place in the corporate ecosphere.

DATABASE DESIGN

The core to a database that functions well is its design. A poorly designed database may be able to serve its purpose, but it will never perform well and will be unable to scale. Database design takes into account several different aspects including the type of database, the level of normalization applied to the design, how relationships are formed, and how data is indexed to increase response time. In addition, security concerns become part of design through the use of encryption at several levels.

In this section, we'll be going over several basic aspects of database design and how they impact the operation of the database. Creating excellent database designs is something that takes a great deal of knowledge about the DBMS being used as well as extensive experience in the database design world. The goal of this chapter is not to teach you how to create the most effective and efficient design for a 400 table relational database, but rather to give you the foundational design principles used to create these database designs. Understanding database design can help you to troubleshoot database performance as well as know where to logically look for data when working with a database.

OLAP, OLTP, and "Big Data"

The first part of database design is the determination of the type of database that should be built. Most of our discussion so far has centered on transactional databases also known as Online Transaction Processing (OLTP) databases. OLTP databases are designed to serve the following purposes:

- Handle large quantities of transactional or operational data
- Be the source system of record for the data that they're storing
- Provide data for business processes or tasks
- Respond to frequent data updates and additions
- Respond to queries quickly with relatively small record sets

This type of database tends to have entirely different database designs and operational procedures compared to other database types. OLTP databases are typically designed to be highly normalized (discussed in the next section) in order to facilitate their rapid response and reduce data storage through de-duplication of data elements. From an operational perspective, OLTP databases tend to be backed up more frequently than other database types and the DBMS has higher availability requirements. Since OLTP databases are usually user-facing as part of an enterprise application, it is critical that these databases be highly available.

Another database type is Online Analytical Processing (OLAP) databases. You may also hear these referred to as "data warehouses" or "enterprise data warehouses." OLAP databases serve a different purpose than OLTP databases and are therefore designed and constructed in a different way. OLTP databases store their information in tables where OLAP databases store their information in "cubes." OLAP databases are intended to perform these tasks:

- Handle large quantities of data for reporting and analysis
- Be a consolidation point for data from one or many OLTP databases
- Provide data to help with analysis and planning of business operations
- Provide views based on multiple dimensions that reflect business concepts
- Accept large quantities of data as fed in through repeated batch processes
- Run large and complex queries to aggregate data across multiple data dimensions
- Support many indexes to facilitate data manipulation

As you can see from this task list, OLAP databases are quite different from OLTP databases. They serve an entirely different business function and are intended to provide information to business so that they can make decisions based on a wide range of data.

For example, an OLTP database may serve the purposes of handling order fulfillment and customer relationship management while another OLTP database could handle supply chain management. If both of these OLTP databases fed their data into an OLAP database, the OLAP database could be used to develop business plans based on both data sets. Making decisions such as where to build a new distribution center could be made by analyzing the data associated with orders such as customer locations in combination with supplier locations from the supply chain management system. This consolidated view of data can greatly help with making informed business decisions.

CORPORATE MEMO...

Using OLTP Databases for Analysis

One of the worst things that can happen to an OLTP database from a performance perspective is to start using it as a source for analytical data. OLTP databases are designed to run very quick transactional queries and they do it quite well. By asking an OLTP database to serve in the role of an OLAP database is just asking for trouble. The database is not designed for these activities and it will not do them well. In addition, it won't be able to perform its core functions well while it's busy trying to do these analytical duties.

In many cases, end users of enterprise applications who, for one reason or another, have access to the database itself can cause this issue. They frequently see the database simply as a data source that can be used for any purpose without understanding what it is they're asking the DBMS to do. For example, the author has seen an enterprise application be slowed to a crawl due to an end user with too much access to the back-end database creating a query to determine all sales of a given product year over year in relation to the credit score of the purchaser and their geographical location. This is a query that makes sense and should be performed to help facilitate making business decisions, but it should be performed against a database built for that purpose and not a Production transactional database.

A popular topic as of the time of this writing is "big data." Big data is another way of referring to data mining in very large sets of data. This can be done using NoSQL DBMSs or traditional relational DBMSs. In general, the concept here is to dig through very large sets of data to try and uncover patterns that can then lead to identifying future trends. The science of this type of data mining and analysis has its foundation in probability and statistics and looks at data in a different way than either OLTP or OLAP.

You might think that OLAP and big data are very similar and you would be correct. The differentiator is how the data is analyzed and presented. For example, you could use an OLAP database to create a multidimensional view of data from several OLTP databases and then use this data to identify the number of sales of a particular product from a certain state. This type of analysis would be used for identifying past sales in the region and help with planning the amount of stock to keep on hand in that area.

However, what if you wanted to also throw in data associated with weather in the area, economic trends, and competitor marketing programs to determine *why* sales in the area performed the way they did? This brings a level of complexity that is difficult to model in traditional OLAP databases and is where the data mining aspects of big data come into play. By having all of this data available, data mining techniques can be used to identify patterns in the data that can then be used for modeling. These models can predict future trends and be used for forecasting what the business will need to do in order to proactively be ready for future events that the data predicts.

All of these database types can be used in concert within corporate enterprises to provide a very powerful amount of information. Let's take a look at another example. Imagine a company that sells tires nationwide. They may have an OLTP database that is used to handle tire orders, customer information, and other sales-related data. This data is then used to populate an OLAP database which is, in turn, used to identify which areas of the country have the largest amount of new and used tire sales. In analyzing this data, it may be discovered that there is a regular uptick in used tire sales in coastal regions on a semiregular basis, but no real indicator as to why.

This data could then be transferred into a big data-type database along with data from a number of different sources. By performing some data mining techniques, it could be seen that there is a trend toward high sales of used tires in coastal regions any time a hurricane is predicted in the area. Based on this, the company may make a decision to ship more used tires to local distribution centers in these areas during hurricane season and set up a more frequent delivery schedule to the area when hurricanes destined for the area are detected.

Using each database type for their intended purpose can provide huge benefits to corporate enterprises. As an enterprise applications administrator, you should know these different database types, their purposes, and where they fit into the enterprise ecosystem. This knowledge can help in planning out system architectures that provide very high value to the business and substantial returns on their technology investments.

Normalization

Normalization is a design concept used to leverage the relationship model of relational DBMSs, reduce data duplication, increase the usability of the database, and provide high database performance through design. Performing database normalization is done while designing the database schema by creating many smaller tables within the database to hold data in segmented chunks rather than a single large table to contain all of the data. This type of design does require that the database work harder by processing more complex queries, but it does help a great deal in reducing wasted space.

Let's take our sample database and imagine a new business object such as orders that we want to track. An order may be composed of a few different data elements including information about the customer placing the order, what the order was for, how many items the order was for, where the order should be shipped, etc. If we were to create a table to hold this data in a nonnormalized manner, we could simply put columns for each of those data elements into a single table. The structure of this could look like that shown in Figure 4.3.

This table layout would certainly be functional and would serve the purpose of holding this data, however, there would be a lot of duplicate data stored in the database. Based on this schema, every time a customer placed a new order, we would record *all* of their information in the orders table including their name and address. Also, any time we sold a given product, it would be listed by name and description, over and over in this table.

You can see how this would lead to inefficient use of space for the database, but what about query speed? If you wanted to generate a list of every product that the company sells, you would have to create a query that goes through every single order which has been recorded, pull out the product name, and then, using a UNIQUE modifier, ensure that only one instance of each product is returned in the query. The same would hold true for listing customers or the association between customers and their addresses.

To further muddy the waters, what about data updates? If we were to rename a product, every single entry in the Orders table referencing that product would have to be updated. The same would hold true for customers who change their name. And how would we handle the case when a customer moves? Would we want to just use the new address with new orders or

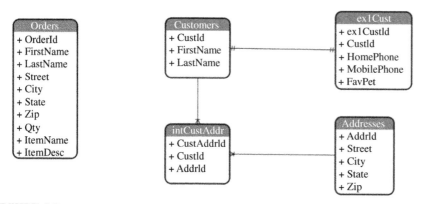

FIGURE 4.3
Nonnormalized schema example.

would we need to update past orders so that they still reference the same customer?

Now, let's take a look at how that schema might be laid out if it was done in a normalized fashion. This is shown in Figure 4.4.

In the revised schema shown in Figure 4.4, you can see that the data in our large Orders table has now been broken up into an Orders table and a Products table. In addition, data available in both the Customers and Addresses tables has been leveraged and new relationships established with those tables. This gives us the ability to list products a single time each in the Products table and simply reference each product from the Orders table. The same applies to both Customers and Addresses. This table could, and probably should, be further normalized by adding a new table to handle order line items. With its present design, each order could only contain one product.

Using normalization is a standard practice in designing OLTP databases. You should keep in mind, however, that OLAP databases are frequently nonnormalized intentionally. Due to the way that OLAP databases work with and present data, normalization can actually cause the database to have to perform more work to transform the data from transactional data to reporting oriented data. In many cases, data from OLTP databases is denormalized into "flattened" tables when it is imported into OLAP databases.

Extension Table

In many cases, database schemas are designed in such a way that they can be easily extended later to hold more data elements without modifying the

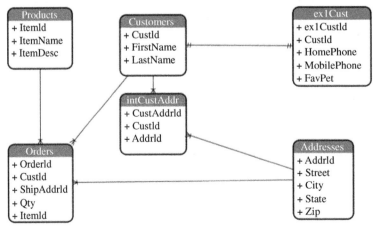

FIGURE 4.4

Normalized schema example.

database schema. This is often the case when dealing with commercial off-the-shelf (COTS) enterprise applications. Also, some enterprise applications restrict you from modifying the core application tables and require the creation of extension tables to hold any new data associated with data elements stored in those core application tables.

In the example schema that we've been referencing thus far in this chapter, our sample database design has an extension table called ex1Cust. This table holds some additional customer data beyond their name and address. As previously mentioned, there isn't really a need to use an extension table in this design, but it's included to illustrate how the relationships with extension tables work. These relationships are one-to-one relationships where there exists one and only one row in the extension table to correspond with each row in its associated base table.

In enterprise applications that offer predefined extension tables, the columns within them are typically named in a very generic manner such as "ExtVarChar1," "ATTRIB_31," or "Column34." This leaves flexibility for the application administrator or developer to use the columns in the extension table for whatever purposes they have in mind for the application. These extension tables are considered "static extension tables" because they have a predefined schema within the database and their structure is left unmodified. Dynamic extension tables, in contrast, are those that are manually defined within the database schema and added to the overall database schema through its one-to-one relationship with the appropriate core or base table.

Intersection Table

An intersection or junction table is used to establish many-to-many relationships between tables in a database schema. The intent of an intersection table is to identify the appropriate rows from each of the linked tables and create a link or intersection between the tables. For example, the table structure that we've been using so far uses an intersection table to create the many-to-many relationship between customers and addresses. This implies that each customer can have multiple addresses and each address can have multiple customers associated with it.

In order to maintain this link, a "key" from each table is used as a reference in the intersection table. We'll talk about keys in more depth next, but for the purposes of this example you should understand that a key is used to uniquely identify a row within a table. The intersection table itself can have many instances of each key referenced within it, but the key will relate to exactly one row in each linked table. This implies that the intersection table itself has a one-to-many relationship with each linked table. It is through this linked set of one-to-many relationships that a many-to-many relationship is formed.

Unique Keys

Unique keys (or simply "keys") are an integral part of using relational databases. The DBMS allows you to assign specific columns within each table to be defined as keys, which are the best way to identify distinct rows of data within the table. Each table can have multiple keys and each defined key can be comprised of multiple columns. The intent is for the DBMS to respond with a single distinct row if the given table is queried using values in a given key. For example, a key could be built based on the combination of the columns FirstName, LastName, and AddrId. If this were done, the database would have to maintain its referential integrity by preventing the addition of any data that would make this key nonunique. That means that you could never have two rows containing the identical first and last names with a reference to the same address.

Out of the keys defined on a database table, one of the keys must be defined as the "primary key." The primary key is the key that other tables should use to reference data within the table. This primary key, like any unique key, cannot be duplicated within the table. In many common databases, the primary key is a single column that uses a uniquely generated value for each row. Our sample database schema includes an ID column in each table that can be used as the primary key.

Foreign Keys

Whenever a table references the data in another table through its primary key, that value is considered the "foreign key." This is simple to remember in that the primary key for any given table will always be called the foreign key when referring to it from the context of any other table. In our sample database schema, you can see many references to other tables through the use of their primary keys. For example, the Orders table has a column called CustId, which is the foreign key to the Customers table. This foreign key relationship is what allows the data between these two tables to be appropriately linked.

Indexes

Indexing is a method used by many DBMSs to speed up the process of querying for data and providing it in the requested format. Similar to the index in a book, a database can contain an index that contains references to all of the data in its tables. To illustrate this, imagine taking this book and manually searching through it for every reference to "indexes." It would take a very long time to look through every page of this book to find that value. Instead, you could turn to the index, rapidly look up the work "indexes" based on the alphabetical order of the index, and identify all of the pages containing this value (including this one). Obviously, this is much, much faster.

Databases use indexes in a similar way. By creating an index that stores references to commonly queried columns, the speed in which the DBMS can return results based on these columns can be greatly increased. This speed increase isn't really generated simply by indexing the values as that doesn't really decrease the amount of data that the DBMS has to sort through. Instead, an index sorts the data that it is indexing in order to help the DBMS rapidly find it. By default, most DBMSs automatically provide this type of index to any primary key in order to facilitate searches based on that key, but other indexes can be manually defined.

There aren't any hard and fast rules as to when an index should be created. In many cases, it will vary based on the DBMS in use, the types of data being stored, and how that data is queried. For example, in our sample database schema from Figure 4.4, let's take a deeper look at that Customers table. In this table, we have a primary key already defined as CustId and, due to the default index, queries against this column will be very fast. But what if the application using this database tends to query by last name more frequently than the customer's ID number? In this case, we could create an index on the LastName field and these queries would see a performance increase. This could be done using the following syntax:

```
ALTER TABLE Customers ADD INDEX ( 'LastName' );
```

Instead of the default order which has last names completely unsorted, the index would have those last names in a sorted order allowing the DBMS to quickly look through the data to find the appropriate rows to return.

The temptation might be there to simply index everything in a database in order to gain tremendous performance benefits. However, there is a downside to indexing. Any time a row is inserted, any indexes using those columns must be updated as well leading to a longer insert time. The same performance loss also applies to data updates when an indexed column is involved. Also, the storage of an index takes up space. If there were an index on every column in a database, every single piece of data stored in the database would be duplicated in the indexes causing the database to double in size. This could be even worse if indexes containing multiple columns are created as well. In every case, the benefits of adding an index must be weighed against the associated detriments.

ACCESS CONTROL

Just as with any information technology, DBMSs need to apply a layer of security through access controls. This is critical due to the often sensitive or private nature of data stored in databases. Each DBMS implements its access control features in different ways, but most use a core set of concepts that are similar across all DBMSs. These are the concepts of users, groups, roles, and permissions. In this section, we'll discuss each of these concepts, how they apply to database security, and how they fit into the overall realm of security in enterprise applications.

Users

From a security perspective, users exist in association with databases in two manners. The first is as a user within the DBMS and secondly as a user within a designated database. Depending on the DBMS in question, these may be one and the same, but it's important to keep the segregated when you consider the overall security of the database. A user of the DBMS may or may not exist in association with a given database hosted by the DBMS and a database-specific user may not have any direct access to the DBMS itself. To segregate these two types of identities, a standard approach is to consider the DBMS account as the "server user ID" and the database account as the "user ID." These are shortened to SUID and UID, respectively.

From an enterprise applications administration perspective, both are important. Typically, end users, application-specific User IDs, and data owners will have a UID, but not an SUID. As an enterprise applications administrator, you may have a need for both in order to perform higher-level administration functions such as determining database cluster status, analyzing server performance metrics, or other tasks related to the core DBMS.

Depending on the operating system, some SUIDs are managed by either the access control mechanism provided by the operating system or an external identity management system. With this being an optional feature in many DBMSs, it is possible to end up with an ID for the server host, an SUID for the DBMS, and a UID for the database all with different permissions and, potentially, different passwords. Consequently, it's important to understand which system or service you are authenticating against and ensure that the correct credentials are used.

Roles

DBMSs support both "groups" and "roles" to simplify the assignment of permissions to the database. These two concepts do not necessarily align to the network account administration view of how users can be grouped together for administration purposes. Much like UIDs, roles can be assigned at the Server level or the Database level. In database administration terminology, database roles are more similar to network groups and database groups are a more static concept that we'll discuss next in this section.

Within a database, a role is an entity that can be assigned specific permissions. These permissions define what activities the role has permission to perform. We'll discuss permissions a little later in this section as well. For now, you need to understand the following concepts around roles:

- Roles are created and maintained at the database or server level
- Roles are in a many-to-many relationship with UIDs
- Permissions are assigned to roles which then apply to UIDs associated with those roles

From an administration point of view, it is generally much easier to assign database privileges to a role and then assign that role to multiple UIDs than to assign the permissions directly to the UIDs. This also helps reduce ongoing maintenance when a permission change needs to be made and allows the assignment of roles and permissions to align with business job functions. For this latter benefit, a role can be created that matches a specific job description, permissions necessary for the job duties associated with that job can be assigned to the role, and the role can be assigned to the appropriate UIDs for the people performing that job. Again, this is very similar to the way that permissions are assigned when performing network account administration.

Groups

Groups are similar to roles in that they can have permissions assigned to them and can be associated with UIDs. However, they differ in that groups are static, built-in to the DBMS, and unable to be changed. There are a few common groups that exist across multiple DBMSs, but for the most part, groups change depending on the DBMS in use. Some example groups or group types are:

- System Admin—Has permissions to modify core functions of the DBMS and has the highest level of DBMS permissions.
- Database Admin—Has responsibility for a single database along with the highest level of permissions associated with that database.
- Database Maintainer—Has the ability to perform a number of system and database functions including those necessary to back up, modify, and control availability of one or many databases.
- Operations Admin—Has permissions to perform basic database operations including startup, shutdown, backup, and restore.
- Security Admin—Has the ability to add, modify, and delete user accounts including the ability to change permissions. Also has the ability to perform audit-related functions.

There are a number of other default groups available with most DBMSs, but these tend to exist in some form across all common DBMS implementations. The names may differ, but the functions are generally very similar.

Similar to roles, groups are assigned to individual UIDs, which then allows for the permissions associated with the group to apply to the UID assigned. In many DBMSs, the permissions assigned to the built-in groups are unable to be changed, so it's important to be absolutely certain that the user associated with the UID should have all of the permissions granted to the group. For example, if you want a UID to have the permissions necessary to back up data but not restore it, you wouldn't want to assign the UID a group such as the Operations Admin group that includes both.

Permissions

Permissions within a DBMS can get complex due to the number of objects that they can be assigned to and the granular level of detail that can be controlled with permissions. From the DBMS perspective, different permissions can be assigned at the system (DBMS), database, or table level. There are also other nonhierarchical areas where permissions can be assigned such as those used for stored procedures, database scripts, and DBMS services. Each of these, naturally, differs depending on the DBMS in use and can vary dramatically in their implementation.

SQL supports a subset of its language specific to security and permission assignment. This is known as Data Control Language (DCL). DCL contains commands used for modifying permissions within the DBMS using the familiar SQL syntax. The two most common commands are GRANT and REVOKE. GRANT is used to allow a security subject such as a UID or role permissions to an object in the DBMS. REVOKE is used to remove a previously granted permission. In addition, some DBMSs support DENY command to allow explicit denial of access to a specified object.

As previously mentioned, permissions can be granted at a number of levels within the DBMS. These levels do operate in a hierarchy with system-level access at the top, followed by database-level access, and finally table-level access. Each level allows for permissions to be granted associated with functions appropriate to that level. For example, the system level allows for permissions to be granted that allow shutting down the system or modifying its log storage location. Database-level permissions could potentially allow the ability to change where the logs for the given database are stored, but not where the DBMS-level logs are stored.

From the enterprise applications administration perspective, it is important to understand at what level permissions need to be granted to perform specific functions. Any function associated with the DBMS itself will have permissions at the system level. The modification of any aspect of a specific database will be at the database level. Granting permissions to modify the tables within a database or control the ability to read and write to those tables will be at the table level. In addition, we have the nonhierarchy areas that we mentioned associated with stored procedures, scripts, and services. Each of these will have permissions available to be assigned in their own respective areas.

At this point we've discussed permissions being assigned within the system->-database-> table hierarchy as well as the side areas of stored procedures, scripts, and services. There is also a level of support within some databases that allow for the control of access to specific data elements. This is known as label-based access control and uses some of the concepts associated with "mandatory access control". By applying a label to specific data elements, the DBMS can apply even more granular permissions including controlling who can read or write data from or into specific rows and columns.

In most corporate environments, the ability to change DBMS permissions is (and should be) very tightly controlled. Only those with the appropriate training and knowledge should be allowed to modify permissions in the DBMS. In many cases, due to the need to segregate duties, even the database administrator is restricted by policy from changing permissions within the DBMS. Instead, a separate security or identity management organization is responsible for ensuring that permission changes are properly requested, approved, and applied to the appropriate DBMS level.

Auditing and ongoing maintenance of permissions is also an important aspect of DBMS security. On a regular basis, all accounts (both SUIDs and UIDs) and permissions should be audited to ensure that the correct level of permission is applied across the board in the DBMS. This ongoing audit may be part of the organization's security functions or it may fall into the role of enterprise applications administration since the administrators are typically the most familiar with the structure of the application's database and are therefore best positioned to understand the appropriate level of permissions at each level. Regardless of the group who performs this audit, it is important that it be done and that constant awareness of appropriate database security implementation be maintained across all administrators responsible for the DBMS and its contents.

TROUBLESHOOTING

In many cases, enterprise applications administrators need to troubleshoot the databases associated with the enterprise application. In this section, we will discuss troubleshooting of databases at multiple levels including getting to the database, permissions within the database, and database performance. Again, this is not intended to give you the expert-level knowledge associated with being a trained and experienced database administrator. Instead, you should gain the knowledge necessary to troubleshoot basic database issues in the context of an enterprise application and be able to successfully communicate with the database administrator to resolve more complex issues.

Finding the Database

When connecting to any given database, the first step is to find it. Different DBMSs use different mechanisms to identify the location of a database. Some of the more common are Open Database Connectivity (ODBC) configuration, local configuration files, proprietary name services, and LDAP. Depending on the DBMS in use, some or all of these may be supported. Each has its own nuances and requires some level of configuration to work correctly. For the purposes of this section, let's talk about what can go wrong with each.

We'll start with ODBC configuration. ODBC is supported by many operating systems and is intended to be an OS agnostic interface for performing database-related communication. The intent is for applications to be able to make a call to an ODBC data source and be able to perform that call in the same way whether they're running on a Windows Server or UNIX-like platform. From a configuration perspective, this means that the ODBC communications layer on top of the OS must be configured to understand the call being sent to it and know where to forward that call in order to communicate with the actual DBMS.

ODBC appears to the operating system and its applications as a driver. The ODBC driver manager allows for configuration of the driver, which then handles the actual work of communicating with the DBMS. The driver manager allows for the creation of Data Source Names (DSNs). The DSN contains all of the information necessary to be able to communicate with the DMBS including the host name, database name, UID, password and other important details. Some of these are considered required by the ODBC driver for the specific DBMS type in use but are optional for the DSN. In these cases, the ODBC driver can then prompt for the appropriate data. This is frequently used for credentials.

The DSN configuration used for ODBC is stored on the local system from which the requests to the DBMS will be made. Therefore, any troubleshooting of the connection to the database should begin there. It's critical to ensure that the DSN configuration is absolutely perfect in order for the database connection to work as expected. This includes the use of the correct ODBC driver for the remote DBMS, which can vary based on version. For example, the ODBC driver for Oracle Database 10g is completely different from that used for Oracle Database 9i.

Other parameters to check for are the network host name for the DBMS, the name of the database hosted by the DBMS, the port being used for communicating to the DBMS, and any credentials stored within the DSN. Errors with any of these parameters can cause difficulty in finding and connecting to the database.

Another potential misconfiguration can occur in the setup of the application using the ODBC driver. The DSN specified in the application configuration must match that used for the DSN in the ODBC configuration. An error in naming here can cause the ODBC layer to be unable to identify the DSN requested by the application and therefore be unable to provide further connection information.

In addition to ODBC, local configuration files can be used for resolving database connection information. Many DBMSs support their own proprietary clients and there are many database clients that exist with the ability to connect to multiple DBMS types. For many of these clients, the information necessary to connect to a remote (or even local) database is stored in configuration files on the machine running the client. As with ODBC, configuration options to look for are DBMS host name, DBMS host port, database name, and credentials as errors with any of these can cause the client to be unable to find or connect to the intended database.

These configuration files differ based on each client and how it is built. While all of the necessary data elements necessary to find and connect to the database will be there, the location of the configuration will vary wildly and its format will be different for just about every database client. While we won't be addressing every variation in configuration here, there are a few core concepts that will work well in troubleshooting across every database client.

- Always check for misspellings
- If a hostname isn't working, try the fully qualified domain name
- Make sure that the port is correct
- Always look at the client logs to see if there is a clue associated with the problem
- If the client configuration allows you to specify an order of name resolution to use, ensure that it matches what you're expecting

Some databases also allow the use of either proprietary name resolution services or leverage LDAP and a centralized directory to store their connection information. This allows for a correctly configured client to use a simplified name to connect to a database have the client automatically pull other critical connection information down from the service performing the resolution.

Clients that use this type of resolution must be configured correctly in order to properly communicate with the appropriate resolution service in the correct way. In addition, the service providing the resolution for the database must have all of the correct database connection details. If there is a misconfiguration in the resolution service, clients may be able to connect to the database directly, but clients using the resolution service will fail. This gives you a troubleshooting step in that you can attempt a "manual" connection to the database using a client to test the availability and accuracy of the resolution service.

Connecting to the Database

After finding the database you're looking for, the next step is connecting to it. We've talked about this a little bit in the prior section regarding finding the database as the two processes are often quite intertwined. The data accumulated when finding the database is subsequently used for creating a connection that your enterprise application can actually use. This means resolving the IP address from the DBMS hostname, sending over the appropriate packets to the correct port to instantiate a connection, and authenticating against the database using the assigned credentials.

The first step is converting the hostname to an IP address. We may have already done a conversion process whereby a database connection name is resolved into a set of connection parameters, but the next layer of establishing this connection actually requires an IP address (within TCP/IP networks of course). This further resolution can be done either locally through a .hosts file or by using DNS as discussed in Chapter 2. All of the troubleshooting steps typically used for resolving issues with name resolution that were discussed in Chapter 2 apply to this situation as well so refer to those steps if you run into issues with DBMS hostname resolution.

With an IP address in hand, the next step is to establish a connection to the appropriate port on the DBMS host. This port varies depending on the version or type of DBMS and can be modified by the database administrator as well. Depending on your corporate environment, your DBMS may use custom ports for its databases. This may be due either to the perception that using a nonstandard port makes the database more secure or because multiple DBMSs are hosted on the same server.

It is critical that your client system is able to successfully establish a connection to the DBMS port on the DBMS host server. As always, confirm with the database administrator that the port information that you have is correct and that your client is configured correctly. Connectivity can be tested by creating a manual connection to the DBMS host port using the Telnet client or another tool that allows for the creation of a TCP connection. If this connection fails, frequent causes are client misconfiguration, DBMS downtime, and firewall configuration (either local or network).

With the connection to the DBMS established, the client then authenticates using the UID provided in its configuration. This can be set in the DSN parameters when ODBC is being used or simply passed as part of a connection string. The DBMS will confirm that the UID exists, that the password matches, and that the UID has sufficient permission to log into the requested database. If any of these checks fails, the DBMS will return an error to the client that is attempting to authenticate.

Each DBMS uses different error codes and messages, but all of them are pretty consistent in letting you know what went wrong. Troubleshooting of this step in the process typically involves reading the error message and checking the source of the problem identified in the message. Some additional complexity can come into play if the DBMS is using a directory service to facilitate authentication. When this is the case, errors that occur between the DBMS and the directory service can have an impact on database client authentication as well.

Post authentication, there are still a couple things that can go wrong when establishing a connection to a database. These may not cause an error with the connection itself, but rather with the transfer of data over that connection. Most DBMSs support multiple languages as well as different formats for text. While in the United States, the standard ASCII character set is sufficient for most communication, other more complex languages require a double-byte or multi-byte character encoding such as Unicode. These present themselves within DBMS configuration as UTF-8, UTF-16, or other encoding options. If the DBMS client is set to use the wrong language, the communication between the client and the DBMS may not work correctly.

Permissions

Permissions were briefly mentioned in the prior section referring to the DBMS checking to ensure that the UID has sufficient privileges to connect to the requested database. This is one of the many checks that the DBMS does to ensure that the UID in question is allowed to perform the action that it is attempting. On initial connection and all subsequent requests the DBMS constantly validates the permissions for the UID, therefore, having the correct permissions assigned is absolutely critical.

When performing troubleshooting, the permissions typically appear as a problem when the UID is unable to perform an operation that it should be able to do. For example, if the UID is attempting to run an INSERT statement and receives an error indicating that it is not allowed to insert data, there is probably a permissions problem. The difficult part may be tracking down where that problem is occurring.

Permissions, as we previously discussed, can be associated directly with a UID, with a role, or with a group. When an operation fails due to a permissions problem, some or all of these areas must be checked. Conflicting permissions and incorrect permissions contribute to the majority of these failures. Based on this, whenever an issue occurs that looks to be associated with a permissions problem, the administrator (whether database administrator or authorized security administrator) should walk through each permission assigned to a UID either directly or via role/group assignment to determine if there is a conflict or a missing permission.

Conflicts arise when permissions are granted via one method and then denied through another. Permissions are generally additive, meaning that each role or permission assignment adds to the overall permissions granted to a UID. However, in some DBMSs, explicit denial permissions can be put in place. An example of this is when a UID has a role assigned granting it a specific privilege and an explicit deny for the same privilege is assigned directly to the UID. The DBMS must then determine which assignment takes priority and apply the correct permission to the UID. In some cases, this doesn't work as expected leading to the need to carefully review permission assignment.

Missing permissions are much easier to troubleshoot, but the fix may be more difficult. When adding a permission that is intended to affect a specific UID, a decision must be made on where to apply the permission. Is this related to the job role of the user and should it therefore be made to the database role? If so, what is the impact to other UIDs assigned the same role? Is this something specific to just one user and if so, should the rule of thumb against assigning direct permissions be broken or should a new role be created? The answers to these questions will vary greatly depending on the rules and policies of the organization and the way that the database or security administrators choose to implement security patterns within the DBMS.

Performance

When working with databases in enterprise environments, database performance is a frequent area of concern. When enterprise applications rely on back-end databases to support them, there is a requirement that the database be available and perform well. In many cases, there are service level agreements (SLAs) or operation level agreements (OLAs) in place that state the maximum acceptable amount of time that specific database queries are allowed to run. When the database is heavily loaded with users and transactions, its response time is not supposed to exceed these maximum allowable times as defined in the SLAs and OLAs. But this does occasionally happen and there are some things that can be done to detect, correct, and prevent these performance issues.

To identify performance issues, best practices would be to monitor and log both the DBMS and the hardware and then correlate the data from both sources. A great example of being able to identify performance issues on an MS SQL server would be running an SQL Trace in SQL Server Profiler and using Performance Monitor (perfmon) to monitor CPU, Memory, and Disk I/O simultaneously throughout an entire day. After this information is collected, open the SQL Trace file in SQL Server Profiler and import the data collection from perfmon. This will allow you to identify what each query or action is doing to the hardware and where bottlenecks exist.

Long Running Queries

One of the more deadly things that can happen to a database is for it to be overloaded with a large number of long running queries. These queries run for a very long time, consuming database resources and holding connections that could otherwise be used by other database users. In many cases, a long running query runs for so long that the client that put in the request stops waiting for a response due to a defined timeout period configured in the client. This, however, doesn't stop the database from continuing to try to fulfill the query that was given to it.

A number of different causes for long running queries exist. In some cases, they occur when joins are made incorrectly and a DBMS is forced to return rows from the same table over and over for each row contained in the joined table. This can be made even worse by adding more than two tables into the poorly formed join. Effectively, every combination of all rows of all the joined tables could be generated as the result of this type of bad query.

Another cause is running large analytical queries against a transactional database. As we discussed previously, OLTP databases are designed to handle many rapid transactions rather than really long queries that perform a great deal of analysis. If these types of queries are performed against an OLTP database, they can run for a very long time and block use of the database. Finally, hardware constraints within the DBMS host could contribute to the duration that a query runs. We'll discuss this more a little later in this section when we talk about host performance.

These long running queries have the effect of consuming system resources, which can cause slowness throughout the system and drive down the speed at which the enterprise application using the database operates. In addition, they can consume connections to the DBMS, preventing connections from other users or systems that may need to connect to and use the DBMS resources. And finally, long running queries can block access to actual data if they are INSERT or UPDATE queries. This can prevent other active connections from being able to read or write data to whichever tables are presently in use by the long running query. This blocking may present itself as an error, or the insert or update being performed in the second request may just hang.

A database administrator through looking at the current database statistics can typically identify long running queries. These should show the duration of each query currently active within the system and those with an excessive run time should be looked at more closely. Depending on the capabilities of the DBMS, the database administrator may be able to gather additional information about the long running query such as which UID executed it, what tables it's using, and potentially the query itself. This can then be used to further analyze exactly what caused the query to run for such an excessive amount of time.

There are a number of tools that exist for database administrators that can analyze a query to determine its potential performance characteristics as well as tools within the DBMS that can trace a given query to figure out exactly how it's running within the context of the real database. These tools can help a great deal in pinpointing the cause for a query being long running and can point you in the direction of how to modify the query so that it performs better. This analysis and query modification is also called tuning and can help to ensure that queries make the best use of the DBMS resources available.

Indexes

We discussed indexes when we went over database design concepts, but they're important to consider in the context of troubleshooting as well. When you determine that there are a number of queries that run slowly when they gather data from certain tables, it may make sense to further analyze those queries to determine exactly why. If the queries are hitting similar data elements, it may be worth considering indexing those data elements.

From a performance perspective, indexes can greatly decrease the amount of time that it takes to query for indexed data. On the other hand, updates to indexed data do take longer. From a performance perspective, you need to weigh the benefits and detriments of an index before implementing it in order to ensure that it will really help. It's possible to reduce overall database performance by adding too many indexes or adding indexes to tables that receive many more writes than reads. Always consider the data being accessed as well as how it is being accessed before deciding on the addition of an index.

Host Performance

A DBMS can only operate as fast as the system that is hosting it; therefore, it pays to ensure that the host can meet the needs of the database. If the host does not have sufficient resources, the DBMS will run slowly which can, in turn, cause the enterprise application that relies on the database to run slowly. Ensuring that the host has enough memory, processor, and I/O resources available can prevent this cascade of poor performance.

Databases are typically implemented in one of two methods. The first is for the DBMS to be installed on a given host with the intent that the database will only perform as well as the host will allow it. This method is often used for smaller databases, nonproduction environments, and other situations where high performance is not a critical need. The second implementation method is to analyze the expected use of the database and size the host accordingly to ensure that it has the resources to handle the needs of the database when running at full capacity.

Regardless of the implementation method, the effectiveness can frequently be determined by running load tests against the database. Load tests simulate a number of connections and perform queries against the database to determine how well it will operate under simulated load. These load tests can be run to simulate the number of connections and queries that are expected to run against the database under normal scenarios, or they can be run to see how much traffic the database can handle before crashing or becoming unusable. Both types of tests are very helpful and can assist in determining if the host's resources are adequate.

Monitoring

Ongoing monitoring of the database is critical to ensuring that it performs well. Monitoring can be done both for availability and performance of the database. Basic availability monitoring ensures that the database host, DBMS, other resources, and the database itself are up and available. This type of monitoring can be used to alert support personnel when a problem occurs so that they can quickly rectify the situation and get the database back up. It also aids in troubleshooting by pinpointing exactly where the issue is without the database administrator having to perform step-by-step troubleshooting to find the trouble area.

Performance monitoring is done to ensure that the database is performing as expected. This type of monitoring can ensure that SLAs and OLAs are being met as well as provide historical information about database performance over time. What time of day is the database the busiest? When would be a good time to perform maintenance? Do batch jobs that run at 4 a.m. appear to cause a performance problem? All of these are questions that can be answered with the performance data being collected through performance monitoring of the database.

In addition, performance monitoring can help in troubleshooting problems before they exist. If a resource is starting to spike in usage unexpectedly, there may be something going on that requires more research. For example, large spikes of processor utilization along with an increase in memory usage may indicate that a long running query has been executed. A large increase in disk I/O may indicate that one drive in an array has failed and that rebuild activities are occurring. These types of indicators can frequently lead administrators into fixing back-end issues before they cause the database to go down entirely.

SUMMARY

In this chapter, we moved our focus to databases and their relationship to enterprise applications. This began by discussing standard terminology associated with databases and clearing up some frequently incorrect usage of terms between databases and DBMSs. By having a solid framework of terminology, we can ensure that we're all discussing the same things as enterprise applications administrators as well as communicate correctly with database administrators.

This moved on to a discussion of SQL, the standard language used by most DBMSs. SQL has a very rich command structure allowing for a large number of operations to be performed within a database. We discussed some of the more common operations including SELECT, INSERT, UPDATE, and DELETE statements for working with data. We also talked about performing modifications to the database schema through the use of CREATE, ALTER, and DROP statements. This section was closed out with a brief discussion of NoSQL DBMSs and how they differ from traditional DBMSs.

What followed was an extensive discussion on the topic of database design. While we didn't go into the level of detail necessary to be a true database designer, we did cover some of the more important basics including the concepts of OLTP versus OLAP database types, database normalization, and how keys are used in databases. This led to a discussion of intersection tables using keys to create many-to-many relationships as well as the use of foreign keys to refer to data from other tables. We finished up this section by discussing indexes and how they are implemented into database designs.

Next on the list was the topic of access control. This discussion centered around security in the database environment and how database access control differs from network resource access control. We discussed the concepts of both SUIDs and UIDs for identifying users and then moved on to how roles and groups can be assigned to UIDs in order to apply permissions. The types of permissions available and how they are granted was discussed in detail. We also talked about the concept of labeling data and how access controls can be incredibly granular when labels are used to identify and control access to data.

Our last section was all about troubleshooting. Troubleshooting of databases is a critical part of being an enterprise applications administrator and so we discussed multiple facets of database troubleshooting. This started with the basic need of finding the database and then moved on to connecting to and communicating with the database. There are many things that can go wrong in this process and we discussed several of them as well as some potential solutions. This moved on into a discussion of troubleshooting and its relation to database security and permissions. Finally, we talked about database performance across the board and how to troubleshoot and resolve performance issues.

Since enterprise applications rely so heavily on their back-end databases, it is important that enterprise applications administrators understand databases and how they work. These skills are critical in being able to properly support the enterprise application as well as communicate with database administrators responsible for the operations or design of databases used by the application. Reading this chapter will not make you a database administrator, but it should give you the information that you need in order to support enterprise applications and the way that they use database technologies.

Information Security

BASIC CONCEPTS

Intertwined with every enterprise application is the security that protects the application and its data. Most enterprise applications contain a large amount of confidential and private data that should not be publicly released. This can be due to a number of needs such as:

- Protecting patient privacy
- Protecting customers' personal information
- Protecting customers' or corporate financial information
- Safeguarding company trade secrets
- Maintaining partner confidentiality

To serve these needs, we turn to information security, which, at its core, is all about protecting information and access to that information.

As information security has evolved over the years, it has gone through many changes in concept, scope, and recognition. This evolution has expanded the concept of information security and caused it to grow from a basic concept of just presenting a password prompt to the huge information security industry that we have today which includes providing security at all levels of all systems. The scope of information security has also grown tremendously.

Whereas the original scope of information security was simply to provide a limited level of protection over some digital assets, it now includes ensuring the confidentiality, the integrity, and the ongoing availability of all data. This scope covers the bases from basic authentication all the way to providing physical security measures and disaster recovery (DR) plans. Finally, the recognition of information security within the enterprise increased tremendously over the years. What was once a small part of the "sysadmin" job is now typically a full department with many people all working exclusively on providing security for the corporate environment.

Information security as it exists today focuses on three main principles: confidentiality, integrity, and availability. This is known as the CIA triad and forms the basis of most corporate security models. This concept is illustrated in Figure 5.1 where you can see how the three parts of the triad fit together to protect data. The intent is for all security models to ensure that confidentiality, integrity, and availability is assured for the data within the scope of the model.

As we go through this chapter, we'll discuss the three parts of the CIA triad, what they mean, and how many information security models address them. In addition, we'll be going over various aspects of information security that you may or may not be familiar with and how they align to the CIA triad. Finally, all of this will be tied together to illustrate how information security practices integrate with all layers of enterprise applications and the various components of those applications.

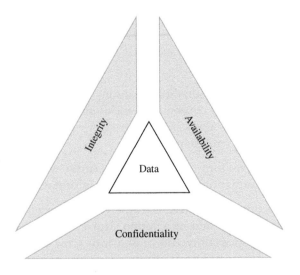

FIGURE 5.1
CIA triad.

Confidentiality

Confidentiality is all about ensuring that data is kept confidential and is not disclosed to those who are not authorized to have it. Some data elements are not necessarily confidential such as a corporation's public financial filings or the member names of their publicly disclosed board of directors. Other data is considered confidential from a business perspective and can include things like trade secrets, private financial information, and even employee names. Another type of confidential data is customer data including customer name, address, date of birth, and age.

In many cases, there are general categorizations of data and policies that drive the protection of this data. For example, data that can identify an individual is known as Personally Identifiable Information (PII) data. Many companies have policies in place regarding the rules and requirements for protecting PII data. Companies that accept credit cards also work with Payment Card Industry (PCI) data and have another set of rules and requirements known as the PCI Data Security Standards (PCI-DSS) for this data. The same also applies to the medical industry with requirements around patient data detailed in the Health Insurance Portability and Accountability Act (HIPAA). There are additional regulations for data protection depending on the company's industry.

Each of these regulations, policies, or guidelines is implemented in different ways in different companies. Most commonly, large enterprises have a dedicated staff tasked with interpreting the required rules, recommending approaches, and auditing results.

From the enterprise applications perspective, this data is frequently stored and accessed through enterprise applications and therefore fall under the responsibility of enterprise applications administrators to implement the appropriate controls around data confidentiality.

Policies for a number of different types of data exist in addition to what we've already discussed. Some organizations, such as government or military, classify data using a much more granular classification system. Classification systems like this use labels to describe the sensitivity of data and implement technological approaches to protect data depending on its sensitivity label. Labels used in this type of classification include options such as unclassified, sensitive, confidential, secret, and top secret. Other classification systems, including those used in many corporations, use labels such as public, sensitive, private, and confidential.

Depending on the type of data being protected, there are multiple risks associated with its accidental release. With customer data, competitors could gain an advantage by using another company's customer list. The customers could be sent unsolicited emails under the guise of a company they have an existing relationship with in order to persuade the customer to give up their account passwords. This is known as phishing and is a common technique used in social engineering attacks. Fraud could be committed using a customer's account information if the customer's login credentials for a company's web site are released. Effectively a large amount of risk exists around the release of customer data.

Even more important is a patient's medical records or a government's top-secret defense data. All types of data like this fall under one or more guidelines or regulations to ensure the confidentiality of the data. While most large enterprises do have information security departments dedicated to ensuring that this confidentiality is maintained, it often falls to technical teams including enterprise applications administrators to properly implement appropriate risk mitigation controls based on guidance from these security departments.

We'll be discussing methods for protecting this type of data later in the chapter, but for now you should understand the concept of data confidentiality, why it's important, and how it fits into the role of enterprise applications administration.

Integrity

Whereas protecting confidentiality focuses on the release of data to unauthorized people, integrity focuses on ensuring the validity of the data. This focus is intended to ensure that unauthorized users do not modify data and that authorized users do not make unauthorized changes. It also focuses on the consistency of data against both internal and external sources. If all of these requirements are met, the integrity of the data is considered to be assured.

Any enterprise application supports a large number of users, but naturally there are people who are not supposed to access a given application. For example, there would be no need for a warehouse worker in a company to access an accounting system. The same applies to anyone who should not have access to any company resources such as external attackers of the company's information systems. From the security perspective, any of these individuals are considered "unauthorized users."

There are a number of ways that unauthorized users can gain access to information systems which we'll discuss later in this chapter. In the event that an unauthorized user does gain access to an enterprise application, the goal of this part of the triad is to prevent that user from modifying any of the data in the application. In essence, this segregates the ability to view data from the ability to change it. Confidentiality addresses the viewing aspect of data protection while ensuring integrity addresses the risk of changing data.

Depending on the data being stored, there are significantly different risks around the modification of data versus the data simply being viewed. For example, with credit card data, more controls should be put around the viewing of the data as changing a customer's credit card number on their account would have a lower risk to the company (and the customer) than the credit card number being viewed and used elsewhere for fraudulent purchases. On the other hand, if medical data is being stored, a patient's dosage for a given medication could be altered leading to the potential of negative health impacts up to and including death.

Data integrity is important from the perspective of authorized users as well. In many cases, authorized users of a system should be able to view data, but not modify it. This requirement may also change based on prior actions of the user. For example, based on the principle of separation of duties (discussed later in this chapter), the employee creating a particular record may not be allowed to modify that record to indicate that it has been approved. Instead, another authorized user may be needed to double-check the first user's work and approve the record. In this case, assuring data integrity would involve putting controls in place to prevent unauthorized changes from being made by authorized users.

Within any given system, it is also important to ensure that the internal integrity of data is maintained. This does not necessarily refer to maintaining referential integrity within a database (although it can), but instead ensuring that data within a system is not changed due to system errors or other technical issues. For example, when migrating data between two tables, it's important to validate that the data in the recipient table is a 100% match to the data in the source table. If there is a difference, something went wrong in the transfer and the integrity of the data has not been maintained. This type of situation can also occur when data is encoded and then decoded. If the data that results after being decoded does not match the original data prior to being encoded, data integrity has been violated. Another example of this from an enterprise application perspective is the possibility of the application changing data incorrectly. If an application is intended to modify a particular subset of data but instead modifies the entire superset of data, the integrity of the data is no longer assured.

Data can also be checked against external sources to assure its integrity. This is known as validating the data's external consistency. External consistency is the assurance that the data matches what exists in the real world. For example, an inventory database should always reflect the actual count of inventory on hand. By performing an audit to determine if there is a match between physical products in the real world and the inventory count in the database, external consistency is being checked. For external consistency, processes must be in place to ensure that the data is kept current and reflects correct real-world values.

Availability

Availability is the third part of the CIA triad and involves ensuring that data is always available to those who need it when they need it. Effectively, the premise is to always ensure timely access to data. In many cases, the work to ensure availability falls to operations groups, but it is considered part of the security function conceptually. From the security perspective, there are a number of attacks such as denial of service (DoS) that are targeted specifically to cause data to be unavailable, which we'll discuss a little later in this chapter.

In order to ensure availability, there are a number of techniques that can be used, most of which are intended to prevent loss of availability through specific means. For example, the approach used to ensure availability when an earthquake occurs will differ from the approach used when there's a power outage. We'll talk about the preventative measures which can be used to assure availability later in this chapter but for now, understand that the general approach is to put multiple methods of ensuring availability into place at multiple layers of the enterprise application. Depending on the criticality of the application, the availability needs may differ and therefore the methods used to ensure that availability may differ as well.

Data availability does not always mean that a system is up and accessible. In the broadest terms, ensuring data availability simply means that the data can be made available within a timely manner as mentioned previously. In the event of an emergency, this may mean that the data is available via off-site backup and can be available within a specific predefined window such as 24 hours. In most large organizations, policies and procedures are in place that provide details on what the required availability level for specific data is and how to provide access to that data under a variety of circumstances.

Controls

Another important concept to understand as it relates to information security is that of controls. Controls are put in place to prevent, detect, or fix issues that can occur with the protection of data. Every part of the CIA triad will typically have multiple controls in place that help to protect data from a variety of threats including naturally occurring disasters, external intruders, and internal unauthorized employees among other things. It is through the use of these controls that threats such as these can be mitigated or have their damage reduced.

All controls are implemented in different ways, but most focus around people, processes, and technology. Each control will typically target one or more of these areas and will reduce threats to information security. For example, a control may be put into place such as segregation of duties, which ensures that someone is unable to both create a transaction and approve that transaction. This is a control that affects people, but is implemented through a specific process. There may also be a technology-based solution in place that ensures that both a "creator" and an "approver" role are not granted to the same person within a specific application.

Controls are also categorized based on the method through which they are implemented. The most common implementation categories are administrative, technical, and physical. Simply put, administrative controls are put in place through policies or procedures, technical controls are put in place through appropriate use of technology, and physical controls are put in place through the use of physical devices such as locks. In some cases, controls span across multiple implementation categories as well.

There are several different types of controls that can be put into place. The most common control types are preventative, detective, and corrective. These are considered high-level control categories as each has a huge number of controls within the category that may or may not be effective under different circumstances. By understanding the types of controls that can be used, you can gain a better understanding of what the purpose of the control is and how it can help provide information security.

Preventative controls are put in place to prevent harmful things from happening to data. Some examples of these controls are firewall installations, ensuring strong authentication processes are in place, and putting a lock on the door to the company's data center. All of these controls focus on preventing occurrences of events that could violate data confidentiality, integrity, or availability. Other types of preventative controls are ensuring that personnel are appropriately trained on the confidentiality of the data that they're working with, putting a process in place to move backed up data off-site on a regular basis, or using an X.509 certificate to ensure the identity of a remote system before transferring data to it. Again, preventative controls, like any other control, can address people, processes, or technology.

Detective controls are those that are put in place to identify when some sort of harmful event has occurred. These controls do not prevent an event from happening. They focus instead on detecting the event and taking some form of action. These actions can be as simple as logging the event or as complex as notifying appropriate personnel and putting additional preventative controls into place automatically. The intent behind detective controls is to track the event and provide sufficient information to those who have to react to those events.

The last primary control category is that of corrective controls. Corrective controls activate after a harmful event has occurred. The purpose of corrective controls is to restore service or repair data after the event in such a manner that the system or data is brought back to its normal operating condition. Some examples of corrective controls are restoring a database from a backup, rerouting traffic through alternative network nodes, or patching a compromised security vulnerability. Again, these controls are not intended to either prevent or detect harmful events, but only provide corrective actions after an event has already occurred and has been detected.

From a controls perspective, there are a number of additional categories that exist. Some of these include deterrent controls, input controls, change controls, and others. Depending on the enterprise that you're working in, control categories such as these or others may be in place. We will not be examining every control category in the scope of this book, but instead focus on the top three control types. If your role involves the creation of or support of controls in additional categories, you are strongly encouraged to research those specific control types so that you can understand their intent and purpose. This will help you to ensure that all appropriate controls for your specific environment are implemented correctly.

AUTHENTICATION, AUTHORIZATION, AND AUDIT

Authentication, authorization, and audit are the "3 As" of access management. In this section, we'll discuss each of these and establish a baseline of what each is and how it relates to enterprise application administration. In some cases, such as with authentication, multiple concepts work together to provide a holistic solution. Authentication, for example, relies on the establishment of identity through identification before moving on to allowing that identity to be proven. We'll discuss these additional concepts within each subsection and examine how they all work together to help wrap a level of security around enterprise applications.

Authentication

Authentication is the process of establishing and verifying a user or system's identity with a high degree of confidence. Depending on the information security need, the confidence level requirements may be higher or lower based on a number of factors. There are many different methods used today to prove that an identity is authentic especially as it becomes easier to forge various types of identity verification.

In this section, we'll be going over the process of identification and methods that can be used to verify identity. We'll also talk about different ways of verifying identity based on the information presented and information that the verifying party already has. Throughout the section, the use of authentication in enterprise applications will be discussed so that you have context around the different forms of authentication and how they can be applied in the real world.

Establishing Identity

In order to perform authentication, there first must be identification. Identification is the act of a user or system professing that they have a specific identity. This could be, at its most basic level, someone telling you his or her name. In this simple case, the person that you're talking to is presenting their identity and you have to determine whether or not that identity is correct. If someone introduces himself or herself as you, you can be fairly certain that they are attempting to fraudulently identify themselves. But to confirm their identity should they present themselves as someone else requires that you have some preexisting knowledge of their identity or they have some sort of proof.

In order to identify themselves, the user or system going through the identification process must present their identity in a form that the verifying party understands. In our example above, you might simply accept their word that they are who they say they are or you might require some sort of proof. That proof could be in the form of an identification card of some type or specific knowledge that only the correct person would have.

In dealing with information security, establishing identity as part of the authentication process is crucial to ensuring confidentiality. Before allowing any user or system to interact with another, the user or system must identify itself and, in many cases, prove that its identity is authentic. This can be done in a variety of ways depending on how certain the verifying party must be that the identity is authentic.

Authenticating Identity

After presenting some sort of identity, the requesting party must usually prove that it really is who it says that it is. The proof that it can present is considered a "factor" in the authentication process. Single-factor authentication is the use of a single piece of proof that the requesting party is who they say they are. This could be the use of a password or passphrase as an example. Single-factor authentication is the easiest to implement, but is not necessarily the most secure.

As you increase the number of factors used, the level of confidence that the requesting party is who they say they are increases. Each additional factor raises the complexity of any intruder fraudulently identifying himself or herself as someone else. Two-factor authentication would use two distinct factors such as a password and a token. Some incredibly secure systems require the use of up to six different factors in order to fully validate a user's identity but this is rare.

Additional factors can include many things, but are frequently categorized as:

- Something you know (password, passphrase, personal information)
- Something you have (token, certificate, ID card)
- Something you are (biometrics such as fingerprint, retina print, iris scan, hand geometry)
- Something you do (pattern detection around specific actions)

After a user or system has presented their identity, the verifying system must determine if the values presented actually correspond to what it knows about the requestor. This is the actual process of authentication.

Decentralized or Local Access Control

It is not always possible or preferable to have a single point for all access control requests. When the access control system is configured in such a way that multiple authentication systems are responsible for the access control requests for a single or small group of systems, it is considered to be a decentralized access control system. This basically means that the access control system is not centralized to a single large access control system. Some examples of this would be a Windows workgroup where access control is handled by every member of the workgroup or a database system that handles its own authentication. These systems do not rely on any other system to perform access control for them.

When working with decentralized access control systems, the individual computer systems performing access control will typically keep a local database of identity information, authentication information, and permissions. This is also referred to as local access control. This does offer the advantage of providing for access control system functionality in cases where connectivity to a centralized access control system may be impossible or intermittent.

It takes a great deal more administrative effort to work with and synchronize a decentralized access control system compared to a centralized access control system. If there is a requirement for users to be able to authenticate against multiple computer systems in a decentralized access control system, the user will have to have an account on each computer system. This can easily cause an administrative nightmare when trying to perform password resets or access control troubleshooting.

Local authentication is common for smaller systems or applications as well as in instances where a high level of independence is required. For example, the system may be architected in a manner that allows for it to remain functional and available even when it cannot contact any remote systems. In this situation, the system will still need to perform authentication and will have to rely on a local data store since it would not have access to a remote authentication system.

In most enterprise applications, centralized authentication services are used for the application as a whole rather than local authentication. However, there are cases where local authentication is used for various components of the enterprise application such as the database or network equipment. Understanding what type of authentication is used for the various components of the enterprise application as well as the enterprise application as a whole is an important part of administering it correctly.

Centralized Access Control

A centralized access control system is based on the concept of all access control queries being directed to a central point of authentication. The central authentication system performs the authentication and forwards the authorization data back to the requesting system. This type of system allows for a single point of administration for the entire access control system. This cuts down a great deal on administrative effort, but does raise costs and/or availability concerns somewhat as each system using the centralized access control system must be able to communicate with the access control system at all times.

Implementing a centralized access control system is somewhat more difficult than implementing a decentralized system, but the benefits are typically worth the extra effort when dealing with enterprise applications due to the decreased administrative effort required for ongoing maintenance tasks. Making a change within the centralized system allows for that change to be reflected on all systems using the access control system. The speed in which that change is propagated throughout the system will vary. For example, the change of a user's last name may take 15 minutes to push out to all the access control servers, while the disabling of a user's account may push out immediately. In addition, centralized authentication can allow for the same credentials to be used across multiple applications or systems as well as providing common enforcement of authentication rules such as timeouts and access attempts.

That's not to say that implementing centralized authentication is always the best solution. In many cases, implementation and ongoing maintenance of a centralized authentication system can take a lot of effort. In addition, there are sometimes issues with compatibility as not all systems or applications will work with all types of centralized authentication providers. Finally, a centralized system means that you can potentially have a single point of failure. If the centralized authentication provider is unavailable and no allowances have been made for local authentication, all authentication requests could fail causing impacts to a large number of systems and applications.

Lightweight Directory Access Protocol

We discussed Lightweight Directory Access Protocol (LDAP) previously in Chapter 2. LDAP can be used with a number of different centralized access control systems as the method for querying and utilizing their authentication and authorization services. For more information on the use of LDAP itself, refer back to the LDAP section in Chapter 2.

When using an LDAP-compatible directory service, the directory service can be connected to and queried using standard LDAP commands. In addition, communication between the authentication requestor (the server requesting authentication services) and the authentication provider (the LDAP server) can be encrypted using Transport Layer Security (TLS). This added layer of security could help to ensure that man-in-the-middle (MitM) attacks are less likely. We'll talk about this type of attack later in this chapter. This standardized protocol allows for different back-end directory service technologies to be used while allowing the authentication requestor to utilize access control services in the same manner.

When configuring an enterprise system to use LDAP, it is critical to properly define all parameters associated with the directory service provider. This may include domain names, IP addresses, ports, server credentials, directory tree information, or other important details. Mistakes in this configuration can cause authentication with the centralized directory service to fail causing availability issues for the application utilizing the centralized services.

Active Directory

In many corporate environments, Microsoft's Active Directory services are implemented and used for centralized access control. While Active Directory is one of many directory services that allow for LDAP to be used for authentication and authorization requests, Active Directory does differ in that it offers some extensions on top of the standard LDAP capabilities. These extensions allow for special functions such as account lockouts, password expiration policy implementation, and others. Microsoft Active Directory also utilizes functionality provided by the Kerberos protocol in addition to using LDAP for requests.

Kerberos

Keep in mind that LDAP is a protocol used for performing authentication as well as directory services queries. It is often used for authentication requests as they are supported by the protocol, but there are more robust protocols that exist solely for authentication purposes. Kerberos is one of these more robust authentication protocols.

Kerberos is used as the preferred network authentication protocol in many medium and large enterprises to authenticate users and services requesting access to resources. This protocol allows for authentication of the requestor by the host providing the requested resource through the use of secure and encrypted keys and tickets (authentication tokens) from the authenticating Key Distribution Center (KDC).

Let's look at how Kerberos works and how it helps secure authentication activities in a network. We'll start by looking at Figure 5.2, which shows the default components of a Kerberos v5 realm.

As can be seen in Figure 5.2, there is an authentication server requirement (the KDC). In a Kerberos realm, whether in a UNIX-based or Windows-based OS, the authentication process is the same. For this purpose, imagine that a

Client
(user, service, or machine)

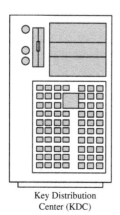

Key Distribution
Center (KDC)

Resource server or
storage

FIGURE 5.2
Kerberos required components.

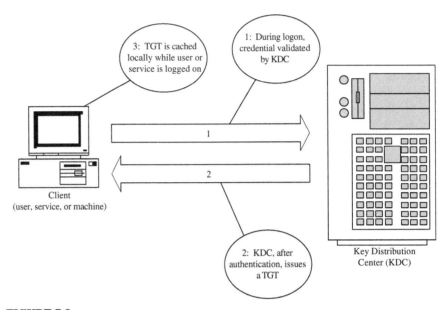

FIGURE 5.3
Authentication path for logon access in a Kerberos realm.

client needs to access a resource on the resource server. Look at Figure 5.3 as we follow the path of the authentication for logon. This continues into Figure 5.4 for accessing the desired resource.

As seen in Figure 5.3, two events occur as credentials are presented (password, Smart Card, biometrics, etc.) to the KDC for authentication. First, the authentication credential is presented to the KDC. Second, the KDC issues a Ticket Granting Ticket (TGT) that is associated with the access token while you are actively logged in and authenticated. This TGT expires when you (or the service) disconnect or log off the network. This TGT is cached locally for use during the active session.

Figure 5.4 shows the process for access control object access in a Kerberos realm. It starts by presenting the previously granted TGT to the authenticating KDC. The authenticating KDC returns a session ticket to the entity requesting access to the access control object. This session ticket is then presented to the remote resource server. The remote resource server, after accepting the session ticket, allows the session to be established to the object.

X.509

X.509 is a *de facto* standard based off of an ITU Telecommunication Standardization Sector (ITU-T) recommendation for authentication using

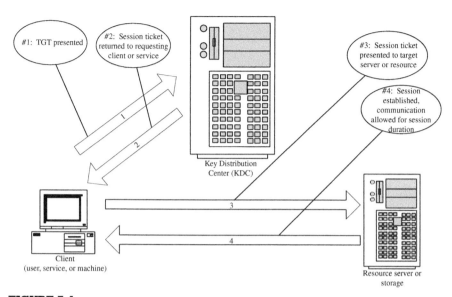

FIGURE 5.4
Resource access in Kerberos realms.

public keys. X.509 bases its authentication off of digitally signed public key certificates issued by a certificate authority (CA). This form of authentication is most commonly used for secure transactions over HTTP, but also has many other uses. For example, it can be used for single sign-on purposes as it allows for an access control subject to be authenticated a single time for multiple connections and allows for nonrepudiation.

Single Sign-On
Single sign-on is a solution frequently deployed to make the authentication process easier for end users. With single sign-on, the user authenticates once, and the fact that they have been authenticated is passed on to each system that they attempt to access. Their initial authentication can take place using any authentication type or combination of types while the authentication to subsequent systems can occur using an entirely different type.

The primary disadvantage of single sign-on technology is that it is very difficult to implement it properly and integrate it with all existing systems that may have their own authentication methods. Many systems have their own proprietary access control system, and each of these systems requires some work to integrate properly with the single sign-on product used. It is also an additional cost that some enterprises choose not to spend money on or are prohibited from implementing by policy.

CORPORATE MEMO...

Single Sign-On Value

Remember that single sign-on is primarily for the convenience of the user. This will help you to put single sign-on into perspective with the actual required portions of access control. Many enterprises feel that the convenience of single sign-on is worth the cost, but others feel that simply using a centralized access control system so that the same credentials work across all systems is sufficient.

Security Assertion Markup Language One of the more common current technologies for dealing with single sign-on is the Security Assertion Markup Language (SAML). SAML is a standard based on XML that allows for the authentication of a user by one system and the subsequent authorization of the user by another system. We'll talk a little more about the authorization process later in this chapter, but for now let's just recognize it as the next step after authentication occurs.

When using SAML, there are a few different pieces of the puzzle that link together in order to make the single sign-on concept work. In the SAML standard, these pieces are the principal, identity provider (IdP), and service provider (SP). The principal is the user or system requesting access, the IdP is the system in charge of authentication, and the service provider is the system providing the service or resource that the principal needs access to. The service provider is also responsible for the authorization part of the access control flow.

The SAML process starts with the principal contacting the service provider to request access to a service or resource. If the principal already has a valid SAML token from an authorized IdP, the service provider can then assume that the presented identity is valid and make an authorization decision. If the principal does not have a valid SAML token, the service provider will tell the principal to contact the IdP to get the token. The IdP will then authenticate the principal based on whatever identification and authentication mechanism has been set up within the IdP. This can be directory based, local authentication, or any other supported authentication type.

After the IdP has authenticated the principal, it signs a SAML token and provides that token to the principal to use with the chosen service provider. The principal then re-requests access to the service or resource from the service provider and offers up the SAML token that it was issued. The service provider validates that the token was signed by an IdP that it recognizes as valid and then grants the principal access to the service or resource based on its authorization process.

Authorization

Authorization is the part of access control that occurs after authentication. It is defined as a process through which specific levels of access are granted to an access control subject (the system or user requesting access). After an access control subject is identified and authenticated, the subject is authorized to have a specific level or type of access to the access control object (the service or resource being requested). The level of access granted depends on the object being accessed and the specific rules defined in the access control system.

These rules are generally based on access control models defined for the enterprise or the specific enterprise application. These models, in turn, allow for implementation of the company's policies, regulations, and standards within the access control mechanism. The three most common access control models are discretionary access control (DAC), mandatory access control (MAC), and role-based access control (RBAC).

Discretionary Access Control

Discretionary Access Control is the most common access control model in use. This model bases security off of the identity of the access control subject. Every access control subject has specific permissions applied to it and based on these permissions has some level of authority.

This access control model is called discretionary because individual users or applications have the option of specifying access control requirements on specific access control objects that they own. In addition, the permission to change these access control requirements can also be delegated. As assigning access control permissions to the access control object is not mandatory, the access control model itself is considered discretionary. Basically, the owner of the access control object is allowed to decide how they want their data protected or shared. The primary use of DAC is to keep specific access control objects restricted from users who are not authorized to access them. The system administrator or end user has complete control over how these permissions are assigned and can change them at will.

DAC allows for a distributed access control system to be used because the owner of the access control object has the ability to change the access control permission on objects without regard to a central authority. Also, centralized access control systems can be used with this as a single authoritative point of authorization with the permissions still being applied at the object level. The ability to use different types of access control systems with this model gives it a great deal of flexibility.

As previously mentioned, this is a very common access control model. It is used in UNIX, Windows, Linux, and many other network operating systems.

These systems use an access control list (ACL) to set permissions on access control objects. These ACLs are basically a list of user IDs or groups with an associated permission level. Every access control object has an ACL, even if it is left at the default after the object is created. Systems do vary in the way the permissions are defined in the ACLs and how the overall access control within the operating system, database, network device, or application works.

Mandatory Access Control

MAC is based off of sensitivity levels rather than ACLs on objects and is frequently used by government systems. In MAC, the security administrator gives every access control object and access control subject a sensitivity label (also known as security labels) and the object owner or system user cannot change this sensitivity label. Based on the sensitivity labels of the access control objects, the access control system decides how all data will be shared and the data is restricted to the access control subjects with the required matching sensitivity label. For example, if an object has a sensitivity label with a classification of "top secret", an access control subject with a label classification of "secret" will be unable to access the object.

MAC is considered to be a more secure access control model than DAC as every subject and object must have a label assigned to it. This model ensures that if a subject is not authorized to access data with a specific sensitivity label, they will not be able to access it. This works well in a strictly defined hierarchy such as the military where subjects are simply not authorized to access any information that is above their classification in the hierarchy.

The major disadvantage to MAC is that it is extremely difficult to implement. There is a great deal of administration involved, as every object must be assigned a sensitivity label by the administrator when it is created. It is also very difficult to program applications to work with MAC due to the way objects are created and used. For example, the guidelines for MAC require that any data or information with a sensitivity classification higher than the object that the data is going to be placed in should be restricted from being placed in that object. This logic is very difficult to work with when designing applications. In addition, whenever output is generated from the data in an object, the output media itself (print job, optical disk, flash drive, etc.) must be labeled with the same sensitivity classification. This makes MAC very difficult to work with which is the primary reason that it is not implemented in most corporate environments. The total cost of ownership for MAC is not justified for most business purposes.

Nondiscretionary

There are several different forms of nondiscretionary access control, and each of these basically assigns specific roles to access control subjects and labels to access control objects specifying which roles are granted access to the object. This access control model is also called role-based access control as it depends on the definition of roles in order to make access control decisions.

RBAC basically assigns users or systems to specific roles and assigns permissions to each role. In addition, there is a hierarchy within RBAC whereby some roles can inherit permissions that are granted to another role. For an example, take a look at the illustration shown in Figure 5.5.

Based on this illustration, you can see how roles can be inherited. In this example, the office assistant role has access to only the patient's contact information. The medical doctor role has permission to view the patient's medical records. However, since the medical doctor role inherits the permissions of the office assistant role, the patient's contact information is accessible as well. The medical specialist has been explicitly granted access to all patient information and therefore has access not only to the contact information and medical records but also anything else in the patient's files.

In a good RBAC implementation, there is also the ability to block inheritance. There are instances where, for security reasons, you would want to limit privileges in the access control hierarchy. For example, in a banking situation, you would want to have someone in the bank teller role have access to balance out his or her register at the end of the day. In addition, you would want to have someone in the floor supervisor role to have access to verify that the teller's balance matches the actual money shown in the final count. However, you really wouldn't want the floor supervisor to be able to balance the register as well; otherwise, the organization would be open to fraud from a single person. You can combat this by blocking inheritance in the hierarchy. This is also an example of segregation of duties.

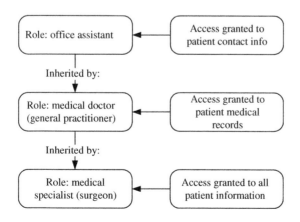

FIGURE 5.5
RBAC inheritance.

Audit

In a many access control systems, the access control system itself is responsible for all identification, authentication, and authorization. Any portion of a system asserting that much control over the operation of the system as a whole must be accountable for its actions. In the context of access control, ensuring that the access control system is accountable for any security-related transaction provides accountability. The security-related changes that the access control system must be accountable for include not only the three parts of granting access but also any transactions occurring and any changes in the way the access control system itself works.

Whenever a transaction controlled by the access control system occurs, it should be logged in some form. This log is known as an audit trail or transaction log. These transactions can include an access control subject creating an access control object, changing an object, or simply viewing an object. Basically, anything that occurs which falls under the domain of access control should be logged in some manner.

An access control system must be aware not only of changes or access requests between the access control subjects and access control objects, but also within itself. For example, the access control system must know when an authorized (or unauthorized) access control subject attempts to change the way that the access control system operates. This could include changing the access control policies, changing the permission requirements on an access control object, or elevating the privileges of an access control subject. Most of these changes will be recorded within the transaction log, but transactions regarding the changing of privileges of access control subjects are important enough to warrant having their own audit trail.

This log is called the privilege elevation audit trail or privilege elevation log. This log is designed to provide accountability for any changes in the privileges of access control subjects. As this is one of the most frequently examined transactions when a security breach occurs, it is very important that the access control system maintain a log of what changes have occurred related to privilege elevation.

Another logging item that needs to be specifically addressed is that of an authentication audit trail or authentication log. This type of log is typically smaller than the overall transaction log, but is very important for providing accountability. Any time that the access control system authenticates a request, it is accepting the proof of identity that the access control subject and object has presented and based on that, grants or denies the request based on its policies or predefined rules. If the decisions made by the access control system are ever questioned, it must have a method of proving that it did exactly what it was supposed to. The authentication audit trail provides for this and allows a system of checks and balances to exist within access control.

Maintaining all of these logs, even if all three are simply part of one large log, is critical to ensuring that the access control system is accountable for all changes that it makes. This provides assurance that the access control system is doing what it is supposed to, and if this is ever questioned, it can be tracked through one of the audit trails. Keep in mind that the audit trails are there to track not only the functionality of the access control system itself but also the administrators of that system. If someone is abusing their administrative privileges, this can be easily tracked and proven by the audit logs. This is yet another way of providing assurance that the overall access control system is safe and effective.

Monitoring your access control system is another part of the overall administration of the system. This includes the constant monitoring of all security and audit logs within the system. The basic monitoring requirement is that all behavior regarding the use of privileges, changes to accounts, and the escalation of privileges should be logged and that a consistent review of those logs must be performed. The monitoring of these logs is critical to ensuring that the access control system remains secure.

ADMINISTRATION OF ACCESS CONTROL

After an appropriate access control system has been chosen, developed, and implemented comes the long-term workload of properly administrating access control. This involves many factors including account administration, determining rights and permissions, management of access control objects, monitoring, securing removable media, and management of any data caches. In this section, we will be going over each of these and examining how each relates to the administration of access control. We'll also discuss some industry best practices for each part of access control administration. Always remember that without ongoing maintenance and administration, access control systems will be ineffective and unable to perform their function.

Account Administration

A major portion of access control administration is that of account administration. This encompasses the administration of all user, system, and service accounts used within the access control system. Account administration can be broken down into three parts: creation, maintenance, and destruction. These three parts encompass the entire lifecycle of an account and is shown in Figure 5.6. A documented process for each part of account administration is a must for a well-designed access control system.

The creation of accounts should be done only with proper approvals from the appropriate management entities. One major vulnerability of access control systems is a lack of good control over the account creation process. This can cause accounts to be created with more rights and permissions than they really need. We will be covering rights and permissions next, but the key to remember at this time is that no account should be created without proper approvals and a specific list of rights and permissions that should be granted to the account.

Ongoing maintenance for access control accounts typically consist of assisting users with password changes and unlocking accounts that have been locked out due to bad passwords. Another important part of account maintenance is the development and implementation of security policies requiring regular password changes and specifying password requirements. Also, if a

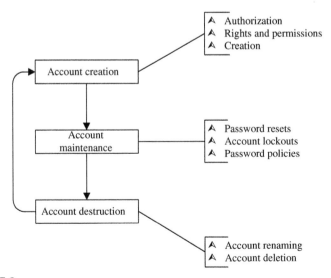

FIGURE 5.6
Access control account lifecycle.

user gets a promotion or hired for a different job within the organization, account maintenance could include changing security groups and updating account information.

Account destruction is the final part of the access control account lifecycle. This does not necessarily mean the deletion of accounts as some access control systems require that accounts never be deleted. A more common practice is to disable and/or rename the account. Whether the access control system used recommends deletion or disabling of accounts, the destruction activity must be accomplished quickly. A very large security vulnerability is created when accounts are left enabled for a time after an employee is terminated. This has the possibility of allowing potentially vindictive ex-employees a method to access the system, which is never a good idea. This is where a centralized access control system can be very beneficial to an organization's security.

One of the best practices for account administration is to work hand-in-hand with the human resources or personnel office of the company. With this relationship in place, accounts can be authorized and created when employees are hired and immediately destroyed when they are dismissed. This security practice goes a long way to decrease vulnerabilities within the company's access control lifecycle.

Determining Rights and Permissions

In most access control systems, the determination and configuration of appropriate rights and permissions for accounts is the most difficult part of the access control process. Any rights and permissions for a specific account should be authorized by the owner of the data that they want to gain access to. This ensures that the owner of the data is aware that the specific account will have access to the data and allows the owner to designate what level of access the account should have. Following this process will ensure that the data that the access control system is meant to protect is properly secured.

One of the most important concepts to apply here is the principle of least privilege. The idea behind the principle of least privilege is to grant all the rights and permissions necessary to an account, but no more than what is needed. For example, if a user needs to gain access to specific log files in a specific directory on a remote server, the best practice is to give them read-only rights to the files in that directory. This way, the user has the level of access necessary to perform the job functions, but no more than that. This helps eliminate many security vulnerabilities that could be caused by accounts having more rights than they need.

Management of Access Control Objects

Working with access control involves management of not only the access control subjects or accounts but also the access control objects. This includes several management processes such as ensuring secure storage, applying appropriate security controls, ensuring proper classification and declassification, and ensuring secure data destruction.

When access control objects are stored on any device, controls must be in place to ensure that the storage place for the access control objects is as secure as possible. This includes not only logical security, but also ensuring that the storage location is physically secure. Both of these security requirements fall under the heading of access control, but there is a third area which must be considered to make sure that the access control object storage location is secure. This is the application of appropriate security processes to eliminate vulnerabilities in the storage location and data transmission itself.

Access control objects that are classified using the methods described in the mandatory access control section of this chapter have additional management which must be performed. Whenever an object is created using MAC, it must be classified with one of the labels used by the MAC system. Ensuring that the data is classified correctly is the responsibility of the security administrator and is a critical part of access control using the MAC system. Another responsibility of this is the declassification of data in the MAC system as needed. Whenever the security requirements of an object change, its classification must change as well. In most environments implementing MAC, this process is well defined and documented as part of the overall access control policy or security policy.

The last part of access control object management is ensuring that when data is supposed to be destroyed, it is truly destroyed without possibility of retrieval. This is a requirement of high-security systems as well as a legal requirement for some standard-security systems. In high-security environments, data destruction ensures that the data will be inaccessible in the event that the system security of the environment is compromised by an intruder. In a legal sense, destroying data beyond a certain timeframe is desirable due to the legal ramifications of retaining old data. The laws for each state differ, but most only require companies to retain data for a certain length of time. Any data older than this timeframe is eligible for destruction. However, if a company retains data for longer than this requirement, that data can then be used against the company if required by legal action. In other words, the company is best served by destroying any data from outside its required retention period so that the contents of the data cannot be held against them later.

Data destruction in this sense means securely deleting the data from any physical media or from system memory. We will cover removable media later in this section. Typical secure data destruction utilities overwrite the area of the media or memory with a sequence of 0's or 1's in order to obscure the previous contents of the media. The most secure data destruction utilities do this a number of times in order to ensure that there is no possibility of recovering the destroyed data. However, dealing with solid state drives will differ from dealing with hard disk drives and may require different procedures.

ASSESSMENT

An important part of ensuring the security of an enterprise application is to assess the application in its entirety. This is done as a multipart process typically performed by experienced application assessment personnel. In most organizations, the application assessors are part of the IT security organization and perform assessments of commercial off-the-shelf (COTS) as well as home-grown applications. While teaching how to perform the full assessment process is outside the scope of this book, we will go over the steps involved as well as some of the critical vulnerabilities that can be found when assessing enterprise applications.

The assessment starts with identifying the assets to be assessed. In the case of an enterprise application, this will typically include all servers associated with the application, all networking components of the application, any databases used by the application, and finally, the application itself. Each asset is clearly identified and the communications channel used between assets is also scoped for assessment.

The next step is the determination of any threats to those assets. Threats can include natural events such as fire, earthquakes, or tornadoes, theft of the asset, compromise of the asset through internal or external sources, and many other possibilities. These threats all impact the application's confidentiality, integrity, or availability and should be clearly defined as part of the assessment. Each threat can impact one or more areas of the CIA triad.

At this stage, the potential impact of each threat is determined as well. Each threat may have a different impact on the organization and the cost associated to that threat may vary. For example, the threat of lost business due to a power outage may be a very costly threat to the company, whereas the threat of a compromised Twitter feed may be considered to be of negligible value. This threat assessment will differ between companies and will reflect their thoughts and opinions on the potential cost of business, reputation impact, and regulatory or legal ramifications.

With the assets and threats defined, the fun work begins! Each asset is examined for vulnerabilities that could lead to a threat being realized. For example, the threat of theft could be made more likely if it's discovered that a data center hosting a server has insufficient outdoor lighting. Every asset should be thoroughly investigated to find as many vulnerabilities as possible. By identifying the vulnerabilities throughout all of the enterprise application assets, you have a better idea of which threats are more likely to be exploited and can work to better understand the risk to the corporate enterprise.

Vulnerability assessment includes the analysis of the enterprise application itself through (potentially) both static analysis and penetration testing activities. Static analysis is a process wherein the application code is run through specialized scanning software to identify common vulnerabilities. These may include areas of the code where commonly exploited functions are used, places where data is not properly sanitized, and a host of other common programming errors. Penetration testing (sometimes referred to as dynamic analysis) is a much more intensive testing process where all aspects of the application are carefully tested to find even more potential vulnerabilities. In ideal cases, highly skilled penetration testers perform basic scans of the application to identify potential trouble areas and then focus on testing those areas very intently. In addition, skilled testers can utilize techniques where multiple vulnerabilities are combined to further compromise the application being tested.

After all of this testing is completed, the risk identification part of the process begins. Each vulnerability identified is paired with its associated threat and the likelihood of the vulnerability being exploited is determined. This likelihood may be high or low depending on the vulnerability itself and the difficulty associated with exploiting it. The risk level is then paired with the cost associated with the threat in order to provide a clear picture of the overall impact of any given vulnerability to the company.

Finally, any safeguards or countermeasures are taken into account. These may already exist, in which case the risk assessment will need to take them into account to lower the risk of a given vulnerability. If appropriate safeguards or countermeasures are not in place, their cost and value can be determined at this stage. That cost can be lined up with the risk assessment to determine if the cost of mitigating the risk is worth it compared to the cost of the vulnerability being exploited.

Vulnerabilities

There are many vulnerabilities which can exist in enterprise applications. For the purposes of this book, we will not delve into the full depth of vulnerabilities which can affect every asset in the enterprise application stack. Instead, we will focus on some of the more common vulnerabilities that can be found in enterprise applications and what they mean. There are thousands of vulnerabilities which exist for enterprise applications, but we'll discuss some of the high-level categories used to group many of them together.

Password Attacks

One of the more common vulnerabilities associated with enterprise applications is in the access control system. Passwords are frequently used for authentication and can be exploited in some cases. While many enterprises are starting to move toward enforcing good password policies, there are frequently problems encountered when these policies are implemented causing them to be reversed or ineffective. These problems can be due to administrative overhead associated with frequent password resets, technology limitations, or simply a lack of security awareness. In addition, there are some attacks that can be used, which specifically target password-based authentication.

Dictionary

If the user does not use a password that is easy to guess, they will sometimes still use common words that are easy for them to remember. This brings into play a simple method of cracking passwords known as a dictionary attack. A dictionary attack basically uses a flat text file containing most of the words out of the dictionary (sometimes in multiple languages) and many other common words. These words are then systematically tried against the user's password until one of them works. In addition, most dictionary attack applications also support adding numerical prefixes or suffixes to the password in case the user tries to obfuscate the password by adding a digit or two to the beginning or end.

Brute Force

Even if the user does use a secure password that is a random or pseudo-random generation of numbers, letters, and symbols, their password can still be broken. A technique for doing this is known as a brute force attack. In this type of attack, every conceivable combination of letters, numbers, and symbols are systematically tried against the password until it is broken. In organizations with good password policies, this may be mitigated by locking the account if too many bad passwords are tried. However, in some cases, a policy exists where the account is unlocked or the bad password count is reset after a specified duration. This leaves a vulnerability where the password can eventually be compromised if the attacker throttles the password checking to happen over a longer duration. Frequently, brute force attacks will not be performed on live systems. Instead, the person performing the attack will download a copy of all the password hashes and will attempt to crack them locally or through a service.

Compromised User Accounts

Another common vulnerability associated with accounts is that of previously compromised user accounts. In many cases, users will utilize the same password across different systems or even different companies. This is quite common and you'll often find where (against all recommendations) a user will have the same password for their email as they do for their enterprise application account which, in turn, is also the same as the password that they use for an external social networking site. Now ask yourself what happens when the account database for that external social networking site is compromised.

If the attacker can identify that the account on the external site is associated with a person at a target company, they can easily try the password that they have against the target company's systems. Some attackers don't put much thought into determining that relationship between user and a target company. Instead, they simply try every user ID/password combination that they have from the compromised site against as many targets as possible. In many cases, this leads them to find valid combinations that work across multiple targets which can then be further leveraged.

SQL Injection

One of the more common methods of compromising a database server is through using applications that connect to the database. If the application does not properly sanitize the input being used to formulate its database queries, it may be vulnerable to a SQL injection (SQLi) attack.

SQLi involves forcing the application to pass specific SQL queries to the back-end database that it wouldn't normally do based on its code. In addition to database access, SQLi can be used to get root access to the remote database system. Through the use of locally executed scripts or other techniques, the database's most useful features can be turned against it and used to give more access than what would normally be available.

SQLi works through a few different methods including what is known as Boolean-based blind SQLi, time-based blind SQLi, error-based SQLi, UNION query SQLi, and stacked queries SQLi. With each of these techniques, specific commands are passed through the application and to the database itself through the SQLi vulnerability. The database executes the queries differently depending on the DBMS software in use, and the results of the queries are either passed back to the calling application or simply executed with no response depending on the specific attack being used.

Imagine an application that simply selected all of the records from the database that matched a specific string. This application could have a URL such as http://victim/cgi-bin/query.cgi?searchstring=SEELY which relates to a snippet of code such as the following:

```
SELECT * from USERS WHERE name = searchstring
```

In this case, the resulting query would be:

```
SELECT * from USERS WHERE name = 'SEELY'
```

We may find that the application fails to sanitize the user's input and falls prone to having input that extends the SQL query such as http://victim/cgi-bin/query.cgi?searchstring=SEELY' DROP USERS. This would change the query sent to the database to the following:

```
SELECT * from USERS WHERE name = "SEELY" DROP USERS
```

Depending on the DBMS in use, this command could be used to drop database tables or perform other malicious activities including compromising the database host server.

Cross-Site Scripting

Cross-site scripting (XSS) vulnerabilities are one of the most commonly found and exploited with literally thousands of these bugs found in web applications. They are also often misunderstood. During a XSS attack, an attacker uses a vulnerable application to send a piece of malicious code, usually JavaScript, to a user of the application. Because this code runs in the context of the application, it has access to objects such as the user's cookie and other private session data for that site. For this reason, most XSS attacks result in some form of cookie theft or data gathering. In some cases, the JavaScript used by attackers can even be key loggers or other malware.

Testing for XSS is reasonably easy to automate, which in part explains the high number of such bugs found on a daily basis. A scanner only has to detect that a piece of script submitted to the server was returned sufficiently unmangled by the server to raise a red flag. This is one of the vulnerabilities that are most frequently scanned for by attackers, not because of the potential to compromise the site or application directly, but because of its ability to gather more information.

From an enterprise application perspective, XSS attacks do not cause the application to give up sensitive information or allow attackers to connect to the host system or underlying database. However, they can be used to gather credentials or other sensitive data from valid users of the application which can then be leveraged to further compromise the system. For example, if an application has an XSS vulnerability, that vulnerability could be used to cause malicious code to run that captures keystrokes. That key logger could then capture the credentials of an administrator logging into the site and forward them to the attacker. The attacker could now potentially log into the application as the administrator and gather more data or cause damage.

Buffer and Stack Overflows

One of the most dangerous vulnerabilities from an application point of view is buffer and stack overflows. These vulnerabilities allow an attacker or even just a malformed request to crash an application or cause it to perform unexpectedly. Depending on how the overflow happens within the application, it may even allow the execution of code that the attacker sends in the request causing the overflow. These vulnerabilities can be used to either cause the application to be unavailable due to the crash or be fully compromised in cases where that arbitrary code can be executed.

A buffer is a temporary holding area for application data. To speed processing, many applications use a memory buffer to store changes to data and then copy the information in the buffer to the system's permanent storage. When more information is put into the buffer than it is able to store, a buffer overflow occurs.

There are two types of overflows: stack overflows and heap overflows. The stack and the heap are two areas of the memory structure that are allocated when a program is executed. Function calls and static variables are stored in the stack and dynamically allocated variables are stored in the heap. A specific amount of memory is allocated for the buffer to use within the appropriate memory area.

Attackers can use buffer overflows in the heap to overwrite a password, a filename, or other variable data. If, for example, the variable for a filename is overwritten, a different file will be opened. If this is an executable file that the primary application process is calling, code will execute that was not intended to be run as the file of the attacker's choosing is opened instead of the intended executable. The substituted program code is often the command interpreter which allows the attacker to execute commands with the privileges associated with the account that the application is executed under. This could include root access depending on the system configuration. Some other attacks send staging code to be executed through the overflow attack because it's small and fast. The stager then downloads additional code from another source to further compromise the system.

To make matters worse, some hardware architectures use the stack to store function return addresses. Thus, the problem is that a buffer overflow can overwrite these return addresses and the computer will still attempt to use them. If the attacker is skilled enough to precisely control what values the return pointers are overwritten with, they can control the computer's next operation by pointing it to an address of their choosing.

Buffer overflows are based on the way the C programming language works. Many function calls don't check to ensure that the buffer will be big enough to hold the data copied to it. Programmers can use calls that do this check to prevent overflows, but many do not.

Creating a buffer overflow attack requires that the hacker understands assembly language as well as technical details about the operating system to be able to write the replacement code to the stack. However, the code for these attacks is often published so that others, who have less technical knowledge, can use it. Some types of firewalls allow buffer overflow attacks through, whereas application gateways (if properly configured), web application firewalls, and other more advanced protection systems can filter out most overflow attacks.

Luckily, buffer overflows are only a problem with languages that must pre-declare their variable storage sizes (such as C and C++). ASP, Perl, and Python all have dynamic variable allocation meaning that the language interpreter itself handles the sizing of variable storage. This makes buffer overflows a moot issue because the language interpreter will increase the size of the variable if there's too much data. However, C and C++ are still widely used languages, and buffer overflows are not bound to disappear anytime soon.

Denial of Service

A DoS attack is an attack against the availability of an application. These attacks attempt to render an application or system inaccessible by flooding it with network packets to the point that it is no longer able to accept valid packets. This works by simply overloading the processor of your network equipment, server, or database by making them attempt to process a number of packets or requests past their limitations.

An alternative attack that is more difficult to defend against is the distributed denial of service (DDoS) attack. This attack is worse because the attack can come from a huge number of computers at the same time. This is accomplished by either the attacker having a large distributed network of systems all over the world or by infecting normal users' computers with malware, which allows the attacker to force the systems to attack targets that they specify without the end user's knowledge.

By doing this, the attacker is able to set up a large number of systems (called Zombies or bots) to form a botnet and have each system perform a DoS attack at the same time. This type of attack constitutes a DDoS attack. By performing an attack in this manner, it is more effective due to the number of packets being sent. In addition, it introduces another layer of systems between the attacker and the target, making the attacker more difficult to trace.

Aside from impacting availability, DoS and DDoS attacks can be useful in masking other activities. When administrators are dealing with an attack of this nature, their attention is naturally drawn to the systems performing the attack. That may cause either the administrators or their intrusion detection systems (IDSs) to miss other attacks that occur at the same time. Because of the "noise" caused by an attack of this nature, it's often easy to slip in some other scanning or attack activities that are virtually unnoticed.

Spoofing and Man in the Middle

Spoofing is a form of attack where the intruder pretends to be another system and attempts to obtain data and communications that were intended for the original system. This can be done in several different ways including IP spoofing, session hijacking, and ARP spoofing. Each of these methods allows an intruder to access data which they would normally be restricted from viewing.

IP spoofing is a fairly simple attack where an intruder configures his or her system to work with the same IP address as a valid system on the network. The intruder then fools any routers or switches into thinking that their system is the actual destination machine. This is done by poisoning the ARP cache of the switch or by sending out WINS broadcasts on the network. In this way, the intruder is able to have any packets intended for the original destination routed to their system. This isn't very useful by itself, but this attack can be combined with other techniques to make it very powerful.

Session hijacking is similar to a normal spoof attack except that this type of attack is intended to intercept specific packets that the source and destination systems are using to maintain a communications session. An example of this is a telnet connection to a host. When the intruder spoofs the address for the user's system, they can continue communications with the host via the same telnet session. By doing so, the intruder effectively bypasses any authentication procedures and is able to access the remote system as if they were the original end user.

The last type of spoofing that we will discuss here is ARP spoofing. We mentioned this earlier as part of IP spoofing, but ARP spoofing is also a standalone technique of its own. An ARP spoof is performed by sending an ARP packet to a switch containing the IP address of the target, but the MAC address of the attacker. By doing an ARP spoof, the attacker can hijack sessions that a client was previously using. This can also be used as a MitM attack between two network devices.

A MitM attack is performed by effectively inserting an intruder's system in the middle of the communications path between two other systems on the network. By doing this, an attacker is able to see both sides of the conversation between the systems and pull data directly from the communications stream. In addition, the intruder can insert data into the communications stream which could allow them to perform extended attacks or obtain even more unauthorized data from the host system.

Figure 5.7 shows the communications path used for normal communications and how this is changed during a MitM attack. The following steps illustrate how to perform a MitM attack by using ARP spoofing.

1. The intruder (I) sends an ARP packet to a client (C1) using the IP address of another client (C2), but the MAC address for the intruder (I).
2. The intruder (I) sends an ARP packet to a client (C2) using the IP address of another client (C1), but the MAC address for the intruder (I).
3. Now both clients have ARP cache entries for each other's IP address, but the MAC address for these entries point to the intruder. The intruder routes packets between C1 and C2 so that communications are not interrupted.
4. The intruder sniffs all packets that it is routing and is able to see all communications between the clients.

This process will allow an intruder to view all traffic between two clients, but ARP spoofing can potentially be more damaging than this. By performing a MitM attack between a router and the switch, an intruder could see all data

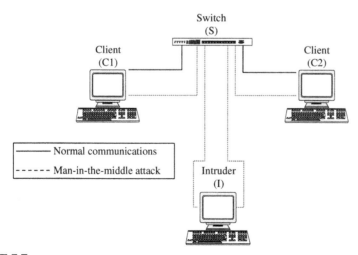

FIGURE 5.7
Man-in-the-middle attack.

coming through the router. In addition, if an intruder replies to every ARP request sent out by the switch, it could intercept traffic going to all clients. This gives the intruder the option of performing a DoS attack by not allowing any client to communicate with the switch, or routing traffic to the intended client and sniffing the data being communicated via the MitM attack.

DEFENSE IN DEPTH

A key concept of information security is that of defense in depth. This means adding in appropriate security controls at every appropriate layer of the information technology stack. The goal here is that each layer of security adds to the overall cumulative security solution increasing the amount of work that any attacker has to perform and reducing the impact of any given attack.

In this section, we'll be discussing some of the preventative measures that can be put in place within each layer of the information technology stack. This includes administrative controls such as standards and procedures as well as technical controls in the various technology areas. By adding layer after layer of protection, you can build a deep security solution that can truly help mitigate a substantial number of risks.

Control Documents

From an administrative perspective, there are a number of controls that can be put in place to help add a layer of security to your information technology stack. These administrative controls take the form of standards, guidelines, policies, and procedures, all of which are intended to help document the appropriate use of technology resources. Depending on the environment, these documents may be incredibly prescriptive and define exactly how work should be done, or vaguer and just provide a general idea of how the technology should be used. They clearly define specific administrative controls and create a comprehensive administrative control layer.

A *standard* is used to ensure that information technology assets are used in a consistent manner within the corporate enterprise. Standards can help reduce support costs and simplify system or application configuration since any relevant system should adhere to the defined standard. For example, the corporation may have specific standards that outline the model and specifications of servers for specific uses. There may also be standards that define which version of an operating system will be installed on the servers and any ancillary software that will be in place. These standards are generally considered to be mandatory.

Guidelines are a little more flexible. Guidelines are general recommendations that the individual user can choose to use if they'd like to. Some examples of this are guidelines around how to create stronger passwords or how to protect your personal information when using the internet. When guidelines are issued within a corporation, the expectation is that they will be used where appropriate and assist in guiding behavior, not mandating it.

When a company needs to mandate a particular behavior, a *policy* is frequently used. A policy sets a direction as defined by the management (or government) and it is required that all personnel in scope of the policy follow it without fail. For example, a company may have an acceptable use policy that defines how information technology assets should be used within a company or it may have a policy addressing the use of illegal substances. Policies must be followed and will typically detail out consequences that will occur if employees do not adhere to the policy. A common phrase used in many policy definitions is "disciplinary action up to and including termination."

A policy will generally be high-level and will not get into very specific details. *Procedures* are very detailed step-by-step instructions on how to perform a specific task or function and take over where policies leave off. Procedures, like policies, are mandatory and are sometimes referred to as standard operating procedures (SOPs). In some cases, procedures need to reference another even more detailed step-by-step document to clearly define how to perform a task in the same way every time. This type of referenced document is known as a *work instruction*.

Administrative Controls

The creation of standards, guidelines, policies, and procedures are all based on general administrative controls. The general process is to determine the administrative control that needs to be implemented and then document the control in the appropriate document type. Some of the more common administrative controls are separation of duties, which we've already touched on briefly, rotation of duties, record retention, and change management. This list is not comprehensive by any means, but includes some of the most basic and common administrative controls which corporations use.

Separation of duties defines an administrative control which prohibits the same person from handling all parts of sensitive transactions. This is commonly seen with call centers where an average customer service representative can take calls and perform basic tasks, but has to call a supervisor in order to credit accounts. It can also be seen in approval processes where a requestor is not allowed to approve their own request. This type of control helps to ensure that a single person cannot perform an end-to-end task that could cause financial or other damage to a company. Instead, at least two people would have to collaborate (or collude) in order to perform the transaction.

Rotation of duties is a similar administrative control with a slightly different purpose. This control can also be called "job rotation" and involves forcing employees to change job roles on a regular basis when they are working in an area associated with sensitive transactions. If the same person always did the same job, the possibility exists that they could gain too many privileges associated with the job role over time. It also increases the likelihood that collusion could happen between two or more people in segregated job roles. While this type of control is not necessarily a good fit for all job roles, it does make sense in some cases and can help in reducing risk to the company. Another similar control is that of mandatory vacation where employees are required to take vacation while other employees temporarily fulfill their job role.

A number of administrative controls around record retention can be defined in order to help keep a good handle on a company's sensitive documents. In many companies, there are specific regulations that must be adhered to in association with record retention. These regulations are often reflected in policies as well as company-specific requirements around record retention. It is common for policies to define the minimum amount of time for a record to be retained due to regulations, but also a maximum retention time based on company requirements.

The final administrative control that we'll discuss is that of data remanence. Data remanence is the data that is left on various types of media after it has been logically erased. There are generally administrative controls put in place that describe when data should be deleted, but data remanence controls can help define *how* to properly delete the data. In some cases, this may involve overwriting the area where the data was stored with random data multiple times in order to reduce the likelihood that it can be restored. In other cases, this type of control may require that the media be physically destroyed and define acceptable destruction methods.

Technical Controls

As you think about the concept of defense in depth, technical controls are usually the first that come to mind. Technical controls can be put into place in all layers of an enterprise application's infrastructure. Each of these controls should address one or more parts of the CIA triad and contribute to the overall security of the application and corporate enterprise. In this section, we'll discuss some of the technical controls that can be put in place at each layer of the application stack.

Network

We'll start by looking at the network used by the enterprise application. When we discussed network hardware and technologies in Chapter 2, we touched on some of the hardware that can help implement these controls, but now we'll focus on that hardware in the context of the security control that it enforces. It is important to think of any security-oriented device in the manner of a device that enforces a control. Just having the device will provide no security to your assets. Instead, a policy must be defined around the appropriate controls and the security device should be configured to enforce that policy.

Intrusion Detection Systems

An IDS is quite simply the high-tech equivalent of a burglar alarm—a burglar alarm configured to monitor access points, hostile activities, and known intruders. There are also network intrusion detection systems (NIDSs) which monitor the entire network. These systems typically trigger on events by referencing network activity against an attack signature database. If a match is made, an alert will take place and will be logged for future reference.

Creating and maintaining the attack signature database is the most difficult part of working with IDS technology. You must always keep your IDS up-to-date with the latest signature database provided by your vendor as well as updating the database with the signatures you find in your own testing. Some IDSs also have the ability to identify patterns in behaviors and alert based on changes to the baseline patterns that it is expecting.

Attack signatures consist of several components used to uniquely describe an attack. An ideal signature would be one that is specific to the attack while being as simple as possible to match with the input data stream (large complex signatures may pose a serious processing burden). Just as there are varying types of attacks, there must be varying types of signatures. Some signatures will define the characteristics of an operation such as that of an nmap portscan, while others will be derived from the actual payload of an attack. Most signatures are constructed by running a known exploit several times, monitoring the data as it appears on the network and looking for a unique pattern that is repeated on every execution. This method works fairly well at ensuring that the signature will consistently match that particular exploit.

Virtual Private Network

One of the most common methods of providing employees with remote connections to the corporate office is through the use virtual private networks (VPNs). A VPN basically allows the end user to create a secure tunnel through an unsecured network in order to connect to the corporate network.

Typically, the user will connect to his or her normal internet service provider (ISP) and then use a software client to create the VPN connection to the corporate network. At that point, the user's system functions as if it were located on the corporate LAN and accesses enterprise applications as if they were at the office.

Firewall

A firewall is the most common device used to protect an internal network from outside intruders. When properly configured, a firewall can block access to your internal network from the outside, as well as blocking users of your internal network from accessing potentially dangerous external networks or ports.

There are three firewall technologies that are commonly used:

1. Packet filtering
2. Application layer gateways/web application firewalls
3. Stateful inspection

All of these technologies have their advantages and disadvantages, and most firewalls now combine or have the ability to combine multiple technologies. For example, the Cisco ASA can provide packet filtering, deep packet inspection (DPI), and application layer filter plus many other functions.

A packet filtering firewall is designed to operate quickly by either allowing or denying packets and works at the network layer of the OSI model. An application layer gateway or web application firewall analyzes each packet, verifies that it contains the correct type of data for the specific application that it is attempting to communicate with, and contains no content that might match an attack signature. A stateful inspection firewall simply checks each packet to verify that it is an expected response to a current communications session.

A packet filtering firewall can be configured to deny or allow access to specific ports or IP addresses. There are two policies that can be followed when creating packet filtering firewall rules. The first is to allow by default. This policy basically allows all traffic to go through the firewall except for that which is specifically denied. The alternative is to deny by default. This policy blocks all traffic through the firewall except for that which is explicitly allowed.

The best security policy is to deny by default; however, this could result in the availability of services or business processes to fail until the firewall is configured properly. This goes along with the general security concept of restricting all access to the minimum level necessary to allow the business needs to be supported. To apply this when configuring a firewall, the best practice is to deny access to all ports except for those which are absolutely necessary. For example, if you are configuring an externally facing firewall for a web server, you may want to deny all ports except for port 443 (the SSL port) in order to require all connections coming in to your DMZ to use HTTPS to connect to your web servers.

A firewall works in two directions, and you should keep this in mind when considering its role in enforcing security controls. It can be used to keep intruders at bay, but also to restrict access to the external network from your internal users. Why would you want to do this? A great example can be found in the way that some Trojan horse programs work. When they are initially installed, they can report back to a centralized location to notify the author or distributor that the program has been activated. Some Trojans do this by reporting to an IRC channel, or by connecting to a specific port on a remote computer. By denying access to these external ports in your firewall configuration, you can prevent these malicious programs from compromising your internal network.

Packet filtering does have both benefits and drawbacks. One of the benefits is speed. Since only the header of a packet is examined and a simple table of rules is checked, this technology is very fast. A second benefit is ease of use. The rules for this type of firewall are easy to define and ports can be opened or closed quickly. In addition, packet filtering firewalls are transparent to network devices. Packets can go through a packet filtering firewall without the sender or receiver of the packet being aware of the extra step. A major bonus of using a packet filtering firewall is that most current routers support packet filtering, so you may not have to purchase a new device to serve this function.

There are really two major drawbacks to packet filtering. The first is that a port is either open or closed. With this configuration, there is no way of simply opening a port in the firewall as a specific application needs it and then closing it when the transaction is complete. When a port has been opened, you always have a hole in your firewall waiting for someone to attack. The second major drawback is that they do not understand the contents of any packet beyond the header. Therefore, if the packet has a valid header, it can contain any payload. This is a very common failing point that is easily exploited.

Application Layer Gateways/Web Application Firewalls
The second firewall technology we'll look at was originally called application filtering or an application layer gateway and later called next-generation firewalls (NGFWs). Over time, this technology evolved into a more web-based application concept and morphed into web application firewalls. This technology is much more advanced than packet filtering as it examines the entire

packet and determines what should be done with the packet based on specific rules that have been defined. For example, with an application layer gateway, if an HTTP packet is sent through the standard FTP port, the firewall can determine this and block the packet if a rule is defined disallowing HTTP traffic. It should be noted that this technology is used by proxy servers to provide application layer filtering to clients going through the proxy.

With web application firewalls, even more protection is offered as the firewall is able to scan inside each packet to see if there is content that matches specific attack signatures. This is a blend of technologies in that it combines concepts associated with intrusion detection along with concepts associated with firewalls. This blend provides a substantial amount of flexibility that can help support the "defense in depth" practice very well.

One of the major benefits of application layer gateway technology is its application layer awareness. Since it can determine much more information from a packet than a simple packet filter can determine, it can use more complex rules to determine the validity of any given packet. These rules take advantage of the fact that application layer gateways can determine whether the data in a packet match what is expected for data going to a specific port. For example, the application layer gateway (in the form of a web application firewall) would be able to tell if packets containing controls for a Trojan horse were being sent to the HTTP port (80) and block them. Based on this, it provides much better security than a packet filter.

In addition to what application layer gateways can do, some NGFWs also have the ability to perform user-based policies by mapping users to local IP addresses and integrating LDAP lookups to define roles. An example of this would be allowing the human resources department to have access to run an HR-specific web-based application and have the ability to visit Facebook and LinkedIn, while other users would not be allowed to.

While the technology behind application layer gateways is much more advanced than packet filtering technology, it does come with drawbacks. Due to the fact that every packet is disassembled completely and then checked against a complex set of rules, application layer gateways are much slower than packet filters. Since application layer gateways actually process the packet at the application layer of the OSI model, the application layer gateway must deconstruct every packet and then rebuild the packet from the top down and send it back out. This can take quite some time when a lot of traffic is being processed.

Stateful Packet Inspection Firewalls

Stateful packet inspection (SPI) is a compromise between these two existing technologies. It overcomes the drawbacks of both simple packet filtering and application layer gateways, while enhancing the security provided by your firewall. Stateful inspection technology supplies application layer awareness without actually breaking the client/server architecture by disassembling and rebuilding the packet. In addition, it's much faster than an application layer gateway due to the way packets are handled. It's also more secure than a packet filtering firewall, due to the application layer awareness as well as the introduction of application and communication-derived state awareness.

The primary feature of stateful inspection is the monitoring of application and communication states. This means that the firewall is aware of specific application communication requests and knows what should be expected out of any given communication session. This information is stored in a dynamically updated state table, and any communication not explicitly allowed by a rule in this table is denied. This allows your firewall to dynamically conform to the needs of your applications and open or close ports as needed. As the ports are closed when the requested transactions are completed, this provides another layer of security by not leaving these ports open to be attacked. To take SPI a step further, Deep packet inspection came along. DPI still performs the same checks that SPI does; however, DPI will also look at the contents of a packet and check it against known patterns or signatures.

Servers

In most corporate environments, there are procedures in place for "hardening" a server when it is built. This hardening process involves setting-specific configuration parameters, disabling unused services, installing monitoring software, and implementing other server-based technical controls. There are hardening guides available for most operating systems, and most corporate IT departments use these guides as a baseline to which they add company-specific changes that further implement their own internal security policies.

We will not be covering all of the hardening options available for each operating system. Instead, just be aware that hardening guides exist both within the corporate sector and within certain government agencies. In many cases, these latter guides are publicly released and can help guide implementations in the corporate world to match those within the government sector. This hardening process should be performed as soon as a server is built and, through the implementation of appropriate change control, the server should be kept up-to-date with changes to the hardening process over time.

Secure Sockets Layer/Transport Layer Security

We talked about TLS as the replacement protocol for Secure Sockets Layer (SSL) in Chapter 2. While this is technically a network protocol, it is important to keep it in mind from a technical controls perspective when you consider communications with and between servers.

SSL and TLS provide a connection between a client and a server, over which any amount of data can be sent securely. Both the server and browser must have SSL or TLS enabled to facilitate secure web connections, while applications generally must have SSL or TLS enabled to allow their use of the secure connection. However, a recent trend is to use dedicated SSL accelerators as VPN terminators, passing the content on to an end server.

For the browser and server to communicate securely, each needs to have the shared session key. SSL/TLS use public key encryption to exchange session keys during communication initialization.

Fault Tolerance and Redundancy

An important aspect of ensuring availability is the appropriate use of fault tolerance and redundancy. We'll discuss both of these topics at length in Chapter 6 when we go over architecture. For now, understand that fault tolerance refers to a system or application's resilience. A fault tolerant system can gracefully handle one or more failures in its capabilities in order to maintain the overall availability of the system. Redundancy refers to having multiple systems (or subsystems) available so that if one fails, the other can take over the work. In many cases, fault tolerance is provided through the use of redundancy. For example, many servers have redundant power supplies. If one power supply fails, the others continue to function and just carry more of the system's load. This makes the server fault tolerant against power supply failures.

Other technical controls that are used to ensure availability include clustering, matrix networking, and disaster recovery. Clustering will be covered in depth in Chapter 6 and we went over matrix networking as a part of network design in Chapter 2. DR is an important technical control that can be put in place in order to provide for availability in the event of a true disaster. In most cases, DR plans are intended to be implemented only if the company's primary hosting facility goes completely down for an extended amount of time.

DR concepts can be implemented in a few different ways depending on how the company wants to address availability. Under the DR umbrella, there are various DR types including cold sites, warm sites, and hot sites. These terms refer to the level of readiness that is available at the facility used for DR. A cold site is typically available, but may or may not have hardware in place and will not have up-to-date data. In order to use the site, hardware may need to be installed and data copied in from a backup. Warm sites will usually have hardware running, but will still need to have the most current data loaded. Finally, hot sites are fully configured and ready to go in the event of a disaster and have current copies of all data in place.

In some instances, companies will create a hot site for DR, but will use it for other purposes when a disaster scenario is not in place. This helps reduce the overall cost of maintaining the facility in that it is at least able to provide a level of value versus just burning power while waiting on a disaster to occur. Typically, these sites will be used as a staging or preproduction environment for enterprise applications and, since the hardware is typically a close match for production, they can also be used to test performance of enterprise applications.

Backups

Another common control used to provide for data integrity or availability is backups. Backups are basically copies of data that are stored in another location and made available for use if the original data is lost or corrupted. These backups may be kept on separate backup media, stored under another file name on the same system, or copied to an off-site storage facility. Regardless of the method used, it is always wise to keep some sort of backup of all data.

The type of threat that you wish to mitigate will drive the type of backup being performed and where the data is stored. For example, if you wish to just protect against accidental corruption of a file, you could simply make a backup of that file to the same system and disk under a different name. If you wish to protect data against the threat of a drive failure, you would need to back that data up to either a different drive or other type of media. Protecting against the threat of fire might involve duplicating the data to an off-site facility. On the extreme side, protecting the data against a nuclear bomb would involve storing it off-site within a radiation-proof structure. Depending on the threat being addressed, different backup approaches should be used as mitigating controls. There have also been numerous cloud-based backup solutions arising which allow companies to back up their data to geographically distributed systems.

Databases

The most common controls applied to databases are typically those around access control. Ensuring that the correct people or systems have access to the correct data in the correct manner is very critical. However, there are some additional controls that can be put in place from a technical perspective to mitigate various risks identified at the database layer of the enterprise application stack.

When it comes to databases, confidentiality is a very key element. While proper access controls go a long way toward protecting data confidentiality, sometimes they aren't enough. What if someone were to gain access to the files that are used by the DBMS to store the data? In theory, someone gaining access to these files could extract the data, therefore eliminating its confidentiality. This threat can be fought to some degree by using database encryption.

Depending on the DBMS in use and the products chosen to provide encryption services, there are a few options that may be available to database administrators. Encryption can be applied at several levels including encrypting the entire database, selected database tables, or even just specific columns. However, it is important to note that encryption of a database can cause drastic slowdowns in the applications using it. In addition, the communications channel between systems that use the database and the DBMS can be encrypted to protect data while it is transferred. All of these options fall under the context of database encryption and provide technical controls at the database layer to protect confidentiality.

Most of the other controls that can be used at the database layer have either been discussed in Chapter 4 when we discussed databases in detail or previously in this chapter. For example, the controls around backups and fault tolerance apply to databases just as they would to other server or data storage technologies.

Enterprise Applications

There are a number of controls that can be put in place within enterprise applications to address various threats. We've already talked about access controls which help protect the confidentiality, integrity, and availability of the data or services associated with enterprise applications. We've also discussed some of the technical controls that can be put in various layers of the enterprise application technology stack. Now it's time to address controls that can be put in place within or around the enterprise applications themselves.

Many of the controls used around enterprise applications include those that we've already discussed. Concepts such as access control, fault tolerance, redundancy, and data storage all apply to enterprise applications and are typically reflected in the technical architecture used by the application as well as the application architecture itself. In addition, the assessment of enterprise applications should fully encompass the areas of both static and dynamic application analysis to uncover potential vulnerabilities in the application. By ensuring that this is done regardless of whether the enterprise application is commercial software or home-grown, you can identify potential trouble areas in the application and determine the best approach for mitigating any risks.

From an enterprise application-specific point of view, there are some other concepts that may need to be looked at in order to add the appropriate level of controls to the application. One of these is nonrepudiation. Nonrepudiation is the assurance that when someone takes an action, appropriate data is recorded to ensure that they cannot later say that they did not take that action. This is frequently implemented within enterprise applications as a control to help ensure both confidentiality and integrity. Along these lines, enterprise applications will frequently have code in place that logs when a user accesses sensitive data even if they don't change it as well as logging any changes to the data. This type of logging is considered a technical control although it frequently falls under a category associated with other audit data.

Another important technical control for enterprise applications is that of application monitoring. While there is frequently monitoring of various assets that make up the enterprise application stack in place, it is a good idea to monitor the enterprise application itself. There are many cases where a piece of technology may be "up" but functioning incorrectly causing the availability of the application using that technology to be impacted. From a mitigation perspective, technical controls around monitoring can be put in place as detective controls so that administrators can be informed of availability issues and rapidly assess and fix the problem.

SUMMARY

This chapter has effectively been a crash course on information security. While we in no way covered all aspects of security, the intent is to get you thinking about various information security topics and how they apply to enterprise applications. Across the board, there is a need for more awareness about information security and this can't be just from people in traditional "security" roles. Enterprise applications administrators are often in the forefront of security associated with the application that they're managing and so it is critical for any enterprise applications administrator to understand basic information security concepts.

In this chapter, we discussed some of the basic concepts and principles associated with information security including the CIA triad and all of its components. Most security concepts revolve around protecting confidentiality, integrity, and availability which was a common theme throughout this chapter. As an enterprise applications administrator, you should focus on these three key areas and make sure that any security strategies used for the enterprise applications that you are responsible for address them.

We also spent some time discussing authentication, authorization, audit, and administration of access control. These four topics tie together to form the access control mechanisms used by most enterprise applications today. By understanding the differences between each part of access control and how each contributes to the overall security of the application, you are better positioned to make good decisions around access control within your role as an enterprise applications administrator.

Most large organizations do have their own information security team which is responsible for assisting with or performing threat and risk assessments. However, they are usually not experts on the enterprise applications that may exist in the enterprise and may be limited as to how deep their assessment can go. This is where an enterprise applications administrator with good information security knowledge can be incredibly helpful. By partnering with the appropriate teams when performing enterprise application security assessments, the insight of an administrator can help uncover more threats and vulnerabilities within the application as well as more clearly define risks.

Finally, we talked about defense in depth. This effectively means applying the appropriate level of security controls at each layer of the enterprise application. Whether it's the network, server, database, or application, the correct controls must be in place to help mitigate risks. Understanding this concept and how properly applied administrative and technical controls can help add layer upon layer of security to the application is critical for enterprise applications administrators. The best approach is to always secure an enterprise application in the most holistic manner possible through the implementation of appropriate controls at all levels, and no one can understand how all those pieces fit together better than the application's administrator.

Architecture

- Architecture Concepts
- Enterprise Architecture
- Solution Architecture
- Application Architecture
- Technical Architecture
- Cloud-Based Architecture

ARCHITECTURE CONCEPTS

When working with enterprise applications, a term that is used quite a bit is "architecture." But what does that mean in the various contexts associated with enterprise applications administration? In this chapter, we will be going over the various types of architecture that play a role in enterprise applications and how the appropriate use of architectural concepts can help improve the operation of enterprise applications. We'll also be going over some of the emerging concepts around cloud-enabled capabilities and their role in enterprise applications.

When you think of architecture, what immediately comes to mind? Is it the design of a building such as a data center? Perhaps it's the layout of network components, servers, and databases that make up an enterprise application. Alternatively, it may be that the logical layout of the enterprise application and its various components or modules pops into your head. Maybe you think of all of the enterprise applications that exist in a corporation and how the data flows between them to keep everything coordinated. All of these are correct and each is just a different aspect of architecture and how architecture plays a role in an enterprise application.

For the purposes of enterprise applications administration, we're going to focus on the architectural areas of technical architecture, application architecture, solution architecture, and enterprise architecture. Other types of architecture include physical architecture such as our data center example, system architecture including how the physical hardware for server systems or even processors is built out, security architecture, network architecture, and software architecture which include coding standards and other programming-specific concepts. We will not be covering these additional architectural areas except for small components of security and network architecture as they relate to technical architecture.

As we look at each architectural area, we will be discussing what concepts are involved in the architecture, how the architectural area relates to the other key areas of enterprise applications administration, and how the architectural area rolls down into the next architectural area. We will be starting with the enterprise architecture and move down through the architectural hierarchy until we get to the technical architecture. When designing a new enterprise application implementation, it is typical to start with the enterprise architecture and work your way down to the technical architecture as this will help ensure that high-level decisions are made before getting down into the finite details associated with applying those decisions.

To illustrate how this is done, we are going to create a set of architecture documents for a hypothetical enterprise application called Fake Linking Application Relationship Prioritizer or FLARP. FLARP is a standard multitier enterprise application comprised of web servers, application servers with various functions, database servers, and a variety of supporting hardware. This application runs in a large enterprise with many other enterprise applications that it must share data with either directly or through the use of data integration hubs. This application will provide critical business services, require a fairly rapid response time, a high level of availability, and integrate well into the existing enterprise while providing new capabilities to the corporation.

ENTERPRISE ARCHITECTURE

Enterprise architecture is a practice within the IT field that is intended to align IT with the strategic direction and vision of the company. Often when developing an enterprise architecture the goal is to help drive down the cost of enterprise technology solutions and reduce the complexity of IT systems. As information technology evolved in corporations over time, many systems were implemented without much regard as to how the system would fit with other existing systems, what value the system provides in comparison to others, and what the long-term value of the system is as the company's business roadmap evolves. It was not uncommon to end up with three or more systems that have the exact same function leading to ongoing maintenance costs for all of the systems as well as ongoing questions as to which one is the source of truth for any given data.

Enterprise architects attempt to drive alignment between information systems and business goals as well as provide guidance around system implementations. This guidance may involve setting specific enterprise patterns for accomplishing tasks, defining which system is the "master" for a given capability or function, as well as ensure that standards around technologies are developed and followed. From a business perspective, most enterprise architecture organizations are tasked with understanding the company's business processes and long-term vision, which they then document and use as a model that can be applied across existing and new information systems.

When working with enterprise architecture, the enterprise architect role is twofold: to guide and to approve. In these two capacities, enterprise architects can assist in ensuring that any information system solution fits well within the enterprise and aligns with where the company is headed from a business perspective. This alignment is critical and where the value of enterprise architecture can be found aside from the cost savings that comes from the appropriate uses of information technology.

Looking at the guidance role of enterprise architecture, most enterprise architecture organizations focus on the business roadmap and strategy, principles of governance, organizational structure, and business processes. By focusing on these key areas, enterprise architects are able to develop a model of what the technology roadmap for the company should look like at a high level and ensure that new system implementations align with the model. For example, if a new system implementation request was submitted for review and it didn't seem to line up with the business strategy, the requestor would need to justify the creation of the system. If the creation were justified, then the enterprise architecture group would work to ensure that the business organizations are ready to adopt the system and align the business processes and system processes as needed.

The role of approver aligns with enterprise architecture's governance focus. It is often the job of enterprise architecture groups to ensure that systems being implemented do follow best practices and align with enterprise strategies and needs. In many cases, it may be faster and (in the short term) cheaper to implement a system without any regard to other systems that already exist in the enterprise. However, it has been proven time and time again that the longer term costs of this practice are much higher than taking an enterprise-wide view initially. From a governance perspective, enterprise architecture groups will typically have the ability to deny or actively shut down implementation projects if they do not align with enterprise standards and patterns. While this may seem to be a preventative measure, the true intent is to help to guide implementations to do things the "right" way from the enterprise architecture point of view in order to drive down information system costs and complexity.

As we look at the creation of our architecture for FLARP, we will make the assumption that the company has an enterprise architecture practice in place and that specific guidelines have been set for enterprise standards. The example shown in Figure 6.1 demonstrates what a company's enterprise architecture could look like from a business capability perspective. In this example, each business capability is broken out into its respective functional area. As new enterprise applications such as FLARP come along, the business capabilities that will be impacted must be determined.

In the example shown in Figure 6.1, there are a number of business capabilities defined and they are organized into the functional areas of back office services, service offerings, customer services, and external services. Most companies that have an enterprise architecture practice will have more functional areas and more capabilities than are shown in this example depending on the size of the organization. For our purposes, this smaller business capability diagram will serve well.

In order to map our enterprise application against the company's business capabilities, we must determine which of these capabilities the application provides. In the case of FLARP, let's say that it provides the ability to apply

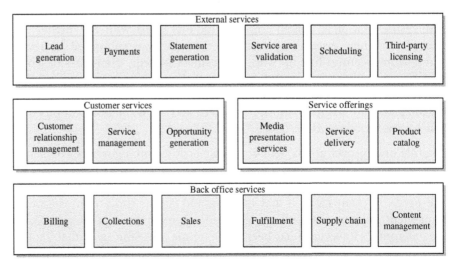

FIGURE 6.1
Fake Inc. enterprise architecture business capabilities.

for a service, manage the service application process, perform a credit check to determine eligibility, and then process an order for service. Each of these capabilities lines up with one or more areas within the enterprise business capability map and must be called out for further analysis in each of those areas. Figure 6.2 shows an example of how this could be done visually.

As you can see in Figure 6.2, the following business capabilities have been impacted with the introduction of FLARP:

- Sales
- Customer Relationship Management
- Billing
- Fulfillment

In many cases, it is up to the enterprise applications administrator to help determine which capability areas are impacted by that enterprise application. This is frequently done with the assistance of enterprise architects or individual capability architects. From the capabilities offered by FLARP, this determination is relatively easy to accomplish in this example. For more complex enterprise applications or for applications where there is more ambiguity in capability, it may require in-depth analysis by enterprise and capability architects to determine the correct business capability area alignment.

Again, with FLARP, this process is fairly easy. The ability to apply for service aligns very well with the sales business capability. Managing the application process implies managing the relationship with a customer as they go

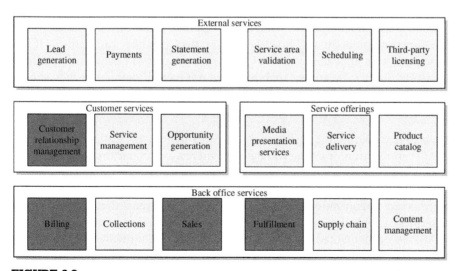

FIGURE 6.2
FLARP business capability map.

through the process therefore falling under the Customer Relationship Management capability. The credit check performed by the application is a little ambiguous as it could fall under a couple of different capabilities. However, since the company has a billing capability, it may make sense for the credit check to fall under that capability since it is credit related. In a different organization, it may be preferable for this capability to fall under a Customer Verification capability or something similar. Finally, we have the order processing capability of the application. The end result of the order processing is typically fulfillment of a product or service so this would fall under the Fulfillment business capability.

CORPORATE MEMO...

Business Capabilities

Keep in mind that each and every one of these alignments that we determined in our example could vary widely between different enterprises depending on how they have their business capabilities defined. There is no solid standard on how a company should build out its business capability list because those capabilities are very individualized.

With any enterprise application, the process used to analyze its business capability alignment is identical. You can look at this as a process that starts with identifying what the enterprise application does, breaking that up into distinct functional areas, and then tying those functional areas with the business capabilities that make the most sense. In cases where the functional area could line up with multiple business capabilities, there are two options. You can align the functional area under the business capability that is closest to the function or align the function under two business capabilities. If the functional area appears to line up under more than two business capabilities, it's likely that the business capabilities are not as well defined as they should be or the functional area has not been broken down to a low enough level of granularity.

Now that we know the business capabilities that we're dealing with for our FLARP application, it's time to take the enterprise architecture analysis down a little deeper. The next step is to identify the other enterprise applications that fall under the impacted business capabilities. In most mature enterprise architecture organizations, there will already be a map that defines which enterprise applications align with each business capability. For example, after FLARP is implemented, the business capabilities identified as impacted by the implementation would have the FLARP application added to their application list. An example business capability to application mapping is shown in Figure 6.3.

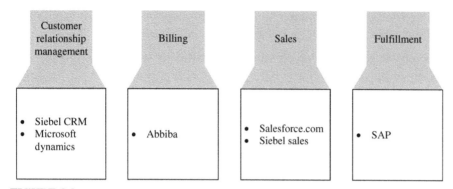

FIGURE 6.3
Applications by business capability.

As you can see in Figure 6.3, the individual impacted business capabilities have been shown along with enterprise applications that already exist within those capability areas. It is at this point that capability architects who specialize within those business capabilities can help in determining the best way to implement this new enterprise application. As each capability is examined, a determination must be made on how to align the functionality provided by the new application with the functionality provided by other applications within that capability.

In cases where the new enterprise application is providing a unique piece of functionality, the decision is simple; implement the enterprise application and consider it the source of record for data associated with that functionality. When there are overlaps between applications, this becomes more difficult and is where the enterprise architecture practice is intended to show the most value. The options available when applications overlap in functionality within a business capability are:

- Do not implement the new enterprise application in this capability due to the conflict
- Implement the new enterprise application and sunset the existing enterprise application
- Implement the new enterprise application and coexist with the existing enterprise application

There are pros and cons for each of these approaches which is why sufficient time and resources should be allocated to ensure that the appropriate level of analysis is done prior to the implementation of any enterprise application. The analysis must consider many factors including feasibility, cost (both short-term and long-term), alignment with the business roadmap, operations supportability, business impact, and others. All of these factors will influence the decisions made around the implementation of enterprise applications and their relationships with other enterprise applications.

Let's look at each option for resolving functionality conflicts starting with the option of not implementing the enterprise application within the capability where there is a conflict. If there is already an enterprise application in place that is performing this function and performing it well, the question really turns into asking why you would replace it. There may be valid reasons for this such as the new enterprise application as a whole is tightly coupled and unable to break this function out without causing the application itself to be unable to function. If that is not the case and the application is designed in a modular fashion, it could make perfect sense to leverage the existing enterprise application providing that function. In this case, the new enterprise application would need to link up its other functions with the external application through the appropriate type of interface. We'll talk about interfaces more when we discuss solution architecture later in this chapter.

Assuming that the decision is made to go ahead and implement the new enterprise application, the next decision that has to be made is whether or not to sunset or shut down the existing enterprise application providing the same functionality. There are situations where this is ideal and others where it is not. If the existing enterprise application is performing this function poorly or is old and could be made more efficient by using the new enterprise application, it may make sense to replace the old with the new. However, any replacement of an enterprise application can be very expensive due to other applications that would have to change in order to support the replacement.

As an example, if you have an existing enterprise application that has five other applications communicating with it for its functions within a capability, all five of those other applications will need to be changed to support the new enterprise application. And what if the old enterprise application falls across more business capabilities than just the one where the conflict exists? Does it make sense to modify every application across all business capability areas due to a conflict in one? It might, but the costs and benefits must be carefully analyzed in order to find out. The main thing to keep in mind with this option is that replacing a legacy enterprise application is typically quite expensive and can involve modifying a huge number of other applications and systems. It may be worth it and make perfect sense, but in the end, the value must justify the costs.

The third option is that of coexistence with both legacy and new enterprise applications. This is one of the areas where enterprise architecture practices have to be incredibly careful since their goals are to reduce costs and complexity. By allowing two enterprise applications with similar or identical functionality to coexist, they are allowing for the ongoing costs associated with both as well as increasing the overall complexity within the enterprise. Decisions like this should not be made lightly and should involve a great deal of analysis.

When two enterprise applications providing identical functions coexist, the issue of data ownership usually arises. Since they perform the same function, it's highly likely that they are working with the same types of data. So which application "owns" the data? When other applications in the enterprise need to get access to that data, which application should they communicate with? And what if they need to update data? Do they update the data in one of the applications, the other application, or both? For coexistence scenarios, these are questions that must be answered.

In most cases, one application is defined as the system of record for the data. That makes it the source of truth and identifies it as the system that all others should rely on when that data needs to be read or written. However, if two applications share the same function and need to share this data, they must be configured in such a way that the integrity of the data is maintained. In this situation, that means ensuring that the primary application is the "master" for any data used by both applications. If the "slave" application needs to update data, it must send it to the master in order to ensure that the data is updated in the correct place. This concept may be difficult to implement for some commercial enterprise applications and may require modifications to be done to the application or interfaces to be put in place to handle the data transfers.

As you can see based on our discussion of these options, making good enterprise architecture decisions is hard and requires a lot of analysis both of application technologies and benefit/cost comparisons. There are tradeoffs to each approach and many pros and cons to consider when looking at every decision. In addition, business has to move fast in order to stay competitive so all of these decisions must be made in a very short amount of time and sometimes with incomplete data. It is often the role of enterprise applications administrators to provide as much information as they possibly can about the functionality of their application to the appropriate architects in order to help make these decisions. Application expertise and enterprise application administration knowledge are very valuable at this phase of architectural analysis in order to provide the right data as a basis for decisions that have a long-term business impact to the company.

SOLUTION ARCHITECTURE

The practice of solution architecture becomes more granular than enterprise architecture and takes into account decisions made at the enterprise architecture level. After an application has been determined as a fit within the enterprise and its appropriate business capability areas defined, a determination must be made on *how* exactly to implement the enterprise application. This is where solution architecture comes into play.

To clarify, solution architecture does involve other work as it relates to implementing applications into corporate environments. In many cases, it is the recommendation of solution architects based on their analysis of business requirements that will lead to the examination of specific enterprise applications for potential fit within the company. Just like many other roles in information technology, there are many aspects to the role of solution architects and those aspects involve working with architecting solutions in two directions. One is from the project direction where business requirements are documented and the solution architect must determine how to meet those requirements. This can, naturally, involve the possibility of implementing new enterprise applications to meet those requirements. The other angle is from the implementation direction where it has been determined that a specific technology or enterprise application must be implemented and the solution architect must figure out how. It is this latter aspect of the solution architecture role that we will be focusing on as it is most applicable to enterprise applications administration.

With that in mind, we know at this point the application that needs to be implemented, the functionality that it provides, and the business capabilities that are impacted by that functionality. In addition, we know what other enterprise applications exist within those business capabilities already and may have some direction from the enterprise architecture perspective on how to handle any conflicts. For this example, let's assume that the only business capability where there is a true conflict of functionality is that of the SAP application in the Fulfillment business capability. The direction from the enterprise architecture practice within the organization is to leverage the existing SAP enterprise application and the modular design of FLARP will support this.

With organizations that have a solution architecture practice whether standalone, as a part of the enterprise architecture group, as part of a business capability silo, or as a part of a dedicated development organization, it is the function of this practice to map out how an enterprise application should be logically implemented within the corporate enterprise. To do so, the solution architect takes into account the functions of the enterprise application, the data that it needs in order to operate, where that data comes from, where it needs to go to, and any external functions that the enterprise application needs to leverage in order to meet the requirements provided by the business. With this data, the solution architect develops a map of how the new enterprise application should fit into the landscape of existing enterprise applications.

Going through this process, the solution architect first gains an understanding of what the enterprise application does and how it does it. Frequently, this will involve working closely with application developers, vendors, and enterprise applications administrators in order to gain as much information about the application as possible. The solution architect needs to know what logic the enterprise application uses when making decisions, what the inbound and outbound data is, and how the application operates at a functional level. This will guide the solution architect on how they can integrate the new enterprise application within the corporation.

Another critical component is understanding what external functions the enterprise application needs in order to work properly. We know already that it needs to integrate to SAP for order fulfillment. But what about the credit check? Does it need to contact a credit agency to perform that check and then interpret the results? Does the order data need to make it into a reporting system for analytics purposes? What if an order is canceled due to a failed credit check or the customer changes their mind? Should those orders be put into another system for future marketing purposes? Finally, does the application have all of the data it needs about the customers, services, product offerings, service areas, and everything else associated with its functionality internally, or does it need to contact other applications to get more information?

It is the practice of solution architecture which is intended to figure out the answers to all of these questions and put together a design that illustrates an overall solution to the implementation. This solution can then be analyzed and approved by the enterprise architecture practice within the company or guidance can be provided on alternative solutions that more closely align with the company's longer term business strategy. As always, the development of this or any architecture is a collaborative effort across many people with their own areas of expertise.

Figure 6.4 shows one possible solution architecture model for the FLARP application. In this architecture, the FLARP application has links to a number of additional applications in order to receive or send data. These interfaces are illustrated with the requesting system using the "open arrow" side of the line and the responding system using the "closed arrow." For example, FLARP requests information from the Credit Check service and the Credit Check service will respond with the information FLARP needs. Note that at this point the types of interfaces have not been defined nor have the individual servers or network components associated with the enterprise application. All of these aspects of the enterprise application will be defined as we go through the application and technical architecture designs.

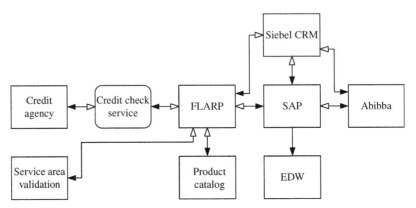

FIGURE 6.4
FLARP solution architecture.

The solution architecture shown in Figure 6.4 draws out a much more detailed view than those used at the enterprise architecture level. The focus has now moved beyond categorization and into the realm of interaction. Solution architecture is all about making sure that the appropriate enterprise applications are able to interact with each other in the best way possible in order to make efficient use of enterprise resources. This also lines up with the enterprise architecture goals of reducing costs and complexity. At the solution architecture level, the guidance provided at the enterprise architecture level begins to manifest itself into the implementation process.

In many cases, there are dozens of ways that a given enterprise application can be implemented within an enterprise, each of which has its own pros and cons. The solution architect takes a look at each approach and makes the best decisions that they can based on the functionality of existing systems, the ability of those systems to conform to the needs of the new enterprise application, the cost of system modification or interfaces, the source of record for any given data element, the requirements defined by the business, and the long-term business capability roadmaps defined by the enterprise architecture practice. In some cases, making these implementation decisions may involve consulting with experts on individual technologies or enterprise applications including other architects or enterprise applications administrators.

When the solution architecture is being defined, it's important to start thinking about how security fits into the enterprise application's architecture. In many organizations, there is a security architect who can work with the solution architect to help ensure that the overall solution complies with the enterprise's security policies and industry best practices. There is generally not a separate architecture document associated with security architecture. Instead, the results of the security architecture work are incorporated into the other architectural documents. In some organizations, the security architect will also provide a review document of some type detailing their assessment of the architecture. It's of critical importance that security be a part of every portion of an enterprise application's architectural design.

In the end, the solution architect should develop an approach similar to that shown in Figure 6.4 that can then be used as a map for building out the implementation of the enterprise application. In some cases, the solution architect may develop multiple options along with a list of pros, cons, and costs associated with each option. It then generally falls to collaboration between the business stakeholders, architects at all levels, company executives, and occasionally enterprise applications administrators to agree to implement one of the defined options. After that decision is made, all of the groups must commit to supporting it and the next two levels of architecture can be developed.

APPLICATION ARCHITECTURE

After the solution architecture design work is done, the technical aspects of designing the enterprise application's architecture can begin. This falls into two primary areas: the application architecture and the technical architecture. In some organizations, there is some confusion between these two types of architecture so, for the purposes of this text, we need to define our usage of these terms.

The application architecture is the overall design and functional flow of the various components of the enterprise application. This is not the software architecture which defines how the code within the application should be written, nor is it the technical architecture which defines the physical and logical map of the enterprise application. The application architecture includes the structure of any modules that make up the application, the flow of data across various parts of the application, and the way the various functions of the application interrelate.

In the case of FLARP, we have several impacted business capabilities as defined by the analysis done for the enterprise architecture fit for the application. As a reminder, these capabilities are:

- Sales
- Customer Relationship Management
- Billing
- Fulfillment

Each capability ties back to a function of the application. This mapping is shown in Figure 6.5.

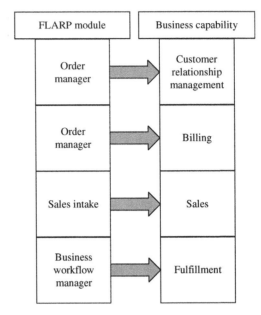

FIGURE 6.5
FLARP function to business capability mapping.

Each of these functions shown in Figure 6.5 should be able to be tied to a specific part of the enterprise application if it has a modular design. In addition, there may be additional parts of the application which provide supporting processes to allow these functions to work and integrate with either other parts of the enterprise application or other applications. Each of these modules or application components can be mapped out in relation to the other application components as part of the application architecture. An example application architecture diagram for FLARP is shown in Figure 6.6.

As you can see in Figure 6.6, the application architecture for FLARP has a number of components that make up the overall enterprise application. These components all communicate through a common communication channel according to this design and route intra-application communications through this channel. In addition, any external communication from an interface perspective routes through another dedicated module of the application. These modules would not be easily identified by just focusing on the functionality of the enterprise application itself; therefore, it is important for any enterprise applications administrator to understand the application architecture in order to support the application correctly.

The application architecture is very detailed from a technology perspective and focuses on how the enterprise application itself is designed and built. With an understanding of the application architecture, it is possible to trace

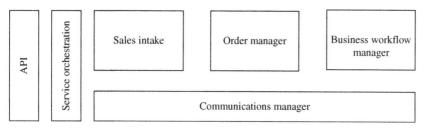

FIGURE 6.6
FLARP application architecture.

issues through the application, know how to interface the application with other applications, and know how to best leverage the functionality provided by the enterprise application. In some cases it is the enterprise applications administrator who draws out this application architecture, but it's usually the software developers and designers who create the application architecture to begin with. Regardless of the source, it is critical for any enterprise applications administrator to be able to both interpret and describe the application architecture for any application that they are responsible for.

TECHNICAL ARCHITECTURE

Technical architecture deals with the most granular level of an enterprise application's architecture. This area of architecture focuses on the individual technologies that make up the application's technology stack including network, server, integration, and database technologies. Each of these elements is identified and documented as part of the enterprise application's technical architecture.

In order to determine the application's technical architecture, we must first determine what the application's needs are at the technical and business levels. These needs are generally presented in the form of technical requirements and nonfunctional requirements. The application's technical requirements refer to the system-specific needs of the application. In the case of FLARP, let's assume that the vendor has told us that it runs on a Linux platform, requires 4 GB of RAM for every 100 users of the interactive part of the application, supports Apache as a web server, and requires an Oracle DBMS back end. These technical requirements tell us exactly what the system needs in order to operate properly.

The application's nonfunctional requirements refer to requirements around capacity, security, and availability. These requirements are generally determined by working with the business units who will be using the application, understanding what their needs are, and putting those needs together with what is possible at a technical level. There is typically some back-and-forth communication on this as cost estimates are put together around what it will take to reach specific levels of availability, etc.

In this case, a lot of the questions that come up when developing a technical architecture are already answered. For example, we already know the operating system to use and some of the supporting software required including Apache and Oracle DBMS. In addition, we already know a little information about capacity and sizing for the application. However, there is still a lot of other information that we need to determine in order to map out this application's technical architecture. As we go through each section in the remainder of this chapter, we'll discuss the requirements necessary to drive the various decisions that must be made in determining the enterprise application's technical architecture.

Servers

All enterprise applications run on servers of some type. Even if the enterprise application is cloud-based or installed on a developer's desktop, the system that it is running on is considered a server. In order to use the correct type of servers for the enterprise application as well as the correct number of servers and design, we must have a solid understanding of the application at a technical level as well as the needs of its users. This knowledge will then help us make decisions on server availability, capacity, network, integrations, and hosting.

To start, let's go over some basics of technical architecture design at the server level. In most cases, an enterprise application will have a number of different functions that it provides, many of which may be broken into individual modules. These modules may have different system requirements depending on what they do and how they work. From a technical architecture perspective, the enterprise applications administrator should understand how the application breaks up into its individual components and how each of those components works together.

FLARP has been described as a "multitier application" in this chapter, and it's in the technical architecture that this design begins to make a difference. Each layer of the application's technical architecture is considered a tier if it can be split out independently from other tier-level components. For example, if an application has a web tier, an application tier, and a database tier and they can all run independently, then it is considered a three-tier application. However, if the web tier and application tier cannot be separated and run on separate servers, then the application will have a web/app tier and a database tier. This would make it a two-tier application in technical architecture terminology.

Within a tier, various pieces of functionality can be further broken down into individual modules in many enterprise applications. For example, the web tier may have different web server instances dedicated to specific segments of the application. The application tier may have some servers dedicated to real-time calls while other servers focus on batch mode processing. These splits within a tier are considered modules or components of the enterprise application and these terms are frequently interchangeable.

With our terminology in place, we can now start discussing design in a consistent manner. Designing an enterprise application's technical architecture can be very straightforward with the appropriate level of in-house knowledge, vendor support, and experience. However, it can also be incredibly complex for larger enterprise applications serving a huge number of end users or in cases where the necessary level of support is unavailable. In the case of FLARP, let's assume that we have some in-house knowledge about the application and that the vendor is able to help provide some of the information that we need to design the technical architecture.

For FLARP, we already discussed some of the modules that exist in the application. As a reminder, these modules are identified as part of the application architecture. Looking back at Figure 6.6, the application architecture for FLARP has a number of components that make up the overall enterprise application. These components all communicate through a common communication channel according to this design and route intra-application communications through this channel. In addition, any external communication from an interface perspective routes through another dedicated module of the application.

Now we must align these individual components of the application with the application's technical architecture. We'll start by just breaking each module out onto its own server and see how that looks. This is shown in Figure 6.7.

The reality is, this technical architecture probably doesn't make sense as-is. We probably have too few of some of the servers and there may be areas where some of the modules can coexist on the same server to make more efficient use of system resources. As we go through the rest of this section, we'll start to refine this design from this baseline and flesh out the technical architecture.

Capacity

Our first focus needs to be around the enterprise application's capacity. We have some details of capacity from the vendor as indicated earlier in the chapter, but there is still a lot of work to do in this area. The vendor information stated that FLARP runs on a Linux platform, requires 4 GB of RAM for every 100 users of the interactive part of the application, supports Apache as

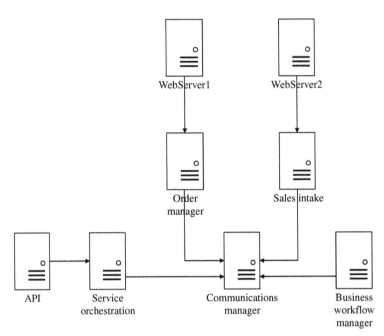

FIGURE 6.7
FLARP components.

a web server, and requires an Oracle DBMS back end. That gives us enough information to start putting together some ideas around the application's capacity after we combine it with more information about the intended use of the application.

When doing high-level capacity planning, there are several questions that you can ask in order to get the information that you need. The most common questions for capacity determination are about the intended use of the application in the short term and long term. These questions will vary somewhat depending on your corporate infrastructure, but a good guideline is given in Table 6.1.

Please keep in mind that the questionnaire given in Table 6.1 is not intended to encompass all of the details necessary to perform a full capacity planning exercise. Capacity planning is a very complex process, requires a substantial number of data points, and generally involves experts with a great deal of experience in order to generate accurate sizing values. The intent, rather, is to give you a general idea of how to start the capacity planning process and perform a rudimentary capacity planning exercise for our example application.

With that disclaimer out of the way, let's take a look at FLARP and how it will be used in our example organization. Through collaboration with the

Table 6.1 Sample Capacity Questionnaire

	Capacity	
	Initial Application Usage	**Usage in 1 Year**
Application usage		
Concurrent LAN users		
Total LAN users		
Concurrent external users		
Total external users		
Concurrent interface users		
Total interface users		
Total concurrent users		
Total overall users		
Application resources		
Application file system disk storage		
Application file system creations per hour		
Average application file system file size		
Core application CPU baseline utilization		
Core application CPU per user		
Core application memory baseline utilization		
Core application memory per user		
Core application network TPS		
Core application network TPS per user		
Core application disk baseline utilization		
Core application disk TPS per user		
Database resources		
Record reads per hour		
Record updates per hour		
Record creations per hour		
Total transactions per hour		
Average record size		

Table 6.2 FLARP Application Usage

Capacity		
	Initial Application Usage	Usage in 1 Year
Application usage		
Concurrent LAN users	100	200
Total LAN users	200	400
Concurrent external users	1000	4990
Total external users	20,000	100,000
Concurrent interface users	10	15
Total interface users	10	15
Total concurrent users	1110	5205
Total overall users	20,210	100,415

business users, you can generally get a pretty good idea of what their plans are for application usage. The application resource usage and database resource usage are more technical and will be based off of the application usage figures. Let's assume that we have the numbers for FLARP's application usage given in Table 6.2.

Let's go over these usage numbers a little bit to understand how they all work together. Any enterprise application will typically have more actual users with access to the application than concurrent users who are using the application simultaneously. This will vary depending on the type of application. In enterprise applications that have a large number of internal employees with access to the application, the total number of LAN users will be high. However, if all of these employees work in shifts or log on and off the application on an as-needed basis, the concurrent user count may be low.

The same concepts apply to external users of the application. The application may have many external users who have access that provides them with the ability to use the application, but it's very unlikely that all of those provisioned users will access the application at the same time. The percentage of the total external users that will be accessing the application simultaneously drives the value for the number of concurrent external users.

The third category in the questionnaire is around interface users. Interfaces are those connections between systems and are generally accounted for separately from interactive users. This is done in order to support the modularized design of most enterprise applications as well as in order to segregate automated system utilization versus utilization based on interactive users of the enterprise application itself. The interfaces in to and out of an application can be driven based on user behavior either within the enterprise applications or within other applications that have a connection to the application that we're analyzing, but the behavior will differ from that of normal interactive user transactions.

In business, it's always important to forecast plans, sales, and results over a long term. This term may vary, but in general, most businesses have at least a 6-month to 1-year forecast. In information technology, it is important that our systems align with the business forecasts. Therefore, when performing capacity planning, we need to understand what the business forecast is for the enterprise application in order to ensure that it will support the required capacity over time. This forecast can go as far out as 5 years but typically 1 year is the minimum forecast period for capacity planning. Based on this, we can get a better understanding of what needs to be built to support future needs.

With the application usage information in mind, let's move on to determining the data needed for the two technical areas of the questionnaire. We'll start by focusing on the application resource utilization. In this area, we need to determine how much disk, CPU, memory, and network capacity is required by the application in order to function correctly. The utilization in each category is split into a baseline as well as a per-user value. The baseline is what the application will consume when just running with no users connected. The per-user value will be multiplied by the number of concurrent users and added to that baseline to get an idea of what the "fully loaded" scenario looks like.

KEY CONCEPTS

Capacity Planning for Mathematicians

There are many brilliant scientists and engineers who, through the years, have developed complex algorithms for determining precise scaling of applications through detailed analysis of millions of individual data points. Any of these individuals will gladly tell you that the capacity planning numbers shown in this book are absolutely incorrect and will not stand up to a thorough analysis of the data. They're right. However, enterprise applications administrators must have some sort of guidelines to use when planning capacity *without* having all of the detailed data necessary to do an incredibly thorough analysis. It is the author's intent to show how to develop and use the guidelines without getting into the heavy number crunching necessary to perform a 100% accurate application utilization analysis.

Again, these methods are guidelines and are intended to help in planning out capacity for enterprise applications in general. In some cases, the addition of more users to an application does not scale resource utilization linearly. Some additional technologies such as database multiplexing may cause the application utilization to follow a wave-like pattern. Just use these suggestions as guidelines and modify them as necessary depending on the utilization patterns of the specific enterprise application that you are working with.

As previously mentioned, determining all of these values will typically require collaboration between enterprise applications administrators, subject matter experts for the application including developers in some cases, and vendor resources for any commercial application. Based on the usage numbers and intimate knowledge of the application, a general idea of the resource utilization can be derived. However, if the appropriate level of knowledge about the application is unavailable, the same information can be determined through test installations and performance testing. We'll discuss performance testing a little later in this section.

Assuming that the technical information that we need is available, we can start filling out this part of the capacity questionnaire for FLARP. The first few questions address the utilization of the application file system. Please note that this is not necessarily the disk where the application is installed nor is it intended to encompass the binary, library, and core files of the application itself! Rather, this intended to address a design principle in enterprise applications where a common file share is set up for storage of application user documents and other media. The application disk needs are addressed at the end of this section of the questionnaire.

Using the memory utilization figures given with the application details earlier in this section as well as hypothetical numbers derived by technical analysis of FLARP or the feedback of application experts, a response to the technical part of the questionnaire might look like that given in Table 6.3.

Some of the values shown in Table 6.3 are self-explanatory, but some may require a few more details. First, the application file system disk storage value starts at 0 since the enterprise application has not yet been implemented. An estimate has been given that over a year, there should be roughly 100 GB of files created within that file system. In addition, the velocity of file creations will increase as usage of the application grows. This is reflected in the increase of application file system creations per hour increasing from 10 to 50 over a 1-year duration. The average file size for these types of files is estimated to be 1 MB according to the questionnaire.

When an application is running with no users, there is a baseline value as previously mentioned. These baselines are reflected in the CPU, memory, and network questions within the questionnaire and have values of 5%, 500 MB, and 10 TPS, respectively, to start. Over time, the baseline stays the same for most of these except the network transactions per second (TPS). This value is shown to increase over the term of a year, presumably due to additional connections between systems as the system scales.

On a per-user basis, there are values for CPU, memory, and network reflected in the questionnaire. If the application scales linearly, we can use the method

Table 6.3 FLARP Application Resource Utilization

Capacity		
	Initial Application Usage	**Usage in 1 Year**
Application usage		
Concurrent LAN users	100	200
Total LAN users	200	400
Concurrent external users	1000	4990
Total external users	20,000	100,000
Concurrent interface users	10	15
Total interface users	10	15
Total concurrent users	1110	5205
Total overall users	20,210	100,415
Application resources		
Application file system disk storage	0	100 GB
Application file system creations per hour	10	50
Average application file system file size	1 MB	1 MB
Core application CPU baseline utilization	5%	5%
Core application CPU per user	1%	1%
Core application memory baseline utilization	500 MB	500 MB
Core application memory per user	41 MB	51 MB
Core application network TPS	10	30
Core application network TPS per user	10	10
Core application disk baseline utilization	300 MB	300 MB
Core application disk TPS per user	10	10

mentioned previously and multiply these values by the number of users and then add the result to the baseline for each category. For example, with 1110 users, we can calculate the processor utilization as $(1110 \times 0.01) + 0.05$. This results in 11.15 or 1115%. If the percentage is reflective of a single processor core with 100% of the processor available for user processes, then we'll need a total of $(11.15/100 = 0.1115)$ approximately 12 cores to support this user load. However, we didn't include any overhead for the operating system itself or anything else that may be running on the server, nor did we include the baseline percentage on a per-server basis. Those values will need to be added in to come up with a solid sizing value. We'll work more on this later in this section.

The same type of calculation can be done for the network TPS, but the memory utilization value needs some closer examination. Over a year term, the memory utilization on a per-user basis increases from 41 to 51 MB. This implies that the application is storing more data per user in memory as the application is used more over time. This increase will need to be accounted for as we do sizing for the application servers.

The other technical area that is listed on the questionnaire is around database utilization. The statistics necessary for very rudimentary database sizing are shown populated in Table 6.4. These figures reflect high-level numbers associated with the transactions that the application will be performing. Table 6.4 now shows all of the values associated with the resource utilization of the FLARP application.

Doing a detailed database capacity plan is a very complex exercise and requires more rigor, database-specific knowledge, and experience than general server sizing. Therefore, we will not be delving into the details on how this capacity planning is performed in this book. Instead, we will make the assumption that hardware recommended by our database administrator at Fake, Inc. will be sufficient to support the application needs and reflect those recommendations on our technical architecture diagram.

Let's focus now on determining our server sizing based on the capacity numbers that we've gathered. Since this is a multitier application, we need to determine the number of servers and the server specifications for each tier as well as for each module within the application tier. The numbers in our questionnaire give us a good idea of what will be necessary for the application tier as well as the database tier (through the recommendations of our DBA); however, there is still the web tier to figure out.

Generally, the sizing of the web tier will vary depending on the number of concurrent users, the design of the web portion of the application, any additional web server modules in use, the web server technology, and other similar factors. For the purposes of this example, we will assume that a current version of Apache is used (as listed in the FLARP application requirements) that uses no additional modules and, based on testing with other applications, will handle 200 concurrent users on a 2-processor, quad-core server with 4 GB of memory.

Using the application usage figures that we have on the questionnaire, we know that we'll start out with 1110 concurrent users and end the year with 5215 concurrent users. For the purposes of our technical architecture, let's plan on scaling to where the application will need to be after 1 year. This

Table 6.4 FLARP Database Resources

	Capacity	
	Initial Application Usage	**Usage in 1 Year**
Application usage		
Concurrent LAN users	100	200
Total LAN users	200	400
Concurrent external users	1000	4990
Total external users	20,000	100,000
Concurrent interface users	10	15
Total interface users	10	15
Total concurrent users	1110	5205
Total overall users	20,210	100,415
Application resources		
Application file system disk storage	0	100 GB
Application file system creations per hour	10	50
Average application file system file size	1 MB	1 MB
Core application CPU baseline utilization	5%	5%
Core application CPU per user	1%	1%
Core application memory baseline utilization	500 MB	500 MB
Core application memory per user	41 MB	51 MB
Core application network TPS	10	30
Core application network TPS per user	10	10
Core application disk baseline utilization	300 MB	300 MB
Core application disk TPS per user	10	10
Database resources		
Record reads per hour	500,000	2,500,000
Record updates per hour	5000	25,000
Record creations per hour	50	250
Total transactions per hour	505,050	2,525,250
Average record size	1K	1K

architecture needs to represent every tier of the application and each associ-ated server. To illustrate the process of this, we'll go through a series of itera-tions and continue to flesh out the overall technical architecture for FLARP through each iteration.

TIPS & TRICKS

Capacity Planning Over Time

The question may come up as to why you need to know the initial application usage values if you're just going to put together a technical architecture that reflects the needs of the appli-cation after a year. What if you needed to plan on a 3-year lifespan for the system hardware? You could use the growth figures between 0 and 1 years to determine the potential growth (if external factors are ignored) over 3 years. In addition, this gives you the ability to implement the enterprise application hardware in a phased manner within that first year if necessary.

Starting with the baseline technical architecture shown in Figure 6.7, let's first make some design assumptions:

- The technical architecture will not reflect interfaces with external systems at this stage
- The technical architecture will not reflect availability decisions at this stage
- Enterprise standard system configurations exist for the following system types:
    - 2-processor/2-core
    - 2-processor/4-core
    - 2-processor/4-core
    - 64-processor/4-core
- Disk and network I/O will not be in scope for this technical architecture
- 15% growth will be used as a basic "unplanned capacity usage" value

All of these assumptions would normally be validated with the business unit(s) that the application will be supporting, the corporate enterprise architecture group, the vendor, and other resources as needed. In addition, there may be other assumptions that have to be made later based on vendor recommendations or "best guess" during the architecture design. Any of these assumptions should be documented and later validated via communication with appropriate parties or testing of the application.

If we start with the diagram shown in Figure 6.7 as a baseline, the first thing to notice is that there are two primary user-facing modules of the applica-tion. These are the Order Manager and Sales Intake components. Per our original technical architecture design, we split out each component individu-ally and both of these are front ended by a web server to allow for user interaction. However, our application usage information only indicates a single value for the number of concurrent users. To move forward with this design, we'll assume that the number of users is split between the two components evenly, but this would be an assumption which would have to be validated and confirmed later.

With that in mind, let's start with the web tier for the user-facing components. We can assume that at the end of the year, we will have 2603 (5205/2) concurrent users on each system. We have web server sizing information already that indicates support of 200 concurrent users on a 2-processor, 4-core server with 4 GB of memory. Some simple division tells us that 2603 users would require 14 servers with these specifications (2603/200 = 13.015). As you can see, you always round up when doing these calculations. However, that doesn't include our 15% of unplanned capacity growth. In this case, we'll add 15% to the user count giving us a theoretical count of approximately 2994 users. Performing the same calculation tells us that we'll need 15 servers to support this user load.

Since we have multiple machine specifications available to us, we can also scale the systems up vertically (bigger machines) to reduce the number of systems. For example, if we move to 2-processor, 4-core systems, the total number of systems reduces to 8. Moving to 4-processor, 4-core systems would allow us to only build four servers. These would have to have 2, 4, and 8 GB of memory, respectively. Depending on the best fit for this environment and excluding all other factors, we can scale up to reduce hardware costs and simplify the architecture. So let's plan on using four 4-processor, 4-core systems with 8 GB of memory for the web tier associated with each of the user-interactive application components.

Now let's address the application tier for these two application components. Again, we'll go with the assumption that we have 2603 concurrent users per component. At this phase, we can do one of two things to reflect our unplanned growth assumption. We can increase the number of concurrent users when starting the calculation, or we can increase the values at the end of the calculation. The results will usually be pretty similar, so it generally comes down to personal preference if there are no other factors that will influence the calculation. We'll go with an upfront user increase in this case just to make sure we don't forget to scale up at the end. Again, that puts us at 2994 users.

For the application tier, we need to calculate CPU, memory, and disk. Let's start with the CPU calculations. We know that we have a 5% baseline for application overhead per server and, based on our early calculations, we'll definitely need multiple servers. Since we know that this will involve multiple servers, we won't use the baseline value in the simple manner previously demonstrated, but instead include it later in our calculations. For the application to support 2994 users we start by calculating the total processor usage for just the user transactions. At 1% utilization per user, we have a utilization percentage of 2994%. Roughly, that's 30-processor cores at 100% utilization per core.

Due to the operating system and application overhead, however, we don't have 100% of a core available for application users. Let's assume that the operating system consumes 10% of a server's resources and the application consumes an additional 5% as indicated on our questionnaire. This means that 15% of the CPU on any given server is consumed by nonapplication user processes. To use this in our calculations, we have to move the per-server overhead to a per-core overhead. Based on our default server specifications, this means that we have the following per-core CPU overhead:

- 2-processor, 2-core = 3.75% overhead per core
- 2-processor, 4-core = 1.88% overhead per core
- 4-processor, 4-core = 0.94% overhead per core

Obviously these are not huge numbers for this particular exercise, but as you work with larger applications, the overhead may be larger and cause a bigger impact on sizing. So to perform our sizing calculation, we must modify the value we use for the available CPU percentage depending on the server specifications that we're using. For example, instead of assuming 100% processor availability for the 2-processor, 2-core systems, we assume a 96.25% processor availability. This changes our equation to be $(2994 \times 0.01)/96.25 = 0.3111$ which rounds up to 32 cores. This will require eight servers with the selected server specification. If we used our prior calculation method without accounting for application overhead on a per-server basis, the result would have been 30 cores putting us in a position where we undersize the servers necessary to run the application.

Using the same method of calculation, we can put together the server requirements if the other server specifications are used. With 2-processor, 4-core systems, the calculation is $(2994 \times 0.01)/98.12 = 31$ cores = 4 servers. With 4-processor, 4-core systems, we use $(2994 \times 0.01)/99.06 = 31$ cores = 2 servers.

Just to further illustrate how this works; let's change the numbers a little. If our application used 5% of the CPU for each user and required 20% of the CPU per server for overhead (15% for application and 5% for operating system), we'd end up with 95% of each core available for user sessions on a 2-processor, 2-core server. To support 10,000 users, we would require $(10,000 \times 0.05)/95 = 527$ cores = 132 servers to support the load. Our original calculation of $(10,000 \times 0.05) + 0.15$ would yield a result of 501 cores or 126 servers. This small change in the way that capacity is calculated has a large impact on the designed technical architecture and can lead to disastrous results with large-scale enterprise applications.

Let's move on to our memory calculations. Based on what we know about the application through the questionnaire, we have a 500 MB baseline memory utilization for the application and an additional 51 MB used per-user at the 1-year point for the application. Similar to the CPU calculations, the memory baseline has to be added on a per-server basis. We know that depending on the server specifications that we use, we will have eight, four, or two servers. With our user count of 2994 (with unplanned growth included), we need a total of $(51 \times 2994 = 152{,}695$ MB$/1024 = 150$ GB) 150 GB of memory to support the concurrent users. Split across servers, i.e., 19, 38, or 75 GB of memory per-server required for the concurrent user load. Add in another 500 MB (rounded up to 1 GB) per-server and you have 20, 39, and 76 GB, respectively. These values would also need to be increased on a per-server basis to include any additional memory utilized by other applications running on the server. With that in mind, we could probably plan around 24, 48, and 92 GB, respectively.

Based on these values, we would be looking at the grid of server specifications shown in Table 6.5.

Table 6.5 FLARP Application Server Options		
Server Specification	**# of Servers**	**Amount of RAM (GB)**
2-proc, 2-core	8	24
2-proc, 4-core	4	48
4-proc, 4-core	2	92

Based on server costs, enterprise standards for server specifications, and other factors, let's assume the best option is the 2-processor, 4-core system with 48 GB of memory. With this specification, we'll need four servers for each application component. Again, this excludes any availability considerations or other important factors. We can now reflect this on our technical architecture diagram.

KEY CONCEPTS

What About Disk?
You'll notice that we have not specified the disk values for these systems yet. Disk values can be determined using the same calculations that we used for CPU and memory. It will be left as an exercise for the reader to determine these values based on the information provided in the questionnaire and the server information determined by the other value calculations. With this in mind, disk values will be left off of the technical architecture diagrams though they would normally be included when the enterprise applications administrator is generating this documentation.

The remaining items from our baseline technical architecture diagram that need to be determined are the database server specifications, communications manager, business workflow manager, and service orchestrator module servers, and the web server front-ending the service orchestrator module. We already know that we have a recommendation from our database administrator for the database server. Let's assume that the recommendation we received was for an IBM server running AIX with 64 processors containing four cores each and 128 GB of memory. For the remaining servers, let's also assume that we have recommendations from the vendor for FLARP. The overall server specifications for our enterprise application are shown in Table 6.6.

Table 6.6 FLARP Server Specifications				
Server Purpose	# of Servers	Server Processors	Processor Cores	Server Memory (GB)
Order Manager Web Server	4	4	4	8
Order Manager App Server	4	2	4	48
Sales Intake Web Server	4	4	4	8
Sales Intake App Server	4	2	4	48
Communications Manager Server	2	4	4	8
Service Orchestration Web Server	1	2	2	4
Service Orchestration App Server	1	2	2	4
Business Workflow Server	1	2	2	4
Database Server	1	64	4	128

Now, let's update our technical architecture diagram with this information. We'll need to reflect the number of servers as well as include the server specifications within the diagram. This can be seen in Figure 6.8.

With the updates shown in Figure 6.8, our technical architecture is beginning to become more reflective of the environment needs for FLARP. As we continue through this section, we'll update the technical architecture diagram to reflect each additional technical area.

Performance Testing
One of the more crucial aspects of developing a solid plan around enterprise application capacity is performance testing. Performance testing involves

simulating a large number of transactions against an enterprise application in order to better understand how the application will perform under load. The goal here is to have solid metrics about application performance prior to the application being subjected to actual user load. In many cases, performance testing is performed prior to the initial implementation of the enterprise application and at various stages of its lifecycle such as when a patch is implemented or an update performed.

Performance Test There are different types of performance testing that can be done. The first is a true performance test that simulates the expected type and number of transactions that the application will be expected to process

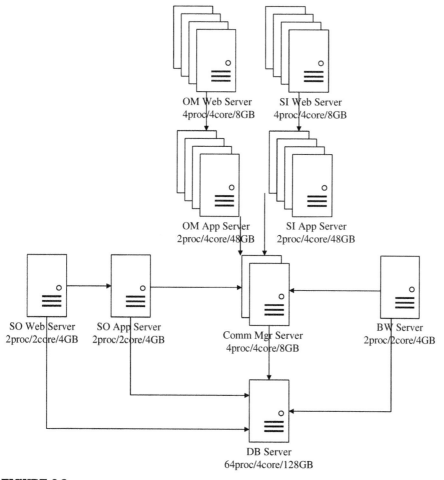

FIGURE 6.8
FLARP technical architecture diagram.

either at normal operating levels or at peak. The transactions in a good performance test will be modeled after actual user behavior and will vary in transaction speed and wait times to mimic what would happen in the real world. Some of the important factors that go into building out a performance test of this type are:

- "Happy path" workflow of the users as they use the application (transaction sequence used when everything works perfectly)
- "Realistic" workflow of the users as they use the application (transaction sequence that involves errors, rework, backing up in the flow, etc.)
- Number of concurrent users
- Typical rate of login/logout
- Average wait times between transactions within a workflow
- Percentage of users with different application access levels

There are other factors that go into a performance testing plan, but these are some of the more important ones to keep in mind to make sure that the test adequately models the usage of the application. The results of the performance test are metrics that tell you how fast transactions process under load, how stable the application is, and whether or not it performs as expected under those conditions. Performance tests can also be used to help establish baselines.

Load Test A second type of performance testing is load testing. In this type of test, a simulated load is again put against the application, but with slightly different goals. Whereas in a standard performance test, you're looking to understand how the application works when under load, in a load test you are putting that full load against the application with the intent of understanding whether or not the application is able to meet the requirements of the business users that it will be supporting. In many organizations, service level agreements (SLAs) are in place that define how fast the enterprise application should respond and how it should perform under normal use. The load test is used to validate that the application can indeed live up to those expectations.

Another type of load test is an endurance test. The load used for an endurance test is typically identical to a normal load test, but the duration changes. In a load test, the test is run for a small specified duration (usually just a few hours) to make sure that the application meets its goals. With an endurance test, the duration is extended sometimes into days or weeks to determine if the application can handle that load in a sustained manner. This can help to determine if certain parts of the application are prone to failure over time due to issues such as memory leaks or if there are areas that need improvement to handle sustained load.

Capacity Test A load test can help to ensure that an application can meet its goals, but a capacity test is used to determine what capacity the application can handle while still meeting those same goals. For example, let's assume the application is supposed to handle 5000 concurrent users with a response time of 50 ms after a piece of data is submitted. With the load testing results, we may have been able to confirm that the application was able to successfully respond within 40 ms when 5000 concurrent users are simulated against it. With a capacity test, we would increase this to 5500, 6000, 7000, etc. and watch to see when the response time goes over 50 ms. When that happens, we have a value that indicates the amount of load that the application can handle while still meeting its SLA goals.

Stress Test A stress test is a type of performance test that is used to see exactly what the application can handle. Whereas the other performance test types that we've discussed focus on what the application is expected to handle, a stress test is used to determine what levels of load the application can handle in a worst case scenario. In other words, what does it take to make the application either break or perform so poorly that it is no longer usable? A stress test will typically continue to increase the load on the application up to and beyond the point that it is no longer able to function.

Different companies implement their performance testing processes in different ways, but most find a great amount of value in executing these types of performance tests against their enterprise applications. A large number of tools are available in the marketplace to simulate user transactions and application loads. These tools may be as simple as a scripted process that keeps sending the same HTTP request to the application over and over or as complex as a tool that simulates button clicks, field changes, and other user interface functions. Choosing the right types of performance testing to execute and the appropriate tools is very important to ensuring the long-term stability of an enterprise application.

Virtualization

We touched briefly on the concept of virtualization in Chapter 3. Now it's time to go into more depth on virtualization and how it affects technical architecture. Virtualization is the concept of creating segmented virtual resources out of a larger physical resource. This very high-level definition is important as virtualization can play a role with almost any physical resource including disk, network, server, memory, or processor resources. In the interest of simplicity, we're going to focus on the concept of virtualization at the server level and discuss how this architecture works and how it applies to enterprise applications.

Server virtualization involves taking a physical server, installing a hypervisor known as the host machine, and then creating virtual machines known as guest machines. There are two types of hypervisors, Type I and Type II. A Type I hypervisor, also known as a bare metal hypervisor, is installed directly on the physical hardware of a server as an operating system and is the first layer on top of that hardware. A Type II hypervisor, also known as a hosted hypervisor, is installed within another operating system running on a server. In this scenario, the server's operating system is the first layer, and the hosted hypervisor is the second layer on top of the hardware. Once the hypervisor is installed, guest machines will then be created on top of the hypervisor. The guest machine will be on the second layer above the hardware in a bare metal hypervisor implementation. Alternatively, the guest machine will be on the third layer with a hosted hypervisor.

A number of different options exist in the marketplace for hypervisors. Some Type I hypervisors would include VMWare ESXi/vSphere, Citrix XenServer, KVM, and Microsoft Hyper-V. Some Type II hypervisors would include Parallels, Virtual Machine Manager, VMWare Player/Workstation, and VirtualBox. These hypervisors run directly on the server's physical hardware or on top of a host operating system depending on the hypervisor type and provide an interface that allows the administrator to build out the virtual machine infrastructure. This infrastructure can include virtual networks as well as virtual servers.

The hierarchy of a virtualized server starts at the physical server, moves into the hypervisor, and then into various virtual servers within that hypervisor. Figure 6.9 shows how this virtual architecture looks when visualized.

As you can see in Figure 6.9, each virtual machine has its own allocated set of processors, memory, network cards, and disk. From the virtual machine perspective, these hardware resources are fully "owned" by the virtual machine operating system and free to use as it sees fit. In reality, the resources are allocated on an as-needed basis by the hypervisor and shared across all virtual machines that are being run within the context of the hypervisor.

While some hypervisors allow you to dedicate specific processors, memory, or other resources directly to a specific virtual machine, the largest gains in resource utilization are typically found by sharing resources on an as-needed basis across many virtual machines. This takes advantage of the fact that in most cases all of the virtual machines will not be 100% utilized all of the time. Those gaps where the virtual machine is not using parts of hardware resources allows those same resources to be allocated to other virtual machines to run their processes. This allows you

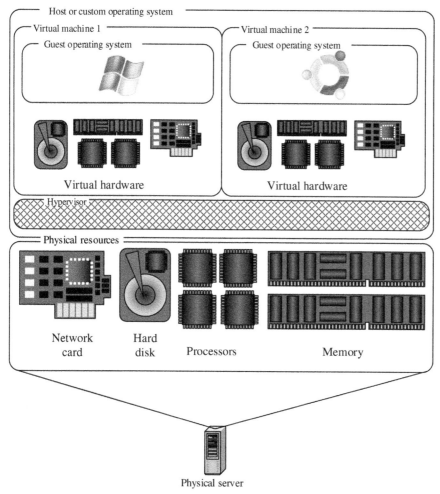

FIGURE 6.9
Virtual server architecture.

to host a larger number of virtual machines on physical hardware than would otherwise be possible without the use of virtualization technologies.

In the past, virtualization was isolated to the realm of development and testing environments. However, over the years as virtualization technologies have improved, more and more companies are finding benefits in using virtualization within their production environments. There are many benefits to virtualization including reduced cost, reduced maintenance work, reduced energy consumption, more efficient use of resources, etc. These benefits have helped drive the tremendous growth of virtualization over the last several years and will continue to drive its growth over time.

There are, naturally, some downsides to using virtualization as well. Any time that you have additional software running on a physical machine, that software consumes some resources as overhead. This is the case for the hypervisors as well. When a hypervisor is in use, some percentage of machine resources are in use just to operate the hypervisor and are therefore unavailable to the virtual machines running under the hypervisor. Also, since system resources are shared, it may happen that processor time is not available when a virtual machine needs it if another virtual machine is already consuming that resource. This is one of the detriments that always exists when sharing a finite amount of resources and takes some planning and consideration to compensate for.

The management of virtual machines does take some skill and expertise especially in larger virtualized environments. Many organizations find that they do not necessarily have staff with the required skills in house and must either train employees on virtualization technologies, hire the appropriately skilled personnel, or contract out the work. This has led to further specialization within information technology where experts on specific virtualization technologies gain certifications on that technology and provide their knowledge and expertise to companies seeking to gain the benefits associated with virtualization.

TIPS & TRICKS

Virtualization Versus "Cloud"

One of the most predominant topics in information technology as of the time of this writing is cloud computing. It is important to clarify the difference between virtualization and cloud computing in order to clearly discuss these two topics. Virtualization is the segmentation of physical resources into smaller virtual resources. Cloud computing, which we'll discuss in detail later, focuses on a complete abstraction between backend infrastructure resources and operating system/application resources. Virtualization is one of the technologies used to allow for this abstraction, but the technologies and concepts behind cloud computing become more complex based on its goals. So to keep it simple, virtualization is the segmentation and virtualization of physical resources into virtual resources while cloud computing is the concept of abstracting physical infrastructure completely from operating systems and applications using virtualization as one of the methods of accomplishing this abstraction.

Let's go back to the technical architecture for FLARP and see if virtualization technologies can apply to this situation. If we take a look at the Service Orchestration web server and application server, we can see that they're pretty small servers compared to the others. Considering that they will be communicating directly with each other a substantial amount, that communication speed could probably be increased by putting them on the same physical host. In addition, it's likely that their resource utilization will probably be sequential in that a call first gets made to the web server consuming web server resources which subsequently calls the application server and utilizes application server resources. These factors make the use of virtualization technologies a good fit for this part of our enterprise application and is reflected in the diagram shown in Figure 6.10.

Some of the other areas to consider virtualization are in the web server layers and application server layers of the FLARP application tiers. However, based on the sizing that has to be done for these tiers, virtualization may not be a good fit unless the physical hosts are very large. In an environment where large physical hosts are available for hosting virtual machines (which is

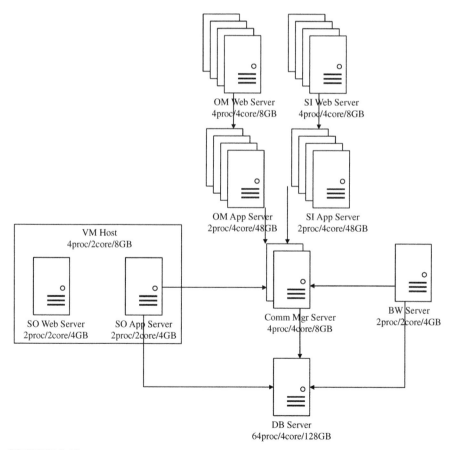

FIGURE 6.10
FLARP technical architecture with virtualization.

becoming more common), this may be a viable option. However, let's assume that we're just using virtualization for the Service Orchestration component of the application at this time.

Availability

A very critical aspect of any enterprise application is its availability. We discussed this in Chapter 5 as it relates to security and overall data availability. Now it's time to focus on availability as an architecture concept. When looking at the technical architecture of any enterprise application, you should always keep an eye out for areas of focus around availability of systems that comprise the enterprise application, its dependencies, and any potential architectural issues that could reduce application availability.

For this discussion, we're going to break up the overall concept of availability into three primary areas. These will be fault tolerance, high availability, and disaster recovery. Each of these looks at enterprise application availability from a slightly different perspective. To ensure the highest level of enterprise application availability, all three availability areas will need to be addressed, however, not all enterprise applications need that level of availability. In addition, each availability area also has varying levels of availability within it depending on the options used.

From an enterprise applications administration perspective, it is important to understand the availability needs of the application based on the requirements of the business users. Every increase in application availability comes with a price tag, and the higher the availability level, the higher the cost. For some enterprise applications, there is a true need for an incredibly high level of availability. As an example, consider an application that provides mapping and routing information to ambulance drivers. This is an application that would have tremendous negative consequences if it fails. On the other hand, consider an application that does reporting of sales information. While inconvenient, it's probably not life threatening if the application is down for a few hours. Tough decisions have to be made when weighing out the benefit of increasing levels of availability versus the cost to ensure those availability levels.

Availability is typically measured on a percentage basis and is a cumulative roll-up of the availability for every system and dependency that make up the overall enterprise application. In many cases, the availability is referred to as the number of 9s that exist in the percentage. For example, 90% availability is "one 9" whereas 99.99% availability is "four 9s." The percentage is derived based on the number of hours in a day, week, month, or year. The chart in Table 6.7 shows some sample availability percentages and their associated downtimes.

Table 6.7 Availability Percentage Chart

Availability (%)	Annual Downtime	Weekly Downtime
90.00000	36.5 days	16.8 h
95.00000	18.25 days	8.4 h
99.00000	3.65 days	1.68 h
99.90000	8.76 h	10.1 min
99.99000	52.56 min	1.01 min
99.99900	5.26 min	6.05 s
99.99990	31.5 s	0.605 s
99.99999	3.15 s	0.0605 s

Most service level agreements do make allowances for scheduled maintenance downtimes and these do not affect the application's availability figures. In many cases, downtime is split between planned and unplanned downtime. Unplanned downtime is considered a hit against the application's availability whereas planned downtime is a maintenance event. This varies depending on the organization and the needs of the application users. Also, there are some SLAs that have different levels of service based on business hours vs. nonbusiness hours. Finally, there are some SLAs that focus on the level of availability during a specific timeframe. For example, some vendors consider the overall hosted system "available" even if only 80% of it is working normally. It's very important to carefully read and understand the terms of any SLA if you are relying on services provided by another party.

CORPORATE MEMO...

Enterprise Application Maintenance

Depending on the availability requirements for the application, there are occasions where planned downtimes are minimized as well and the application's technical architecture is built in such a way that the application never has to be completely down even when maintenance is being performed. This is one of the most expensive levels of availability to implement, but is a valid requirement for some enterprise applications.

Fault Tolerance

The first of the three areas of availability that we'll discuss is fault tolerance. Fault tolerance is a system's ability to handle hardware faults without causing a full system failure. This is done through the use of redundant systems or components as well as specific fault-tolerance technologies. The use of fault tolerance at a system level allows for the reality that any physical component will eventually fail. Age, wear, manufacturing defects, or simple random events can all cause failures and building fault-tolerant systems reduces the impact of these failures.

Looking at the primary components of a server, fault tolerance typically takes a view of which components are most complex or most likely to fail and then increases their redundancy by adding one or more identical components. For example, a server may have multiple processors, memory modules, power supplies, disks, fans, or other components. By having more than one of these components, the server can be built to handle failures of individual components.

Just because a server has multiple components of a specific type does not automatically make it fault tolerant. With no further configuration, a server with multiple processors will probably crash if one of the processors fail. Additional configuration in the form of fault-tolerant operating systems, hypervisors, or other technologies is required in order to ensure that the system can handle the failure of a component gracefully. In addition, the system must know what to do if the component fails. Should it just keep working? Or should it set off an alarm and email an alert to someone? In most cases, fault-tolerant systems have the ability to use notifications to alert an administrator to the component failure.

Along with redundant components to handle failures, another part of fault tolerance is the ability to replace components without taking the system down. This is known as a "hot swap" capability implying that the component replacement can occur while the system is "hot" or powered on and running. Different systems support different levels of hot swap capability. Some will allow for hot swapping of disks or power supplies, but nothing else. In others, you can replace practically every component (one at a time) while the system is up and running.

One additional thing to keep in mind about fault tolerance is that even if the server supports fault tolerance, the operating systems or applications running on it may not. For example, a server may support hot swapping of a processor, but the operating system may not recognize the newly available processing resources without a restart. This varies based on the manufacturer and design of each server as well as its operating system. It's important to understand the fault-tolerance capabilities of the servers that you're working with in order to correctly understand the availability of the server and thereby meet your enterprise application's availability goals.

High Availability

While fault tolerance focuses on a server or device's ability to cleanly handle hardware faults, the concept of high-availability applies more to the overall system and application tiers of the architecture. Technically, a fault-tolerant system can be "highly available," but there is a need to separate fault-tolerant systems from architectures that are also fault tolerant. From a terminology perspective, therefore, we refer to internal server or device fault tolerance as "fault tolerance" and system or application-wide fault tolerance as "high availability."

High availability is achieved by taking the same concepts used for fault tolerance and moving them up a level. Where you would have multiple identical components for fault tolerance, you would have multiple identical servers for high availability. The idea with high availability is to reduce architectural failure points within the enterprise application. Any point of failure in the application should be examined and a determination made on whether or not a potential failure at that point would cause the entire application to fail or just a part of it. From there it needs to be determined if that failure would be acceptable from an availability perspective or if it makes sense to put money towards eliminating the failure point if possible.

Mitigation of failure points at the application level can be done through the use of redundant systems or clustering. Redundant systems simply means that multiple devices are performing the same function. It's important to use the clarifying term of "devices" here as redundant systems can involve servers, network equipment, electrical lines, etc. By having a sufficient number of systems performing the same function with sufficient capacity on each, failures can typically be handled more smoothly than if the application relied on a single system.

Two important factors to keep in mind as you look at redundant systems are capacity and capability. If the technical architecture for the enterprise application has implemented redundant systems, but the systems are fully utilized to handle user traffic, then the failure of one of the systems would still cause an outage. Sufficient capacity above and beyond the ongoing needs of the application must be allocated in order for redundant systems to contribute to the application's availability. This is normally known as an "$N + x$" architecture, where "N" is the number of systems needed to handle normal capacity and "x" are the number of additional systems in place to provide for availability in the case of failure. For example an "$N + 1$" architecture is one where the application has sufficient systems to handle normal concurrent load plus one extra system.

The second factor is capability. Not all enterprise applications have an application architecture that supports redundant systems. In cases where session state is only available on the server where a user is connected, the user's session could be lost if the system went down. In addition, some applications or some components of them cannot support being run on multiple systems simultaneously. It's important to understand the application architecture and its relation to redundant systems when planning out the availability aspect of your application's technical architecture.

In the case of the FLARP application, we already have redundant systems in a few areas including both the web and the application tiers. Based on capacity, however, our redundancy does not contribute to our availability. Capacity-based redundancy will help handle the load, but will not help the application to stay up in the event of a system's failure. Let's go ahead and plan on using an $N + 1$ level of system redundancy in order to meet the availability requirements of our business users. To do this, we'll add an extra server to each stack in the web and application tier throughout the application.

What about the database? There are a couple of options for increasing database availability. We can use replication where a copy of the database is made and kept constantly up to date or we can use clustering. Clustering is similar to system redundancy, but can work in places where the application architecture does not support redundant systems. For example, if an application component cannot be duplicated due to the application architecture, it becomes a single point of failure. This can be mitigated by clustering the application component instead of just duplicating it.

There are two different kinds of clustering: active–passive and active–active. Active–passive clustering means that there are one or more "spare" systems within the cluster that are available in the event that the primary system fails. These spare systems are therefore considered the "secondary" node within the cluster. Active–passive clusters are used when there can only be one instance of the clustered component running at any given time.

In cases where the application component does not natively support running on redundant systems but has the ability to function with multiple instances running, active–active clustering may be an option. Active–active clustering makes more effective use of system resources because all nodes within the cluster are up and available at the same time. This allows for the capacity of the component to be increased since it is running on multiple systems. As with redundant systems, active–active cluster nodes are referred to as $N + x$ depending on the number of nodes available within the cluster and their capacity.

Disaster Recovery

We talked about disaster recovery in Chapter 5 when we discussed the availability component of enterprise application security. It is important to recognize that this is an important aspect of an application's technical architecture as well. While typically not called out directly on the technical architecture diagram, it is important to plan around disaster recovery when determining your technical architecture strategy. In many cases, a disaster recovery environment can be used for performance testing or other purposes and will therefore be part of your overall technical architecture even if it's not included explicitly on the Production technical architecture diagram.

Most disaster recovery environments are architected either as an exact duplicate of the Production environment or a scaled down version. In either case, the same technical architecture will apply but the number of systems may differ. Therefore, you should always keep in mind that modifying the technical architecture of the Production environment will typically require an identical modification to the disaster recovery environment as well.

Business Continuity

Business continuity is a topic that is very closely related to disaster recovery. From the technical perspective, we generally put most of our focus into our information systems and how we will recover them in the event of a disaster. However, from the business perspective, business can't stop just because the information systems are not available. Most large organizations also make business continuity plans that define how the business will keep running in the event that information systems are unavailable. These plans may include the use of paper-based systems, manual processes, and other nontechnical solutions. In addition, good business continuity plans also include details on how the business will transition back to the information systems when they're available again. This may include recording paper-based transactions electronically and other means of getting the data generated during the outage back into the enterprise applications.

Network

Next, we'll consider the networking aspect of the technical architecture. We discussed networking hardware at length in Chapter 2 but now it's time to talk about how that networking hardware fits into the technical architecture for our enterprise application. Keep in mind that network design is a very complex topic and requires many years of experience to master. Consequently, we'll assume that the primary work of designing the network and networking standards for the company has already been done. From the enterprise applications administrator perspective, we'll focus on how to apply those designs to our technical architecture and reflect them on the technical architecture diagram.

With our enterprise application, we already know that there will be a number of servers communicating with each other. We also know that there will be external users accessing FLARP via web servers. There will also be connections to other systems based on our solution architecture diagram. While we have not discussed interfaces yet and how they work, we can still reflect the network connectivity between our FLARP application and other applications that it must communicate with.

Let's start by looking at our application and its tiered architecture. A demilitarized zone (DMZ) is often used as part of an enterprise application's technical architecture in order to improve the overall security of the application. In the case of FLARP, we do have externally facing web servers and it is appropriate to implement those within a DMZ. Many corporate DMZs are designed to reflect application tiers and have a series of firewalls that protect each layer of the application. This architectural design is shown in Figure 6.11.

Along with the implementation of the correct network hardware to support the security aspect of the architecture, we also need to examine the hardware necessary to support the general functionality of the enterprise application. In our technical design so far, we have a number of web servers working together to support the required capacity and redundancy. To route traffic to all of these servers, we could use a technique such as DNS round robin or we could put a more fully featured solution in place such as a load balancer. For the purposes of this enterprise application, a load balancer would probably

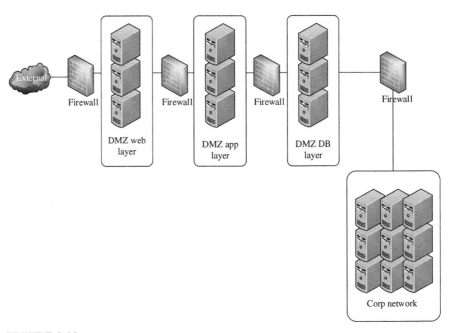

FIGURE 6.11
Standard enterprise network security architecture.

be the appropriate solution and we'll reflect that on our technical architecture diagram.

To summarize, at this point we'll need to show the various security zones used for the enterprise application, the firewalls in place to provide protection, and the load balancers that distribute connections between servers. To correctly identify each system on the architecture, we'll also need to show its server name and IP address. This will help any groups utilizing the technical architecture document to understand the identity of the servers associated with the enterprise application. The architecture with these additional components is shown in Figure 6.12. Please note that some network connections have been simplified to reduce the "noise" level of the diagram.

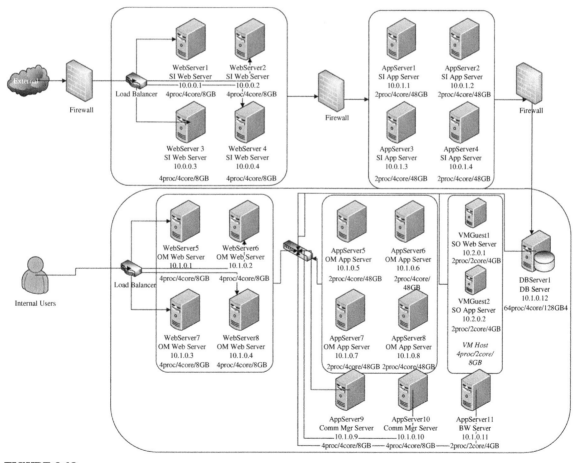

FIGURE 6.12
FLARP technical architecture with networking.

Integrations

Integration between multiple enterprise applications is a very complex topic. Over time, real-time application integration has morphed from a tightly coupled interface pair where each application is explicitly programmed to communicate with each other to more loosely coupled service-oriented architecture (SOA) and then to a resource-oriented architecture (ROA). In addition, batch interfaces, where large amounts of data are transmitted as a single scheduled transfer, have changed over time as well. In this section, we're going to briefly touch on some of the more common types of integrations and integration architectures without going into depth on how the architectural concepts work on the back end.

Real-Time Interfaces

Real-time interfaces are designed to transfer data on an as-needed basis. When an application needs to either send or request data immediately, a real-time interface is used. As previously mentioned, the architecture used for these real-time interfaces has changed a lot over the years and it will continue to evolve over time. Two of the more popular interface architectures currently in use are SOA and ROA.

With SOA, interfaces are designed in such a way that they support specific distinct services. For example, a service might be created to retrieve a customer's account information. An entirely separate service would be created to associate new products with that account. SOA is based on the concept of taking each type of interaction and exposing it as a unique service. These services are then tied together through the use of orchestration. Whereas a service performs a distinct function, orchestration calls multiple services in the correct manner to accomplish a specific business function.

ROA instead focuses on specific objects such as accounts as a data object or state transactions. The concept with ROA is to expose each resource in a reusable manner and allow the consumer of that resource to consume it via a consistent interface. There are some obvious similarities between SOA and ROA, but there are many differences as well. Each architecture has its benefits and detriments and the discussion of these typically turns into a religious debate between interface architects. Generally the best approach is to choose the architecture that best fits in any given situation after carefully considering all factors.

Along with the architecture comes the communication method. Most SOA architectures use a number of standards developed for web services known as the WS-* standards. This naming comes from the standard convention used for many of these services such as WS-Security, WS-Policy, and WS-Discovery. The standards for web services associated with the SOA architecture come from a number of different organizations and cover a wide range of topics associated with how various services should operate. Standards such as Simple Object Access Protocol (SOAP), Web Services Description Language (WSDL), and Universal Description, Discovery, and Integration (UDDI) are also associated with SOA architectures.

For ROA, the most common standard is that of Representational State Transfer (REST). REST is basically architectural principles applied as a standard for real-time interfaces. It's based on some of the foundational principles used for most web-based communications and is easier to use and faster to implement than the highly rigid and structured standards associated with SOA. REST is designed to support the resource based architecture concept through an understanding of data objects and utilizing those objects through simple commands, such as GET or PUT.

As we look at real-time interfaces from an enterprise application perspective, they are responsible for any of the immediate movement of data that the enterprise application needs. These needs are expressed through the use of interface calls and allow the enterprise application to appropriately communicate with any of its dependency systems.

The servers used for this communication are typically reflected on a technical architecture diagram by the server that the application is actually communicating with. This differs from the solution architecture where the path between enterprise applications is shown as lines between the applications themselves. With some real-time interfaces, a broker or messaging bus may be used to consolidate traffic between different applications, provide orchestration, or even provide an extra layer of security. On the technical architecture diagram, these connections must be called out so that the appropriate connections can be made between systems. This illustration would cause our technical architecture diagram to be difficult to read in print, so consider the additional connections as additional servers and reflect them in this manner on your own diagrams with an appropriate level of detail.

Batch Integrations

Batch integrations are used when real-time interfaces are unnecessary or unwanted. In some cases, it makes sense to do a large load of data at a specific time rather than making a large number of calls against a real-time interface. Batch integrations are also used frequently when data has to be transformed and moved at specific times due to dependencies on other systems or processing times for the data.

When working with enterprise applications, it's critical to know what batch integrations exist within the system, when the batch jobs initiate, and when they're expected to terminate. One of the more common issues that enterprise applications administrators have to deal with is the failure of batch jobs to run as expected or performance problems that occur when the batch job runs during normal working hours causing performance degradation across the application.

One of the most common types of batch integrations is an Extract, Transform, and Load (ETL) process. An ETL process takes data from a source system (extract), modifies it in the appropriate manner depending on the integration needs (transform), and then inserts the data into the destination system (load). This process is frequently used for loading data warehouses or supplying a data mart with the appropriate source data.

CLOUD-BASED ARCHITECTURE

Cloud-based architecture is an emerging trend in the information technology field and is beginning to be adopted for more and more enterprise applications. The concept of cloud-based architecture is to abstract the infrastructure component of running applications from the operating system or application. The focus moves away from ensuring that you have enough hardware in place or have sized it perfectly and into making sure that the enterprise application is running correctly and operating as expected.

All cloud-based architectures take advantage of some form of virtualization as mentioned previously in this chapter, but cloud-based architecture and virtualization are still two separate concepts. Most cloud-based architectures focus on a specific service or set of services that they offer to customers and build their infrastructure and management systems in such a way that they are transparent to the customer. For example, the customer should just be able to deploy a Java application in a Platform as a Service (PaaS) offering without concern as to the backend operating system, server, or network design. In the eyes of the customer, it should "just work."

There are benefits and detriments to using cloud-based architecture. In some cases, the cost of using cloud-based services is more expensive than running the equivalent hardware and software within your own data centers, but that can also be offset with reduced maintenance costs associated with some of the cloud-based service offerings. Another area to look at when considering cloud-based architecture is maintenance. With some cloud-based service offerings, a degree of maintenance of hardware and other components is included within the service cost. This does vary depending on the type of service however. For example, in a PaaS service offering, maintenance of the development platform, operating system, and hardware is included, but in an Infrastructure as a Service (IaaS) offering, the client is responsible for maintenance of their own operating system and development platform.

One huge advantage of many cloud-based service offerings is the ease and automation of provisioning systems. In addition, scaling the cloud-based service up or down to handle load on an as-needed basis is typically much easier. These ease-of-use scenarios are very appealing to business users who are more familiar with the long turnaround times for getting systems or services provisioned through traditional information technology departments.

A big area of concern with cloud-based architectures is the same that exists for virtualization, but on a larger scale. As with virtualization, cloud-based services share hardware resources across multiple customers. This sharing is subject to the same usage spikes that would be seen in any other traditional system utilization scenario. Consequently, a usage spike from one customer can affect the service performance for another.

With all of these factors in mind, application design has to change to accommodate the concepts associated with cloud-based architecture. For example, the potential latency inherent in a shared environment should be accounted for in the application's interface architecture. The ability to scale up or down automatically can be built into the application design to facilitate easier capacity management. Applications have to be designed to be hardware, operating system, or platform agnostic in order to be mobile between different cloud-based service providers.

The topic of cloud-based architecture is huge and growing all the time as this capability evolves. For the remainder of this section, we'll discuss some of the more common cloud-based service offerings and what they mean. As a collective group, cloud-based services are typically referred to as "XaaS" or "Something as a Service" offerings. The X defines the specific service being offered and implies what that particular service is supposed to help the customer accomplish.

Software as a Service

Software as a Service (SaaS) is the concept of a full cloud-based enterprise application. The customer of the cloud service provider simply has to subscribe and use the application. In some cases, the cloud service provider will allow for interfaces into and out of the application but in others, the application is completely stand alone. When using a SaaS solution, the cloud service provider is responsible for ensuring that the service meets the SLAs defined in their contract with the customer and the work that they do to meet those SLAs is transparent to the customer. The cloud service provider may have to add hardware, change operating system versions, or patch the application as needed and the customer will typically not be aware of the change if all works as planned.

Data Analytics as a Service

Data Analytics as a Service (DAaaS) moves the realm of "big data" analytics into a cloud-based service. With a DAaaS offering, the cloud service provider puts into place the appropriate infrastructure and software to perform analytical analysis of large collections of data. With this service, the customer simply transports the data to the cloud service provider in a supported manner, defines the type of analysis that they need to have done, and the cloud service provider does the necessary data analysis. This is very similar to a SaaS offering, but is specifically targeted for big data analytics.

Storage as a Service

In some cases, all a cloud customer needs is a place to put their data. This need may include transferring the data to another party, making it available to a cloud-based application, or simply providing an off-site location to backup important information. Cloud providers offer Storage as a Service (STaaS) to support this need. STaaS is effectively a cloud-based disk that can be used by your enterprise application. In some cases, there is native integration to the cloud provider available, but in other cases some sort of data copy process must be used. Depending on how the cloud provider offers the service, the consumer may have the ability to choose how much space they are limited to, where the data is stored, and how (or if) the data is backed up.

Platform as a Service

If you look at cloud service offerings as a hierarchy, SaaS, DAaaS, and STaaS are at the top of the list with the highest cost investment for the customer and the least amount of work necessary for maintenance. As you go down that hierarchy, the service costs may reduce, but more work is left to the customer to perform. This generally equates to more flexibility for the customer as well.

The next level down in this hierarchy is the Platform as a Service offering. With PaaS, the application is not built on the cloud service provider's infrastructure by default. Instead, a development platform is provided where the customer can upload their own custom application code. This gives the customer all of the flexibility of using cloud services while allowing them to still design, develop, and deploy their own custom application. The cloud service provider in this instance is responsible for maintaining the development platform software, the host operating system, and the hosting infrastructure whereas the customer only has to maintain the application.

Infrastructure as a Service

IaaS takes these cloud service offering to the next level down. With IaaS, the cloud service provider offers up their infrastructure and the customer will upload their own custom virtual machine image or use the cloud service provider's virtual machine templates. Generally, the customer is responsible for maintenance of the operating system within the virtual machine as well as any software installed within the virtual machine. The cloud service provider is just responsible for operating and maintaining the hardware that is hosting the virtual infrastructure. Some cloud service providers do offer managed services agreements where they are also willing to offer their professional services to maintain the operating system or perform technical tasks. This, however, is an added service and is not included in the IaaS offering.

SUMMARY

Our focus for this chapter has been many of the architectural aspects of enterprise applications. This includes enterprise architecture, solution architecture, and technical architecture among others. As we looked through these three main architecture types, we discussed how each relates to enterprise applications, how their concepts translate into real-world scenarios, and how to document each through an appropriate architecture diagram.

The most technically detailed part of architecture is, naturally, the technical architecture. In order to properly design and implement a strong technical architecture, many considerations must come into play. Some of the considerations that we discussed are server sizing, capacity requirements, performance testing, and virtualization. We also talked about increasing the availability of our enterprise application through the use of fault tolerance, high availability, and disaster recovery planning. Networks and integrations were the final focus of our technical architecture discussion. Throughout the chapter, our technical architecture diagram evolved from a simple illustration to a comprehensive technical architecture.

Finally, we shifted to discussing one of the more popular topics of conversation at present in the architectural world, cloud-based architecture. This involves a number of different service offerings available through cloud providers, such as SaaS, PaaS, IaaS, among others. These are collectively known as XaaS. Each service offering has its own benefits and should be evaluated as you look at hosting options for your enterprise application.

CHAPTER 7

Enterprise Applications Administration Teams

BUILDING A TEAM

All of the chapters in this book so far have focused on information relevant to both enterprise applications administrators and those leading enterprise applications administration teams. This chapter is intended more for the latter and those who are interested in becoming leaders of this type of technical team during their career. We will be focusing on the people aspect of enterprise applications administration and some best practices that can be used to build and lead a solid administration team.

The methods and techniques used within this chapter will, by necessity, vary based on the company guidelines, culture, and internal processes used by the corporate enterprise in which the team is built. In general, most of the information discussed here can be modified to fit the requirements of the company while maintaining their core effectiveness. In addition, not all of this information applies to every situation or circumstance. It's important to learn what works best in your organization from experience and tailor your leadership methods to fit them.

With that in mind, the people in the role of enterprise applications administrators are one of the most important assets of any company and it's critical that the correct people be put into these positions. It's also important to ensure that the enterprise applications administration team itself be put in a position to provide maximum value. In Chapter 1, we discussed enterprise applications administration in general as well as some of the benefits derived from enterprise applications administration teams. We will not be going over that again here, but it is important to note that these teams need to be positioned correctly organizationally to fit the roles that they are intended to fulfill within the corporate enterprise.

Team Building Basics

When building an enterprise applications administration team, you must start with a solid idea of what you're looking for both at the team and at the individual level. Your requirements will vary tremendously based on the types of applications that need to be administered, the number of administrators that will be members of the team, and any overarching requirements based on company policies or guidelines. In general, the first step in fleshing out an existing enterprise applications administration team or building a new one is to understand and detail out the specific requirements that the team as a whole must meet. An example of these requirements could be:

- Provide 24 × 7 on-call support
- Support development, testing, and production environments
- Be able to:
  - Troubleshoot issues
  - Install software
  - Assist developers
  - Administer user accounts
- Create technical documentation
- Deliver end-user training
- Monitor ongoing application availability and performance

This, obviously, is a very small snapshot of the requirements for an administration team. The key is to develop a full understanding of what it is that the team is expected to do and what their deliverables are. We discussed many of the roles that enterprise applications administrators can play in Chapter 1, and these serve as a good baseline to start from when determining the team requirements.

Team Structure

With the team requirements in place, you must then determine the layout and structure of the team. This will be based heavily on the requirements and what you need the team to do. For example, if the team is going to be doing both project work and support work across a large number of applications or very complex applications, it may make sense to segment the team into subgroups that concentrate on each area. In addition, there may be a regulatory requirement for segregation of duties in a particular administrative area, so you may need to carve out part of the team to focus on audit or verification tasks.

When defining this structure, it helps to make a high-level list of any subgroups that need to be created and furthermore, depending on the size of the administration team, any subgroups of those subgroups. This is best looked at in a format similar to a document outline. An example might be:

- Enterprise applications administration
  - Integration
    - Project team
    - Support team
  - Reporting
    - Project team
    - Support team
      - ☐ Ad-hoc reporting
  - Enterprise applications operations
    - Project team
      - ☐ Special projects
    - Support team

This high-level structure segments out the full enterprise applications administration team into manageable subgroups allowing for a concentrated focus on individual administration areas. This level of segmentation may work well in larger organizations, but is overly bloated for small administration teams. When you're working with a smaller organization, simply prune down the team structure as necessary while still maintaining the necessary segmentation defined by regulations or guidelines.

TIPS & TRICKS

Team Growth

As your team continues to grow, it's always a good idea to do a reality check and make sure that the team structure is still effective. Like anything else, organizational structure needs to morph over time to best support the needs of the organization. Performing an organizational structure review from time to time is a good idea and allows you to ensure that your structure still works as the team expands.

Staffing Requirements

With the high-level team structure defined, you can start moving on to determining the appropriate staffing requirements for the team. Just like the team structure itself, this is something that will vary tremendously based on the company's needs and budget. There are a few things that should be kept in mind as you look at developing the staffing requirements that are universal across all companies, and we'll discuss those here.

First, staffing should always be done with an eye toward team capacity. There are only 26 hours in an enterprise applications administration day (which obviously varies from the 24 hours that exist in a normal human's day), and somehow all of the work that needs to be done must fit within those hours. All joking aside, it's important to understand the amount of work that needs to be done and how long that work will take to accomplish based on the skills and experience expected of those doing the work. This can be done by putting together something akin to a "budget" of hours for a given position. Out of our "budget," we can put a baseline number of hours and calculate various "bills" that have to be paid from those hours such as vacation time, sick time, training time, and so on. An example of this is given in Table 7.1.

As you can see in Table 7.1, there is a substantial difference between the base work hours per year and the real available hours to perform work. These calculations will vary depending on geography, company policies, and other factors. For this example, a typical US 40-hours workweek was used with 3 weeks of vacation, 1 week of sick leave, and 12 holidays. Many company policies will vary these values depending on laws in their geography, religious observances, and employee benefits. For example, it may make sense to add bereavement hours into the calculation if this is part of your company's policy. The "other" category is intended to cover some of the miscellaneous time spent per day doing nonwork tasks and this too will vary widely. The goal is to come up with a general idea of how many work hours are available and, based on this example, we have roughly 25 real work hours of capacity per employee, per week.

Table 7.1 Productive Hours Estimate		
	Time Allocation	**Available Hours**
Work hours per year		2080
Vacation	120	1960
Illness	40	1920
Holiday (12 holidays per year)	96	1824
Breaks (30 min per day)	130	1694
Training	120	1574
Mandatory meetings (two per week @ 1 h)	104	1470
Other (30 min per day)	130	1340
Weekly available hours		25.76923077

The next step is to determine the amount of work that needs to be done. This is an incredibly complex task and will vary widely depending on the types of work being performed, the skill level and work ethics of the employees, and the intended roles that the administrators are intended to play. The best way to approach this estimation is to break the work down to its individual parts much like we did for the available hours and see what the result is. An example is shown in Table 7.2.

As you can see in the example shown in Table 7.2, many of the tasks that an administrator may need to perform are defined and estimated in detail. As usual, this will vary in every organization. You'll notice that there is minimal project-related work defined in this list. In many organizations, projects are funded from capital (versus expense) budgets and require a more detailed

Table 7.2 Work Estimates

Task	Hours to Perform	Frequency per Week	Hours per Week
Consult with development teams	1	5	5
Research issues	1	10	10
Answer support calls	0.25	25	6.25
Answer support emails	0.25	50	12.5
Perform application maintenance	1	5	5
Audit application logs	1	5	5
Perform user administration	0.25	50	12.5
Perform code deployments	0.5	10	5
Perform break-fix operations	2	3	6
Migrate data	2	1	2
Perform data fixes	0.5	15	7.5
Install patches	3	1	3
Coordinate cross-team efforts	1	5	5
		Total hours per week	84.75
		Available hours per week	25
		Required personnel (rounded up)	4

task analysis. In general, the type of estimate given in Table 7.2 will work for ongoing maintenance overhead, but project work should be estimated separately in a similar manner.

It's also important to note that these values reflect the amount of time the tasks may take if the individual can dedicate their time to that task in a contiguous period. If there are interruptions or the enterprise applications administrator must switch between tasks frequently, there is a loss of efficiency, and the time to complete a task increases. Consider the amount of time that it may take to respond to the interruption, take care of the cause of the interruption, remember what you were doing, catch back up on exactly where you were in the task, and begin execution again. Depending on the level of difficulty of the task, the time that it takes to get back on track can be substantial. If your team suffers from frequent interruption, you may need to increase the amount of time associated with some tasks to compensate.

Now that we have a general idea of the workload, we can calculate the number of people that it will take to accomplish this. If you look at the bottom of Table 7.2, you'll see that this calculation has already been done. With 84.75 h of work needed per week and 25 h of available work time per person, you end up needing around 3.4 people. While you could bring on a part-time person to fill that 0.4 need, it's generally advisable to round up to the next "whole person." This means that we'll need four people to manage this workload.

There are a few other factors that do need to be understood before we solidify on this team size. First, is there a need for the team to perform on-call duties and, if so, how frequently will they be called to perform work? This has an impact as you can assume that any time an on-call person is contacted after work, you will lose at least some amount of productive work time the next day. This is typically due to either follow-up work required in association with the on-call work or lost rest time leading to a delayed start on the next day. Make sure to "budget" for this when putting together your work estimates.

Also, depending on the way that security and work is handled in your organization, you may need (or want) to implement a "second set of eyes" strategy. This means that any time an administrative command is run or a software install performed, one person performs the operation while another watches. This is a good method to ensure that the team is cross-trained and that an administrator does not abuse their privileges (without collusion). However, this does pull productive time from another person and will need to be accounted for in your work estimates.

Lastly, in larger teams, you will need to allocate time for team leads to perform their duties. Team leads are typically used to help lesser-skilled team members with questions, allocate work efforts across multiple team members, review and provide feedback on team member's work, and other duties along those lines. By utilizing team leads, the team manager can focus on more administrative work while delegating any technical work to the team leads. Again, this will vary depending on your organization and its methods of getting work done.

Building the Organizational Chart

Let's assume that we have no on-call needs, that this particular team will not be using the "second set of eyes" strategy, and that the team manager will also perform team lead tasks for this smaller enterprise applications administration team. If that is the case, we can now start on the next step toward putting together our organizational chart. We need to align our projected workload between the various roles defined in the organization and put these on an organizational chart.

Since our organizational structure is broader than the number of team members planned (eight "teams" across four team members), we need to combine some roles. In some cases this is fairly easy. Since we intentionally excluded project work from our estimate, we can skip the project-related positions in the structure. With that in mind, we can plan on one team member for each area across integration, reporting, and operations. That gives us another team member to deploy in the correct location based on workload. Chances are good that this will be in the operations team, so we'll place the extra position within that team. This gives an organization that looks similar to the chart shown in Figure 7.1.

As you can see in Figure 7.1, we have a single available position set aside within each team but have reflected the overall organizational structure. By using this model, we can expand the team as needed to support both projects and growth in the future. We can add new positions within the appropriate

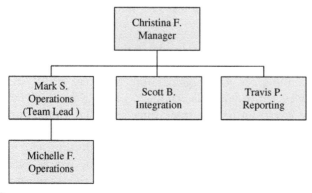

FIGURE 7.1
Sample organizational chart.

column to grow out the team as well as identify team leads or other critical organizational information.

Hiring

One of the more difficult tasks associated with building enterprise applications administration teams is recruiting and hiring qualified individuals. Depending on your organization, there may be specific recruiting practices in place including internal recruiters, use of recruiting web sites, use of job fairs or college campus recruiting exercises, and others. Regardless of the recruitment method used, remember that it's important to find a candidate qualified to fill the role and motivate them to join your organization.

In the next section, we'll talk about putting together a skill list for the particular role that you're looking to fill. It's important that you have a clear understanding of what skills and expertise you're looking for in a candidate. This will help to guide your recruiting efforts as well as provide a baseline that can be used to gauge a candidate's technical fit for the position. A high-level listing of the required skills, experience, industry certifications, and expectations should be included within the job description posted and distributed for the position.

You'll frequently receive a very large number of candidate applications for any given position. Many of these will not be qualified for the position, but will be using the "shotgun" approach of applying for jobs where they try to apply for as many as possible in the hopes that one fits. You'll likely also receive resumes from candidates who are under-qualified, don't understand the position being offered, or lack skills that you've listed as required. These submissions are pretty easy to dismiss and reduce the number of candidates that you have to consider further. However, if you are using a recruiting service, it is important to pass these back to the service with feedback so that they understand why the candidates did not fit your expectations. This can help them to tailor their search to better fit your needs.

When you've decided on the candidates that you think are qualified and should be considered for the position, it's time to determine your interview strategy. Depending on your organization, this may already be defined for you or it may be left to your discretion. A common strategy is to perform an initial phone screening to ask basic questions that would quickly exclude them from consideration. Having the candidate explain their past work in specific technical areas works well for this. In addition, you may consider asking questions that have the candidate describe detailed technical work that they've done in various areas associated with the technical needs for the position. This may also be a good time to call the candidate's references and see what their past associates have to say about their work. Generally, a person's references always speak positively about the candidate, but you may be able to derive some information about their work habits from the reference.

After the initial screening, you may be able to reduce the candidate pool further. You could then move on to a more extensive interview. This may be with just the hiring manager, a panel of interviewers, or multiple individual interviewers. At this next level, the candidate should be asked questions that clearly demonstrate their fit for a position. Some hiring managers will use technical tests, others will require the candidate to solve problems on a whiteboard, and others may ask behavioral interview questions that force the candidate to explain how they approach various problems.

Your interview may consist of some or all of these techniques. The goal is to understand what the candidate knows, what they can do, and how they think. Pay close attention to how they answer the questions that they're presented with. Do they sound like they're reciting memorized knowledge or do they sound like they've actually performed work in this area? Can they organize their thoughts and walk you through how they approach and solve a problem? Are they able to describe their own contributions to an organization versus a collective team's contribution?

After this level of interviewing, you should have a pretty good idea of each candidate's qualifications. This should weed out the candidates that lie on their resume, don't have the required knowledge or skills, or would be a bad fit for the team. Making a decision on who to hire is your next step and may be very difficult. In many cases, you will not find a "perfect" fit for the position but rather candidates who are a close fit and can grow into the position. There may be skill gaps in some areas that can be filled with appropriate training or knowledge transfer. There may also be gaps in experience that can be filled by simply having them perform the job. Don't hold out for the perfect candidate, but also don't be afraid to cast your net again to try and find other qualified candidates if none seem to be a good fit.

Organically Grown Teams

When building an enterprise applications administration team, it's very rare that you will be starting from scratch and building an entirely new team from the ground up. This happens, but not very frequently. It is much more common for an enterprise applications administration team to be formed by existing company employees that are working in other areas but have skills that are a good fit for enterprise applications administration. For example, many teams are formed by taking developers or server/operating system administrators and teaching them either systems administration or application knowledge, respectively.

This is not necessarily a bad approach, but it does require some work to ensure that the correct mix of skills and knowledge is available across the team. For example, if the team is formed exclusively by individuals with a developer background, will they know how to specify a cluster configuration? Would they have an understanding of how to install software within a Linux environment? These and many other tasks may be required and is knowledge that a developer moving into this role must gain.

The converse is also true for systems administrators that become enterprise applications administrators. They may understand how roles work within Microsoft Active Directory, but do they know how those roles translate into application permissions? Or which part of the application actually provides the Active Directory link necessary to utilize those credentials? Again, there is a knowledge gap that must be filled in order for the application to be correctly administered.

With this in mind, you need to put together a plan on how you will ensure that each member of the team has the knowledge and skills necessary to perform this role. The plan should include a detailed list of required knowledge or skills, a comparison of those requirements against the team member's current knowledge and skills, and a roadmap that details out how any gaps will be filled. This can include shadowing, on-the-job training, formal training, and even practice sessions or lab time to gain experience.

The basis for the plan has to be a list of tasks that the team member is expected to perform as well as the knowledge or skills necessary to perform those tasks. For example, to install an application on a Linux operating system, the team member may need the following knowledge or skills:

- Linux Operating System basic navigation
- Usage of SSH
- Usage of X Window installers
- Usage of UNIX file editing tools

With these basic skills, an application install could probably be performed. Any application-specific settings would require additional guidance or knowledge of the application being installed. If a list similar to this is developed for each task expected of the team member, you will have a very clear picture of what they need to know at a minimum in order to adequately fulfill their role.

The next step is to put together a list of what skills the team member already has. An easy method of doing this is to take the required skills list as a baseline, mark the items that the team member knows or has done before, and add any other knowledge or skills that they have to the list. These additional items may not be needed now, but they might be necessary in the future, and it's always a good idea to understand what your people are capable of doing.

The gaps that need to be filled are the knowledge or skill areas that are required but unknown by the team member. For each of these, you will need to determine the best way to teach the team member the necessary knowledge and how to help them gain the appropriate skills. As previously mentioned, this can involve shadowing someone else who has the knowledge or skills, learning through on-the-job training, or attending a formal class on the subject.

TIPS & TRICKS

Learning Methods

Everybody learns in different ways. Some people learn best when they read information out of a book, whereas others learn better by listening to someone read or teach material. Others do their best learning by seeing something done and then repeating the process. Still others only learn by practicing and trying something until they get it right. Understanding different learning methods and which methods work best with your team members is critical to understanding how to best train them.

Onboarding

Bringing on new team members is frequently challenging. When it's an internal employee of the company migrating, it's a little easier, but there is always paperwork to do, systems to set up, access to be granted or removed, training to administer, and information to share. In order to go through this process as efficiently as possible, it helps to have an onboarding plan that you use to ensure that the new team member has everything that they need and have a clean transition into your organization.

This plan can generally be broken up into two parts: a part that you as the manager or a team lead must do, and a part that the new team member must do. This ensures that each person is aware of their responsibilities and takes ownership of the onboarding tasks associated with their role. For example, you wouldn't want the new team member to have to send out their own cross-team introduction email and you wouldn't want to have to schedule a meeting with the company's benefits department on their behalf.

Onboarding Plans for Managers

With that in mind, you can begin putting together plans for each role. These plans can include scheduled activities, a checklist of things that need to be done or even references to informational sheets and work instructions for the team member to perform. A sample of what an onboarding checklist might look like for a manager is given in Table 7.3.

Table 7.3 Sample of Manager's Onboarding Checklist

Pre-Start Date	
Complete?	**Task**
X	Complete background check
X	Complete substance abuse check
X	Finalize HR paperwork
X	Create badge request
	Allocate desk space
	Order office supplies
	Request phone
	Request laptop
X	Request user ID
	Submit application access requests
	Submit network access requests
	Request VPN access
X	Create critical training list
X	Print out employee onboarding document
	Assign an orientation partner
	Schedule new employee orientation

Start Date	
Complete?	**Task**
	Meet employee @ 8 a.m.
	Meet with security @ 8:30 (badge photo)
	Tour of facility
	Introduce to team members
	Show desk location
	Deliver new employee gift
	Deliver laptop
	Deliver training list
	Deliver onboarding document
	Review job description, responsibilities, and expectations
	Review basic expectations (dress code, working hours, lunch, time off processes)
	Review organizational structure and department functions
	Schedule one-to-one meetings
	Review security and safety requirements

Post-Start Date	
Complete?	**Task**
	Touch base to answer any questions and address concerns
	Review performance/salary process and incentive programs
	Arrange team lunch
	Ensure that all required forms are complete and signed
	Discuss effectiveness of and improvements to onboarding process

As you can see in Table 7.3, there are a number of tasks that need to be completed before the employee starts, on their start date, and sometime after they've started. This latter category is typically intended to reflect a timeframe of 1−2 weeks after the start date. In some cases, this timeframe can go up to a month, but after that point, it's generally a good idea to use an ongoing employee engagement process rather than considering the tasks part of onboarding. This can include things like quarterly, biannual, or annual performance reviews, one-to-one meetings, and so on.

There are a few tasks on this checklist that require special attention. The first are the tasks around access requests. In general, most corporations require that an initial user ID be set up prior to submitting requests for a person to have access to specific applications. Once configured, the user ID can be used as the identifier for the person to be granted access to the various applications and network locations that they need in order to perform their job. For any manager, it is important to have a list of which applications and network locations your new team member will need access to as well as the level of access required for those resources. This list can be used to ensure that all of the correct accounts and permissions are set up.

Next is the employee onboarding document. We'll discuss this in a little more detail later in this section, but it's very important that this document exists and is detailed enough to help ensure that the employee is able to get going quickly. In some organizations, it can take as long as 30 days for an employee to be fully brought up to speed on the basics and begin performing work. This is a waste of valuable time and can be mitigated by having a solid onboarding document for the employee to follow in order to quickly set up everything that they need.

Finally, there are several references to touching base with the new team member, scheduling one-to-one meetings, and answering questions. Changing roles or starting a new job is a very difficult process for anyone and is often made worse if the manager does not spend sufficient time working directly with the new team member to get them oriented. Many managers use a "hands-off" approach to onboarding where they give the employee a stack of documents, some equipment, a desk, and then leave them on their own to flounder about. This does not help to establish a good relationship with the employee and leaves them in a bad starting position. A good manager always ensures that they spend adequate time working directly with new team members so they are able to perform at their best.

Onboarding Plans for New Team Members

For new team members, whether employee or contractor, joining a new team is full of unique challenges. Aside from merging into the team from a personality perspective, there are many logistics associated with coming up to speed with the rest of the team. These logistics can be made easier through the use of onboarding plans for the new team members. These are similar to the onboarding plans used by the manager, but focus more on specific actions that the new team member needs to take.

One of the primary differences between managerial and individual contributor onboarding plans is the level of detail. While the managerial plan may be primarily a checklist, the plan for the new team member needs to include a huge amount of critical information. This can include links to online resources, step-by-step instructions on how to access and use tools, contact information for frequently contacted individuals or departments, links to standard operating procedures or work instructions, reference material for enterprise applications or their infrastructure, and other useful information. This is on top of a checklist similar to that shown for managers in Table 7.3 to ensure that all critical tasks are taken care of.

In many cases, this onboarding plan should be a formalized document that includes a checklist that the new team member can follow. The structure of the document will obviously vary based on the needs of the organization, but should include the following sections at a minimum:

- Onboarding Checklist
- Links to Informational Resources
- Links to Documentation
- Organizational Information
- Frequent Contacts

These can be expanded and reference external documents as needed to keep the onboarding plan lightweight.

Leading Technical Teams

A team of four as discussed in our prior examples isn't too difficult to manage, but there are some aspects to managing technical personnel that are critically different than managing people in other professions. Professionals in the information technology field have grown to have slightly different expectations and needs compared to those in other fields. While this could probably be said for almost any role, it seems exceptionally prevalent in the science and technology fields.

When building an enterprise applications administration team, it's important to have the right mix of knowledge and skills across the team members. For example, if the tasks that your team is responsible for include areas where both development and database knowledge could be helpful, you'll want to ensure that your team members have those skills. In many cases, this may not be one person initially, but instead be split across two or more. This is generally the starting point for enterprise applications administration teams, but an end goal of having the entire team proficient in all required technical areas should be set.

Training

With this in mind, cross training and solid knowledge transfer between team members is critical. From a team management standpoint, you cannot rely on any single team member to be the single point of knowledge or skill in a technical area. The same concept of "single point of failure" that is applied to system architecture applies to the team structure as well. Setting up an ongoing plan for performing solid documentation, cross training, and knowledge transfer is critical to eliminating this potential issue.

We'll talk about documentation at length in another chapter and focus on cross training and knowledge transfer here. These two topics are split because cross training focuses on the actual skill, whereas knowledge transfer focuses (obviously) on the knowledge. Within any technical field, there is a distinct difference between having knowledge on a subject and being skilled in that subject. This is frequently seen as the difference between education and experience.

Knowledge transfer is exactly that—a defined method of transferring knowledge. This can be done through documentation, public training sessions, and one-on-one training sessions. In some cases, it's a combination of some or all of these techniques. The idea with knowledge transfer is to teach someone about a particular topic much like it is the author's intent with this book to teach you about enterprise applications administration. By performing knowledge transfer, you're effectively teaching someone something that they didn't know before or a new way of thinking about things that they did already know.

Cross training is more complex and involves more work. Typically, knowledge transfer is performed first in order to teach the material that will be used in the cross training exercise. In order to develop a skill and experience, cross training is the practical application of the knowledge that was transferred. For example, if knowledge transfer has been done on basic SQL, cross training could be performed by having the student perform a number of different types of queries against a database.

It's important to note that there are a number of ways to perform cross training. One of the most common is to have the student perform the activities associated with a knowledge transfer within a nonproduction or less critical environment. With this technique, risks of damage being caused through the cross training process is minimized while still allowing the student to gather practical experience. To use this technique, a knowledgeable team member trains the student in whatever fashion works best and then provides a task or tasks to be performed. Key points here are that a skill cannot be gained through knowledge transfer alone and that performing cross training without a task to be executed tends to be ineffective.

Another less common, but very effective technique is to perform cross training through "fire." This technique works well for team members who learn more effectively by researching and learning about topics without formal knowledge transfer. To use this technique within enterprise applications administration teams, a need to perform tasks in a specific knowledge area is assigned to someone with minimal or no knowledge in that area. This should be done only in cases where the risk of any issues arising from mistakes is minimal or nonexistent and the work isn't urgent. In addition, a knowledgeable and skilled person should be available to the student to ask questions of or to validate what the student has learned. In some cases, this can be considered an inefficient technique, but with some individuals, it is the best way to cross train a new topic.

This leads into the concept of learning techniques. Just as different techniques can be used to teach a topic, each individual tends to have a slightly different method of learning. Some people can learn a topic very well by just reading about it. Others learn better by listening to someone speak about the topic. In some cases, individuals are unable to learn from either of these methods and have to actually perform an activity hands-on in order to learn it. And finally, combinations of any or all of these may be the most effective approach for some team members. As an enterprise applications administration team manager, it is important to understand how your team members learn best and ensure that they receive training in the method or methods that suit their learning style. It doesn't make sense to spend thousands of dollars on formal training if the student won't learn from it, and it also doesn't make sense to withhold formalized training funding if that's the best way for a team member to understand a topic.

Task Allocation

When managing an enterprise applications administration team, it's critical to properly balance workload amongst the team members. This requires maintaining a careful balance between utilizing appropriate expertise, ensuring that work gets done correctly, meeting timelines, and maintaining team member interest. In larger teams, the role of task manager will frequently fall to a team lead, but in smaller teams the manager is responsible for this effort. In addition, team leads often need to be coached by the manager on the most effective way of working with the teams and implementing the manager's intentions.

The most obvious method of task allocation is simply to assign all tasks of a particular nature to someone who is an expert at the associated technology. For example, any task that involves troubleshooting network issues could be assigned to a team member with a network administration background. However, this can lead to some long-term problems. When the number of tasks associated with a specialized technical area exceeds the bandwidth of the person that they're being assigned to, that individual may be overloaded and be unable to deliver their work on time. In the meantime, another team member that specialized in another technical area may be underutilized. This situation leads to unhappy team members as well as unhappy customers or clients.

Your task allocation technique must also account for quality of work. In reality, some people are simply better at performing certain tasks than others. This may not be due to technical expertise as much as attention to detail and other softer skills. In this situation, it can be tempting to assign more tasks to the person who does them better since you will be assured of high-quality work. In this case, you're effectively encouraging poor quality by reducing the workload of people who do lower quality work. Instead, the focus should be on improving the quality of each team member's work so that it is consistent amongst all team members.

Managing timelines is another critical part of task allocation. If an individual has a lot of tasks to perform that each require extensive dedicated time to complete, there is the possibility that they will not always be done. When assigning tasks, it is important to include a mix of longer-term tasks and shorter-term tasks with each team member. In addition, task prioritization may be necessary when multiple tasks are assigned so that the team member knows which ones to work on first. It shouldn't always be the case that short-term tasks get completed before longer-term tasks. In some cases, the longer-term task may be more important and require more attention.

Finally, you should always keep an eye on the human aspect of team members when you are performing task allocation. People are not machines and simply cannot perform the same monotonous task over and over without any change. This can quickly lead to burnout within the team. Assign tasks that keep each person learning and interested in their job. A job cannot be rewarding if it isn't interesting and challenging, so keep that in mind when assigning tasks. In addition, changing up the tasks assigned to specific individuals can help fulfill security controls by providing for job rotation as well as maintaining the team member's interest.

Career Growth

In some fields, career growth is an organic thing that simply happens based on tenure in a specific type of position. This is not usually the case for technical people in today's workforce. Most individuals in the information technology field take a great deal of interest in their own career path and want to know what their future holds. As the manager of an enterprise applications administration team, it is important to understand this and to be able to support your team members in achieving their career growth ambitions.

In some cases, this can be as simple as having a team member that wants to see a solid progression of money and incentives over time. When this is the case, a career plan can be drawn out that helps the employee achieve ongoing raises and promotions throughout their career within your organization. This plan will need to include what is necessary from the team member in order to earn these raises and promotions. Quite frankly, in today's economy, performing the same task in the same way day after day with no improvement does not justify substantial raises and promotions in the information technology field. Instead, the team member must continue to grow in value in order for them to continue to progress financially. The team member's career plan should outline where they have opportunities to provide more value whether it's gaining knowledge or skills in various areas, mentoring other team members, or demonstrating methods of reducing cost within the organization. By achieving goals such as this, the team member has demonstrated growth and can reap the benefits of that growth.

Other team members may not be motivated by money but rather by the opportunity to move up the organizational ladder. Granted, there are generally financial incentives associated with these moves, but those are sometimes secondary to the opportunity to gain higher levels within the organization. These team members may be more enticed by a new job title than a slight raise or they may prefer the opportunity to act in a leadership role within the organization. It's important to understand the team member's motivation behind their career growth goals and tailor their career plan with the intent to fulfill those motivational needs.

The last type of career growth basis that we'll discuss is around those employees who crave knowledge. Within this field, it's very common to have team members who want nothing more than to learn all that they can about as many topics as they can. These are some of the best types of team members within enterprise applications administration teams as they have a personal desire to fit the enterprise applications administrator mold. They can be a specialist in multiple technical areas and a generalist in many more which makes for an excellent administrator. With this type of team member, you can help them reach their career growth goals by supporting their education and learning needs. This can be done through both the utilization of formal training as well as the other training techniques discussed previously in this section.

Regardless of the career growth needs of your team members, it is important to recognize those needs and support them. An enterprise applications administrator will do their best work when they recognize that their needs are important to their manager and that the manager is collaborating with them to help them achieve their goals. That may involve forcing frank conversations with your employees as they may, by nature, be reticent to talk about what they want to do or whether or not their current work is fulfilling. By having these conversations and putting together a solid career growth plan with goals, steps to achieve those goals, and incentives, you can support the team member's needs while continually improving the enterprise applications administration team as a whole.

Personality, Culture, and Diversity

One of the key indicators of a high-performing enterprise applications administration team is the ability for the team members to work together well and collaborate. By bouncing ideas off of each other, the team members are able to enhance and refine their thoughts and come up with a better overall result than working alone. This is one of the reasons that people like to work in teams and one of the benefits of this type of organizational structure.

However, it's easy to cancel out these benefits if the team members do not mesh well and work together effectively. The most destructive element to any team is personality conflict between team members. It is impossible for all team members to get along at all times, but it is important that the personalities of the individual team members be compatible and conductive to a high-performing team. For example, if there is a team member that presents a negative attitude at all times, this will bring down the overall team morale and will lead to the other team members being unhappy. As a manager, you must be able to recognize any issues that the team members are having interacting with each other and work with the team as a whole or one-on-one to ensure that the team is able to work together well.

It is important for the team to be diverse as each team member must bring their own style, knowledge, skills, and background to the team in order for it to be an effective enterprise applications administration organization. In no other type of technical team is this as crucial as it is for administrators dealing with a variety of technologies. However, that diversity can lead to conflict and you must be prepared to deal with any conflicts that arise. In most corporations, the human resources department can help with diversity training for employees as well as provide suggestions and recommendations to managers working with diverse teams.

In addition to the background cultures of individuals, there are also the factors of corporate cultures and team cultures to keep in mind when managing enterprise applications administration teams. Every company has their own culture, and team members in every organization must be able to work within and with the culture of the company that they're employed by. Within enterprise applications administration teams, it is typical for the team to develop their own internal culture that differs somewhat from other teams within the information technology organization. This is generally a good thing, but care must be taken to ensure that the team's culture is complementary to the company culture and takes into account the background cultures of each individual team member.

TEAM STANDARDS

With enterprise applications administration teams, it is important to have standards for the team to adhere to. In this instance, we are not referring to standard operating procedures as much as the team's cultural standards. It is the development of these standards that sets the bar that the enterprise applications administration team must meet in order to continually show their value to the organization as a whole. As the manager of this type of technical team, setting standards gives your team members clear guidance on how various situations should be handled as well as setting a clear expectation that can be followed.

On ships, a ship captain will create a document called "Standing Orders" which tells other officers on the ship what the captain's expectations are when the captain is not on deck. These standing orders dictate everything from what the officer of the watch is responsible for to instructions as to under which circumstances the captain should be awakened for further orders. Setting standards for your team is no different. The manager cannot be involved in every decision nor should they be. Instead, the team members should be empowered to make appropriate decisions based on the guidance of the team's manager. This guidance can frequently be set through the documentation of standards for the team.

In addition, there may be specific procedures and protocols that the team must follow under certain circumstances. For example, there may be specific actions that have to be taken when a team member receives a phone call alerting them to an issue with the enterprise applications after normal working hours. There may also be specific requirements around how quickly an on-call team member must respond to attempts to contact them. While some of these may fall under standard operating procedure documents which we'll discuss in more detail in a later chapter, others may be less formalized organizationally and fall under general team standards instead.

As previously mentioned, most enterprise applications administration teams grow to have their own culture. While it's not necessary to document what this culture is or how exactly it works, it does help to clearly define the expectations of team members and the standards that the team members should meet. For example, the following are some general team standards that could exist for an enterprise applications administration team:

- Hosting effective meetings
  - Timing
    - The start times of meetings should be scheduled for 9 a.m. until 3 p.m.
    - The meeting organizer should provide meeting objectives/agenda prior to meeting (optional for standing meetings depending on purpose).
    - Budget time in meeting for transition between meetings.
    - Commitment is to start/stop on time.
    - 50-min duration for 1-h meeting; 25 min duration for half-hour meetings.
    - Meeting notices should be sent a minimum of 48 h in advance when possible.
    - Avoid scheduling over lunch hours if possible.
    - Schedule based on current calendars for most critical attendees.
  - Location
    - When in the same building, commit to meet in person when possible.
    - When people are located in other buildings, it is okay to teleconference for a meeting.
  - Response
    - When a meeting is accepted, the expectation is that you attend, otherwise decline or respond as tentative at least 24 h in advance.
    - If you don't think you should be invited to a meeting, confirm with the organizer or decline and notify why you're not attending.
- Team collaboration
  - We all have different backgrounds and skills. If you need help with a problem or just want to know what has been done before… ASK!
    - This avoids rework, ensures that we are consistent in our approach, and adds to our personal knowledge.
  - Ensure that all team members know which environments/servers you are working on
  - Document, document, document!
    - If it's a "one-time" process and required some analysis that is out of the norm or unique knowledge, document it.

- If it's a process that will be used on a recurring basis, document it.
- If it's a "tip or trick" that you've discovered, document it.
- We have a priority to ourselves also. Make sure you take the time to answer questions and help teammates
- Engaging with other teams
  - The primary method of engagement with any other team is through the ticketing process
  - Follow-up with a phone call if the need is very urgent from a support perspective
  - If the need is urgent from a project perspective, have the project manager follow up with the appropriate party
  - Always engage other teams in a courteous, respectful, professional manner
  - Some teams may request additional information through another process. If this is necessary, work with the appropriate teams to get this done as efficiently as possible. If the process is not efficient, discuss it with your team lead
- On-call duties
  - Schedule
    - Each administrator is expected to participate in a rotating on-call schedule.
    - The schedule for each month will be posted to the team intranet site and will take into account any posted vacation/leave time recorded on the site calendar.
    - Your shift will run from 9 a.m. Central time on your scheduled start date until 9 a.m. Central time on the next scheduled person's start date.
    - On-call services are to be provided 24×7 during your scheduled week.
    - If you receive a call during normal business hours and have worked late the night before, you can do a warm handoff to another administrator in the office.
  - Response time
    - You must respond to any call within 15 min of the call.
    - You should be able to be online within an hour of being contacted.

These standards are examples that you can use within any enterprise applications administration team. They will need to be tailored to fit the culture and standards of your company and your team in order to be effective. They should reflect the guiding principles of your team and clearly outline what the expectations are for your team members. Standards such as this go beyond the corporate policies and guidelines that are required by most company's human resources department and allow you to define appropriate behaviors within your team while still adhering to any corporate, legal, or regulatory requirements.

IMPLEMENTATION VERSUS SUPPORT

In many enterprise applications administration teams, the team is responsible for providing ongoing support of enterprise applications as well as implementing new applications or enhancing existing applications. We talked about this a little in Chapter 1 when we talked about the role of enterprise applications administration teams. As you look at the role of your team, it is important to understand how this model fits and what your team is responsible for as it relates to the enterprise applications that it supports. Segregating between support and implementation may be one part of this.

Enterprise applications administration teams that do both support and implementation run into unique challenges. These challenges are similar to those experienced by other technical teams that perform both support and implementation activities, but they are exacerbated by the fact that enterprise applications administrators are typically either directly responsible for multiple technology areas or assisting with troubleshooting and integration of those other technology areas within the enterprise application ecosystem. In order to address these challenges, it is important to clearly understand the differences between support and implementation and the impact that these two distinct roles can have on a team.

Implementation Projects

In most cases, the implementation of enterprise applications is performed as a project. This can be done formally with the assignment of a project manager, the creation of a detailed cross-team project plan, and full project financial management processes or it can be done informally as a "mini project" led by the enterprise applications administration team itself. As a best practice, even the smallest implementation projects should have some level of project management even if it's only internal to the team. This helps to ensure a consistent implementation process and clearly defines what needs to be done by the team.

In larger projects, the enterprise applications administration team plays a role in a number of different areas. Depending on the development methodology used or the implementation process for the company, this role will differ and the deliverables from the enterprise applications administration team will change. In a waterfall methodology, for example, there may be distinct scoping, design, development, testing, and delivery phases for a project. Agile projects may require ongoing repetition of some of these phases based on their methodology. Regardless, many of the same deliverables exist but their timing and format may differ.

Scoping

During scoping phases, the enterprise applications administrator typically contributes in two primary ways. They assist in determining what nonfunctional requirements need to be accounted for, and they support the project team as a subject matter expert on the enterprise application that the project is working with. In this role, the enterprise applications administrator must use their knowledge of the enterprise application as well as underlying infrastructure, integrations, and other technologies in use to ensure that any potential issues are discovered and addressed as early on in the project as possible.

In many cases, the requirements gathering process of project teams focus on understanding exactly what the business needs the system to do. The requirements associated with this are all functional requirements and define what the system has to do from a functional perspective. Another critical piece of scoping is the determination of nonfunctional requirements. These are requirements that define how the systems should provide the functionality requested. Nonfunctional requirements also specify any technical limitations that need to be reflected in the design as well as other critical system characteristics.

Some examples of nonfunctional requirements where the enterprise applications administrator could provide input are:

- Availability requirements including scheduled maintenance windows or timeframes for downtime, redundancy, and disaster recovery
- Resource utilization requirements that indicate maximum limits for utilization of disk, processor, memory, etc. on affected systems
- Security requirements around user authentication, authorization, data protection, auditing, etc.
- Performance requirements that detail how fast the system needs to process particular pieces of data or execute specific tasks
- Error handling requirements that define how the system handles errors, which conditions should be handled in an automated fashion versus those that require human intervention, and what to do when unexpected errors occur
- Scalability requirements that define how the system should be defined to scale in order to handle increased load. This may include requirements for both vertical and horizontal scaling.

While many of these requirements may necessitate input from the business groups who will be using the enterprise application, the enterprise applications administrator is typically the individual who is best positioned to understand what is really needed and how that translates into appropriate nonfunctional requirements. For example, the business groups may want the system to respond back with data in less than a second, but the enterprise applications administrator may know that due to the number of subsidiary systems that must be called, sub-second response is unrealistic. This knowledge can help drive the nonfunctional requirements to include a realistic response time that meets the business needs and is technically feasible.

This type of expertise bleeds over into the enterprise applications administrator's other role during the scoping phase. By acting as an expert-level resource with technical knowledge about the enterprise application and its foundational infrastructure, the enterprise applications administrator can help ensure that all requirements gathered during the scoping phase (both functional and nonfunctional) make technical sense and are achievable. It has been the author's experience that in some cases the business groups using an enterprise application don't fully understand what it is and is not capable of doing. It is therefore up to the enterprise applications administrator to help educate as well as ensure that any requirements gathered make sense within the confines of available technology.

Design

During the design phase, the enterprise applications administrator has a number of tasks that are critical to ensuring that a solid design is developed. To keep things simple, we'll focus just on the design phase in general and not the split between high-level and detailed design. In practice, most organizations start by performing a high-level design for any enterprise application development or implementation project and then drill in deeper to create a detailed design.

It's during the design phase that the enterprise applications administrator can help ensure that design decisions align with the needs of the application to run in an enterprise environment. In many cases, the development or basic implementation process for an application is focused only on basic functionality and does not account for the special needs associated with an enterprise application running in a large, complex environment. For example, in a development environment, an enterprise application may be running within a smaller scale than production and simply have all components of the application locally installed on a single server. In the production environment, this may be distributed across multiple servers and the application may have to be designed to handle session state transitions across servers, etc. During the design process, the enterprise applications administrator can help ensure that designs are made that reflect the end-state implementation of the enterprise application.

Based on the requirements that have been determined for the application, the enterprise applications administrator may need to start engaging with various teams and individuals to get infrastructure needs for the application in place while the application is being designed. In most cases, a technical architecture will need to be built around the application and multiple teams engaged to implement that architecture. The alignment between the application architecture and technical architecture is critical as we discussed in Chapter 6. These designs can be built out during this project phase, and any lead times for infrastructure work can be accommodated by engaging the appropriate people as early on in the implementation process as possible.

Finally, as the application goes through its design phases, the enterprise applications administrator typically helps to ensure that the developers have a place available to test new ideas, perform proof-of-concepts, and demonstrate new capabilities. In many organizations, there is a split between operational support of production environments and ongoing support of development environments, but it is typically enterprise applications administrators who are responsible for both in the end.

This is especially critical during design and development phases of project implementations. While many operations organizations identify that there is a direct budget impact associated with downtime in production environments, most project teams recognize that there is also a substantial financial impact caused by any downtime in development or test environments. Every hour that developers are unable to develop or testers are unable to test costs the project money as they are paying the development or testing teams to do nothing and then have to pay for the work that should have been done during the downtime at a later time. When you consider a large development team consisting of dozens or hundreds of developers, an hour of downtime can have a very significant cost associated with it.

Development

We've already talked about the support of lower environments during the design and development phases, but there are other activities that enterprise applications administrators do during this phase that are critical to the success of any implementation project. As always, it is the experience and the cross-platform technical knowledge of the administrator that provides the greatest value and their role as a consultant during the development phase can greatly assist any developer. As questions arise around various technologies or ways to accomplish things on different platforms, the enterprise applications administrator can serve as a guide to the developers and help them to understand what the end state of the application infrastructure will be and how to best leverage its technical capabilities.

In some cases, the enterprise applications administrator can also help the developers in various aspects of the development process. With the current state of development practices, it is becoming more and more common to create development environments that automatically compile (if necessary), deploy, and test code as soon as it has been developed. This automated environment is very helpful in quickly identifying code problems, testing out potential ways to meet requirements through code, and ensuring that the enterprise application works as expected. However, any automated system does require effort to set up and maintain. As with the enterprise application's lower environments, it is often the enterprise applications administrator who is responsible for building and maintaining these automatic-build environments and ensuring that they are working as expected.

Testing

During any testing phase, there is a constant process taking place where a given bug or defect has to be determined to be a code problem or a problem caused by the environment that the code is being tested in. In many cases, a feature will work perfectly in development environments but fail during the same testing scenario when performed in a test environment. This can be due to how the code is written and differences between what was done in the development environment and the test environment. On the other hand, it could also be due to differences between the configuration, architecture, or setup of the two environments. Often, the only person with enough insight into the application and system configuration to help make this determination is the enterprise applications administrator responsible for maintaining those environments.

In situations such as these, it is typically a joint effort between the enterprise applications administrator and the developer to research the cause for a bug or defect and make a determination as to whether that cause is code based or environment based. Even when the issue is determined to be environment based, there may be a code change necessary in order to compensate for the environmental difference. This is critical under some circumstances as it's possible that the production environment is more architecturally similar to the test environment than the development environment, and the code needs to reflect the end state of the application architecture and configuration.

It is also during the testing phase (usually toward the end of this phase) that performance testing is done for enterprise applications. We've already discussed performance testing and the detailed assessment of performance that must be done in order to understand capacity within the enterprise application. In order to facilitate that performance testing process, it is typical for enterprise applications administrators to provide assistance in defining the tests, monitoring the systems, and interpreting the test results. This also gives the administrator a great deal of insight into how the application performs under load and can assist them in making architectural design decisions in later implementation projects.

Deployment

We talked about segregation of duties in Chapter 5 when we discussed information security. In most corporate environments, this is heavily enforced when it comes to the deployment of code or any changes to production environments. In some cases, regulatory requirements such as the Sarbanes–Oxley Act expect that segregation of duty rules be complied with during these deployments. This is where the enterprise applications administrator comes in as a method of compliance for these types of rules. In most cases, the requirement is that the person who developed the code cannot be the person who deploys the code. By having the administrator responsible for deployment, the corporation can comply with the appropriate security controls.

In addition, deployment of code for enterprise applications can be a very complex process especially in very large implementations. It's possible that code will have to be deployed across hundreds of systems in order to do a complete deployment to the environment. In addition, many code deployments must be done in a specific sequence with certain prerequisites in place before the deployment process can continue to the next step. Finally, there may be infrastructure changes associated with a deployment that must be made at specific times during the deployment process. Due to their understanding of all of the technologies which comprise the enterprise application, it is generally the enterprise application administrator who is best positioned to orchestrate, coordinate, and perform this complex deployment process. In some cases, they may need to work with other teams to accomplish all of the required steps, but in the end, the enterprise applications administrator should be able to handle both the coordination aspects and the technical aspects of code and enterprise application deployment.

Non-Waterfall Development Methodologies

The steps that we've been discussing so far in this section align more closely with the waterfall method of application development rather than other methodologies which may be in use. Many companies are finding value through the use of Agile, Iterative, Extreme Programming, and other alternate development methodologies. This book is not intended to be a debate as to which methodology is the best or even which one works best under different circumstances. Instead, we have chosen to illustrate the enterprise applications administration tasks and roles associated with the waterfall development methodology because those same tasks and roles exist within all development methodologies but with different timing and methods of interacting.

Whereas with the waterfall methodology there are distinct phases that a project goes through such as scoping, design, development, testing, and deployment, in other development methodologies these phases work very differently. For example, in the Agile methodology, development work occurs in rapid "sprints" that occur over a relatively short amount of time such as 1—2 weeks. The goal of each sprint is to create a specific feature that can then be deployed and demonstrated to the requesting business unit. To support this, there are different steps that have to be done within the implementation process to support the rapid-fire approach of development that must be done in order to quickly design, build, test, and deploy these features.

The role of the enterprise applications administrator in these alternative methodologies doesn't really change, but the way that they engage may. For example, the nonfunctional requirements that the administrator works with the developers on during the scoping phase may turn into "stories" that define what needs to be built within an Agile methodology. In essence, the same work has to be done from the enterprise applications administrator perspective; it just may have to be done in a slightly different way to support the organization's chosen method of performing development and project implementations.

Operations Support

In most organizations, the primary role of enterprise applications administrators is performing a level of operations support. As discussed in Chapter 1, the level of support varies between companies and the exact role of an enterprise applications administrator will vary. However, in almost all cases, the need for application experts that also have substantial knowledge in multiple technology areas is apparent and fulfilled through the use of enterprise applications administrators.

In their support role, enterprise applications administrators are responsible for a number of activities that ensure the ongoing availability of the enterprise applications. We called out quite a few of these in Chapter 1 and went into detail on some of those tasks. There are a few tasks which are critical and tend to exist across all enterprise applications administration teams that we should discuss further. These are key components of building out a solid enterprise applications administration team and showing that team's value over time.

The first are the support activities around performing maintenance to the enterprise applications and their dependencies. We touched on this previously, but it's important to note that when it comes to ongoing maintenance, it is critical that maintenance tasks be documented, understood, and executed consistently. There are many cases where the author has heard statements such as, "Joe can't be fired because any time he's gone, SuperDuper Application fails!" This is not an acceptable position for any company to be in. Whatever tasks "Joe" is doing need to be documented and consistently executed as they are obviously critical maintenance tasks for the application. We'll talk about the automation of those tasks in Chapter 8.

As part of these maintenance efforts, it is a good practice to develop runbooks that the organization can use to consistently execute these maintenance tasks within the enterprise application. Runbooks are detailed documents that outline various scenarios and point to work instructions that should be executed when those scenarios occur. In some cases, the scenario can be as simple as the passage of time. An example of this would be a task that must be performed weekly. We'll go over runbooks in detail when we dig into documentation more thoroughly, but you should consider them an important part of the enterprise applications administrator's role in ongoing operations support.

Monitoring of the application is another support role that is frequently fulfilled by enterprise applications administrators. This monitoring role can be at different levels depending on the organizational needs. For example, it may be the enterprise applications administrator who defines what needs to be monitored and the method of monitoring while responding to alerts is performed by other personnel. In other organizations, it may be the enterprise applications administrator who is responsible for watching over every aspect of the application to ensure that any component failures are quickly identified and rectified. We'll go over monitoring more in a later chapter.

When it comes to operations support, one of the more common areas where enterprise applications administrators provide a huge amount of value is in troubleshooting access control issues. While dedicated identity and access management teams may be responsible for setting up user accounts and ensuring that the correct security controls are applied, there is usually a need for someone to help troubleshoot issues when things don't work as expected. In most enterprise applications administration organizations, a fair amount of time is spent trying to understand and fix user access issues. This type of work is often best performed by the enterprise applications administrator as it requires an understanding of security controls, application logic, and potentially other technology areas in order to fully diagnose and fix access issues.

This leads to the primary role of enterprise applications administrators who perform operations support; the analysis and troubleshooting of deeply rooted issues within the application are where an enterprise applications administrator has to use all of their skills across multiple technology areas to provide a level of support that no one else can. In some cases, this may involve looking through captured network traffic, operating system configurations, database records, and application logs to determine exactly where a problem is occurring. The enterprise applications administrator is uniquely positioned to be able to work through all of these aspects of the application and tie the data together in order to determine the cause of the problem. They then turn their skills into attempting to find a fix that will correct the identified problem and prevent it from occurring again in the future.

It is this analysis and troubleshooting capability that truly illustrates the value of enterprise applications administration organizations as they are able to tie together all of the technologies that an application consists of and dig through those technologies themselves to find the problem or work with subject matter experts in each technology to coordinate the troubleshooting efforts. In either case, the central point for ensuring that the cause for the problem gets found across whatever technologies are necessary is the enterprise applications administrator.

The final task that we'll discuss for the enterprise applications administrator in this role is that of production control. This was described in Chapter 1 and is effectively the responsibility of protecting the production environment for an enterprise application. This protection may require ensuring that maintenance events don't occur outside of a specific window or it may involve preventing code from going into the production environment until it has been proven to be adequately tested. There is a lot of responsibility associated with production control, and each company will have different guidelines that they follow to ensure the integrity in this environment. In many cases, it is the role of the enterprise applications administrator to enforce those guidelines and be the last line of defense on behalf of the application's availability.

TEAM BUDGETING AND COST ESTIMATION

One of the more difficult tasks for any manager is the process of cost estimation and budgeting for their team. This process will vary widely between companies and even within different parts of the company's organizational structure. One common thread across most enterprise applications administration teams is the need to create solid budget values using very little information and do this quickly and accurately. To do this properly requires a great deal of experience as well as in-depth knowledge as to the team's capabilities, the company needs, the responsibilities of the team, and the complexity of the enterprise applications that they are responsible for.

The intent of this section is to provide some baseline concepts associated with cost estimation and budgeting that you may be able to apply to your team. Again, the budgeting and cost estimation process will be very different at every single company, but there are some general techniques that you can use to make the process a little easier. These techniques can be tweaked to fit your specific circumstances and used to help you to provide the most accurate cost estimates or budgets possible.

The approach that we're going to take toward this process is going to be splitting up the concepts of budgeting separately from the concepts of cost estimation. The term "budget" in this concept will be used to refer to the annual budget that is required to operate and maintain an enterprise applications administration team. The term "cost estimate" will be used to describe a project or initiative-specific estimate of cost that can be used to enhance the enterprise applications administration team in order to accomplish a given set of tasks or perform a charge-back against other parts of the organization for performing specific work efforts.

Team Budgets

Developing a team budget involves several steps that culminate in the creation of a mostly accurate budget. Any budget can only be as accurate as the data that is used to form it and unknown factors or changing factors may cause the actual financial spend to be greater than or less than expected. For example, if an employee takes an unpaid leave of absence in the middle of the year, you will spend less on personnel costs than you originally budgeted. On the other hand, if enterprise application maintenance contracts are within the scope of your budget and the cost of a contract increases unexpectedly, you may be spending more than you budgeted. In many cases, these factors can be balanced out without too much effort, but in others you may have to make difficult decisions on what does or does not get paid for.

The general idea behind this method of budget creation is to use the best data that you can, cover as many scenarios as possible, and estimate the results of those scenarios from a financial impact perspective. After all of this is done, you will have some solid numbers that can be used for your team and presented to the organization for approval. If approved, part of your role in managing your team is to manage the finances in accordance with the budget with the intent of staying as close to your projected numbers as possible.

CORPORATE MEMO...

Budget Cuts

It seems like every year there is a challenge across the industry to "do more with less" and cut budgets regularly. This may be the reality of the situation at your company as well. Rarely does a budget come back to a manager in this day and age without a memo indicating that another 5%, 10%, or 30% has to be cut. You must be ready to face this challenge, understand the best areas to cut in your budget (hint: it isn't training), and justify the budgetary needs in critical areas.

Detailing the Budget

Putting together a budget begins with determining everything that the budget needs to encompass. This is very similar to a scoping exercise for an implementation project. Ask yourself, "What elements do I need to include in this budget for it to be complete?" Do you need to account solely for personnel costs? If so, does that mean including just their salary or salary, benefits, and incentives? What about the hardware for them to use such as laptops, phones, accessories, and printers? As it relates to personnel, do you need to include training costs as part of your budget or are those costs covered by a larger organization-wide budget? As you can see, simply accounting for personnel costs quickly grows outside of their salary and can add quite a few dollars to your budgeting needs.

Your team may also be comprised of a mix between employees and contractors. While you typically will not have to account for benefits or training associated with contractors, you will need to include their contract rate within your budget if it's expected that you'll continue to contract out your needs over time. These contracts may also include allowances for travel and expenses which will need to be reflected in your budget. Any equipment that needs to be supplied to the contractor usually comes out of your team budget as well and will need to be included.

If your team works at multiple facilities or you plan on having employees travel for any reason, those travel costs will need to be included in your budget. Travel costs consist of the cost of transportation (which may include paying the employee for mileage if they drive their own vehicle when traveling for business), the cost of accommodations if overnight travel is required, appropriate per-diems to cover meals and entertainment, rental vehicles or taxis, and even costs of telephone calls from the hotel in some cases. Travel can be very expensive when all of these items are added together and can contribute to a substantial part of your budget if a lot of travel is necessary.

Some organizations also require teams to contribute to the cost of the facility where they are housed. This can be considered the renting of office space (and services) and would need to account for any desk space, conference rooms, physical storage, and other space-related needs. These costs may also be covered by other parts of the organization such as a facilities department, but again, this will vary across different companies.

Office supplies are another budget item that is often forgotten. When many people think of office supplies, they often think of notepads, staples, paper, and pens. However, there are some higher dollar items that fall into this category such as dry erase boards, projectors, chairs, and shredders. In addition, there may be the need to pay for office services such as copying and binding services, shipping, and secure document storage. All of these costs should be considered for your budget as well.

Finally, enterprise applications administration teams also pose a unique challenge in budgeting due to their application management responsibilities. In some organizations, since this team is responsible for managing the enterprise applications, they're also responsible for any vendor maintenance contracts, external support agreements, hardware service contracts, development software, knowledgebase subscriptions, and other similar costs. Depending on the software and hardware in use, this can be millions of dollars in costs that must be included in the budget for the organization. When this is the case, it's also typically the responsibility of the team to try to minimize these costs as much as possible and drive them down through vendor negotiation. Depending on the company, this may also involve engaging other departments within the company such as a procurement department or a dedicated vendor relationship management team.

Developing a Baseline

With all of the elements of the budget determined, the next step is to start off with a baseline for each item. Table 7.4 gives a sample list of items for a hypothetical budget. You'll note that in this table, there are columns allocated to show the prior year's budgeted amount as well as the actual amount spent. By tracking these values over time, you can get a general idea as to how well the budget aligns with the actual spend as well as the growth or reduction trend over time. These can be used as the beginning of the baseline, but there are also other pieces of data that we can include into our budgeting baselines in order to better predict our budgeting needs.

In order to understand how the organization is performing from a budgetary standpoint, it's important to have solid metrics related to what the team is doing. For example, if your team is responsible for performing support tasks, you should be keeping a record of how many requests the team is receiving, how much time is spent resolving each request, and what the request volume trend looks like over time. Using these values can tell you whether the

Table 7.4 Sample Budget Item List

Budget Item	Prior Year Estimate ($)	Prior Year Actual ($)	Current Year Estimate ($)
Salaries	425,000.00	427,950.00	437,388.50
Benefits	127,500.00	145,503.00	153,085.98
Training	15,000.00	14,196.00	14,500.00
Equipment	19,283.00	22,963.00	20,500.00
Travel	15,000.00	24,310.00	15,000.00
Facilities	10,000.00	10,000.00	12,000.00
Telephony	5,000.00	5,624.00	5,700.00
Office supplies	20,000.00	19,872.00	20,000.00
Maintenance contracts	13,450,500.00	13,980,500.00	15,797,965.00
Total	14,087,283.00	14,650,918.00	16,476,139.48

amount of time necessary to resolve tasks is increasing, decreasing, or staying the same. In addition, you can see what the volume trend looks like and use this data to project what the volume in the future might look like.

Estimating Growth

Growth is a natural process for enterprise applications administration organizations. In general, you can always assume that the use of enterprise applications will increase, that the support needs over time will increase, and that the number of enterprise applications in an organization will continue to grow. But the real question is, how will this growth affect my budget and what should I plan for? To answer this, you need to look at the trend of data associated with the past as well as gather information from other parts of the organization related to what their expectations are for the coming year.

Depending on what is planned for the company in the next year, you may need to account for supporting new applications, adding staff to support additional support needs, or plan for additional licenses for the applications that your team is responsible for. You may also need to plan around increased maintenance costs, supporting a larger number of support hours (e.g., supporting international growth of an application by providing support during working hours of the new geographical location) and supporting an increasing number of enterprise application issues if a great deal of development work is planned for the year.

To estimate this, you can look at growth in two ways. These are the concepts of organic growth and planned expansion. If you'll recall our previous discussion related to the growth of system capacity needs over time, this may seem familiar. Just as system usage grows both organically and through planned expansion, support needs grow in the same manner. From an estimation standpoint, you should always try to understand the growth trend of support needs over time and ensure that your estimate includes funding to pay for any organic growth that will occur in the coming year. In addition, by working with the various business units within your organization, you should be able to get an idea of any planned expansion and estimate your budget number to scale appropriately based on additional work that the enterprise application administration team will need to perform.

Keep in mind that as you scale up your budget to support growth, you should look at multiple budget line items. Scaling up a budget for growth does not involve just adding money to the personnel salary budget! Instead, each line item will have to be increased to account for the expected growth accordingly. Everything from training costs to office supplies should be reexamined and an appropriate growth value added to each as needed. This can also include support contracts or maintenance contracts if the number of software licenses, hardware configurations, or support needs is expected to change due to either organic or planned growth.

Estimating Personnel Costs

At this point you should have a baseline list of budget items, prior year budgeted and spent numbers if available, and an understanding of what growth you're expecting for your team in the coming year. Now you can start putting numbers into your budget to reflect your best estimate of costs for the coming year. This will, of course, include both personnel costs and other ancillary costs associated with the ongoing enterprise applications administration role.

When estimating the budget for personnel costs, there are a few things to take into account. Most companies have a planned performance structure that includes an annual raise based on employee performance. In addition, many also have both short-term and long-term incentive programs that are intended to help retain talented employees. The budgeting for these raises and incentives is sometimes difficult as it is generally unknown as to what the company's guidance for raises and incentive percentages is until well after budgets are approved. This is generally solved either by having raises and incentives come out of a separate budget at the appropriate time or by accounting for rough estimates for these values during the budgeting process. In some cases, the process is a blend of these where raises are accounted for in the team budget but incentives are accounted for in a separate budget.

If your organization is one that requires individual teams to include raises and/or incentives in their budget, they will generally provide some guidance on what percentages should be used as a placeholder value. In addition, they'll generally have an idea as to when the salary changes will take effect. This will help you to understand when the salary cost of the employees will go up and from there you can determine how much to add to your budget. For example, if your budget is due in January and salary changes take effect in August, you only have to plan on paying the additional amount for half of the year.

When planning on personnel costs for expanding the team, there are also several factors that come into play. The salary to add to your budget will vary based on the level of employee that you're looking to hire, the current job market, and even the reputation of the company. If a company has a really good reputation amongst the information technology workforce, they can actually offer a slightly smaller salary than average because people have a strong desire to work there. Of course, this reputation is usually gained by other tangible and intangible benefits that the company provides, so there is a cost associated with the reputation as well.

In most cases, corporations have salary grades or bands that define the low, median, and high salary levels for any given position or title within the company. If you base your budget on the median level for any given position, you are usually in a good spot from a financial aspect for hiring an average employee. If you are looking to recruit the best employees in the marketplace, you'll probably want to budget for a higher salary as well as higher benefit costs. Basically, the budgeting process for hiring should reflect the quality of the employee that you wish to have.

TIPS & TRICKS

Diamonds in the Rough

In some very rare cases, you come across an amazing employee who you recruited at a low cost because they didn't recognize their own value. This doesn't happen often, but it is actually a challenging situation when it does. In some cases, the company does not have a good method in place for promoting employees to the level that they deserve based on their skill and requires a long process (years) to move an employee like this up the salary scale. In the meantime, other organizations may become aware of the skills of this employee and attempt to recruit them with higher salaries than you can offer. It's important to recognize the skills of your employees and let the employees know how much you appreciate their work, their knowledge, and their skills. When money can't retain a talented individual, sometimes loyalty will.

On the other hand, there are times when you must also recognize that it may not be in the employee's best interest to stay at a company that cannot reward them appropriately. In this situation, you must make a call on whether to advise the employee that they could progress their career better through another company. Any human resource department will tell you

that you should never take this approach, but the reality is that honesty (within legal requirements) is the best policy. The employee may decide to stay with the company anyway just
because of your honest assessment.

Estimating Other Costs

Outside of personnel costs, there are many other costs listed on your budget.
We've already talked about accounting for growth of some of these related to
enterprise application growth such as maintenance and support contracts. But
there are frequently changes that have to be made to other budgetary numbers
due to other reasons. For example, due to inflation, the cost of office supplies
regularly increases each year. This has an impact to any office supply budget.
The same type of change may also be reflected in office space costs depending
on the contracts associated with the office space. Services such as trash removal
or, for those companies which offer this perk, free-to-employees coffee and tea
tend to also increase in cost over time and need to be reflected in your budget.
These increases aren't necessarily due to growth, but natural inflation.

If you have an idea of what the inflation increase is going to be based on
contracts or past increases, this can be reflected in your budget easily. If not,
you can try to estimate an increase based on what the current rate of inflation is for your country. Alternatively, you can guess that there will be an
increase of 1.5−3% and hope that the increases do not exceed that amount.

When developing any budget, there is always room for error. It is very bad to
get your estimates wrong and run out of money due to budgeting insufficient
funds. On the other hand, if you over-budget and have money left over at the
end of the year, this will call into question your estimation skills and may
cause you to have your funds reduced the following year. Because of this, it's
usually wise to add a line item to cover potential estimation errors. In the
author's experience, a value of around 5% is usually adequate without being
excessive. Some managers choose to add this "oops" percentage into each line
item so that it is not explicitly called out. Some companies actually prefer that
approach while others consider it dishonest since you are, effectively, saying
that any given line item will cost more than it should. Accounting and finance
departments will sometimes call this out indicating that the line items are
inaccurate leading to the perception that you were inflating your numbers.
The correct approach will vary based on the company, but the generally
accepted practice is to call out a contingency line item separately.

Cost Estimates

When performing implementation work, it's common for enterprise applications administration teams to have to put together a cost estimate for their

work on the project. These estimates are generally requested at a very early phase in the project when you may or may not have much information about what the project entails. Because of this, your estimate may not accurately reflect the actual cost associated with the project. The goal is for the estimate to be as close as possible to what the real cost will be within the accuracy requirements of your organization.

Each organization has different accuracy requirements depending on the project phase and the level of information available. During some of the initial ideation around a project before its full scope is known, the cost estimates are generally considered a "rough order of magnitude" (ROM). This type of cost estimate is intended to generalize the cost of the project and give a basic idea of what the costs will be in relation to other projects that have been done in the past. ROM estimates can be dollar based or sizing based. If they are dollar based, then they will typically come in a scale similar to the following:

- < $50,000
- $50,000–100,000
- $100,000–500,000
- $500,000–1,000,000
- $1,000,000–5,000,000
- > $5,000,000

This scale will differ depending on your organization. Some projects will go into the hundreds of millions of dollars, but split the project into phases so that the estimation can be a little more accurately determined.

If the ROM is based on sizing, you may have a scale similar to this:

- X-Small
- Small
- Medium
- Large
- X-Large

This type of scale tells the requestor of the estimate whether they're asking for a fairly substantial effort or something smaller. This allows them to determine a starting point for the project and make determinations on whether the project is worth scoping in more detail. If there is a small budget and each cost estimate comes back as X-Large, there is a possibility that the project would be cancelled and the business unit would move on to something else.

The next level of an estimate beyond the ROM is a budget estimate. Similar to a working budget, this budget for implementation should include all costs associated with the implementation from the perspective of the enterprise applications administration team. We'll talk about scoping next in this section and that will help define what needs to be accounted for in the budget estimate. In general, the accuracy of the budget estimate is expected to be much better than the ROM and should be delivered with an accuracy estimate as well. These will typically range between 10% and 50% depending on the organization and their estimation process.

The last estimation level is the definitive estimate or final estimate. These are generally delivered after the implementation project is fully understood, all scope is determined, and any estimates from vendors or other third-party providers have been gathered in order to roll up into the overall estimate. Generally, these estimates are expected to be accurate to within 5–10% depending on the organization.

Keep in mind that your estimate is coming from the perspective of enterprise applications administration. Unless your team is instantiating the project and executing it internally, your estimate will roll up into an overall project estimate that includes estimates from multiple teams. You may be responsible for including estimates from other teams such as infrastructure teams within your cost estimate when you deliver it to the project team. Make sure that you have a clear understanding of what should be included within your estimate to ensure that nothing in the way of project costs is missed.

Finally, there are always multiple ways to solve a problem. Some projects operate in phases where basic functionality is added first and then expanded upon. Other projects are initially planned to deliver a huge amount of new capabilities and then are scaled down prior to implementation. In order to support this type of activity, it sometimes helps to deliver your costs estimates with a number of options. The first option could include everything that the requestor asked for while the second option scales down what is being delivered in order to lower the cost. You may also want to include an option that expands upon the original request in order to put infrastructure in place to support future project needs. On the other hand, you may need to put together an option that covers the absolute bare minimum required to support the project. It's always good to have options and this can save you some rework later if the implementation project team requests revisions to lower costs.

Scoping the Project

When developing your cost estimate, it's important to understand exactly what needs to be included within the estimate. Obviously, you'll need to include estimates for the personnel who will be involved in the project (if your company uses a charge-back model, labor accounting, or contract staff augmentation), but you may also need to include a number of other elements. Just like developing a budget for operations support, developing an implementation cost estimate involves identifying all of the appropriate elements to include within the estimate.

For example, if the project is intended to be relatively nonintrusive from an infrastructure perspective and not require any additional software, you may need to provide a labor-only estimate. However, if there is any change to the underlying enterprise application technical architecture, you may need to account for hardware costs, maintenance contracts for the hardware, hardware implementation and configuration costs, software licensing, software maintenance and support contracts, and other details. The most important part of this is to understand the true scope of the project, identify everything that will be impacted by the project, and determine the scope of that impact. By doing so, you are positioned to understand what the actual project costs will be from the enterprise applications administration perspective and can relay this information to the project team.

Estimating Direct Project Work

As you look at a project, the bulk of the estimation process generally involves putting together a good idea of what tasks your team will be involved with and how long they will take. Tasks that are done in direct support of the project such as performing a software install or creating a database are considered direct project work. Direct project work is intended to encompass the execution of project-specific tasks. While you may be required to deliver your estimate prior to the development of a full project plan with detailed tasks, you should be able to put together a general idea of what tasks will be required and develop the estimate from that understanding.

When estimating direct project work, it's important to understand that the same task will usually not take the exact amount of time each time it's executed and may also vary depending on who is executing the task. In addition, there is always a level of ramp-up time that is associated to any project when the assigned personnel are learning about the project and gaining an understanding of what they need to do. This is the case for both new and experienced personnel as each new project does bring new challenges and new situations that have to be handled.

With that in mind, it's helpful to put together a chart that illustrates the best-case and worst-case scenarios for any given task on a per-person basis. This allows you to understand the productivity of each team member, account for ramp-up time, better understand who you want to assign to a given project depending on availability, and deliver a more accurate cost estimate to the project team. The grid shown in Table 7.5 is one way of doing this.

Table 7.5 Personnel Cost Estimate Grid

Task: Server Install

Name	Hourly Rate ($)	Best Case (Hours)	Best Case (Cost, in $)	Worst Case (Hours)	Worst Case (Cost, in $)	Average Case (Hours)	Average Case (Cost, in $)	Estimate ($)
Travis	100	3	300	18	1800	10.5	1050	1425
Scott	101	3	303	18	1818	10.5	1061	1439
Christina	90	5	450	40	3600	22.5	2025	2813
Mike	90	5	450	40	3600	22.5	2025	2813
Sean	90	6	540	40	3600	23	2070	2835
Albert	90	7	630	20	1800	13.5	1215	1508
Praneeth	90	6	540	28	2520	17	1530	2025

In Table 7.5, you can see that there are a lot of values that we're dealing with in order to develop this labor cost estimate. First, we have to identify the specific task that this is for (server install) and the personnel who are able to perform this activity. While it may seem excessive to track personnel productivity data to this level of granularity, it does help when determining accurate costs for estimates. In some cases, you may prefer to roll up tasks into higher-level task bundles for simplicity.

Next, we take into account hourly cost for each person. Some organizations track costs on a per-person basis and others do a blended rate which averages out the cost across all of their personnel. Naturally, use the method that works best for you and for your organization. This value is then used in combination with our best-case and worst-case durations for each person performing these tasks. By multiplying these figures, we now know the best-case and worst-case cost for any given task depending on who we assign to execute the task.

Next is a little more math to fine-tune our estimate. The most obvious choice to develop an estimate would be to average the best-case and worst-case scenarios to determine what the average cost would be. However, in practice, you'll find that you very rarely have a task accomplished within the best-case, worst-case, or average-case timelines. From an estimation perspective, you don't want to estimate too low, but estimating for the worst case can over-inflate your cost estimate. A better method is to take the average cost and then average that with the worst-case cost. This gives you an estimated cost a little higher than the average, but not as high as the worst-case scenario. Using this method tends to lead to more accurate cost estimation for direct project work.

Estimating Indirect Project Work

The last topic that we'll cover for implementation cost estimation is that of indirect project work. While there are obvious tasks that can easily be called out on a project plan such as software installation, database creation, SQL tuning, load testing, and so on, there are also other tasks that aren't so easily categorized. These types of tasks are indirect project work and can include items such as:

- Infrastructure team coordination
- Developer support
- Subject matter expert consulting
- Request for change (RFC) process leadership
- Deployment and back-out plan documentation
- Knowledge transfer
- Monitoring setup
- Vendor research

This list can become incredibly extensive as you look at all of the general tasks that an enterprise applications administration team performs in support of a given project. These tasks, while indirect, are related to the project and should therefore be reflected in your cost estimates. This can be done by estimating the number of hours necessary to perform these tasks based on the scope of the project, metrics related to the amount of work needed for projects before this one, and an understanding of the complexity for the implementation project. Another method is to simply add a line item to the cost estimate titled "enterprise applications administration support" and add a percentage of the total cost estimate to account for these indirect tasks. For example, if the cost estimate before adding this in is $100,000, you may want to add an additional $10,000 or 10% to cover overhead. This percentage will vary widely depending on your organization, the tasks that your team performs, and the complexity of any given project.

SUMMARY

This chapter has focused more on the management aspect of enterprise applications administration. This starts with building a team of enterprise applications administrators and ensuring that they have the knowledge and skills necessary to do their job effectively. You always want to do everything you can to support your team including training them, giving them the tools that they need to succeed, and providing them interesting and rewarding work to do. This requires that any enterprise applications administration team manager put a great deal of focus into not only the day-to-day task management of their team, but also into the long-term career planning and ambitions of each team member.

In order to ensure that your team performs to your expectations, it's also important to set the standards for your team and detail out what those expectations are. Most team members want to do their best to contribute to the team and its success, but they may not be clear as to what is needed to do so. By clearly laying out the standards and expectations for your team, you can ensure that there is no question as to what is required and what each team member should do to contribute to the team in the most effective manner possible.

From the managerial perspective, it's very important to understand the type of work that an enterprise applications administration team does. Day-to-day operations support differs substantially from implementation projects and requires a different perspective depending on the type of work being performed. In order to effectively lead your team, you need to understand what the differences between support and implementation are and how to handle the tasks associated with each. This then, of course, ties into the financial aspect of running an enterprise applications administration team and estimating both an operating budget as well as implementation project cost estimates. In this chapter, we went over all of this in detail and gave some best practices on building these estimates based on how your organization expects costs to be determined.

Automation and Monitoring

PROCESS AUTOMATION

For enterprise applications administrators, a major goal should always be to work themselves out of a job. This may seem a little counterintuitive, but there is logic to this statement. With enterprise applications, there is a never-ending list of work that must be done and never enough time or people to accomplish it all. By putting process automation in place, working themselves out of a job, enterprise applications administrators can reduce the amount of time that they spend on repetitive tasks, improve the quality and consistency of the tasks, and increase the amount of time and attention that they can put towards more technically challenging work. Putting time and attention towards ensuring that you don't have to perform certain repetitive tasks manually saves the company money and gives enterprise applications administrators more interesting work to do in the long run.

Not all processes can be automated. Some require too much manual intervention or real-time decisions to be good candidates for automation. Automation of others may be prevented due to technical or administrative limitations. Almost as important as automating the processes themselves is determining which processes can and should be automated. There are a few rules that can be followed to help with this determination process.

- Is the process going to be performed at least three times?
- Is the process free of complex real-time decisions?

- Does the process have a need to run at specific times or intervals?
- Is the process consistent in flow each time it is executed or use variances in flow that can be determined by specific factors?
- Can the process be automated without violating any security controls?

If the answer to all of these is "yes" then the process should probably be automated if possible. If the answer to any of them is "no," the process should be looked at closely to see if it could still be a candidate for automation or if the issue preventing automation can be eliminated. We'll dig into this a little deeper in the next section as we look at how to define an automatable process.

There are different ways that processes can be automated and it's important to solidly understand how this is done. Regardless of the technology used, there are key terms associated with process automation that you need to know in order to ensure that we're speaking the same language. This was referred to in Chapter 1 when we talked about consistency in our approaches and terminology throughout the book. With this in mind, we'll be discussing the differences between frameworks, processes, and tasks and how they all relate to process automation. Each has a part to play in this type of work and their roles should be clearly understood.

In order to automate something, you have to fully understand it. In the case of information technology, this means breaking any given task into its various components which are individually small enough and simple enough that even a computer can understand it. This can be illustrated through a simple exercise. Describe, as you would to someone who has never done it before, the process of going to get a drink of water. An example of this could be:

1. Stand up
2. Walk into kitchen
3. Walk to sink
4. Use left hand to open cabinet door
5. Get glass with left hand
6. Use right hand to turn valve for cold water
7. Wait for water to reach desired temperature
8. Use left hand to move glass under water flow
9. Use left hand to move glass when full
10. Use right hand to turn cold water valve off
11. Use left hand to raise glass to mouth
12. Drink water
13. Move left hand down
14. Place glass into sink with left hand
15. Leave kitchen
16. Walk to chair
17. Sit down

Notice how many individual steps there are in a simple process like this and keep in mind that we still used predefined processes such as "stand up" rather than describing the process of standing up. This is how detailed the individual tasks which make up a process must be defined. We'll take a look at this specific process and how to document it and others in the Documentation section.

Finally, we'll cover how to automate specific tasks through a discussion of best practices and some real-world examples. We will not be going into an in-depth discussion on various scripting languages, their pros and cons, or how to use them as that is outside of the scope of this book. Instead, we'll continue to focus on the general concepts and process of automation rather than digging into the dirty details of the scripting languages.

Defining an Automatable Process

We defined an automatable process previously as one which can answer "yes" to the following questions:

- Is the process going to be performed at least three times?
- Is the process free of complex real-time decisions?
- Does the process have a need to run at specific times or intervals?
- Is the process consistent in flow each time it is executed or use variances in flow that can be determined by specific factors?
- Can the process be automated without violating any security controls?

The reality is that the criteria can be more selective than this and there are always exceptions to the rules. To better understand which processes you should automate, let's talk about these criteria, understand their basis, and discuss valid exception scenarios.

The first question is, "is the process going to be performed at least three times?" Generally the three occurrence "rule" is used as a baseline for the need to repeat a process, but that's a general practice and not a real rule. The actual intent of this is to determine the value of automating the process. We're effectively trying to determine whether or not the time spent automating the process provides value over the long run. This is especially important in cases where quality and consistency are not large concerns and labor is cheap. If the value proposition isn't there, there is no justification for automating the process. To go back to a simple concept, is the juice worth the squeeze?

Let's break that down a little further as the value of automating a process is typically found through time savings as well as improvements in consistency and accuracy. As we refine the question, we can break it down into further questions to better understand the value of automating the process:

- How long does it take to execute the process?
- How much does it cost (based on time) to execute the process?
- How often is the process performed?
- What is the cost in effort to automate the process?
- What is the cost of an error being made in the process?
- How frequently is an error made?
- What is the cost of inconsistency in performance of the process?
- How frequently is the process performed inconsistently?

At this point, we've removed any subjectivity out of the decision-making process and boiled it down to simple facts and numbers. Using this, we can put

Table 8.1 Example Process Automation Valuation Answers

Questions	Responses	Notes
How long does it take to execute the process?	0.5 h	
How much does it cost (based on time) to execute the process?	$33	Contractor @ $65/h
How often is the process performed?	70 times per week	
What is the cost in effort to automate the process?	40 h	Time to set up remote access, automate authentication securely, and test thoroughly
What is the cost in dollars to automate the process?	$3400	Contractor @ $85/h
What is the cost in effort of an error being made in the process?	0.75 h	0.25 h to recognize problem and fix, 0.5 h for another execution
What is the cost in dollars of an error being made in the process?	$49	Contractor @ $65/h
How frequently is an error made?	3 times per week	
What is the cost in effort of inconsistency in performance of the process?	0.75 h	0.25 h to identify out-of-order restart, 0.5 h for another execution
What is the cost in dollars of inconsistency in performance of the process?	$49	Contractor @ $65/h
How frequently is the process performed inconsistently?	2 times per week	

together a quick valuation equation. Let's answer the questions above using a hypothetical process for restarting a server. Table 8.1 shows what the answers could look like.

As you can see in Table 8.1, some additional questions were added to ensure that costs in both time and dollars are captured. Time has a cost that will vary depending on the cost associated with the person or people performing the work. Table 8.1 shows a different cost for the contractor who performs the reboots versus the contractor with the higher skill level required to perform the automation.

With the required information around the process being considered for automation, we can now calculate whether or not it's worth the effort. We do this by determining the cost of the process executions today including the time to execute and frequency, the time and frequency of errors, and the time and frequency of inconsistency to set a baseline. We then calculate the cost of automating the process. In some cases, a process cannot be fully automated and requires some manual effort within the process automation. If this effort is substantial, it can be added into the cost of the automated process as a standalone value. Otherwise, a general rule of thumb is to assume that for any automated process, approximately 5–10% of the time to execute the process manually is still involved in the automated version of the process. This is reflected in the calculations shown in Table 8.2 to ensure that manual work is still accounted for.

With the calculations shown in Table 8.2, we now know that the current process is costing us a total of $2555 per week after effort, errors, and inconsistency are accounted for. The automated process will cost approximately $231 per week to execute after the initial cost of $3400 to perform the process automation. With this in mind, the effort of automating the process will pay for itself within 2 weeks. There is no question that automating this process makes sense from a financial perspective.

This type of calculation can be performed for any manual process and will generally show that it's worth taking on the initial cost to automate the process based on the longer term savings. In more complex processes, the frequency of errors may increase causing the savings due to automation to be even more substantial. In addition, processes that occur to critical systems may have additional factors included into the cost of errors, such as system downtimes and lost business. These additional factors can further reinforce the value of process automation and clearly demonstrate the savings associated with the automation.

Tasks Versus Processes Versus Frameworks

Performing process automation should be a part of day-to-day operations for an enterprise applications administrator. With that in mind, you will be creating a lot of scripts or application code to facilitate automating the processes

Table 8.2 Example Process Automation Valuation Costs

	Hours	Dollars	Notes
Current Process Cost			
Execution of process	0.5	$ 33.00	Contractor @65/Hr.
Frequency of execution (per week)	70		
	35	$ 2,310.00	
Costs related to errors being made in the process	0.75	$ 49.00	.25 Hour to recognize problem and fix, .5 hour for another execution. Contractor @ $65/hr
Frequency of errors (per week)	3		
	2.25	$ 147.00	
Costs related to inconsistency in performance of process	0.75	$ 49.00	.25 Hour to identify out-of-order restart, 5 hour for another execution. Contractor @ $65/hr
Frequency of inconsistent performance of process (per week)	2		
	15	$ 98.00	
Total Weekly Cost		$ 2,555.00	
Automated Process Cost			
Cost to implement automate process	40	$ 3,400.00	Time to set up remote access, automate authentication securely, and test thoroughly. Contractor @ $85/hr
Cost to admin automated process (per week)	3.55	$ 231.00	

that you perform on a regular basis. As you do this, you'll identify various parts of a process that can be automated individually, create scripts for those parts, and then orchestrate them as part of the overall process automation. In addition, you may find the need to perform certain functions over and over or perform higher level process automation when you act on automating a specific process. It's important to understand the terminology associated with these aspects of process automation so that we have a shared vocabulary and can be consistent throughout this discussion.

The smallest part of a process is an individual *task*. A task is typically one of many parts that make up an overall *process*. In our example earlier in the chapter, some individual tasks might be "stand up," "walk into kitchen," and "walk to sink." Each of these tasks should be examined to see if they can be automated as part of the overall process automation. Some tasks may require different scripts or technologies to be used for various tasks that make up the process. As you examine each task, you can make this determination based on how the task must be performed.

Individual tasks that can be automated typically need to be tied to other tasks. Since the individual tasks are all part of the same process, there is generally a given sequence of events that must happen in order for the process to execute successfully. This process-level view is necessary to understand how to link the scripts or application code together so that the process functions correctly end-to-end. This is sometimes done through passing data from task to task or from using a higher level task to orchestrate other subtasks.

As you look at the process as a whole, you may decide that you can't automate every part of the process. Again, using our example from earlier in the chapter, you may decide that you can automate "walk to the kitchen" and "walk to sink" but not "stand up." The "stand up" task may require manual intervention to execute which could then call automation for the next two tasks in the process. In a case like this, it's generally best to look over the entire process flow, determine which tasks can be automated, and determine a method of passing information between those that can and those that can't. This may mean having an administrator review a log file to determine whether the next step in a process should be started or it could be sending the administrator a message for the same purpose. Both push and pull techniques are valid for passing this type of information and should be considered as part of your process automation design.

With the concepts of tasks and their relationship to a process in mind, let's move on to discussing *frameworks*. In the development world, a framework is something that makes doing development easier by having predefined, reusable code already in place that the developer can leverage rather than rewrite themselves. The same concept can apply to process automation. When you look at the tasks associated with processes, you will often find that the same type of task has to be performed for multiple processes. The specific criteria or options for the task may change, but the general concept may be the same. This is where the application of a framework can help in reducing the amount of coding required to automate the process.

In addition, there may be overarching needs that span across multiple processes. For example, each process may need to be scheduled to run at a specific time or based on specific variables versus being manually initiated. Other common cross-process needs are logging, security functions such as authentication and authorization, task management associated with process flows, and user interface functions. All of these are things that could fit in a process automation framework to ease the implementation of the automation.

Depending on the needs of the enterprise, a commercial off-the-shelf (COTS) solution may work for some parts of the process automation framework while other parts are created by the organization. For example, many tools exist that allow for scheduling of tasks, monitoring the completion of tasks, and following the task execution through a process flow. Some of these also include capabilities for logging and security functions as well as a user interface. However, there are sometimes gaps in the commercial offerings that do require coding or scripting on the part of the enterprise applications administrator in order to fully meet the requirements associated with the process.

These COTS offerings do sometimes offer the ability to reuse defined tasks as well and allow you to modify the execution of the task based on variables and parameters. For those that don't, you may need to define code or scripts associated with a task in such a way that you can "wrap" the task execution within another script which is then used by the COTS framework. For example, you may create a task of "walk" and then apply wrapper tasks that pass appropriate variables of "to the kitchen" and "to sink" in order to execute the "walk" task correctly depending on the situation.

Documentation

In order to properly automate a process, it's critical that you have the correct information about the process to start with. Earlier in this chapter, we discussed determining the sequence of events for a given process, but there is a lot more to fully documenting a process in order to prepare it for automation. Accounting for what the process is supposed to do as well as handling cases where things don't go as planned are equally important in process automation and should be reflected in your documentation. In this section, we'll be looking at how to properly document a process in preparation for automation as well as how to use that documentation to understand the process even better than when you began.

Let's start by taking a look at the example that we used earlier in the chapter for going to get a drink of water. As a reminder, these are the steps that we initially documented.

1. Stand up
2. Walk into kitchen
3. Walk to sink
4. Use left hand to open cabinet door
5. Get glass with left hand

6. Use right hand to turn valve for cold water
7. Wait for water to reach desired temperature
8. Use left hand to move glass under water flow
9. Use left hand to move glass when full
10. Use right hand to turn cold water valve off
11. Use left hand to raise glass to mouth
12. Drink water
13. Move left hand down
14. Place glass into sink with left hand
15. Leave kitchen
16. Walk to chair
17. Sit down

With details being this granular, it's also very easy to make mistakes. Did you notice that we left the cabinet open? Were there any other mistakes in this process flow? In many cases, even with very close scrutiny, tasks within a process are forgotten or missed. It's always very important to walk through the process and make sure that you've accounted for as many tasks as possible. Then test the process by following the document repeatedly.

With the process documented in this format, it can be looked at as a top-down process flow. From a diagram perspective, you could illustrate this as shown in Figure 8.1.

As you can see in the diagram shown in Figure 8.1, our process flows simply from beginning to end with no variance or decisions. But that's not how real processes work. Using this example, there are multiple decision points that must be accounted for. As examples, consider determining the temperature of water that you would like or how full you would like the glass to be. In any process, the existence of decisions needs to be determined and the criteria to answer those decisions must be defined. We could add decision points into our process diagram as shown in Figure 8.2 to reflect this.

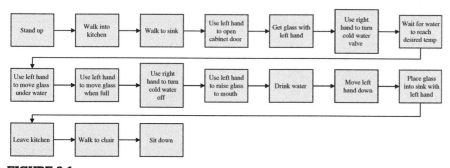

FIGURE 8.1
Basic process flow diagram.

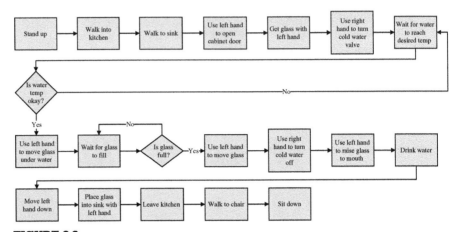

FIGURE 8.2
Basic process flow diagram with decisions.

The data necessary to drive the process through the decisions can be determined either when the process starts or throughout the process. In some cases, you will know up front what the answers are in which case they can be fed through the process to the appropriate decisions. In other cases, the decision must be made based on events that occur as part of the process itself. For example, we may know what temperature we want the water to be up front, but there may be a decision process to determine if the water has actually reached that temperature. In this case, the current temperature of the water must match the predefined temperature that we decided on prior to starting the process. This changes our process flow a little bit as shown in Figure 8.3.

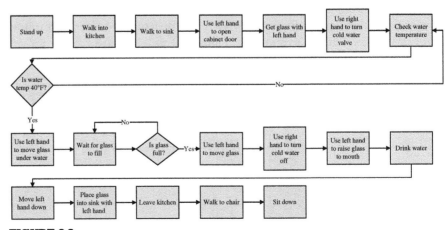

FIGURE 8.3
Basic process flow diagram with predetermined and real-time values.

After the process has been well defined through a process flow, it's time to take the step of improving the process through automation. One of the advantages of automating processes is that you can add steps to the process that enhance it without impacting the amount of effort that the person executing the process has to perform. For example, we might determine that it's easier to drink if we use our right hand instead of our left. To make this change, we can just modify the process flow to include moving the glass between hands prior to raising the glass and change the hand that will be raising the glass. As you look at process flows, it's always important to keep an eye out for places where improvements can be made.

TIPS & TRICKS

Documenting for Improvement

In almost every case, documenting a process shows you obvious places for improvement that may not be easily identified when the process isn't documented. Humans always understand things better when they are presented in an analog or visual format than when they are presented digitally. By forming a picture of how the process works, it is natural for potential improvements to be more easily identifiable. With this in mind, it may make sense to document processes that are being performed even if there is no intent to automate them. The act of visualization associated with documenting the process may help to improve that process through the identification of additional efficiencies.

As you think about improvements in a process, consider the flow of the process itself. In this case, we have a very linear process where one step follows the next. In many processes, additional efficiencies can be gained through the use of multithreading or executing multiple tasks within the process simultaneously. This does not work in all cases such as when a subsequent task relies on data coming from a prior task, but can work in some situations. Some care should also be taken to ensure that not too many tasks are executed at the same time as this can strain the system executing the process. Going back to our example, it might make sense to turn the valve on while getting the glass at the same time. However, if we tried to walk to the sink, get the glass, and turn on the water at the same time, the process would fail. We can't easily turn on the valve before we reach the sink. We can reflect these simultaneous tasks in our process flow diagram as shown in Figure 8.4.

At this point, our process flow diagram should be close to complete. To ensure that the document is accurate, we should walk through the process a few times and correct any mistakes. Fixing errors during the documentation phase of process automation is much easier than trying to fix those errors after the script or code has been written. After all tasks and decisions associated with the process

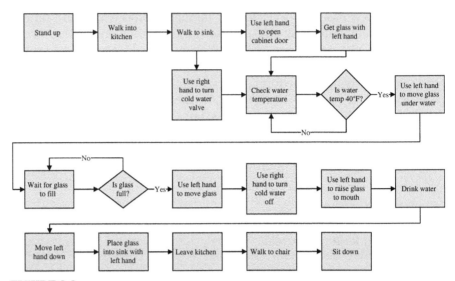

FIGURE 8.4
Basic process flow diagram with multithreading.

flow have been accurately documented, it's time to start making allowances for things to go wrong.

The documented process flow is really a best-case scenario. If everything works exactly as you want it to, this process will function without fail in either a manual or automated fashion. However, in real life, things happen that cause processes to fail or have to change. With our example, what if the cabinet is found to be empty? What if we turn on the valve and the water does not start flowing? What if we drop the glass? These are all events that we can correct for when we manually execute a process, but an automated process must either be told how to correct for unexpected events or be told how to handle the event in such a way that someone else can come and fix it.

This is very similar to documentation associated with application development. The process flow diagram would be considered a "use case" and details out how the process should work. The walk-throughs of the process could be considered "test cases" and demonstrate whether or not the process has been documented properly. The capture of unexpected events aligns with the concept of "destructive testing" where the tester intentionally tries to break the application to see what happens. In the information security world, this would be considered "fuzzing." In the world of process automation, we call it "error pattern modeling."

We have already determined a few errors that could occur within our process. These can be reflected either as defined or expected errors in the process flow or as unexpected errors. Let's go ahead and view the cabinet being empty as an expected error and handle it appropriately in our process flow. This can be done in a manner similar to that shown in Figure 8.5.

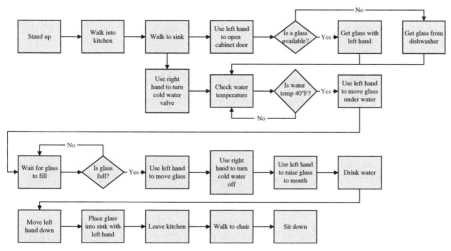

FIGURE 8.5
Basic process flow diagram with autocorrection.

So why would we handle this specific error automatically through the process and not the others? Generally, this determination is made based on two factors. The first is the frequency and probability of the error occurring. If it's an error that is likely to happen on a regular basis, you should probably expect it and ensure that it is handled properly within the automated process. The second factor is the ability for the process to perform automated error correction for the error in question. If the error can be easily corrected for by the process flow with no additional interaction required, it may also make sense to change the process flow to reflect this and consider the error a candidate for automatic error correction.

The other two errors that we determined for this process are less likely to occur and will require additional effort to correct. These can fall into the realm of expected errors because we know that they may happen, but because of their complexity or likelihood of occurrence, they may not be candidate for automatic error correction. We would go ahead and consider them expected errors and perhaps assign them a given error code, but we would not change the process flow to perform autocorrection. Instead, we would identify that the error occurred, report it, and halt the process or move on to another part of the process. This could be illustrated as shown in Figure 8.6.

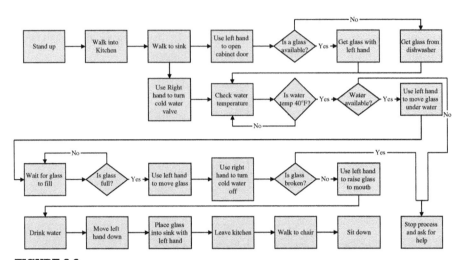

FIGURE 8.6
Basic process flow diagram with expected errors.

Finally, we have the concept of unexpected errors. These are errors that we didn't necessarily think of as we were designing the process that may happen as it's being executed. These errors could be anything from finding out that our leg is broken to finding fire coming from the faucet when we turn the valve. Any error that occurs which is not explicitly expected is, obviously, unexpected. As you develop a process flow, you can put mechanisms in place to handle these unexpected errors. From a development perspective, one of the worst things that can happen with an application is an "unhandled exception" and this is also true of process automation.

To fix this in the development world, it's common to wrap the code being executed in an error handling framework and instruct it to take specific actions if any error occurs that it doesn't know how to deal with. The same is true for process automation. In this case, our process flow should identify a set of tasks to execute in the event that something unexpected goes wrong during the execution of the process. We could add decision blocks after every action that state, "Did this work?" and based on the answer, direct the process accordingly. This makes the process flow diagram very difficult to read and follow, however, so what is normally done is to add an unknown exception handling section to the diagram that details out the tasks to execute when an unhandled exception occurs. When we actually go to code these tasks in a script, we can use the scripting language's error handling capability to direct the task execution accordingly. This is shown in Figure 8.7.

Now the process flow diagram reflects exactly what we want the process to do, which tasks need to be executed when, and how to handle various errors.

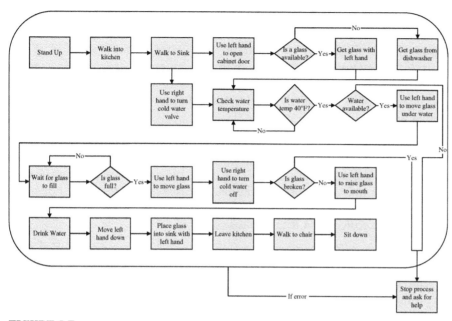

FIGURE 8.7
Basic process flow diagram with unhandled exceptions.

We can further enhance our documentation with various artifacts used for formal development processes, such as clearly defined test cases, performance testing plans, and other documents if needed. However, most process automation work performed by enterprise applications administrators do not go to this level of rigor and are generally less formal than normal development projects. At this point, we have sufficient documentation to begin automating our process.

Automating the Process

With our process flow diagram in place, we can begin the actual process automation work. How this is done will vary a great deal depending on the environment that you're working in, the operating systems that will need to execute the process, how you want to interact with the automated process, and a myriad of other factors. It is beyond the scope of this book to detail out how to handle process automation under every circumstance or language. Instead we will focus on some of the basic principles and best practices used when performing process automation and provide some examples in a couple of different languages just to illustrate various points.

We'll start by going back to the definition of terms that we went through earlier in the chapter. We talked about tasks being the individual steps of a process which in turn can be executed in a framework. As you look at process automation, you need to determine whether the automated process will be truly standalone or if it will be part of an overall process automation framework. This decision can be based on a number of factors including the intended long-term purpose of the automated process, environment requirements around security or logging, the existence of a framework, and whether the process could potentially involve tasks that are reusable by future automated processes.

In some cases, an automated process may need to be executed only a very few number of times within a brief timeframe. This is very common when it comes to data conversion processes or other processes where automation is required, but only for short-term needs. In cases like this, it may not make sense to include the process into an overarching framework as the process will not be executed on a regular basis.

This process-specific requirement can, of course, be overruled by corporate policies. Some companies require that all automated processes run within a specific framework in order to ensure that the security and integrity of the environment is maintained. This framework may include scheduling and logging capabilities, the ability to insert passwords or other credentials unknown to the person executing the process, and other controls that are important to the corporate enterprise. If it is required by policy, the automated process should be developed to run within the appropriate framework.

In some cases, your enterprise applications administration team may be relatively new and may not have an established process automation framework in place already. When this is the case, it's difficult to justify building out a full framework just to handle the execution of a few automation scripts. While the framework may be valuable long term, most teams struggle with getting funding or time allocated for longer term solutions such as this. To address this, you can develop your automated process in a modular fashion so that it can either be plugged into a framework easily at a later time or evolve into a framework of its own.

For example, you might build out a separate script or code segment to handle logging and include that as a module in any script that you write to automate a process. Later, you could replace the calls to the logging modules with calls to the logging module included in a framework or make the logging module that you've already written part of your own framework. Either way, there are savings in cost and time to future process automation without the upfront cost of building out a full process automation framework.

Best Practices

As we look at process automation, there are some best practices that should be considered as you determine how to write your scripts and automate your processes. We've already talked about the concept of frameworks and how they apply to process automation. A general best practice around frameworks is simply to implement a framework around your process automation if it makes sense. If implementing a framework does not make sense for your process automation, use a modular design so that a framework can be implemented easily later if needed.

Some other high-level best practices that we can discuss involve selecting a scripting language, using best practices within the scripting language, determining how to execute your scripts, how to automate transition between tasks within the process, and how to properly manage your automated processes. This is a very broad list of best practices, but they should be sufficient to guide you in the planning, design, development, and implementation of your automated processes. In all cases, the best practices that you adopt should align with best practices that already exist within your corporate enterprise.

Choosing a Scripting Language

There are a number of scripting languages that can be used for process automation. Depending on your process automation needs, one language may be preferable over others or multiple languages may be a good fit. To start determining the language to use, you should start with understanding what type of systems your process will be working with. For example, if the tasks being executed are going to be executing on Microsoft Windows-based systems, you may find that Microsoft's proprietary scripting language, PowerShell, is a perfect fit for your needs. PowerShell, leverages the .NET framework and provides a great deal of power and flexibility for process automation.

If you're working in an environment that is primarily UNIX-based, it may make sense to use a UNIX-based scripting language like shell scripts. These scripting languages are typically specific to a particular shell interpreter and often won't transfer easily between different UNIX shells. In addition, shell scripts are unable to transition to Microsoft Windows systems in the same way that Microsoft PowerShell scripts cannot transition to UNIX-based systems.

This illustrates one of the greatest issues with using operating system-specific scripting languages. The scripts tend not to be portable between different operating systems. This may not be a problem if your process automation focuses on only one operating system, but larger enterprises deal with heterogeneous environments that have a number of operating systems. When this is the case, it may make more sense to choose a scripting language that works across multiple operating system platforms.

TIPS & TRICKS

Cross-Platform Scripting

While the scripting language that you use may work well across multiple platforms, there may still be operating system-specific differences that cause issues with your scripts. For example, the direction of the "slash" character in UNIX-based and Windows-based systems differs. Any calls to an external function can also fail due to differences in the dependencies available for each operating system. An example of this would be calls to the WMI functions on Windows failing on a UNIX-based system because that dependency does not exist. Keep this in mind as you are designing scripts that are intended to execute across multiple operating systems.

There are a number of languages that exist in this space, but some of the more popular among enterprise applications administrators are Perl, Python, Ruby, and PHP. There is constant debate about which language is best for which purpose, but for the most part, you can accomplish most process automation tasks using any of these. If you choose to use a cross-platform scripting language such as one of these, the language choice boils down to determining which one has the capability to easily perform the functions that you need to accomplish, which one is used for other process automation that has already been performed, and which one you're most familiar with.

KEY CONCEPTS

Script Interpreters

One of the main differences between scripts and compiled code is the use of an interpreter. Compiled code is typically compiled into machine code that can execute directly on a server with no interpreter necessary. This is not the case for scripting languages. In scripting languages, the code is not compiled and an interpreter must be present to perform just-in-time compilation and execution of the script. This does cause script performance to be slower than compiled code, but the performance difference is often negligible. However, it does mean that you have to ensure that the destination system has the correct script interpreter and the correct version of that interpreter. Changes between interpreter versions can cause issues with the execution of your scripts as internal functions are changed or removed.

Some scripting languages have built in functions or installable modules that make performing certain tasks easier. The availability of these functions or modules may influence your language choice. For example, the Perl language uses modules available through the Comprehensive Perl Archive Network (CPAN) to expand its functionality. If you need to gather information from a Cisco product and parse its version information, you could manually write code for that as part of your process automation, or you can use the

Cisco::Version module from CPAN to do the work for you. A code example showing this is:

```
use strict;
use Cisco::Version;
## Load the output of the "show version" command into a string
my $show_version = $inbound_data;
## Create a new Cisco::Version object
my $sv = Cisco::Version->new($show_version);
## Parse the output
$sv->parse();
## Print the amount of RAM found
print "total DRAM memory = ", $sv->get_memory(), "/n";
```

Each scripting language has its own libraries of modules, its own built-in functions, a variety of tutorials, and a community of support available. If you are using the approach of selecting a language based on available modules or functions, you should determine what it is that you need the script to do and then determine what resources are available to accomplish that. There may be a scripting language which is a great fit based on what you find.

If you or someone else in your organization has already done some process automation using a specific scripting language, it may make sense to use the same language. By introducing a variety of languages into an organization, you do gain the flexibility and capability associated with each of those languages, but you begin to fragment your organizational expertise. Think to yourself about your own role as an enterprise applications administrator and how easy it is to support a variety of applications versus specialize on a single application. The same applies to choosing a scripting language. If the team is already familiar with the use of one language, it may make sense to go ahead and use that language even if it isn't necessarily the best fit just to make future supportability easier. If, however, there is a driving reason as to why a preexisting language will not work, then it may be worthwhile to introduce a new scripting language to the team.

Finally, your own familiarity with a scripting language does play a part in the language selection process. If you're very good at coding in Python, it may make sense to stick with what you know and automate your processes using Python. On the other hand, it's sometimes useful to learn new languages as well to expand your own expertise. This will often come down to how willing you are to learn something new and how much additional time it will take to learn the new scripting language.

Coding Best Practices

Coding best practices exist for every scripting language that has ever been developed. Some of these best practices are considered absolute requirements, others are considered optional, and others are under constant debate as to whether they should be followed at all. Determining language-specific best practices that you will implement when performing process automation can be a long and arduous process of analyzing a variety of best practice recommendations, determining which fit best with your needs, and documenting required best practices for your specific organization. Alternatively, you can simply find a convenient best practices guide and use it as is. Your choice here will depend on the amount of rigor that you wish to put into the implementation of best practices into your process automation work.

Some general best practices are relatively universal. There are always cases where implementing these don't make sense, but for the most part, they will fit into just about any script and help keep them standardized and efficient. Some of the more universal standards are:

- Use variables that make sense—Name them based on what they're used for.
- If a script can be executed standalone and requires arguments or variables, respond with what those requirements are if the script is executed without them.
- Test every script to make sure it does what you're expecting.
- Validate all of your input.
- If you are scripting as part of a team, document a style guide or best practices document to define the minimal requirements for your scripts. This will help you to understand each other's work easier.
- Always include comments within your code that explain what it is doing. This may seem unnecessary when you're coding, but a year later when you have to fix that script or someone else's, you'll appreciate the comments.
- Include any dependencies for the script to execute within the comments. You may need a particular library or module installed and it helps to document that for posterity.
- Use modular coding techniques so that your code can be reused for other purposes.
- Produce useful error messages with enough information to actually understand what they mean.
- Don't include modules that you don't need just because you might need them sometime in the distant future.
- Make your code readable based on the requirements of the scripting language that you're using. Proper indentation may be either required or optional, but it is recommended.

- When you're writing a script, put debugging points in place where you can see what the script is doing and what data it's dealing with, but make sure that these are removed before the script is released into the wild.
- Name your script something that makes sense. "foo-bar.php" has been done and is rarely appreciated.
- Make sure that your script includes version information either in the comments or in the naming. It's important to keep track of what has changed with a script over time so a changelog may make sense as well.
- When writing a script, think about what you appreciate in scripts that you've used written by others and include those elements. It's always good to learn from experience.

Some of these best practices need a little more elaboration, so let's discuss a few of them. We'll start with the best practices around commenting your code. This is an area that tends to be hotly debated because some feel that it's important to put as many comments in a script as possible and others feel that there should be none. Both are right depending on the circumstances. If you are working with a lot of junior enterprise applications administrators or those who do not have a lot of scripting experience, extensive comments in the code can help them to learn a great deal. People with more scripting experience may not require as many comments in order to follow what is happening, but when a particularly difficult problem is solved or the code itself is unclear, comments will help them to understand what you did.

On the other hand, people will sometimes do odd things like include passwords or confidential information within code comments. This can, of course, be a security risk if those scripts are ever read by someone who isn't supposed to see that information. Some security practitioners therefore recommend including no comments in code as that can eliminate the risk associated with dangerous data being included in the comments. Again, a middle ground should be reached where enough information is included to be useful, but no confidential data is exposed through code comments.

Another best practice aligns with something we've already discussed, modular code. When you develop a script to automate a task within a process, it should always be designed using a modular pattern. Even if the code module is specific to the script being executed, other parts of that same script can reuse the code if it's modular. For example, rather than putting the code to perform a server restart as part of your primary script code, make a function that performs a restart and accepts the appropriate variables. In this way, if you need to perform multiple restarts, you can simply call the function as appropriate rather than duplicating the code.

When designing a script, always trap your errors. The worst kind of error for any script or code is an unhandled exception. All exceptions should be handled in some fashion even if that handling is as simple as logging the error and gracefully stopping the script. This can also help when dealing with the overall process automation as the failure of a single scripted task may not require the failure of the entire process if it's handled correctly. If, as part of an automated process, you are dealing with responses from multiple task scripts, you may make the determination that it's okay if certain tasks fail and the process can continue with or without flow changes based on the failure of the executed task script. This isn't possible without good error trapping and handling so it's important to make this part of every script that you design.

Script Management Best Practices

Execution of an automated process is generally done in one of two ways. Either the process is executed based on a schedule or it's executed manually as needed. If the script is executed based on a schedule, you should ensure that allowances are made within the script to handle situations where the schedule has been changed either intentionally or unintentionally. For example, if the script requires that data exist which is prepared at a specific time, even if the script is scheduled to run after the data preparation time, a check should be done to ensure that the data was actually prepared. Basically, never trust a scheduled task to execute precisely on time every time. Ensure that your script is able to handle situations where mistakes in scheduling happen.

If the script is designed to be executed on an as-needed basis, there are still some best practices which should be followed to ensure that the script executes correctly. In many cases, the user context in which the script runs will make a difference as to whether or not it has permission to perform its tasks as planned. Therefore, you should provide for a check within the script to ensure that it is actually running within the correct user context or has the required execution permissions. Most scripts should be designed to run within a user context appropriate to the task that it is performing to ensure that the security and integrity of the system is maintained.

There is also a big difference between local script execution and remote script execution. When developing a script, you're typically working on a local workstation and developing all of the code to run within that local workstation's operating environment. A remote system may have different security controls, installed software, and configuration. You need to have a solid understanding as to what the true dependencies for your script are and ensure that the destination remote machine has what is necessary for the script to work correctly. In some cases, the only way to be absolutely certain is to test the script on the remote system. When this is the case, ensure that any destructive parts of the script are disabled and test, test, test!

Another important part of script automation is the transition between the tasks that make up the process. In some cases, multiple tasks will be handled within a single script, but frequently multiple scripts are required or desired. In this case, you need to ensure that the correct information is passed between each script within the process. The information passed can be as simple as a return code indicating the successful execution of a script or as complex as data gathered from one script that the next script requires as a parameter. Regardless, it's important to make sure that the script generating the output does so in a consistent and secure manner. In addition, the recipient script should validate the input in every case to ensure that it is receiving what is expected. A very common flaw in scripted processes is the failure to validate input.

An advantage of automated processes is the ability to multithread the process causing multiple tasks to execute simultaneously. With this capability comes some additional complexity. The script that executed the subscripts must ensure that they execute correctly and that events associated with the subscripts are handled appropriately. For example, if a single script executes a remote restart on 50 servers via a subscript, the script should watch for appropriate response codes coming back to ensure that each subscript executed correctly. In the event that there was a problem, the master script should have logic built in to handle the failure. In our example, this could be a retry on only the machines where the restart failed or an error notification to indicate that a failure of some sort occurred.

Just as code within the script should be designed in a modular pattern, the scripts themselves should follow a similar pattern. When designing a script, you should always plan for the script to be reusable. Rather than developing a script that is very specific to the process or task that you're automating, develop a script that can perform specific functions based on input and then incorporate those functions into your script. This has already been mentioned in this chapter, but it bears repeating. Don't give in to the temptation to quickly throw together a script that does exactly what the process or task requires. Put some thought into it and be proactive by thinking about what additional scripts may follow. If you're building a function that's even remotely reusable in the future, ensure that you create it in a manner that ensures its reusability in a relatively simple manner.

Logging is a critical part of process automation. When someone is doing something manually, they can watch it happen and make sure that everything works perfectly. This isn't the case with automated processes. Instead, the enterprise applications administrator is stuck in a spectator role and has to let the script perform the work. While it's sometimes possible to watch a script execute just to make sure everything works perfectly, this is not always the case and shouldn't be the general practice. Manually watching a script eliminates some of the benefits of automating the process, such as allowing it to run in the middle of the night with no intervention. This also consumes unnecessary time while the administrator is watching the script.

To work around this, the best practice is to log all relevant data from the script so that verification of its successful execution can be done. In addition, it may be worthwhile to log additional data to aid in troubleshooting in the event that something does go wrong. When writing a script, think about how the script will be executed and where in that execution you would want to know that something worked correctly. For example, you may want to know that a script successfully connected to a remote system, authenticated without any issues, and was able to successfully write a file. In this case, you would log each of these events as well as relevant error data in the event that a problem occurred.

KEY CONCEPTS

Logging Security

While it's important to log details around the operation of a script, there are some things that should never be logged. Credentials passed through scripts should not be recorded in log files. This is valid for username/password combinations, certificates, or other pieces of data that could be used for authentication. Always think of log files as being sources of information to people who attack enterprise applications both internally and externally. It is always the responsibility of an enterprise applications administrator to ensure the security of the application and eliminating data such as this from process automation log files is critical.

In some cases, the execution of a script will need to be monitored to ensure that it worked correctly. This is generally done either through notification mechanisms built into the script itself or through an external script or process that monitors your automated process. If the notification mechanism is internal, ensure that the notification will still work even if there is a catastrophic failure in the script's ability to execute correctly. This can be difficult as it's impossible for a script to send out a notification that it failed to execute if the script sending the notification doesn't execute at all. To handle this, it's sometimes possible to put the script within a notification wrapper or a framework that handles the notifications in the event that the script doesn't execute.

Following these best practices will help to ensure that your process automation works as expected and is able to save the most time and money possible. Between best practices around selecting your scripting language, coding best practices, and script management best practices, you should have a good idea of how to perform basic process automation in a structured and consistent fashion. As you perform this type of activity on a regular basis, you're certain to develop your own best practices and you should document those for sharing with others. As more and more processes are automated within your organization, more time is made available for performing interesting work versus repetitious and monotonous tasks.

MONITORING

One of the more critical aspects of maintaining an enterprise application is knowing what is happening with the enterprise application ecosystem as a whole. The term "ecosystem" here is important because you have to be aware of every component that makes up the enterprise application including the enterprise application itself, the servers that it runs on, the network infrastructure that it uses, the database it connects to, and any other dependencies that exist for the system as a whole. As an enterprise applications administrator, you should be aware of a problem with your application before the application users whenever possible.

To bring that level of awareness, monitoring of the enterprise application and its components is crucial. This monitoring can take place in a few different ways including infrastructure monitoring, application monitoring, and performance monitoring. In this section, we'll be discussing these types of monitoring, how they are done, and how to use the results. We'll also talk about things to watch for that could indicate potential problems in the enterprise application so that you can fix it before it gets worse.

You'll note that there are a lot of similarities between operational monitoring and the type of monitoring that is performed as part of load testing and capacity planning. Obviously there are a lot of similarities in the data, but the real difference is in the need for alerting. We'll talk about alerting a little as well and how you can manage and leverage alerts based on data provided by your monitoring system.

Infrastructure Monitoring

Throughout this book, we've talked about a lot of different hardware and infrastructure components including network devices, server hardware, database software, and others. These are the components that make up your enterprise application infrastructure and you should have a solid understanding of how each of them contribute to the enterprise application ecosystem at this point. Understanding how well each of these components is functioning will help you to understand how well the enterprise application as a whole is operating.

As you look at each infrastructure component of the enterprise application, you need to know a few things about its status. First, you need to know the availability status of the component. The availability of a specific infrastructure component may not necessarily be based on whether the component itself is up or down, but could also be based on connectivity issues, name resolution problems, or a host of other areas. However, the basic "up or down" check will at least tell you if the component appears to be available for the application to use.

Next, you need to know if the component is functioning normally. Even though a component may technically be "up" that doesn't mean that it's working the way that it is supposed to. The general approach to this type of monitoring is to run a test or monitor a real-time transaction that will tell you the functional status of a specific infrastructure component. As an example, you can look at the various stages of use associated with a database. The database may be "up" but you may be unable to connect to it. If you can connect to it, that doesn't necessarily mean that it is able to respond properly to queries. Ensuring functionality at all levels of an infrastructure component is an important aspect of monitoring an enterprise application.

Finally, you need to understand the capacity characteristics of the infrastructure component. The component may be up and functional, but in danger of reaching its maximum capacity. For example, a server may be processing transactions just fine but be running at 99% of its available memory. If any additional load hits the server, it will impact the performance of the enterprise application and you need to be aware of this. From a monitoring perspective, the capacity of all of the infrastructure components should be known and you should be aware of how much of that capacity is used. This is considered utilization monitoring and will help you to proactively take actions to reduce load or increase capacity of the infrastructure components.

In many cases, monitoring of infrastructure components is done by using agents installed on the infrastructure component itself. These agents communicate with a centralized monitoring system which is used as a console to understand the status of each component. Most centralized monitoring systems also support the concept of thresholds and alerting which we'll talk about later in this chapter. Each agent monitors various aspects of the infrastructure component and reports back to the centralized console which analyzes the gathered data. The central console will often have the ability to remotely control the agents as well, sending them various commands to perform tasks or change which elements they are monitoring.

This agent-based monitoring does take up some resources on the monitored infrastructure as the agent itself consumes processor, memory, disk, and network resources. As monitoring agents have improved over the years, they've gotten better at minimizing the amount of resources they need and reducing their impact on the infrastructure that they're monitoring, but it's still something to be aware of. Most agent-based monitoring systems strive to be as low impact as possible, but there always is at least a little negative impact made by the monitoring agent even if it is working perfectly. Errors can also happen with monitoring agents that cause them to behave poorly and consume a great deal of resources on the system so it's always wise to pay attention to the performance of the monitoring agent as well as the infrastructure that it's monitoring.

To eliminate the potential impact associated with agent-based monitoring, another type of monitoring called agent-less monitoring is possible. With this type of monitoring, no agent is used, but instead, various infrastructure components forward their log information over to a centralized log analysis and correlation system. These systems accept the incoming log and will typically provide the ability to comb through the logged data to find useful information about the availability, functionality, and usage of the monitored infrastructure component. The level of detail associated with agent-less monitoring is typically not as high as that available with agent-based monitoring, but it can potentially have less of a system impact. Deciding which to use is a decision that should be made carefully based on the level of detail that you need as well as how much risk you are willing to accept. Just like anything else, you should always test your monitoring solution very well before implementing it into a Production environment.

In many companies, all security-related log data must be sent to a centralized Security Incident and Event Management (SIEM) system. This type of system collects security-related events from many pieces of infrastructure within the environment and allows for the analysis of forensic data should a security-related event occur. For example, if an attacker penetrated the corporate environment, the security team could theoretically trace their actions through the logs that were sent over to the SIEM system. This also allows this critical log data to reside in a place other than the system where the activity occurred to prevent the logged data from being modified by the attacker.

Enterprise Application Monitoring

Monitoring the infrastructure will help you to know whether or not the infrastructure dependencies of the application are working properly and have sufficient capacity, but the enterprise application itself must be monitored as well. This level of monitoring is typically more complex and requires more work to implement than infrastructure monitoring. This is due to its need to not only understand application-level events but also to gain access to the appropriate data from the enterprise application.

When monitoring enterprise applications, an approach similar to that of infrastructure monitoring can be used. That is, you should be aware of the availability, functionality, and utilization of the enterprise application. This typically starts with ensuring that the application itself is up and running. In most cases, this check can be done by validating the existence of core application processes running on the host server. For example, if your application relies on a process called "entapp.exe" to be running, your monitoring solution should be validating that the "entapp.exe" process shows up in the server process list.

With large enterprise applications, there may be multiple processes that have to be running across a number of infrastructure components in order for the application to be considered "up." A good enterprise application monitoring solution will need to check for all processes across all systems and provide the administrator visibility into their individual availability. In addition, this will need to tie into alerting functions similar to the monitoring of infrastructure components. Some processes used by enterprise applications are ancillary and it may not be absolutely necessary that they are running in order for the application to be available. In some cases, these may be instantiated by the enterprise application on an as-needed basis or may not be needed due to other redundant processes. A good working knowledge of the enterprise application will help you to know which processes must be monitored to ensure availability of the application.

In addition to the core and ancillary application processes, the enterprise application may rely on other processes in order to be available. These other processes may be third-party applications or other parts of the enterprise application. As you look at the application architecture, you should have a general idea of what needs to be running and can then tie those application concepts back to executable processes. Monitoring of those processes can then be done to ensure that the application has all of the components that it needs in order to be available.

Where enterprise application monitoring has to be more intelligent than infrastructure monitoring is in validating the functionality of the enterprise application. In order to ensure that something is functioning normally, you have to know what "normal" looks like. In enterprise applications, this can be very complex. When we discussed functional monitoring for a database in the last section, we talked about ensuring that the database server is available, that it is accepting and authenticating connections, and that queries can successfully be executed against the database. With an enterprise application, there are typically many more functions that must be validated to show whether or not the application is functioning normally.

In some cases, this type of functional check can be performed by closely monitoring log files for the enterprise application. Depending on the application, use of various parts of the application may be recorded in the application log. Existence of these records may be an indicator that the application component being logged is functional. However, the lack of this log data could indicate that the component is nonfunctional *or* that it simply isn't being used. This introduces the possibility of false positives in the monitoring system where simple lack of use of a component might cause the monitoring system to think that the component is down.

An alternative approach is monitoring of the enterprise application log files for errors and implying its functional capability based on the errors that do and do not appear in the log files. In many cases, enterprise applications will put messages into the log files that indicate errors with various components of the applications, parts of a transaction, or other issues that could happen with the application. These log files should always be monitored as they are an excellent source of information about the application. However, you should always keep in mind that a component cannot generate log data if it is completely nonfunctional, so relying on enterprise application log files exclusively is generally not the best approach.

Another method of monitoring enterprise applications for functionality is through the use of synthetic or robotic transactions. These transactions are intended to simulate the actual use of the application and exercise its various components through the execution of the transaction. Typically, the transaction will be modeled off of the actual use cases for the enterprise application and provide input similar to that of what an actual application user would. The results of each part of these synthetic transactions can be monitored and anomalies can indicate that the application is not functioning normally.

TIPS & TRICKS

Log File Formatting

When performing monitoring of enterprise applications, a lot of both availability and functional information can be derived from data in log files. However, the formatting of these log files can differ tremendously between applications and even components within the same application. There are tools like Microsoft's Log Parser that can be used to make parsing and pulling data out of these log files much easier. For further information, you can view more details on this topic in the book "*Microsoft Log Parser Toolkit: A Complete Toolkit for Microsoft's Undocumented Log Analysis Tool*" (Syngress, ISBN: 1932266526) which was co-written by this author.

For enterprise applications monitoring, the final monitoring point is also the same as it is for infrastructure monitoring, monitoring of the application's performance. This can give you a good idea as to how close to the application's maximum capacity it is running and how well it is handling the present load. While these performance characteristics will be reliant on the underlying infrastructure components, the application itself is what the end users see and it is from the perspective of the application that most performance characteristics should be derived.

As with functional monitoring, this can be done via both log-based monitoring and with synthetic transactions. If the application logging level is verbose enough, the application may log performance characteristics that you can then track to understand how well it is performing. This level of logging, however, can potentially have a performance impact itself as the log writes will consume memory, processor, disk, and I/O resources. Depending on the situation, it may be viable to turn on the additional monitoring associated with application performance for a short time while troubleshooting a problem or checking the application performance, and then turn it back off.

With synthetic transactions, each part of the transaction can be logged and the amount of time that it took to perform the transaction can be analyzed to determine the performance of the enterprise application. With this type of monitoring, you can get a solid point-in-time snapshot as to the performance characteristics of a particular type of transaction so that you can better understand how the application as a whole is performing. By performing the synthetic transaction on a regular interval, you can build up a dataset that can give insight into ongoing performance degradation of the application and an understanding as to whether or not the service level agreements for application response times are being met appropriately.

CORPORATE MEMO...

Synthetic Transactions

It's important to note that synthetic transactions can never fully emulate what a user does in an enterprise application. Just as in application testing, real users will always follow different process flows, enter different data, and perform different actions than what you expect. In addition, synthetic transactions are often limited in what actions they can perform. For example, you wouldn't want a synthetic transaction to enter invalid data into the enterprise application, so many synthetic transactions are generated to perform read-only transactions. This limits their ability to test transactions that require writing data which may also exclude testing of certain workflows within the application.

While the monitoring of enterprise applications is typically more complex than the monitoring of the infrastructure components that they rely on, the same monitoring framework can often be used for both purposes. Many of the same functions of scanning for data, correlating it, presenting it, and using it for alert generation are common across both infrastructure and enterprise application monitoring. With this in mind, those functions can all be provided by a combined framework using data sources from both the infrastructure components and the enterprise application.

Reporting

Monitoring is an excellent source for real-time information that can guide operations activities for enterprise applications, but the same data can be used for other purposes as well. By examining monitoring data over time and reporting on that data, you can see trends within the enterprise application and use the resulting information to make decisions associated with future plans for the application. The creation of useful reports is very important from both a planning perspective as well as creating an excellent visualization of what the enterprise applications administration team does.

Reporting can take the form of detailed operational reports, higher level reports that illustrate the ongoing status of an enterprise application, or even instantaneous reports of errors in the enterprise application. This last type of reporting is also called alerting and has been alluded to previously in this chapter. While it's uncommon to think of alerts and reports in the same context, consider that they use the same data, present that data in a similar manner, and provide information that helps to guide activities associated with the enterprise application. The primary difference between real-time alerts and the traditional concept of reporting is the speed at which they must be generated and responded to.

When working with either traditional reports or alerting, it's important to understand exactly what data to use to provide the appropriate information to the consumer of the report. Whether that is showing the availability of the enterprise application over a specific timeframe or a detailed error message identifying something going wrong in the application, the correct information is crucial to the effectiveness of any report. As we look at some of the reporting that can be done for enterprise applications, we must also look at key performance indicators (KPIs). These are the data elements that can be used to identify the necessary characteristics of the enterprise application over time.

Key Performance Indicators

With an enterprise application, there are specific pieces of data that, when looked at holistically, define the performance of that application over time. These are called KPIs and are frequently used to give an overview into the operational status of any given enterprise application. From the infrastructure level and the enterprise application level, KPIs can be defined which roll up into simple to understand status reports for executives, business partners, or other individuals interested in the status of an enterprise application.

The idea behind KPIs is that they collectively create a picture of what the enterprise application looks like from a status and performance perspective. Individually, each KPI may address a single part of the enterprise application stack, but it's difficult to derive the status of the entire application from a single metric. By combining these with other KPIs throughout the application stack, a clearer picture emerges showing what the overall status of the application is. KPI data maintained over time can also provide this same view of the application status from a historical view so that trends in the application can be easily identified.

So what are some common KPIs that we should be concerned with? From the infrastructure perspective, the following items are generally considered KPIs that should roll up into your overall reporting:

- Infrastructure component availability
- Processor utilization
- Memory utilization
- Disk I/O utilization
- Disk space utilization
- Network I/O utilization
- Network latency
- Operating system-specific metrics
- Database transactions per second

There are certainly many more KPIs that can illustrate the health of the enterprise application's infrastructure, but these example items are a good baseline. As you work with a given enterprise application, you'll identify which infrastructure components make a difference in the overall application performance leading you to the use of those related data elements as KPIs. An example of what this type of reporting could look like as part of an overall enterprise application performance dashboard is shown in Figure 8.8.

From the enterprise application point of view, there are other KPIs that should also be considered. For each component of the application, availability is a KPI just as it is with infrastructure components. In addition, there is a lot of focus that should be given to specific portions of the enterprise application component that you're working with. As each enterprise application differs widely on its application architecture, specifics cannot be defined without a firm understanding of the enterprise application. However, some general baseline KPIs might be:

- Application component availability
- Number of connected users
- Max connected users in X timeframe
- Application component resource utilization
  - CPU
  - Memory
  - Disk
  - I/O
- Application component transactions per second
- Application errors per second/minute/hour/day

These and other KPIs can draw a good picture of your enterprise application and illustrate the application's performance. In addition, each of these KPIs make good candidates for alerts which can help enterprise applications administrators respond to potential issues in the application before they become catastrophic.

Alerting

Alerting is effectively real-time reporting of infrastructure and enterprise application KPIs in such a manner as to allow for enterprise applications administrators to take action on erroneous events. In many cases, the enterprise applications administrator is able to respond to these events fast enough to prevent a larger application impact due to appropriate alerting techniques. It is always a goal for the administrator to be aware of application issues before the end users have to report them and alerting on KPIs is the best method of accomplishing this.

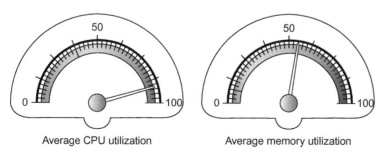

FIGURE 8.8

Infrastructure KPI dashboard.

Depending on your monitoring system, alerts can be configured in a number of ways. Some of the most important aspects of alerts are the KPI being alerted on, the threshold number of errors or utilization percentage that justifies an alert, and any automated actions to take based on the alert. We'll go through a few different KPIs, discuss the types of alerts that could be associated with them, and discuss the concept of thresholds and how they contribute to your overall monitoring and alerting strategy.

We'll start by taking a few KPIs to use for examples. From the infrastructure perspective, let's use server availability, server CPU utilization, and server memory utilization. From the enterprise application point of view, we'll take component availability, component transactions per second, and component memory utilization. Each of these KPIs can help us to be aware of the overall status of the enterprise application and may require administrative intervention in the event that there is a problem.

Let's first take a look at the server availability and application component availability KPIs. These KPIs should generally report that the server or application component is up or down. This would be viewed on a dashboard as a simple green or red light depending on the KPI status. The most simplistic approach to alerting on this KPI would be to send an alert when the KPI indicates that the server or application component is down. However, this doesn't take into account potential temporary network issues, problems with the monitoring solution, or other issues that could cause a false positive for this metric. A better approach is to set a retry count value and a retry interval prior to sending an alert. This is most applicable in cases where absolute immediate response is not needed. In extremely critical enterprise application, you may need to respond immediately to any potential issues.

A retry count value is how many times the monitoring tool should get a negative (or down) response from the server or application component prior to sending an alert. For example, you may want to try to contact the server or application component three times before you consider it down. The time between contact attempts is the retry interval. Depending on the environment that you're working in and the technology that you're dealing with, this retry interval could be anything from a few seconds to a few minutes. Assuming a retry count value of three and a retry interval of 5 s, the following sequence of events would occur:

1. Monitoring system attempts to contact server or application component
2. Server or application component does not respond
3. Monitoring system waits 5 s
4. Monitoring system attempts to contact server or application component
5. Server or application component does not respond
6. Monitoring system waits 5 s

7. Monitoring system attempts to contact server or application component
8. Server or application component does not respond
9. Monitoring system waits 5 s
10. Monitoring system attempts to contact server or application component
11. Server or application component does not respond
12. Monitoring system sends an availability alert

If the server or application component responds as up during one of the retries, the monitoring solution should not send an alert about the server or application component's availability.

The next KPIs that we'll take a look at are the server CPU and memory utilization. These KPIs are generally monitored on a basis of percentage utilized. The closer that you get to 100% utilized, the closer the server is getting to its maximum capacity. Reaching maximum capacity may not cause the server to crash, but could potentially degrade performance of applications running on the server. Consequently, these are important KPIs to monitor and receive alerts on.

With KPIs like this, alerting typically isn't based on a simple yes/no question like availability. Instead, the monitoring system has to understand the ebb and flow of system utilization and ensure that it doesn't send an alert when there isn't really a problem. On the other hand, it's important with KPIs like this to know about a problem in enough time to be able to react to that problem and do something about it. To handle situations like this, monitoring systems use a concept of thresholds to control alerting based on KPIs that use measurements based on percentage values.

Thresholds are based on ranges and where values exist within each range. For example, you may set a range of "normal" and indicate that values between 0% and 75% are within that range. The range from 76% to 85% may be labeled as a "warning" range. And finally, you may decide that the range from 86% to 100% is the "critical" range for your servers. When the value of a monitored KPI passes between ranges, it is said to cross the threshold into a new range and the monitoring system needs to take action appropriately.

Just as with the availability KPIs, you may set a minimum occurrence value for KPIs using a threshold monitoring process. This is similar to the concept of the retry count and retry interval for availability KPIs. You may only want the monitoring system to alert you if the server KPI crosses the threshold a certain number of times within a specific timeframe. For example, a server CPU may spike occasionally when some activities occur on the server, but it may not indicate that there's an actual problem. However, if the CPU hits over 90% 10 times within a 5-min window, there may be an issue that warrants further investigation.

Another KPI that we mentioned for example purposes is the application transactions per second value. This type of KPI may have the need for alerts to trigger on both ends of the value range. If the transactions per second value is too low, it may indicate that the application is having issues processing transactions. On the other hand, if the value is too high, it may indicate that the system is nearing capacity and some action may need to be taken in order to reduce the application workload or increase the application capacity. This KPI range is also probably defined by actual numbers rather than percentages like other KPIs. For example, the range may be 1 to 100 tps for the "low" label, 101 to 6000 tps for "normal," and 6001 to 7000 tps for "high." In this case, you may want to set alerts to occur whenever the KPI value is in the low or high ranges.

The last KPI that we'll use for example purposes is the application memory utilization value. This KPI is generally measured in the same way as the server memory utilization value, but has a slightly different meaning. While the server memory utilization may be normal, the memory utilization of a specific process running within that memory space may be too high and cause issues with your application. Some applications set a specific amount of memory that the process can consume. If the process attempts to consume more than its allocated amount, it may crash, exhibit unusual behavior, or degrade in performance. With this in mind, it may be wise to monitor and alert on the memory utilization of a specific process used by the enterprise application rather than simply relying on the KPI value for the overall server memory utilization.

TIPS & TRICKS

The Christmas Tree Effect

One issue that tends to occur when a monitoring system is put in place for the first time is known as the "Christmas Tree Effect." When a monitoring system has a number of default rules in place, normal system operations may violate some of those default rules and cause the monitoring solution to light up like a Christmas tree. Because of this, it's a good approach to implement a monitoring solution and then tune it carefully to match the needs of your environment before turning on any alerting capabilities.

When an alert is generated by a monitoring system, typically several actions are available. The monitoring system can usually generate the alert via multiple mechanisms including SMS messaging, email, and sometimes even an automated phone call. The intent of alerts like this is to notify an administrator so that corrective actions can be taken and the problem causing the KPI value to be abnormal can be resolved. Some monitoring systems also allow for automated actions to be taken based on alerts as well to automate actions that an administrator might have to do manually.

As an example, if an alert is generated based on a server CPU threshold being exceeded, the monitoring tool may execute a script that captures a list of processes running on the system and the amount of CPU that each was consuming at the point that the alert was generated. This data would then be available to the administrator in order to aid in diagnosing the issue. Other automated actions are also possible such as application component restarts, automated server capacity increases through autoprovisioning mechanisms, and other actions as needed. It's important to keep in mind that some actions that an administrator may take are relatively destructive, such as server reboots, and it may be wise to ensure that someone is actually performing this activity with intent versus relying on automated activities performed by the monitoring system.

Monitoring Data Analysis

A lot of information can be derived from the data collected during enterprise application monitoring. Besides viewing basic trends and alerting on events, this data can be used for capacity planning, failure analysis, and even finding usage patterns that can help improve the application. Appropriate mining of the monitored data is very helpful and should be a part of the services performed by the enterprise application administration team.

There is a lot of discussion around "big data" as of the time of this writing and this was mentioned previously in the book when we discussed databases. Data analytics is not only for business-related data however. The same principles used for data mining of business data can also be applied to data coming from enterprise application logs, server logs, and other data that is typically gathered as part of your standard monitoring practice. Even security-related data being sent to a SIEM system can be leveraged along with all of the other application data to provide a very large dataset for mining.

So what are you looking for in this large pile of data? Primarily you are looking for patterns in the data that tell stories. For example, do you see an unusually high spike in utilization of various components of the enterprise application at specific times? Through mining of the application data and correlation with other data throughout the corporate enterprise, you may be able to determine the cause and use that to ensure that the application is prepared for the additional load. Is there a pattern of security events that occurs immediately following an application release on a regular basis? That may indicate that someone is aware of your release schedule and is probing your application for vulnerabilities based on that schedule.

All sorts of patterns can be found in enterprise application log data when it is analyzed, especially if data from other sources is added in and correlated. There are a few tools in the market today that can help assist with this effort and it should be something that you examine as part of the ongoing maintenance of your enterprise application. By finding patterns such as these, you can be prepared for future events that may affect the applications that you are responsible for.

SUMMARY

In this chapter, we discussed two very important aspects of enterprise applications administration. We started with process automation. Through good process automation, an enterprise applications administrator's job can be made easier, execution of tasks can be made more consistent and faster, and more time can be spent working on the more difficult tasks that must be completed. As part of this discussion, we went over how to determine if a process should be automated, how to document the process in preparation for automation, and how to do the actual automation.

For enterprise applications, processes are typically automated through the use of a variety of scripting languages. Depending on the language used, there are a number of best practices that should be followed to ensure that the scripts are created in a consistent, understandable, and reusable manner. We talked through some of these best practices as well as how to choose the right scripting language for the job. We also discussed the differences between tasks, processes, and frameworks and how all of these work together to perform process automation.

The second part of the chapter was all about monitoring of enterprise applications. This is comprised not only of monitoring the application itself but also the infrastructure components that host the application. In order to monitor the correct information, it's important to define KPIs that give insight into the enterprise application. These KPIs can be used for monitoring the application's performance over time as well as for determining when to alert the enterprise applications administrator to potential problems within the application. We talked about these alerts as well and how to properly tune alerts through the selection of appropriate KPIs as well as determination of retry counts and intervals. By using these techniques, you should be able to know about issues within the enterprise application before the end users and gain the opportunity to fix them before a negative impact is caused to your company's business functions.

CHAPTER 9

Documentation

- Documentation Concepts
- Document Types

DOCUMENTATION CONCEPTS

One of the most important jobs of any enterprise applications administrator is that of documentation. It's also probably one of the least-enjoyed tasks by most administrators as well. In this chapter, we'll talk about some of the basic concepts around documentation, why it's important, when to create or modify documents, what you should document, and how you should document it. With those basics out of the way, we'll move on to focusing on a variety of document types and discuss them in detail.

Why to Document

Let's start with discussing why documentation is important. Most enterprise applications administrators recognize the criticality of good documentation as they gain experience throughout their career. Over time, they gain an understanding of the value provided by documentation that they or others create. In this section, we're going to talk about some of that value and why good documentation is so important.

First and foremost, documentation is about sharing knowledge. At its most basic, we document things in order to teach others. This book, for example, is written to teach others the skills and knowledge that they need in order to be great enterprise applications administrators. The documentation that you create while performing those duties has the same purpose. The knowledge that you gain should be documented so that others can learn from you and your experiences.

As more and more work is done over time, there is a natural tendency to forget things that we've done before. We may remember the general actions that we took when completing a task or recall events happening, but with most individuals, specific details tend to be forgotten over time unless they are repeated frequently. Documentation can serve as a reminder of actions that you've taken in the past or give explicit details on what you've done so that you can precisely repeat the process no matter how much time has elapsed.

From a record-keeping point of view, accurate documentation can give a solid historical record of things that have happened over time. For example, the configuration of a server or enterprise application may morph over time as it grows or changes and documentation can show what those changes were and when they happened. This can both explain past events as well as allow for prediction of future changes that may be needed for the system or application.

This historical tracking may be necessary not only from an informational point of view but also from a regulatory point of view. Depending on the regulatory guidelines that a company or enterprise application falls under, a certain minimum standard of documentation may be required to demonstrate strong change management or configuration management practices. In addition, there may be a need from this compliance perspective for a quality assurance review of work performed based on documentation provided as part of the work effort.

Finally, as you look at any given aspect of an enterprise application, there are dozens of ways that specific tasks can be accomplished. In order to clearly understand how to perform a task in a consistent manner, it is important to remove any ambiguity from the execution of that task. Documenting the steps necessary to accomplish the task as well as explaining why a particular method of execution was chosen can help to clear up that ambiguity. This can be helpful when considering similar work that needs to be done and can be used as a baseline for how to execute other tasks in a consistent manner.

All of these purposes for performing documentation are valid and provide a general understanding of why documentation should be performed. What isn't clear by strict definition is how critical documentation can be within the enterprise application environment. When any enterprise applications administrator is thrust into a critical situation, it is important that they are quickly able to access the information that they need to resolve an issue. The documentation associated with the enterprise application is absolutely essential as an information source when accurate information is needed quickly.

By having accurate documentation available, enterprise applications administrators can respond faster, troubleshoot issues more rapidly, and fix problems with more ease than if the appropriate documentation does not exist.

When to Document

Documentation is not a one-time task. Instead, documentation has its own lifecycle of creation, refinement, approval, and ongoing review. Later in its lifecycle, a document can be retired if necessary, but our focus is more toward those living documents that can help an enterprise applications administrator in their day to day work. With that in mind, let's discuss documentation from a timing and lifecycle perspective.

Since documentation is generally a task that most enterprise applications administrators don't enjoy, the temptation exists to wait until a given project or task is complete and then perform the documentation at the end of the process. This practice results in two problems that make the documentation effort fail. First, it's easy to procrastinate on the documentation creation to the point that it never actually gets completed. Second, by the time the process is complete or the project is finished, there may be steps taken along the way that are forgotten by the time that the documentation is put together.

KEY CONCEPTS

Procrastination Elimination

Almost every enterprise applications administrator that the author has worked with tends to procrastinate the duty of creating documentation. This includes the author himself! When information is fresh in your head, it is truly much easier to document and the work is less of a chore than if you document the information when it's starting to fade from your memory. A technique that can be helpful is to set aside a specific time of day on a recurring basis to go through and complete any outstanding documentation tasks. Depending on your workload and how much documentation you have to do, this could be done by setting up an hour per week or an hour per day. Give yourself enough time to get the work done and make sure that you can do the work in an environment where you cannot be easily distracted. Eliminating procrastination from your documentation routine can go a long way toward making the task of documenting easier and increase the quality of your work.

With this in mind, it's important to address the creation of documentation throughout the lifecycle of a given project or task. When the work effort is initially started, it is generally a good idea to determine the types of documentation that will be required and put together some draft documents that can function as templates as the work effort continues. These rough drafts may not contain much useful data initially, but they can be added to throughout the work effort so that they contain more and more relevant information.

In some projects that enterprise applications administrators work on, there is an element of planning that occurs even prior to the work effort beginning. This planning effort will typically create some information which may be needed later, whether in the form of reference information or in the form of an execution plan. Much like the work effort itself, this planning information should be appropriately documented and included as part of the initial stages of the project or work effort. Just as with technical documentation, this planning documentation may change over time and should be updated as the work effort progresses.

This ongoing evolution of documentation is one of the tenets of creating useful and relevant documentation that provides value over time. Always consider documents as a living concept where the document is updated as you move through a process or project. You gain more knowledge over time, and your documentation should reflect this. If there is one failing point of documentation, it's when documentation is done at a particular stage of a project and never updated again. By properly focusing on the document lifecycle and ensuring that documentation is kept current over time, you can prevent the documentation from becoming stagnant and useless.

Every document should have a point where it's considered "locked" for a specific version, however. There is a danger in keeping a document in a state where it's never complete enough to be usable as well. Consequently, you should pick an appropriate point in the document evolution where it is finalized for a particular revision. Changes can, of course, still be made to the document, but they lead to the creation of the next version of the document rather than add information to the current version.

After a document version is finalized, there is typically a level of review and approval that should be done. In most enterprises, collaboration must happen between both individual team members and teams. It is rare for someone to work in a completely isolated fashion, therefore, other people will need to be able to see and use the documentation that you create. With this in mind, you should always ensure that someone else reviews your documentation to ensure its accuracy, readability, and usability. The feedback that you receive as a part of documentation review can help you to improve your documentation skills and generate better documentation.

As part of the review process, or even before, there is an additional step that is very useful for technical documentation. This is similar to the software development lifecycle in that a document gets created, but it then needs to be tested to ensure that it is accurate. In the case of technical documentation, you can typically use the document to repeat a given process if it's a work instruction (WI), do an exercise to ensure that the steps documented are valid if it's a standard operating procedure (SOP), or validate all of the data contained within the document if it's a technical architecture diagram. This level of testing ensures that the document is accurate and includes all of the information necessary to be useful.

In addition, due to internal policy or regulatory requirements, it is common for documents to have to go through an approval process. This process ensures that the document has been accepted by those who are stakeholders or are responsible for the information contained in the document. For example, policy documents typically need to be approved by a high-ranking employee of the company whereas technical documentation may only need to be approved by a manager one level above the creator of the document.

After a document version is locked, reviewed, and approved, that version should remain unchanged. However, it is still important to update the document with new information as the project or technology changes. These changes would all be reflected in a new version of the document which would then go through the same lifecycle. The point to remember is that just because a specific version of a document is "final," it does not mean that the document itself is done and is not to be revisited. In order for documentation to be useful over time, it must be kept current.

In some cases, documentation can be updated as part of the natural process of change to a project or technology. However, changes may be made that are more organic in nature and are not recognized as true changes to the environment in which you're working. Another possibility is that a change is made and the person making the change simply does not think of or forgets to update the appropriate documentation. To cover this situation, it is important to have regularly scheduled reviews for every document that is created. These reviews can occur monthly, biannually, or annually depending on the needs of your organization and the nature of the document. Regardless of the schedule, it is critical that these reviews be done in order to maintain the accuracy and relevancy of documentation.

Finally, just like in any technical lifecycle, it is natural for documents to lose relevance and usefulness over time. When this happens, documentation can be retired and intentionally marked as no longer in use. When a document version or the entire document is retired, this should be reflected within the document as well as within any document management system. This labeling ensures that people know that a document or a version of that document is no longer relevant, no longer updated, and should not be considered as a reliable source of information.

What to Document

The specific document elements that are required for any given type of document will vary greatly depending on the document type. However, there are a few common elements that should exist across most, if not all, documents that you create. We'll discuss some of those common elements in this section and move on to discussing document type-specific elements later in this chapter within the common document types section.

All documents should start with a stated purpose. This purpose could be as simple as "provide detailed technical information about the FLARP application" or as complex as "provide step-by-step instructions on the method and process of transferring fiber optic cable between two core switches during a disaster situation." The purpose of the document defines what the entire document is going to be about and lets the reader understand the intent of the author. This document element may be given through the titling of the document, through a single statement, or through a paragraph or two explaining the overall document purpose depending on the type of document being created.

TIPS & TRICKS

Document Element Labeling

In some cases, you will be identifying a specific section of a document by a label such as "Purpose," "Table of Contents," or other descriptive labels. In others, the labeling either varies from the true document element or is implied. For example, the "Purpose" document element may be labeled as "Introduction and Objectives" or the "Change History" may be labeled as "Versioning." For some document elements such as "Audience," the element may not be individually labeled or specified but may be implied. It's unlikely that a nontechnical individual would assume that a document titled "Technical Implementation Methodology for the Ghost Operating System Framework" is recreational reading material, thus, the intended audience is implied through the document title.

Another common document element is the audience for the document. When a document is written, it should be written with a specific audience in mind. The writing style and information given for executives will differ greatly from that used for enterprise applications administration staff. Knowing who the audience is helps the author properly communicate their information, and it also helps the reader to understand what point of view they should take when reading the document. As an example, a document with a stated audience of technical professionals might be given to a nontechnical person such as an attorney to review for any legal issues that may exist in the document. With the audience specified, the attorney can better understand how they should approach the information included in the document and what level of review may be needed.

The change history is a document element that can be used to track revisions and modifications made to a document over time. As with any of the other document elements, this element may be presented in a number of ways varying from a detailed change log to a simple table showing the revision number, author, and change date. This element is very important for any document as it explains to the reader which version of the document they're using and other information that may be critical to their use of the document. By matching this with other data available such as through a document management system, they can understand whether they're reading the appropriate version of the document or if they are dealing with something that is out of date.

While not included with all documents, a table of contents is very helpful in allowing the reader to quickly find the information that they need in a document. Many applications used for creating documents allow of the automatic creation of tables of contents based on the formatting and styles used for the headers of various sections as the document is written. By utilizing a table of contents, the reader can gain a quick overview as to the general information included in the document, identify where the information that they need exists within the document, and quickly access the relevant document section.

Within technical documentation, there is a need to simplify the expression of concepts through the use of acronyms. While these are often overused, there is value to them within many industries. Throughout this book, we have used a number of acronyms to reduce the amount of space needed to get information across to you as the reader. When this is done within this writing style, the author will state the full text of the acronym followed by the acronym in parenthesis. Future references to that information will then frequently use the acronym rather than spelling out the full name. An alternative to this method that is frequently used for technical documents is to simply include a table that shows every acronym used in the document and its definition. This type of glossary can also be used to provide definitions of technical terms.

A similar document element exists in the form of a traditional glossary. In some cases, it may be important to explain the meaning of specific words or phrases to ensure that the audience of the document is clear as to the author's intent and use of the word or phrase. To provide for this, a glossary can be included as an optional document element and allows the author to identify the word or phrase and associate it with an appropriate definition associated with the context of the document.

Finally, some documentation requires some sort of summary or conclusion to wrap up the document. In many cases, the summary will be based on the stated purpose of the document and explain how the author accomplished the purpose through the use of the information in the document. In others, it may concisely summarize the high level information included in the document and give the reader a quick recap of what was covered. This element brings the document to a close and allows the author the opportunity to enforce key ideas and illustrate points made within the document.

How to Document

We've covered why, when, and what to document, so let's move on to discussing how to create good documents. Depending on the type of document that you're creating, there are several techniques you can use that will help you to generate relevant, useful documentation that fits the needs and expectations of the reader. By utilizing these techniques, you can create documentation that truly fulfills its intended purpose while following straightforward guidelines that ease the process of creating the document.

We'll start by setting the stage for the document. Two of the documentation elements that we discussed are the document's purpose and audience. By fully understanding what the document is intended to accomplish and who it's intended for, the author can correctly tune the document to fit the need. Therefore, when creating documentation, the first thing that you should try to understand is what you need to accomplish and who you should be writing for.

The purpose of the document may be defined by the documentation type. For example, a "Disaster Recovery Plan" is obviously a plan that is intended to be used in the event of a disaster. In other cases, the purpose of a document may be less obvious. As the author of documentation, find out what your document will be used for and keep that purpose in mind throughout your creation of the document. Everything written within the document should be able to be tied back to the purpose of the document and align with that purpose. If it doesn't, you should consider whether or not the information needs to be included. Understanding the purpose of the document and maintaining alignment with that purpose goes a long way toward ensuring that the document is able to be used as intended.

The audience that the document is intended for is one of the most crucial elements that you should use in determining how to write your document. You shouldn't go into an incredible amount of technical details in a document intended for nontechnical people. On the other hand, you don't want to include too much marketing information or other details that technical people will not find relevant in a document intended for technical people.

Understand what the audience of your document is and then understand what that particular audience needs in order to gain the most from a given document. This may change the word choices you make, the information that you include, or even the style used for the document.

When you have developed an understanding of your document's intended purpose and audience, you can determine the correct level of detail for the document. Some documents may be designed as high-level overviews where you go into a little depth, but not much, on the topics included in the document. This level of detail might include identifying the topic, explaining what it is, and how it is relevant to what you're documenting. High-level overviews are not necessarily just used to explain technical details to non-technical individuals however. In some cases, you may be making the assumption that the reader of the document has a certain baseline of knowledge already and only need to cover certain topics at a high level since it's assumed that the reader already has knowledge on the topic.

The level of detail within certain parts of the document or on specific topics within the document may need to differ as well. For example, you may need to do a high-level overview related to the need to perform specific activities, and then move into a detailed explanation of those activities. As you go through the writing process for a given document, ensure that you understand the appropriate level of detail that should be used for each section and topic so that the document is detailed enough in the right areas without going into too much detail where it's unnecessary.

As you look at the level of detail used for a document, you may do a high-level overview using expert-level detail on some topics. In other cases, you may need to write a true step-by-step level of detail in order for the document to achieve its purpose. This is common for documents used for training, those used to teach very specific information, and those used for validation or quality assurance. When going to this level of detail, it is important to ensure that you accurately record the steps within the document. The more detailed a document is, the more likely it is that errors will occur during the writing of the document. This is important to keep in mind as you write content using a granular level of detail.

For some documentation, it's important to graphically illustrate some points. This may be through the use of graphs, images, or screenshots of important information. The purpose of these visual aids is to clearly convey information to the document audience in a manner that is easy to understand. From the perspective of graphs, it may be the analog display of digital data. For images, the purpose may simply be to get a point across in a strong or illustrative manner. Screenshots frequently answer the question, "What should it look like when I do this?" By using these visual techniques, you can help get your points across in a relevant and appropriate manner tied back, as always, to the document's intended purpose and audience.

COMMON DOCUMENT TYPES

There are countless numbers of document types that exist. A simple search for templates available through your favorite search engine will return thousands of results. You may have a need over time to create hundreds of different styles of documents yourself as part of your role. However, there are a few key document types used by enterprise applications administrators in the course of their work. In this section, we'll be going over a few of those most common document types, explaining what they are and what they're used for, and giving some examples of what these documents could look like.

Please note that this is not intended to be an all-inclusive guide to all of the documents that you will need to use in the course of your work. These are simply some key document types that are most commonly used by enterprise applications administration groups. In addition, the content, format, style, and other characteristics of each document will vary between companies and even between iterations of the document type over time. Again, the intent is to give you a general understanding of some of the most common document types used so that you can use that foundational knowledge in your work as an enterprise applications administrator.

Checklists

One of the most common document types used in enterprise applications administration is checklists. Checklists are documents that are intended to guide specific activities, sometimes in a specific order, and ensure that all aspects of those activities are completed. In addition, they can be used as a quality assurance mechanism to sign off on a piece of work with the checklist serving as a list of what was completed.

Checklists can be valuable over time as they can show what was done at a specific point of time. At the time the checklist is signed-off or marked completed, the items checked signify those that are complete as of that time. In the future, more work may be performed, but with the checklist, there is a clear indicator that what is marked on the checklist is what was done. Figure 9.1 shows an example checklist document.

SERVER BUILD
- [ ] Server Racked
- [ ] Network Run
- [ ] Drives Installed
- [ ] SAN Connected
- [ ] Inventory Recorded
- [ ] Lights-Out Management Configured
- [ ] Power Run
- [ ] PDU Configured
- [ ] Labeled
- [ ] Burn-In Test Completed

OPERATING SYSTEM BUILD
- [ ] Base OS Installed
- [ ] OS Security Hardening Completed
- [ ] Network Configuration Completed
- [ ] Permissions Set
- [ ] SAN Configured
- [ ] Cluster Configured
- [ ] Monitoring Installed
- [ ] Core Applications Installed
- [ ] Agents Installed
- [ ] SIEM Integration Completed
- [ ] Default Users Deleted
- [ ] OS Toolset Enabled
- [ ] Monitoring Server Configured
- [ ] CMDB Updated

APPLICATION PRE-REQS
- [ ] Reporting Software Installed
- [ ] Office Software Installed
- [ ] Secondary Partition Configured
- [ ] Service Account Added
- [ ] Permissions Set
- [ ] Configuration Worksheet Completed
- [ ] Core Dependencies Configured
- [ ] Core File Copies Completed
- [ ] Handoff Worksheet Completed
- [ ] Backdoor Installed|

FIGURE 9.1

Example checklist document.

With checklists, the checklist is typically created in advance of any work associated with the items shown on the checklist being completed. This may be done by the person performing the work and completing the checklist, or the checklist could be created by an entirely different individual. With this in mind, a checklist is typically a two-part document. The initial part is the creation of the checklist with all appropriate items being included and a series of checkboxes being added to the document. The second part is the completion of the checklist in association to the work it references. The checklist is completed and appropriate checkboxes marked when the work is done.

A frequent example of a checklist is that of a "build checklist" used to ensure that a server is built correctly or that software is installed correctly. This checklist will typically show all of the available options or required steps for the build and the person performing the work marks off each task as it's completed. In addition, there are usually fields on the checklist which allow for the addition of text associated with the build process. This could include service account names, installation directories, or other information that cannot be known until the time that the build is performed. The example shown in Figure 9.1 is a build checklist.

Diagrams

We discussed diagrams extensively in several of the preceding chapters. Diagrams are a very useful document type used for a number of different purposes in enterprise applications administration. With diagrams, a great deal of information is shown in a relatively small amount of space in a way that makes it descriptive yet easy to understand. We won't be discussing the specific diagrams already covered throughout this book again, but rather focusing on some of the ways that diagrams differ from other document types both in form and content.

With diagrams, your focus is typically very narrow and each diagram will typically represent a single idea or concept. For example, a technical architecture diagram is very focused on providing the important aspects of a given technical architecture. This type of diagram typically wouldn't include any extraneous data that does not tightly align with the selected technical architecture. In rare cases, you will see a diagram that combines two different concepts such as a technical architecture diagram with an application architecture diagram overlay for context, but this is unusual and can make the diagram difficult to follow if not done correctly.

Most of the document elements that we discussed in the previous section are either not explicitly shown or included in a minimized fashion within diagrams. For example, the revision information may be a small table in the corner of the diagram or even on a different page. The purpose is generally defined through the document title or the file naming convention used. The audience for diagrams is generally inferred. This minimization of nontopical data for diagrams allows them to provide the information that needs to be expressed without cluttering the picture with data that is not strictly necessary for understanding the content.

Informational Presentations

As an enterprise applications administrator, you may have the need to perform a variety of presentations on different topics. These may range from presenting the need to invest in server upgrades to showing the work that your team has accomplished over the last year. These informational presentations are frequently done in the form of slide decks and can either be presented in a formal manner or simply communicated through the distribution of the slide deck itself. Depending on the intended presentation style, there may be some changes in approach that you use when developing the informational presentation.

If you will be presenting the slide deck in a formal manner such as an oral presentation, it is generally a best practice to show key points within the slide deck but not include a great deal of detail. The idea here is that the slides should serve as a method of illustrating your points while the detailed information should be included within your oral presentation. For example, Figure 9.2 shows a sample slide with some basic key points shown on it. In an oral presentation, these key points could consume 2−5 min of time as the presenter expands on the ideas illustrated by the points. A generally

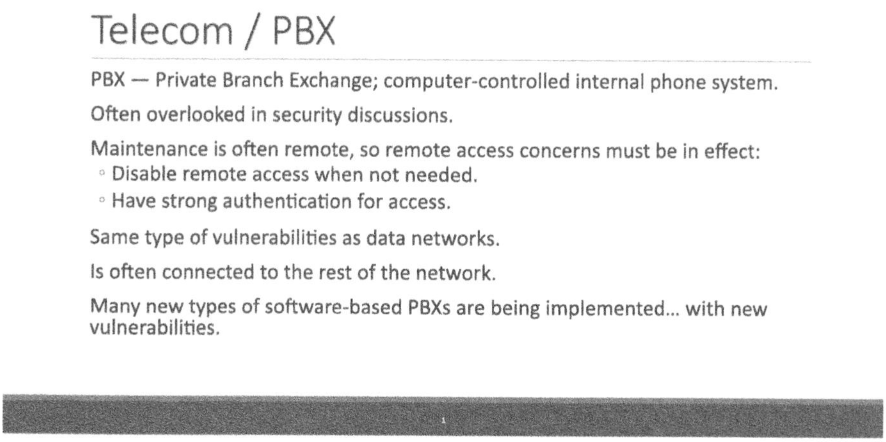

Telecom / PBX

PBX — Private Branch Exchange; computer-controlled internal phone system.

Often overlooked in security discussions.

Maintenance is often remote, so remote access concerns must be in effect:
  ◦ Disable remote access when not needed.
  ◦ Have strong authentication for access.

Same type of vulnerabilities as data networks.

Is often connected to the rest of the network.

Many new types of software-based PBXs are being implemented... with new vulnerabilities.

FIGURE 9.2
Sample key points slide.

accepted best practice is to not include too much detail in the slides as they become unreadable and cause the audience to lose focus.

On the other hand, if the slide deck will not have an accompanying oral presentation, you may need to include enough detail in the slides so that they can be easily understood without the accompanying verbal detail. This may mean including more information on each slide or, if the presentation program you use supports it, including notes with each slide that contain the additional detail. Both of these methods are good, but support of slide notes is not universal and is therefore less frequently used. This additional level of detail may make the informational presentation less usable for future oral presentations, so it may be useful to keep two versions of your informational presentation. One of these versions could be used for oral presentations and the other as a standalone presentation that does not need oral accompaniment.

TIPS & TRICKS

Animations and Effects

Some slide presentation applications allow for the use of animations and special effects within a presentation. These can be very eye-catching and may seem like they add a great deal of pizzazz to a presentation. While that may be true, they will tend to distract from the key message that you're trying to convey as part of the presentation. If you feel the need to add animations or special effects to your presentation, do so in a limited manner and in such a way that the viewer can still focus on your message without becoming distracted.

A third scenario is that of a blended presentation. This type of presentation is a combination of both the prior types in which you present your information with oral accompaniment but distribute the slide deck afterward to the audience for their notes. In this situation, it's important to develop a good blend of key points and details within the presentation. Again, notes within the presentation can be used but may not be effective due to both supportability and readability in the event that you print the presentation for handouts. As with any other document, determine your purpose and audience when developing the level of detail that you need to include in your slides.

Legal Agreements and Contracts

In most cases, enterprise applications administrators are not responsible for creating legal agreements or contracts. However, they may be responsible for reviewing them for accuracy and to ensure that they accomplish the intended purpose. The initial drafts of these documents will typically be created by attorneys and then modified to fit the needs of the companies forging the agreement. The attorneys typically understand law and the legal ramifications of the agreements being executed, but they don't usually understand the technologies associated with agreements involving technical topics. This is where enterprise applications administrators can assist to ensure that the legal document correctly covers the technical aspects of the topic at hand.

From a review perspective, enterprise applications administrators will typically collaborate with the attorneys representing their company in two areas. The first is around the technical accuracy of the legal agreement. The enterprise applications administrator can help to ensure that any auditing requirements are technically feasible, that the services or products described in the agreement are accurate from a technical point of view, or that the wording used to describe various technologies is accurate. It is very important that any contractual agreement be as accurate as possible since your company may be held tightly to the terms of the agreement. Mistakes made in the drawing up of legal agreements can cost the company millions of dollars depending on the scope of the error so it's important to verify accuracy to the best of your ability.

The second role of enterprise applications administrators related to contractual agreements is to ensure that the content of the agreement contains everything that is needed from a technical point of view. Many of the agreements involving enterprise applications administrators focus on topics associated with the enterprise applications that they're responsible for, services associated with those applications, or other products that are used with the enterprise application. With agreements like this, the enterprise applications administrator is best positioned to understand what exactly is needed in the way of products and services and can help to ensure that the agreement adequately reflects this need.

For example, many agreements that you may deal with as an enterprise applications administrator may relate to third-party services that are needed to support and maintain an enterprise application. Contracts like this will generally identify who is providing the services, what services are being provided, how the services will be provided, any assumptions made by either company, what the responsibilities of each company are, how the company providing the services will be paid, how disputes are handled, and a plethora of other details. Enterprise applications administrators may need to confirm that the assumptions detailed in the contract are accurate, that the services being provided are actually those that are needed, that sufficient services are provided to meet the intent of the agreement, and that the method of providing the services will work within the company's technical environment. In addition, the enterprise applications administrator may need to make sure that any checkpoints or deliverables associated with payments are valid and make sense in relation to the services being provided.

This type of review can appear complex and this is further exacerbated by the language used within legal agreements. They tend to be very difficult to understand and are frequently referred to within technical circles as being "full of legalese." Just like learning technical jargon and methods of communication, it isn't too difficult to learn how these documents are structured and to be able to derive the relevant information from the documents. If you are required to review contractual agreements on a regular basis, you should be able to catch on to how they work fairly quickly by reusing the skills that you've already used to master understanding the language used to communicate regarding technical topics.

OLAs and SLAs

Operation-level agreements (OLAs), within this context, are internal agreements between various technical or nontechnical teams which describe how the teams will interact and work together to maintain enterprise applications. They are typically not structured as full and binding legal agreements but rather focus on the interaction between teams. For example, the database support team and the server support team within a corporate enterprise may have an OLA in place which defines how each team should contact each other in the event that they need assistance, how long it will take for the contacted team to respond, and other details that help to guide or set expectations on cross-team work.

Service-level agreements (SLAs) on the other hand can be legal agreements and define the guaranteed level of service provided by a service provider. This may include a guaranteed level of availability, response time, or issue resolution time. The SLA can be seen as a contract between a service provider and a service consumer and will generally include responsibilities for both parties, metrics that services will be judged against, and potentially remedies available in the event that the terms of the SLA are violated. These SLAs may contain much of the same information as an OLA but are intended to exist between a service provider and a service consumer rather than the service provider and other service providers. In this context, service providers can be external parties or even internal teams. For example, IT organizations may have an SLA with a business unit, but OLAs between the individual technical teams.

From an enterprise applications administration standpoint, it is typically the enterprise applications administration team who is customer facing from a service point of view. This will often put the enterprise applications administration team in the position of being the service provider supporting a SLA between the service consumer and the enterprise applications administration team. On the other side, the enterprise applications administration team will generally have a number of OLAs in place with teams providing supporting technical services such as database, network, server, and other administration teams.

With this perspective of the enterprise applications administration team as the pivot point for all of these agreements, it is important to understand the content of the agreements and ensure that all of them align with the needs of the enterprise and the customer. For example, if your SLA with your customer states that your service must have 99.99% uptime but your OLA with the server administration team specifies a 99.9% uptime for server services, you may be unable to meet your SLA because of the terms of your OLA. The same situation can arise in regards to response time and resolution time. If your SLA guarantees a resolution of any issue within 1 hour, but your OLAs have a 45-minute response time, you may fail to meet your SLA if the issue takes more than 15 minutes to resolve by the team that you have the OLA with.

Maintenance of systems and applications is another important topic frequently addressed through the use of SLAs and OLAs. Every technology has a need for some degree of maintenance and this maintenance typically involves a level of downtime from time to time. The impact of this may be reduced through the use of highly available architectures, but if the environment is not sufficiently highly available, downtimes may still be involved. In these cases, it is important to ensure that maintenance windows or downtimes defined in the OLAs are structured in alignment with SLAs. If each team that you have an OLA with has a 1-hour downtime window per week, for example, that may violate the terms of your SLA if only 2 hours per week of maintenance downtime is allowed. Staggering maintenance between teams or doing maintenance on multiple technologies simultaneously are two methods of mitigating this, but, due to technical limitations, they may not always be possible to implement. It is very important to thoroughly plan out the maintenance windows needed within your SLAs and OLAs to ensure that conflicts do not arise.

Policies and Standards

We've discussed policies and standards throughout this book as they relate to the work an enterprise applications administrator performs. In most cases, these policies are reflected in official documents generated by the company's legal, human resource, or other teams. From the enterprise applications administrator point of view, it is often the job of the administrator to follow and enforce these policies. They may range from security policies tying back to controls that the enterprise applications administrator must ensure exist within their applications to regulatory policies that determine how specific work must be accomplished. Policies are tied to the goals and missions of the organization, and should be technology agnostic.

Standards, on the other hand, are often written and used by enterprise applications administrators regularly through the course of their work. Standards can be used to specify a minimally acceptable hardware specification, a standardized set of software that must be installed on a system, or even a minimum educational requirement for job applicants. Regardless of the stated purpose, it is important that any standards created by enterprise applications administrators clearly state what the standard applies to, what the standard is, and how the standard relates to other standards within the organization.

Project Plans

Project plans are documents that explicitly detail out how a project should be accomplished, the timing of specific steps associated with a project, resource allocation associated with the project, and other important project-related information. Enterprise applications administrators typically use project plans in two primary ways. The first is as a project participant where they contribute to and use project plans managed by other individuals as a part of their work effort on a given project. The second is as a method of scheduling and detailing their own work efforts where the enterprise applications administrator plays the role of project manager and manages the project plan themselves.

In the first use case, an enterprise applications administrator is typically part of a project team and participates in specific tasks associated with the project. Depending on the scale of the project, the project plan may be managed by a single individual project manager or a team of project managers responsible for the project. These project managers are typically held accountable for keeping the project on track from a schedule, financial, and scope perspective. The project plan is a tool used as part of the project to help the project manager track and manage these factors. In addition, it helps project team members know what is expected of them and when it is expected.

Enterprise applications administrators contribute to the project plan as both a planning resource as well as a work resource. When project managers are developing or working through a project plan, they will often need to understand the dependencies, timing, and outcomes of technical work that enterprise applications administrators either perform or coordinate. The project manager may or may not have sufficient technical background to understand all of the details associated with the work effort and will therefore rely on technical experts such as enterprise applications administrators to help ensure that the project plan accurately reflects the technical needs of the project. This may involve helping the project manager to understand how various technical tasks must chain together in order, explaining the timing of the technical tasks, and showing how the technical tasks relate to other aspects of the project.

CORPORATE MEMO...

Roles of Project Managers

In project management, the project manager is usually responsible for much more than simply managing the project plan. They will generally act as a facilitator between teams, keep stakeholders updated on the project status, work through funding issues, and help to remove roadblocks that could prevent the success of the project. As an enterprise applications administrator, good project managers can help you to get the things that you need in order to do your work associated with the project to the best of your abilities. Don't be afraid to ask the project manager for assistance in various areas associated with their role in order to make your job easier. They are responsible for the success of the project and can be a great ally to ensure you have what you need to help the project be successful.

From the work resource point of view, the enterprise applications administrator may have specific tasks on the project plan assigned to them. The enterprise applications administrator is then responsible for completing the assigned tasks at the time scheduled and within the allotted time to support the project. If there are any issues with the completion of the task, it is critical that they work closely with the project manager to update the project plan or take appropriate steps to resolve any issues preventing the completion of the tasks.

When performing internal projects or work efforts, project plans can help enterprise applications administrators to organize their work and ensure that these projects go well. Generally, project efforts managed directly by these administrators are not as large-scale as those that have dedicated project management resources, but the same techniques used by project managers can help in those smaller projects as well. By taking any given technical work effort, breaking it into steps, and documenting it in a project plan, an enterprise applications administrator can ensure that each task is appropriately scheduled and track the overall completion status of the work effort. In addition, when managing enterprise applications administration teams, project plans can help in resource allocation and ensuring that the correct team members are assigned to the correct tasks.

Managing internal work efforts using project plans can also have other benefits. For example, if a work effort must be repeated regularly, the project plan can serve as a checklist for the tasks and show how long the overall work effort will take. If the work effort is spread across multiple team members, the project plan can be used as a coordination tool to ensure that team members appropriately transition work between each other. The project plan can also be used as a source for metrics or reporting information to show what the team is accomplishing and how efficiently tasks are being completed within the team.

Roadmaps

Roadmaps are documents that are intended to show the future direction for a given product, enterprise application, or service. A roadmap focuses on a longer-term view of things that will be provided by or accomplished by its subject with various stages along the way. They will typically encompass a range of time from 1 to 5 years and show the current state, multiple intermediary states, and a long-term state that aligns with the last date shown on the roadmap. Future versions of the roadmap as it's updated over time will depreciate information associated with prior states and set new future directions for its subject. An example roadmap is shown in Figure 9.3.

In Figure 9.3, you can see that the roadmap is reflected as an actual road with signposts along the way. This roadmap document takes the term literally and shows the ongoing evolution and plan for its subject in relation to the road. Other roadmaps may not be as literal and can simply be a timeline

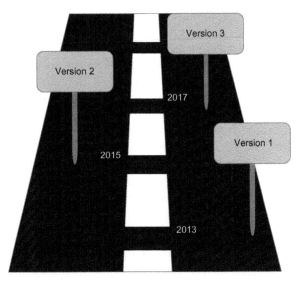

FIGURE 9.3
Example roadmap document.

showing various stages of evolution for the subject in a less illustrative manner.

Roadmaps can be very useful for planning purposes. By understanding what the long-term vision for a specific enterprise application is, you can ensure that any current or planned work efforts align with that vision. For example, if an application that you're administering will be commercialized in the next 3 years, work that you perform today could be done in a manner to make that commercialization effort easier when the appropriate time comes. This can help a great deal in minimizing future work as architectural decisions and other important changes can be made with a longer-term approach in mind.

Roadmaps can reflect enterprise applications very well, but they can also be used to illustrate the changes to an organization over time. Most organizations and teams grow over time, responsibilities change, and the services provided morph to match the needs of the company. The long-term plans of an enterprise applications administration team can also be reflected using a roadmap to illustrate the current team state, intermediary steps where the team takes on responsibility for additional enterprise applications or provides new services, and the long-term goals for the team. Using this documentation method, the enterprise applications administration team manager can show other parts of the organization what the team is doing and what they'll be doing in the future. Just as with technology roadmaps, organizational roadmaps can help in making decisions in such a way that they align with the long-term vision for the organization.

Runbooks

A runbook is a concept that goes back to the more structured operational procedures frequently associated with managing large mainframe computing environments. However, this concept also works well in today's world of distributed computing as well as cloud-based environments. A runbook is effectively a collection of documentation that encompasses build checklists, point-in-time versioned copies of installation WIs used to build an enterprise application, processes or procedures used to accomplish specific tasks within the environment in the past, and instructions on how to accomplish specific tasks in the future.

A runbook can be developed in one of two manners. It can be designed as a point-in-time reference for an enterprise application showing how the application was built and implemented and how to manage it in its as-built state. Alternatively, a runbook can be maintained and kept up to date over time as the single point of reference for all checklists, SOPs, WIs, SLAs, OLAs, and other documents associated with the ongoing operations and maintenance of the enterprise application. Depending on the documentation methodology used by the enterprise applications administration team, it may be most effective to generate the runbook as a one-time exercise as a historical document or it may be used as the point of reference for every document associated with the enterprise application.

If the runbook is designed as a one-time document and used as a historical record, it is important to ensure that all appropriate details are captured within the document before it is finalized. There should be no sections of the document that are incomplete or contain inaccurate information. In addition, there should be a clear indicator within the document that subsequent updates will be handled through other documentation sources and potentially include a reference to where those future documents will be stored or managed. This runbook may be used by future enterprise applications administrators to understand how and why an enterprise application was constructed in a particular manner and be used to plan future iterations of the application or build new ones in a similar manner. In addition, the runbook can be used as a transition document to transition the enterprise application from the build team to an operational team.

TIPS & TRICKS

Runbook Updates

If the runbook is to be maintained over time as a single point of reference for documentation associated with the enterprise application, it may make sense to break the runbook up into distinct sections. Each section can potentially have its own update timeline, review timeframe, and approver list. This can ease the update process for the runbook by allowing for updates to occur for each section rather than requiring an update to the entire runbook each time a small section needs to be changed.

Runbooks can also serve as a master index or collection of documents associated with the ongoing maintenance of the enterprise application. Using the runbook in this manner requires that it is updated whenever there is a change to any of the technologies, SOPs, WIs, SLAs, or OLAs associated with the enterprise application. This may mean that the runbook is updated on a weekly basis in environments where changes occur frequently. When working in this type of environment, it may be more beneficial to make high-level references to other documents within the runbook and include a link to those external documents. Effectively, the runbook operates as an index and points to documents covering specific topics needed within the runbook. When an update occurs to the referenced document, the runbook may need be updated to point to the new version.

Standard Operating Procedures

SOPs are documents that outline general procedures and define what should happen based on specific criteria. They are considered a higher-level document than WIs and typically do not include step-by-step instructions on how to accomplish specific tasks. Instead, they focus on the overall process flow associated with a task and explain how the task should be done. Typical elements of an SOP are:

- Why the procedure should be executed
- When to execute the procedure
- Who should execute the procedure
- What the executor should do

In general, SOPs are considered guidelines rather than step-by-step instructions. For example, the SOP may have a statement indicating that the executor should "reboot a server." The SOP will not explain how that reboot should be done but will expect the executor to rely on more detailed documentation to ensure that the task is executed correctly. SOPs are often used to guide activities involving many steps so that the steps are cleanly organized within a single document.

Another common element of SOPs is a workflow diagram. Since the SOP is describing a specific sequence of steps, there may be value in showing those steps in a sequence along with decision points, alternative branches, and other design elements associated with a workflow diagram. Including this type of diagram within an SOP can help the reader or executor quickly understand the process flow described by the SOP and execute the procedure more easily.

User Manuals

In some organizations, dedicated teams are responsible for training of enterprise application end users and they develop all of the necessary training materials to accomplish this. In others, the enterprise applications administration team may play a role in training end users or teaching them how to properly use the enterprise application. One of the most valuable documents associated with this exercise is the user manual. This manual is intended to walk the user through how to properly perform specific tasks within the application to accomplish their needs. It is often based on the use cases used for testing the enterprise application and aligns with "correct" usage of the application.

When developing user manuals, it's important to remember that the technical level of enterprise application end users is typically not very high. This means that the user manual should try to avoid technical terms or jargon that may confuse the user of the enterprise application. As with any documentation effort, understanding the audience for the document is very important and should be reflected in the terminology and style used within the document. In most cases, enterprise application end users are not as interested in the technology as they are in how to accomplish their specific job. If the user manual focuses on that perspective, it will be more successful in accomplishing the goal of training the end user.

Enterprise application user manuals differ from what many of us think of as your average product manual. Rather than putting a focus on the capabilities and functions of the enterprise application, the better user manuals focus on the tasks that need to be accomplished and the best way to accomplish them. This workflow-based methodology allows for the creation of user manuals that fit the needs of the enterprise application end users, explain what they need to know to them in an easy-to-understand manner, and leave the technical jargon for the technical personnel to deal with.

Work Instructions

WIs are one of the most detailed technical documents. Typically SOPs and WIs work together to give a full end-to-end description of technical tasks that should be done and how to do them. The SOP, as previously mentioned, focuses on the flow of tasks and a higher-level view of what needs to be done and when. WIs, on the other hand, focus on step-by-step procedures on how to perform specific tasks. WIs can be incredibly granular and show through text and images exactly what the person executing the tasks needs to do.

This allows for a great deal of consistency in task execution and ensures that the task can be done the same way every time, regardless of who performs the task. In addition, WIs provide a good basis for task automation by clearly detailing the exact steps that need to be accomplished and therefore automated as part of the task automation exercise. These tasks would then roll up into an SOP that would define the overall workflow for a series of automated tasks. By looking at WIs as the detailed instructions and SOPs as higher-level process flows, you can ensure that you get the correct information in each document and link them together accordingly.

SUMMARY

In this chapter, we discussed one of the least-liked aspects of enterprise applications administration work, documentation. In the first section, we discussed the reason why good documentation is so important and how it applies to daily life for enterprise applications administrators. From providing historical information to meeting regulatory compliance obligations, documentation is a critical part of administration work. There are specific techniques associated with when, what, and how to document various pieces of information that we discussed as well as some tricks to make documenting information a little easier for the enterprise applications administrator.

From there, we moved on to discussing some of the most common types of documents that may be written or used by enterprise applications administrators. These documents include various types of technical documents, process-related documents, presentations, and even manuals intended for enterprise application end users. Each of these documents has specific elements that make them unique and can be used to convey different information in specific ways. A few examples of various document types were reviewed and each document was tied back to its function and purpose.

With this information in mind, hopefully the process of documentation will be a little more clear and, while no less of a chore, its purpose understandable. Documentation is the single common thread that exists across all technical areas that enterprise applications administrators work with. By understanding the key concepts, techniques, and document types, enterprise applications administrators can apply their documentation knowledge across every technology they encounter. Successful implementation of this knowledge can aid in communicating critical ideas, sharing information, and removing ambiguity from complex tasks.

Index

Note: Page numbers followed by "*f*" and "*t*" refer to figures and tables, respectively.

Printed and bound by CPI Group (UK) Ltd, Croydon, CR0 4YY

03/10/2024

01040327-0010